THE INFANCY OF
NAZISM

ALSO BY WILLIAM SHERIDAN ALLEN
The Nazi Seizure of Power:
The Experience of a Single German Town, 1930–1935

THE INFANCY OF
NAZISM

THE MEMOIRS OF
EX-GAULEITER ALBERT KREBS
1923-1933

EDITED AND TRANSLATED BY
WILLIAM SHERIDAN ALLEN

New Viewpoints
A Division of Franklin Watts
New York   London   1976

New Viewpoints
A Division of Franklin Watts
730 Fifth Avenue
New York, New York 10019

Library of Congress Cataloging in Publication
Data

Krebs, Albert, 1899–
    The infancy of Nazism.
    Translation of Tendenzen und Gestalten der
    NSDAP.
    Bibliography: p.
    Includes index.
    1. Krebs, Albert, 1899–   2. Nationalsozialis-
tische Deutsche Arbeiter-Partei.   3. Germany—
Politics and government—1918–1933.   I. Allen,
William Sheridan.   II. Title.
DD247.K73A3713   943.085′092′4   75-29153
ISBN 0-531-05376-8
ISBN 0-531-05583-3 pbk.

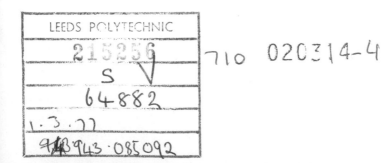

CONTENTS

Editor's Introduction   vii

PART ONE: EXPERIENCES

CHAPTER 1   Between Nazism and Trade Unionism,
1925–1934   3

CHAPTER 2   Nazi Gauleiter of Hamburg,
1926–1928   38

CHAPTER 3   The Nazi Shop-Cell Organization in Hamburg, 1930–1931   75

CHAPTER 4   Nazi Newspaper Editor,
1929–1932   87

PART TWO: ENCOUNTERS

CHAPTER 5   Adolf Hitler   141

CHAPTER 6   Dr. Joseph Goebbels   191

CHAPTER 7   Rudolf Hess   206

CHAPTER 8   Alfred Rosenberg   215

CHAPTER 9   Gregor Strasser   224

CHAPTER 10   Other Leading Nazis
                 (Amann, Bouhler, Buch, Buttmann,
                 Brückner, Ellendt, Esser, Feder,
                 Frick, Haupt, Himmler, Lohse, Ludin,
                 Marschler, Pfeffer von Salomon,
                 Reventlow, Röver, Rust, von Schirach,
                 Schwarz van Berk, Streicher, Telschow,
                 Wegener)   242

For Further Reading   316

Index   321

EDITOR'S INTRODUCTION

In the rise of Nazism the critically significant years were those from 1925 to 1930, the period when Hitler acquired the organizational cadres and the techniques that were to stay with him throughout the Third Reich. The initial years of Nazism, 1919 to 1923, proved to be a false start, though they provided the party with its basic ideology, its distinctive format as a revolutionary *political* movement, and its commitment to Hitler. But then came the great fumbled opportunity of 1923: Nazism failed to exploit a "revolutionary objective situation" *par excellence*. Inadequate organization led to the abortive "Beer Hall" *Putsch* which culminated in Hitler's imprisonment and the prohibition of his party.[1]

But this was only the end of the beginning. In 1925 Hitler, fresh from prison, refounded the Nazi party and made it for the first time a nationwide movement. He also found new leaders and techniques of organization vastly more effective than before. It took five years of slow development, years in which his party had an average membership of only fifty thousand and only 2 percent of the vote, before Nazism again became a serious threat to Germany's democracy. But by the onset of the depression of 1929 the

[1] On the genesis of Nazism, apart from the primary source of *Mein Kampf* (best translated by Ralph Mannheim, in paperback), the most accurate monographs are William A. Jenks, *Vienna and the Young Hitler* (New York, 1960); Bradley F. Smith, *Adolf Hitler: His Family, Childhood, and Youth* (Stanford, Calif., 1967); Werner Maser, *Hitler: Legend, Myth, and Reality* (New York, 1973); and Joachim Fest, *Hitler* (New York, 1974). The scholarly journals have numerous articles on this era; several are listed in the bibliography at the back of this book. The best overview is Karl D. Bracher, *The German Dictatorship* (paperback), while the best study of the 1923 fiasco is Harold J. Gordon, *Hitler and the Beerhall Putsch* (Princeton, 1972).

Nazis were ready to exploit the resultant economic and social chaos. The methods and personnel now on hand enabled Hitler to win the backing of a third of the nation, to parlay that mass backing into an appointment as head of the government in 1933, and from there to turn himself rapidly into the dictator of the Third Reich.[2]

Furthermore, the traits developed by Nazism during its rise to power became the major characteristics of its exercise of power: charismatic leadership, unrelenting propaganda, "institutional Darwinism," advancement of opportunists, and the infiltration of the socioeconomic infrastructure. These and other factors have been analyzed in scholarly monographs, many available in English. What we have not had are detailed and trustworthy eyewitness accounts of the inner workings of the Nazi party—the kind of honest testimony that could produce empathetic understanding. In fact there are hardly any objective memoirs for these years even in German. Propagandistically inspired testimonies abound, but it takes a specialist to sift through them.[3] The memoirs of Albert

---

[2] This period is well covered by monographs in English. The most comprehensive, though flawed by occasional factual and interpretive errors, is Dietrich Orlow, *The History of the Nazi Party, 1919 to 1933* (Pittsburgh, 1969). The most instructive regional studies are Jeremy Noakes, *The Nazi Party in Lower Saxony, 1921–1933* (Oxford, 1971), and Geoffrey Pridham, *Hitler's Rise to Power: The Nazi Movement in Bavaria, 1923–1933* (London, 1973). An older study of Schleswig-Holstein, stressing the Nazi appeal to farmers, is Rudolf Heberle, *From Democracy to Nazism: A Regional Case Study on Political Parties in Germany* (Baton Rouge, La., 1945; revised paperback edition, New York, 1970). For a local study see William Sheridan Allen, *The Nazi Seizure of Power: The Experience of a Single German Town, 1930–1935* (Chicago, 1965, and paperback). On the nature of the Nazi membership see Theodore Abel, *The Nazi Movement: Why Hitler Came Into Power* (New York, 1966, paperback); the same material has been restudied and revised in Peter H. Merkl, *Political Violence Under the Swastika: 581 Early Nazis* (Princeton, 1975).

[3] Ernst Hanfstaengel, *Unheard Witness* (Philadelphia, 1957), is a self-serving apologia; Otto Strasser, *Hitler and I* (Boston, 1940), is slanted to justify the author's political position; Hermann Rauschnigg, *Hitler Speaks* (London, 1939) and *The Revolution of Nihilism* (New York, 1937), are valuable but narrow in focus. The "diaries" of Joseph Goebbels, *My Part in Germany's Struggle* (London, 1934) and *The Early Goebbels Diaries* (Helmut Heiber, ed.; New York, 1963), suffer from their author's inability to write anything but propaganda and must be used with the utmost caution.

Krebs, however, provide an intimate picture of the infancy of
Nazism by an insider whose singular attitude made him an excep-
tionally honest reporter.

Dr. Albert Krebs had almost all the attributes of the typical
Nazi leader from those early years.[4] He was young (born in 1899),
middle class (son of a middle rank civil servant), and even a
Bavarian (raised in Amorbach, a small town southwest of Würzburg). He served as a volunteer in World War I and then entered
the university (to study history and literature) at a time when
hypernationalism dominated student attitudes. He had been in the
Youth Movement and the *Freikorps*, both favorite Nazi recruiting
grounds. By 1923 he was a Stormtroop leader, though he was not
involved in the "Beer Hall" Putsch, and when the Nazi party was
outlawed he became a minor leader in one of its temporary successors, the Völkisch-Sozialer Block.

In 1925, after he received his Ph.D., Krebs became an official in
Germany's largest white-collar-workers union, a position that gave
him insights increasingly divergent from orthodox Nazism, but
which also made him potentially valuable to the Nazi party, which
he had rejoined in 1926. Shortly thereafter he was elected party
leader in Hamburg, Germany's second largest city.[5] After a year of
vigorous effort he was elevated to the rank of *Gauleiter*. That is, he
became one of the thirty-five district leaders who were the basic
regional executives of Nazism's nationwide organization. At that
time there were fewer than five hundred Nazis among Hamburg's
million and a quarter inhabitants; it was possible for Krebs to
know his local organization closely.

After two years in this role Krebs became so disillusioned by the
infighting in the party and by what he already saw emerging as
"perverting tendencies" within Nazism that he resigned his post as
Gauleiter. He then took the editorship of what was to become one
of the major Nazi newspapers, the *Hamburger Tageblatt*, which he
used to express his often critical views of Hitler's policies and his
own conception of what Nazism ought to be and do. For two years

---

[4] For a comparative profile see Daniel Lerner, "The Nazi Elite," in Harold
Lasswell and Daniel Lerner, *World Revolutionary Elites: Studies in Coercive
Ideological Movements* (Cambridge, Mass., 1966), pp. 194–318.

[5] Background data on the city may be found in Richard A. Comfort, *Revolutionary Hamburg* (Stanford, Calif., 1966).

(1930–31) he was also Hamburg's leader of the Shop-Cell Organization, Nazism's instrument for the attempted recruitment of the working class.[6] And all this time he continued as a paid official of his own union, which, since it played a significant part in national politics, gave him a bird's-eye view of the death agony of the Weimar Republic.[7]

Though based in Hamburg, Krebs traveled all over Germany, had frequent dealings with the party's Munich headquarters, and came to know many Nazi leaders intimately. He belonged to Gregor Strasser's "left wing" faction,[8] having originally been attracted to Nazism partly by his interest in social reforms, which he thought the party would promote. This led him into increasing conflict with Hitler until, in 1932, on the eve of the Third Reich, Krebs was finally purged. On that occasion he issued the following press release:

> *My expulsion is directed against the German spirit of freedom of conscience. The Nazi party permits no one in its ranks who thinks independently and dares to express those thoughts. The* Hamburger Tageblatt *was practically the last Nazi newspaper which, disregarding the tactic of wooing certain economic circles, tried to express socialistic views of Nazism. In the future that will now cease. The Nazi party has, in order to maintain the benevolence of business barons and reactionary cliques, thrown out one of its oldest members. That affects the party, not me. I remain what I was at the beginning of my political endeavors: a national socialist.*

But the strain of remaining a "national socialist" while becoming increasingly opposed to Nazism took its toll: Shortly after leaving the party Krebs suffered a nervous breakdown, which immobilized him during the final collapse of the republic and the first,

---

[6] Despite its problematical conceptualization, the best book in English on this is Max H. Kele, *Nazis and Workers* (Chapel Hill, N.C., 1972).

[7] For the political background, Erich Eyck, *A History of the Weimar Republic*, 2 Volumes (paperback).

[8] As yet there is no biography of Strasser in English, but there is an unpublished Ph.D. dissertation (Stanford University, 1966), which is available through University Microfilms of Ann Arbor: Joseph Dixon, "Gregor Strasser and the Organization of the Nazi Party, 1925 to 1932."

bloody months of the Third Reich. This may also have saved his life. He never rejoined the party but lived out the Nazi years holding various minor jobs. He got involved in the anti-Nazi resistance through his old union friends but managed to elude the Gestapo,[9] survived the collapse of the Third Reich, and came to write his memoirs in the 1950s at the instigation of the Research Center for the History of National Socialism in Hamburg.

In composing these memoirs Krebs drew upon his diaries, correspondence files, the office files of his former newspaper, and documents from the Hamburg Research Center's archives. But his major asset was his own independence of mind and his amazingly resentment-free understanding of the early Nazi party.

Albert Krebs' attitude remains difficult to understand, even fifty years after his espousal of Nazism. It is easier to comprehend the brutal venality of a freebooter like Hermann Goering or the warped fanaticism of a monster like Heinrich Himmler than it is to comprehend how a man of intelligence, idealism, and explicit moral standards, such as Dr. Krebs clearly represents, could ever have been drawn to Nazism. To conclude—on the evidence of Krebs' constant quarreling with the Nazi leaders and his ultimate expulsion from the party—that his was simply a youthful malperception extended through stubbornness is to miss the point. An empathetic comprehension of what Nazism meant to men like Krebs must go further.

In the 1920s there were many Germans who found Nazism attractive because they thought it represented unselfish patriotism in a time of their country's denigration, a philosophical alternative to communism in an ideologically polarized era, an integrative venture in a period of extraordinary social cleavage. Their delusion helped produce one of the most dreadful monstrosities of human history. Hitler's Third Reich was not a perversion of Nazi methods, goals, and concepts. It was the logical culmination of them.

Yet Krebs exemplifies the attractiveness of the Nazi idea to young Germans, and it is precisely his selective idealization of Nazism that provided him with the critical detachment that makes his memoirs almost uniquely valuable today. These memoirs are

[9] His resistance associations led him to write a biography of one of those hanged by the Gestapo: Albert Krebs, *Fritz-Dietlof Graf von der Schulenburg. Zwischen Staatsraison und Hochverrat* (Hamburg, 1964).

not a self-justifying apologia (like Albert Speer's[10]) but are the profoundly honest work of a man who—even today—appears convinced of the desirability of a "national socialism," which he thinks Hitler perverted.

Perceptive readers will recognize, however, that while many of Dr. Krebs' insights derive from his adherence to one of the factional wings of the Nazi party, this also leads to the greatest fault of his retrospection: his idealization of all those who were opponents of Hitler, who conformed in one way or another to his own original vision of what "national socialism" ought to be. This causes him, despite his desire to portray the early Nazi movement as it really was, warts and all, to emphasize those characteristics of the movement that were ultimately incompatible with what Hitler subsequently created. The result is a minor distortion in its own right: The attempt to show "the other side" of the early Nazi party may be so convincing that we forget how this "other side" also contained sufficient elements to enable Hitler to forge his movement. Granted that many of the early Nazis did not intend to foster what Hitler unleashed upon the world, the fact remains that they contributed to his success.

Therefore the readers of these memoirs must supplement their insights with a broader typology of the early Nazi leaders. I have tried to suggest, in introductory sections and footnotes, the sources available in English for this since we still lack any universally accepted analysis. Two points should be kept in focus: Very few people joined the Nazi party in expectation that it would do what it ultimately did; those who joined were acting on the basis of an ideology that was very likely to produce what Nazism ultimately delivered.

Krebs' memoirs come very close to capturing the schizoid quality of these apparently contradictory assessments. He came to realize the gruesome tragedy of Nazism, that it set out to better the lot of men but wound up diminishing the quality of mankind. If he leans toward an emphasis upon the former, that is perhaps inevitable, since he shared that hope. No one needs to emphasize the second aspect of Nazism: It is evident now to all what was abhor-

---

[10] See the review of *Inside the Third Reich* in *The New York Review of Books,* January 7, 1971.

rent about its deeds. What is most important to understand is how the ultimate qualities of Nazism were implicit in its original ideas and methods. Thus Dr. Krebs does us the great service of reminding us that the early Nazis were not all freakish aberrations so totally foreign as to be comfortably discounted but fellow human beings with understandable aspirations who took a dreadfully wrong approach. Some were simply swine. Many others are more frightening because they were not monsters but men with whom we find at least a modicum of identity.

On the basis of this recognition we can begin to sort out what made them go wrong. This, I believe, is the basic purpose that led Dr. Krebs to write his memoirs in the first place. If he leans too much toward exonerating those who did not really desire what Hitler subsequently produced, then we benefit by having his judgment to set alongside the results that we all know were the consequence of their peculiar delusions.

In editing Dr. Kreb's memoirs I have tried to correct, by footnotes, those instances where historical scholarship has advanced beyond or corroborated his data. But most of the notes are designed to provide background information for readers unfamiliar with the details of the period. Except where references to books in German were unavoidable, I have also used the notes to indicate works in English so that those interested in further reading will know where to turn. In one or two instances the footnotes derive from my correspondence with Dr. Krebs, cases in which he detected errors in his own recollections. Such notes are identified as his; all others are my own.

I would have found it very difficult to complete the laborious work of translating this book without the moral support and critical suggestions of my wife, Luella, for which I would like to thank her publicly.

WILLIAM SHERIDAN ALLEN

State University of New York
Buffalo, 1975

THE INFANCY OF
NAZISM

PART ONE
EXPERIENCES

CHAPTER 1

Between Nazism and Trade Unionism,
1925–1934

Editor's note: *It may seem strange that Krebs begins his memoirs with his experiences in a white-collar-workers union—even though this shaped his attitudes strongly—rather than with his encounters with Hitler and other prominent Nazis. But in fact his stress upon the relationship between what was essentially a middle-class-interest organization and the Nazi party has been duplicated by historians in recent research on the rise of Nazism. Increasingly, Nazism has come to be interpreted largely in terms of the crisis of the German middle class. Hitler's leadership was significant, but the Nazi party succeeded primarily because it took almost all the voters away from the other middle-class parties and concentrated them behind Hitler.*[1]

The Nazis were able to do this partly because of the troubled social and economic situation of the German middle class in the 1920s. Furthermore, the middle class was unable to unite in defense of its social status because it embodied strongly divergent economic interests.[2] *But the objective situation was only part of the reason for Nazi success. The rest of it included the Nazi ability to penetrate and capture the sub-organizations and interest groups of the middle class and here is where Krebs' experience becomes directly pertinent.*

The politics of the Weimar Republic involved not only the

[1] For a summary of the literature see Geoffrey Barraclough, "Farewell to Hitler," *The New York Review of Books* (April 3, 1975), pp. 11–17. On recent German scholarship see Henry Ashby Turner's "Review Article," *Central European History* (March 1974), pp. 84–90.

[2] Larry Eugene Jones, " 'The Dying Middle': Weimar Germany and the Fragmentation of Bourgeois Politics," *Central European History* (March 1972), pp. 23–54.

activities of the various parties but also those of an almost bewildering array of pressure groups. These indoctrinated their memberships, promoted legislation, and endorsed candidates or tried to get their own members elected to political office through the regular parties. Dr. Krebs' union is a typical example. It also became a target of Nazi subversion, but despite its ideological affinity with Nazism, Krebs' union succeeded in maintaining its organizational independence. Called the German Nationalist Merchant Apprentices' Association (DHV), it was the largest white-collar union in Germany with a membership of about 300,000 store clerks and office workers.[3] In sharp contrast to the great majority of German unions, which were proletarian and socialist, the DHV was nationalistic, anti-Marxist, and middle class in consciousness and orientation. Its economic attitude harkened back to the medieval guild system; its ideology was racialist (völkisch).

In other words, the DHV's members were precisely the kind of Germans who formed the core of the Nazi movement, even though the DHV was jealous of its independence and combated Nazism politically. Krebs' experience of being simultaneously a member of the Nazi party and of the DHV thus illustrates the dilemma of the German middle class. From it we learn how interest groups such as the DHV intervened powerfully in national politics and yet could not effectively forestall the rise of Nazism.

In January 1925 I had a job interview with Max Habermann and Benno Ziegler at St. John's Lutheran Institute in Berlin. In question was whether I should be taken on as the technical specialist of Section 17 (Civic Education) of the DHV. These gentlemen knew me through my fraternity brother Hellmuth Meyer, who had met Ziegler at a Youth Movement convention. Benno Ziegler, the then director of Section 17, was also the national leader of a group of DHV members called the "Traveling Journeymen," which stressed Youth Movement ideals. Ziegler was looking for assistants and my fraternity brother, who knew of my interest in educational, social, and cultural matters, had given him my name.

As far as the job was concerned, the interview raised no particu-

---

[3] For background on the DHV see George L. Mosse, *The Crisis of German Ideology* (New York, 1964).

lar problems. I believed I could fulfill the tasks that Habermann outlined, and could do so, moreover, with a sense of personal satisfaction. But the intellectual and political goals involved in the work were not clear to me. I understood that the work was fundamentally concerned with politics, and since I had hitherto known the DHV only by name, I connected it with the German Nationalist party, which had a very similar sounding name.[4] And so I felt obliged at the end of the interview to inquire into the nature of this apparent connection and also to affirm my sympathy for the Nazi party (even though I was not, at that moment, a formal member of it).

Both men smiled at my declaration. Habermann informed me that the union was politically neutral, though decidedly anti-Marxist, and that it had borne the designation "German National" many decades before the German National People's party had even been founded. As for the Nazi party, he was of the opinion that for the moment it was a kind of political *enfant terrible*. At best it had the role of spokesman for the partly good and noble but partly wild, uncontrolled, and even evil sentiments of a confused youth and disoriented nation. In its present stage of development, he said, a stage that had a distinct similarity to that which the union itself had happily overcome (though not without difficulty) in the years before the World War, the Nazi party could hardly be considered a serious factor in German politics. Furthermore, it seemed more than doubtful whether Herr Hitler, after his lamentable fiasco in the Munich Putsch of November 1923, could ever make a successful reentry into national politics whenever he was released from prison. But, continued Habermann, he did not want these views of his to destroy my faith in Nazism. In the DHV every man could seek political salvation in his own way. To be sure, insofar as anyone became politically active for the union, or in its name, he would have to put the goals and interests of the DHV above those of partisan politics. This condition naturally applied to my future position also.

These remarks closed the interview and I agreed to take the job. It was decided that I should begin my duties very shortly: at the

[4] German Nationalist People's Party (DNVP), the reactionary and monarchist successor to the Conservative party of the Kaiser's era.

beginning of March. Since my doubts increased after I returned to my home in southern Germany, I did not adhere to this date. As an excuse I pleaded the aftereffects of a wound that I had received in Frankfurt at a political meeting featuring Julius Streicher.[5] (I was clubbed in the head for a remark that I had whispered to a friend standing near me about the ridiculous nonsense being spouted by the speaker; the remark was unfortunately overheard.) But I ultimately began my work in Berlin two weeks later, after my father had put considerable moral pressure on me. His view was that one would never have serious experiences or useful activities unless one kept promises and took risks.

Today it occasionally seems to me that this little episode at the beginning of my work with the DHV had a symbolic character— not the least part of which was the blow with the blackjack that I, a Nazi, had received from another Nazi.

In that spring of 1925 the DHV was shifting the emphasis of its work. The immediate postwar years had been primarily devoted to rebuilding the organization and securing a firm position within the entire trade union movement. This involved struggles with opposing unions and employer associations plus difficult negotiations with parties, cabinet ministries, and all sorts of other institutions and individuals. Beyond that, the DHV was constantly embroiled in the tumultuous events of those years: the Spartacist uprisings, the Kapp Putsch, the French occupation of the Ruhr, the Great Inflation, and the Hitler Putsch. What with all these concerns, the internal work of formulating spiritual goals for the union and providing the proper training and education of its members had been given rather short shrift. But now that the political situation had returned to relative calm and stability, all this was to be consciously and systematically made good. The DHV convention of 1924 had so directed, and to carry out this directive the four education sections (14 to 17) were beefed up and housed together in St. John's Lutheran Institute, Spandau, Berlin.

Section 17's work was to be based on objectives expounded in

---

[5] Nazi Gauleiter of Nuremberg and editor of the pornographic anti-Semitic newspaper *Der Stürmer*. He is described below, in the chapter on "Other Leading Nazis." Since the Nazi party was temporarily dissolved at this time, the meeting, while obviously attracting Nazi types, could not have been under the formal auspices of the party.

Habermann's speech to the 1924 DHV convention ("Education Into a German Man") plus the concepts contained in an essay on "civic education" written by Dr. Stapel. In theory this gave us an extremely wide scope. In practice, since we were opposed to such an abstruse approach, we limited ourselves to matters growing out of current problems affecting the economic and social position of German white-collar workers. These we viewed as calling for cultural, political, and patriotic education. Even within these categories matters affecting daily life were given preference. Thus we were much more likely to discuss problems of interior decoration than those of modern art. Our political study groups throughout the nation examined the programs and actions of the parties represented in the Reichstag, but left untouched such basic questions as monarchy vs. republic. Our historical booklets, our slide lectures on border Germandom, town planning, local folkways, our articles on literature, films, theater, music—none of these made any pretension to scholarly completeness but aimed instead at answering day-to-day questions. We never insisted upon uniformity; there was no objection to contradictory interpretations in the material sent out by our section to the members, as long as the basic intellectual position was maintained. In retrospect I would describe that basic position as one of wanting to give the profession of white-collar worker, as represented within the DHV, a form and a status.

This was necessary since the mass of white-collar workers had lost their sense of position in society. The industrialization and commercialization of life had ripped them out of their previous small town and rural environment. We believed we could help reposition them by teaching our members to recognize and appreciate their responsibilities toward their own profession, their historic heritage, and their present duties to their nation. What the DHV was attempting to do was to give a sense of position to a faceless and historyless mass, to secure them a functionally and sociologically justifiable and just role in the national order, to fill them with a consciousness of their place within the historical continuum. I am still convinced that this was a worthwhile task and one that has not yet been completed no matter how much it has since been promoted.

It was relatively rare when the work of our section led to difficulties with the Nazi party or with Nazi members of the union. It might be that in one of the political study groups there would be a massive conflict over the desirability of sending prominent DHV officials into the middle-class "Fulfillment Parties,"[6] and ultimately the appropriate technical assistant from our section would be asked to render an opinion. Occasionally our reference packets or the texts of our slide lectures were criticized for their lack of "strong" language and unambiguously radical demands. Very frequently we heard objections to our tepid and cowardly objectivity. Some attacked us for including the *Communist Manifesto* in one of the document folders. Others were outraged because we continued to circulate the writings of Paul Bröcker ("a notorious Freemason"), while on the other hand we had not yet brought out a new reference collection on the Jewish Question.

Yet these occasional complaints remained within bounds that permitted them to be either answered or ignored. This was partly because the activist workers in the educational sectors of our Local Groups were rarely also Nazi activists. Another reason was that the DHV and the Nazi party appeared to have common views on certain basic questions. Like the Nazis, the DHV attacked the Treaty of Versailles and all its consequences. The DHV viewed the fictions and artificialities of the Weimar constitution as something less than a culmination of German democratic constitutionalism. It fought against Marxist socialism and liberal capitalism, the latter being portrayed most typically as international finance capitalism. It demanded, in the place of a citified and covertly cosmopolitan culture, an organically developed folk culture.

Finally, the DHV declared itself to be anti-Semitic, though already by the middle of the 1920s this anti-Semitism showed an essentially different character from that of the Nazi party. It was limited to a disagreement with Judaism as a whole and concluded from this that Jews should be refused membership in the DHV. It never attacked individual Jewish persons or organizations except when it thought this necessary to defend German interests from threat or injury.

---

[6] Since the Nazis thought of themselves as revolutionaries, they scorned parties that promoted middle-class interests. "Fulfillment Parties," in Nazi parlance, were those supporting Gustav Stresemann's policy of undoing the Treaty of Versailles through compliance and negotiation rather than open defiance.

To the superficial observer, therefore, it might have appeared that the differences between the union and the party were only differences of method and of areas of activity. But in reality the differences ran deeper, as was soon to become evident with the growth of the Nazi party and its concomitantly stronger emphasis on practical politics rather than theoretical pronouncements.

One of the first big conflicts came in autumn 1928. At that time the Nazi Reichstag Deputy, Wilhelm Kube, attacked the leadership of the DHV and its Reichstag delegation (excepting Franz Stöhr[7]) in a series of mass meetings in North German cities. Kube accused the union's leadership, especially its chairman, Hans Bechly, of being too closely connected with Gustav Stresemann's German People's party (tainted with Judaism and high finance) and charged that DHV delegates had voted for the Dawes Plan.[8] Apart from that, however, Kube declared himself a friend of the union and of its earlier leaders, Shack and Döring, whom he characterized as upright fighters and anti-Semites. He gave the Nazi members the slogan "Conquer the DHV!"

These Nazi mass meetings were not without effect, as attested to by the numerous letters, both pro and con, that flooded the offices of both the union and the party. Nevertheless, the general impression was that Kube had acted without justification and had behaved like a bull in a china shop.

Far more significant, in cause, course, and consequence was the uproar engendered by the Young Plan, the referendum against it, and the founding of the Popular Conservative League.[9] Max

[7] There were DHV members in several of the center and right-wing parties' Reichstag delegations; Stöhr was a Nazi Reichstag deputy who belonged to the DHV.

[8] The Dawes Plan, approved in 1924, was a temporary renegotiation of reparations payments. The Nazis opposed *any* reparations payments.

[9] The Young Plan of 1929 was another renegotiation of reparations payments. The Nazis and the Nationalists sponsored a referendum against its acceptance. About the same time Count Westarp, Gottfried Treviranus, and Walter Lambach (a DHV leader) split from the Nationalist party to form the Popular Conservative League. This moderate rightist party was backed by the DHV but suffered a disastrous defeat at the polls in September 1930 and therefore collapsed, though Treviranus became a minister in the Brüning cabinet. See A. Chanady, "The Disintegration of the German National People's Party, 1924–30," *Journal of Modern History* (March 1967), pp. 65–90.

Habermann had written an article in the DHV's *Handelswacht* of
June 1929 sharply opposed to the Young Plan, which he described
as intolerable for the German people and especially so for German
employees. Nevertheless, when Hitler, Hugenberg, and Seldte[10]
initiated a referendum against the Young Plan that autumn, the
DHV refused to participate. The union's leadership justified this
by declaring that it had no confidence in the success of such a
referendum and therefore considered it to be more harmful than
useful to the German resistance policy. Beyond that, ran the argument, the DHV's participation would injure its political image.
The referendum alliance was so ideologically divided and its decisive string-pullers had demonstrated such reactionary tendencies
that the DHV could not afford to lay its own good reputation on
the line by collaborating with them.

Naturally the Nazi leaders were not disposed to accept such reasoning. Their alliance with Hugenberg already had few friends in
their own rank and file. Thus simply to forestall defections, the
Nazi leaders had to repudiate as false and slanderous the references
to ideological divisions and reactionary tendencies. Moreover, the
party's leadership doubted the sincerity of the DHV's stance on
the resignation of Walther Lambach from the Nationalist party
and the subsequent founding of the Popular Conservative League.
This action had been long brewing and was not connected with
the Young Plan referendum either in timing or in content. Rather,
it grew out of the growing differences between Lambach and
Hugenberg over social legislation. But the particular moment in
which the split occurred would make it look to an ill-informed
observer, even if he were unbiased, like a deliberate torpedoing of
the Young Plan referendum.

Furthermore, the organizational, financial, and propaganda support given to the Popular Conservatives by the DHV did go well
beyond the bounds of political neutrality. Naturally the DHV's
leaders justified their actions by claiming that they would demonstrate once and for all their opposition to socially reactionary
forces, no matter how patriotic they might claim to be. And just as
naturally the Nazi party rejected this justification and even denied
the truth of the facts on which it was based. On December 7,

---

[10] Alfred Hugenberg was head of the Nationalist party, Franz Seldte of the
"Steel Helmets," a nationalistic paramilitary veterans' organization closely
linked to the Nationalists.

1929, just two weeks before the referendum, the Nazi theoretician Alfred Rosenberg wrote an editorial in the *Völkischer Beobachter* entitled "In Upheaval." In addition to bitterly attacking the parties that refused to back the referendum, he criticized sharply the attitude of the DHV's Reichstag delegates. He blasted delegate Otto Thiel for belonging to the "pro-Jewish, High Finance People's Party." He spoke of the "pitiful weakness of Lambach and company." He concluded: "Most untrue of all is Herr Lambach's explanation that only Hugenberg's policies have kept the struggle against Marxism from being effective."

Rosenberg's article caused a powerful response in both the Nazi party and the DHV. Declarations and counterdeclarations poured forth, but the chief result was that groups of Nazi DHV members now tried to carry out Kube's slogan of the previous year: "Conquer the DHV!" In various Local Groups, including Hamburg, this led to highly unpleasant scenes and sometimes outright brawls. The only thing this accomplished was that those responsible, primarily younger members, were speedily expelled from the union. The DHV's leaders hoped thereby to demonstrate with maximum clarity their determination to prevent caucus tactics or opposition through violence. Since there was no repetition of these tactics until the spring of 1933, these energetic steps were obviously the right thing to do, though at the time I did not believe so.

In order to meet the Nazi challenge more effectively the DHV also initiated certain organizational and educational measures. The so-called "F-Service" was established, consisting of newsletters circulated to all politically active or otherwise interested union members. Within the League of Traveling Journeymen far more attention was given to political discussion. Throughout the country our study groups likewise emphasized political themes. In our political bureau in Berlin, led by Benno Ziegler, an attempt was made to coordinate our numerous political relationships (the system of cross-connections) and to provide a common day-to-day political line. The task of working out that political line and of explaining it to individual members and to the general public had been undertaken since the spring of 1928 by Habermann's column in the *Handelswacht*, entitled "This Month's Politics."

Though these measures were not aimed exclusively at the Nazis, it was the Nazis who were our chief concern since relations with the older parties and political groups (such as the Young Germanic Order, Steel Helmets, etc.) had long since been normalized. We knew what to expect from them. But the only thing known with certainty about the Nazi party was that it was growing in size and influence and was therefore enormously ruthless. Its program and tactical methods, apart from a few primary demands, remained totally inscrutable and erratic. Therefore the DHV's own goals *vis-à-vis* Nazism had to be open and flexible at first. The only thing that could be clearly and decisively proclaimed was the union's determination to defend its own independence and integrity against every attack.

These attacks were not simply launched over matters of national politics; they also occurred in the arena of purely union affairs. The ultimate Nazi goal here was to lay the basis for the social order they intended to establish in the future. For this reason they increasingly entered their own lists of candidates in shop steward elections. Since this drew votes primarily away from the DHV and from the Employees Trade Union League but not from the Socialists' union—the *Zentralverband der Angestellten*—it constituted a splintering of the anti-Marxist front and was exasperating and stupid even in terms of its immediate results.

Perhaps under normal circumstances we could simply have let the passage of time demonstrate who was better entitled to the confidence of the workers: the union member schooled in matters of social policy or the party man armed with his general political demands. But conditions were not normal. The soaring growth of Nazism could have brought the party into the government at any moment, thus giving its leaders the power of decision. Then we would be faced with the prospect that the attitudes and intentions which today brought the Nazis into shop steward elections might tomorrow lead to new social legislation detrimental to the unions. These intentions were by no means clear. Still, it was a fair assumption that they would follow the ideas propagated by Dr. Otto Wagener, the chief of staff for the Stormtroopers and subsequent economic specialist for Organizational Section II of the Nazi national administration: the concept of industrial "community of interest."[11]

---

[11] A corporate economic organization on the Italian fascist model, which would abolish both unions and employer associations.

Therefore the DHV immediately began to campaign against the separate Nazi candidates in the shop elections and against the "community of interest" concept. Nor was this counterattack limited only to written propaganda; appeals were made in person in the shops and in our Local Groups, on a district and on a national level, in order to assure that the DHV's ideas would prevail.

As far as the ideological struggle is concerned, the DHV was able to restrain Nazi leaders and their publications. The "community of interest" concept did not become a fixed part of the Nazi program but rather remained a matter for discussion. As such it was criticized and rejected even by some within the Nazi party, including the newspaper of the Nazi shop-cell organization, *Workerdom*, edited by Reinhold Muchow and Walter Schuhmann. Of course, this did not keep similar ideas from appearing once again in the "German Labor Front" after Hitler came to power. The only difference was that Dr. Ley's plan at least put obligations and responsibilities upon the employer too, while Dr. Wagener, with his pseudo-solutions, would have specifically exempted them.

The Nazi election victory of September 1930, and the appointment of Dr. Heinrich Brüning of the Center party as chancellor of the Reich opened a new chapter in the history of the relationship between the DHV and the Nazi party. Before attempting to describe this, however, I must explain my own position between the party and the union. Despite Max Habermann's caustic remarks about Hitler and the Nazis during my job interview, I joined the party again in the early summer of 1926. In August, shortly after our Education Sections were moved from Berlin to Hamburg, I attended the Nazi convention at Weimar, and in November I was elected Nazi Local Group Leader of Hamburg.

As far as it is possible to reconstruct the basis for a decision made a quarter of a century ago, I was moved by the following considerations: The union's accomplishments are certainly exemplary and irreplaceable. But the nature of a union is such that its efforts must be directed toward a rather closely circumscribed and small portion of the nation which is, moreover, affected only in some aspects of life. From this standpoint alone work for and through the party is necessary in order to affect the nation as a whole. Beyond this, the party can say and do things which the union, because of the nature of its task, cannot. These things must be said and done in order to awaken that innermost strength of

the nation so necessary to master the historical situation and to
move the nation toward a goal. If this occasionally requires crudeness and brutality, then that is the price that must be paid. Revolutionaries cannot adhere to the standards of decency of an era
whose spiritual basis they intend to destroy. Even the DHV itself
had to go through a period of "storm and stress" with tumultuous
mass meetings and wildly radical demands. Finally, in a period of
latent or open civil war one has to conduct oneself in a militant
manner.

These thoughts kept me from a conflict of conscience for
approximately two years. The DHV gave me full freedom for my
political activity under the condition that this should not impinge
on my professional activity. For my part I always gave the union
prior notice of my intentions and decisions in order to satisfy the
obligation of mutual trust.

But by the beginning of summer 1928, my experiences as Nazi
Local Group Leader for Hamburg, plus the more precise understanding of the DHV and its field of action that I had gained over
the years, led me to reexamine my previous viewpoint. This did
not produce any basically different conclusions. Then, as before, I
viewed both organizations as necessary and desirable forms in Germany's political life. But I began to realize that my prior assumptions about the differences between the two simply in terms of
divergent areas of activity and different levels of organizational
maturity did not adequately reflect reality. It was not just that the
one appeared limited to a single stratum while the other was concerned with the entire nation; there were also divergent concepts
of goals and tasks. It was this that led inevitably to the differences
in method—the amount of prior political experience was a negligi-
ble factor. This same inevitable difference would therefore produce
mounting tension and ever more frequent clashes between Nazism
and the DHV. As these were likely to be sharpened by fanaticism
or clumsiness on both sides, the future of Germany's state and
society would be threatened with grave injuries. Preventing this
became the goal of a kind of broker's activity which I undertook
seriously after my resignation as Gauleiter early in the summer of
1928. It was to be a tiresome, thankless, and—except for some
temporary successes—largely unproductive activity.

As prologue there was one enterprise in February of that same
year which succeeded so quickly and easily that it gave me over-

confidence in my ventures. Hitler had come to Hamburg for the city elections, and at the request of the DHV's leaders, I took the opportunity to propose a pact for the Reichstag elections, due in May. The DHV hoped that in the Reichstag districts of its delegates Thiel, Gerig, Lambach, and Glatzel, the Nazi party would not put up competing candidates who were also DHV members. Hitler agreed, on condition that the same arrangement would apply to delegate Stöhr (a Nazi). He was even willing to promise that the party would not push the campaign to the full against the DHV candidates.

It was not Hitler's fault that this second promise was not fully kept. The DHV gave its candidates such strong backing, not just by financial contributions but by leaflets, advertisements, and personal campaigning by union officials, that a reaction from the Nazis was bound to be forthcoming. This was particularly true in the DHV's Lower-Rhine-Westphalian district, where the union's campaign for Frank Glatzel (who was running on the People's party ticket) undoubtedly went far beyond even the most generously interpreted standards of "neutrality." The Nazi charge that certain union politicians were turning the DHV into a one-sided political instrument was not without substance.

To be sure, this flowed inevitably from the difficult position of the DHV delegates inside the bourgeois parties. To begin with, their position depended less on what they did for their party than on their nomination by the union as employee representatives. If they had any hope of eventually accomplishing anything in the way of legislation for employees, after their election, they had to make concessions in other areas, for example, foreign policy. Beyond that, they had to attempt to gain support for these concessions through the committees of the DHV. To put it concretely: Delegate Thiel would be able to get the People's party to back employee insurance, hours regulation, and protection for older employees only if he voted for the Locarno Pact and the Dawes Plan and at the same time appeared at least theoretically able to deliver a certain number of votes in the next election. Naturally it was not just delegates Thiel or Lambach who were interested in the success of this political horsetrading, but the mass of DHV members and all employees in Germany.

But it was precisely this that the Nazi members could not and would not see. It was partly that they could not grasp the connec-

tion and partly also that they viewed the delegates' activities in the
bourgeois parties as wholly superfluous since the Nazi party was
going to satisfy completely all just social demands once it gained
power. Above all, however, most of them felt that personal and
professional goals should be sacrificed for the general need of the
fatherland. The revolutionary struggle for national liberation must
ignore the interests of the individual. Beyond that, any social measures accomplished by the Weimar "system" would be vitiated by
the burden of reparations, in their view.

These last considerations played an essential role in the reaction,
mentioned above, to the union's campaign on behalf of Glatzel in
Lower Rhine-Westphalia. The reaction came primarily from a
group of serious young unionists led by Peter Berns, of Mettmann,
who was to become the national leader of one of the youth movements a year later. Since I knew Berns, I began my first efforts as
organizational broker in Lower Rhine-Westphalia.

My hope was to find capable, trustworthy Nazi members in each
of the twenty-seven DHV districts, men who would be influential
and respected in both the party and the union. These in turn
would create a network of local agents, hopefully also with good
connections in both organizations, who would be able to gather
around them in loose form the Nazi members of the DHV. I
wanted no true, stringently organized cell system, since this would
not have helped to reconcile differences: The leaders of both the
union and the party, with whom I had to deal, had made it clear
that they opposed the formation of cells within their organizations.
This apparatus of contact men and agents was to develop a
common outlook and purpose by exchanging reports, experiences,
and advice. Then, in the event of conflict, they were to work upon
the appropriate offices of either the party or the union.

As "intellectual foundation" I wrote an article entitled "Party
and Trade Union" in November 1928 for the *Nationalsozialistischen Briefe* (Vol. IV, No. 10). I had already presented essentially the same ideas in a lecture at a Nazi leadership conference in
October 1928.[12] My article, following Dr. Stapel's distinction
between "state" and "society," attempted to derive the different
areas of activity of the party and the union from their involvement

---

[12] Actually in August: see Dietrich Orlow, *The History of the Nazi Party,
1919 to 1933* (Pittsburgh, 1969), p. 139.

in these two levels of concern. The party has a state function; it is masculine, militant, directed toward discipline and duty. It deals with domestic and foreign affairs, if necessary by revolutionary means. It plans the future and thereby has only limited concern for the single individual. The trade union has a social-popular function. Like a mother, it provides for daily needs and for every single member. It moves toward the goal of an organically developed community spirit through its shepherding of the emotionally perceived values of civilization. With its organs of self-administration and self-help it is the great school of social-political leadership for the broad stratum of workers. To put it briefly: The union (along with other professional organizations) preserves and fosters materially and spiritually the substance of the nation for whose state form and preservation the party fights. Viewed biologically, society (the union) has preeminence. Viewed politically, the state (party) does. Both realms find unifying synthesis in the concept of the nation.

From this basic, if perhaps overdrawn, schematization I drew the following conclusions for the party's policies: "One can never lead a revolutionary struggle for state power through a trade union. Its concern for its members drives it into daily compromises, into hundreds of public and private entanglements with the ruling system. The party demands sacrifices of its members, but with unions it is results that count. The party has its roots in ideals, while the union has its roots primarily in the material. All the differences which exist between state and society also exist between party and union. These will become capable of being bridged only in a new *Reich*. Today every entanglement, every taint from our own establishment must be avoided. . . . Insofar as we need the temporary support of the union as a stage in the course of our political struggles, we must attempt to reach a *modus vivendi* with the Christian-National unions and the DHV. . . . Insofar as we need to win workers for our ideals and conception of the state, we shall have to work through the formation of industrial cells. Organization of the shops is the militant method in the attack upon the state. . . ."[13]

This article and the previously mentioned lecture at the leader-

---

[13] Hitler reached the same conclusion earlier and for mostly similar reasons; see *Mein Kampf* (Mannheim translation, Boston, 1962), pp. 596–606.

ship conference had good effects. For one thing, all attempts to form Nazi unions were henceforth officially prohibited and the national leadership began serious preparation for the establishment of the National Socialist Shop-Cell Organization (NSBO). But most important was that I now had more or less official party approval for my own work in building a network of agents.

The DHV, on the other hand, was far less enchanted by my formulation. They did not consider themselves to be a "stage in the struggle" and had no desire to become one for the Nazi party in the future. Also one could properly have pointed out that the DHV, even if it did have a motherly, protective function, still showed far more manly clarity and decisiveness in its structure and attitude than did the Nazi party, which like most mass movements showed strongly feminine, emotionalistic characteristics. But on the other hand, the tactical usefulness of my formulation was perceived. Hence there was no protest or rebuttal issued.

The organization of Nazi liaison men in the DHV did not develop as planned. Apart from personnel problems the chief difficulty was the open mistrust of the Nazis and the covert opposition of some DHV officials whose attitude apparently derived from the still unsettled leadership struggle in the union between Bechly and Habermann. Ultimately district liaison men were established in only four of the twenty-seven districts. And even in these, despite extensive, difficult, and "clandestine" correspondence, the results were meager: a few clarifying conversations, the dissipation of some quarrels, and finally cooperation in a secondary action: the arrangement of numerous weekend conferences and indoctrination workshops all over Germany for Nazi DHV members. These were carried out through Section 17 and the District Education Offices. Local party officials were informed; the liaison men collaborated.

The weekend conferences usually began in a tense atmosphere. The participants arrived loaded with complaints, ready to pound on the table and demand redress—preferably the resignation of Bechly and the entire DHV administration. With the introductory lecture, which regularly put forth the thesis of the two areas of endeavor from my article "Party and Union," the basis was already laid for a more objective and fruitful discussion. Insofar as the participants accepted this thesis they were able to work out the tactical consequences of it for day-to-day politics. Even when this did not immediately settle all disagreements, at least it permitted them to be ranked in order of importance and it helped separate the valid political concerns from the emotionalistic eruptions.

The charges (lumped under the general heading of "corruption"), which dealt with the salaries of union officials, the construction of the new office building in Hamburg, the purchase of expensive automobiles, ceased to play a significant part in the discussions. On the other hand there was strong emphasis on demands that had been made by the party and rejected by the union: for compulsory savings, an industrial community of interest, and action to combat department stores and cooperatives. There were also heated discussions on the policies pursued by the DHV's delegates in the bourgeois parties as well as the union's attitude toward "fulfillment."

The common denominator was usually that in matters of purely social or trade union policy the Nazi members had practically unlimited trust in the DHV and were even willing, on such questions, to take stands contrary to the party's. When properly informed of the need for tactical cooperation with bourgeois parties they accepted this so fully that they declared the party's attacks in these areas to be harmful or, at the very least, uncalled for. Of course, this toleration had limits. It was temporary and moreover would countenance no violation of "fundamental principles." Thus, for example, the complaints against the DHV's connections with the "Jewish-finance-capitalistic" People's Party were far more frequent than those against our collaboration with the Catholic Center party. Finally, the participants were always extremely sensitive about any action that could be construed as treason against the national cause.

Surprisingly enough it was the younger participants in the conferences who were the least trouble, even though they were usually also party activists or Stormtroopers. They were generally well informed and receptive to objective and reasonable considerations so long as these were not intellectually arrogant sophistries. Beyond that, their desire for honest objectivity occasionally enabled them to find fault in actions by the union which really were faulty. All told, this first generation of young Nazis possessed a much greater internal freedom and critical ability than most of their successors who came out of the Hitler Youth system of education.

The indoctrination workshops, of which I recall five being held in the years 1928 to 1931, had a much broader purpose and were far less involved with immediate issues than the weekend conferences. They were supposed to provide young cadres with a broad enough vision of the entire political situation to enable them to function with political sophistication whether within the party or the union. For pedagogical, psychological, and political reasons I conducted these workshops alone, giving up my original plan to invite officials from the party and the union as participants. The results of these workshops, however (apart from some pleasant personal experiences), did not justify either my efforts or my expectations. The participants were chosen by mutually mistrustful local officials of the party and the union and thus were rarely really capable colleagues. But it was precisely those few able people who most needed theoretical training and guidance in practical affairs. Thus when the workshops were over, the ideas and techniques that had been transmitted largely went to waste, as did the personal relationships that had been established. It was only after my expulsion from the Nazi party that I learned—through many letters— that my efforts had not been wholly feckless.

My efforts toward reconciling the party and the DHV by stressing their different areas of activity were not limited to indoctrination within the union. I also explained my position to Nazi leaders by constant speaking and writing. In the sphere of purely social policy, where other Nazis in the DHV worked toward the same goal (such men as Stöhr, Marschler, Murr, and many minor Local Group leaders), there was some success. Especially Gregor Strasser and his circle, the leaders of the Nazi Shop-Cell Organization, were receptive to such arguments. This was the prime reason why Strasser wanted me to become technical specialist for social policy in the Nazi national office in December 1930.

Alfred Rosenberg and Baldur von Schirach[14] also showed a surprisingly benevolent interest in the DHV. Both were primarily impressed by the union's cultural achievements: our library, our two publishing houses (the Albert Langen and Hanseatic Press), our youth education, our development of new social forms, etc.

[14] Respectively editor of the chief Nazi newspaper, *Völkischer Beobachter*, and national leader of the Hitler Youth. Both are described below, respectively, in Chapters 8 and 10.

Schirach's interest had no practical consequences, but Rosenberg made me a promise, in November 1930, not to attack the DHV in its capacity as a union through the pages of the *Völkischer Beobachter* without really compelling reasons. He did not abandon this policy until the presidential elections of 1932. Rudolf Hess[15] was also always ready to listen to my views on the DHV and its problems. But since he felt himself to be nothing more than Hitler's instrument, he carefully avoided taking any personal stance or decision.

The party treasurer, Franz Xaver Schwarz, was another friend of the DHV within the national administrative offices. His benevolence was not because of me but because of the "economic dictator" of the DHV, General Manager Winter. He and Schwarz had professional contact stemming from the refinancing of the Stormtrooper insurance through the Deutsche Ring. Through this business connection both men developed first respect, then affection for one another. Schwarz's feelings extended also to the DHV, though Winter, a Swabian democrat, had little use for Nazism.

From the spring of 1930 a new situation began to affect relationships between the party and the union. The DHV had joined with the Christian Trade Unions, the Center party, the Army, and the free conservative forces within the Peasant Movement in getting Brüning chosen as Reich Chancellor. "The DHV" meant primarily Max Habermann, who had established himself as the union's "foreign minister." Habermann told me of his hopes for Brüning in a long conversation that we had immediately following the unofficial conference between the "kingmakers" and President von Hindenburg's aides. Brüning's chancellorship, he said, would have to bring about that decisive change in German politics which could no longer be postponed in view of the constantly growing revolutionary threat. If this change did not occur, then the future would belong to dark and violent forces. To be sure, the chancellor would have to make harsh demands on the German people, and especially on the political parties—demands of a material nature, but also intellectual demands. The happy little parliamentary game of musical chairs could not continue without destroying the last remnants of the state's authority. There must be an end to the

---

[15] Deputy leader of the Nazi party. He is described in Chapter 7.

all too comfortable trick of blaming everything on the Treaty of Versailles and reparations while avoiding any real solution to the reparations problem. And finally, it was high time to fight the opposition not just with new laws but with a spirit of self-criticism. As soon as honest tendencies became manifest within the revolutionary opposition, then responsible political leaders would have to seek out the serious roots. They would have to eradicate their own mistakes and convert any healthy and justified concerns of the revolutionaries into fruitful state policy. This fundamental approach was now to be applied to the Nazi party. And what, Habermann asked, did I think of this approach?

This was a question Habermann often asked, even before Brüning became chancellor, and one which I could never answer clearly —primarily because we spoke different languages on these matters. For Habermann, the Nazi party was like all the other parties and should be judged by the statements of its speakers and its press, its parliamentary activity, and its program. He could not see that an understanding of these surface phenomena would not produce an understanding of the forces that actually moved the party. His clear, candid, North German manner, which operated through a strict and highly schematic mental discipline, gave him no access to areas where inordinate desires, directionless and formless feelings, drives, and yearnings were predominant.

He could not comprehend the chiliastic hopes that hundreds of thousands of honest German men and women put into this movement as the ultimate fulfillment of their ancient prayers, hopes, and struggles for the rebirth of the German nation. Even ten years later, after so many hard experiences,[16] he still could not understand that demonic quality, so scornful of traditional moral values, that gripped the inner circles of the Nazi party.

My answers were thus hardly comprehensible to him, since they derived from my deeper acquaintance with the underlying attitudes of the party's leaders, especially Hitler. I had hoped that the powerful forces of the masses, summoned up by the Nazis and cut loose from old particularist and class allegiances, that this inchoate faith in and striving for the future could be integrated into an

[16] Habermann was arrested for his part in the "July 20" plot against Hitler and committed suicide in prison in October 1944.

organic development. But I had no concept of how that was to be accomplished.

Hitler, in any event, would be primarily interested in finding coalition partners who would be weaker—in numbers, in energy, and in skill. Where was the German politician who could—so to speak with a submachine gun in one hand—force Hitler into a coalition of honest equality and honorable cooperation? Was Brüning the man? Habermann, who always thought of Hitler as only a tribune of the people, had no doubt of Brüning's ability to do this. To be sure, he believed that Brüning was not yet thinking of a coalition and was hardly making any overtures before the September 1930 elections. But after that the matter ought to be given serious consideration. One could, perhaps, at least gain acceptance of the union's position in the area of social policy.

I was skeptical about this, too. As long as the DHV conducted politics through its obvious system of cross connections and the tactical maneuvers that stemmed from them, there was not much to be gained from simply negotiating with the Nazis, in my estimation. These cross connections and maneuvers would continually cause arguments between the party and the union, with the DHV at a perpetual disadvantage. I believed only a voluntary self-limitation to the arena of pure union affairs (perhaps temporarily) could put the DHV in a position to hold discussions with the Nazi party. Even then any negotiations would still involve recriminations and demands. I was thinking of the development and publication of a general social program which, solely through its objective significance, would force the party into a response. I suggested that even if one did not take the party seriously, at least its members had to be taken seriously. The childishly silly or arrogantly blasé talk, in the major newspapers, about primitives and rowdies simply lacked any force of conviction.

Habermann was receptive to my views but decided that I was asking a bit too much of the DHV. For the time being, therefore, he would continue to operate according to tried and true methods.

A start in this direction was made in July 1930 when the DHV endorsed the candidacy of Albert Forster for the Reichstag elections. Six months beforehand Forster had been transferred from Nuremberg to the DHV accounts office in Hamburg so that from the home office he could acquire a more comprehensive insight into the union's total work. He had, nevertheless, made no effort to accomplish this. Instead, he spent all his free time and half his working hours traveling around Schleswig-Holstein as Gau speaker for the Nazis (he was not welcome in Gau Hamburg). In gratitude, Hinrich Lohse (the Gauleiter of Schleswig-Holstein) gave him a sure spot on the Schleswig-Holstein candidate list, while at the same time, at Hitler's special request, he was put on the national list, too.[17] Hitler liked Forster for precisely those qualities in him which irritated everyone else: his rhetoric, his gestures of "faith in victory," his complete lack of independent thought or judgment, and his boundless combativeness. Forster was not especially malicious or domineering; furthermore he had good common sense, even though he lacked formal education. He was essentially what is called "a big dumb guy" who vainly took himself for an accomplished politician.

This young man thus became, along with Stöhr, an official Reichstag candidate of the DHV, which included him in its campaign literature and made the customary financial contribution to the Nazi party for him. Naturally he was required to resign his union job which so surprised and terrified him that he came to my office quite pale to beg for my support in getting him a conditional rehiring agreement from Bechly and Habermann. "After all, it could be a flop," he stuttered; "maybe Adolf will lose his nerve and make another Putsch, like in 1923. Or we may not have any luck with the voters any more. The people may see that things are getting better and then . . . then I sure wouldn't want to wind up on unemployment pay, you know."

So the strong, victorious fighter had highly petty bourgeois qualms. I made no attempt to assuage them; on the contrary, I made it clear to him that he ought to be ashamed of himself. In

---

[17] In Weimar Germany's proportional representation system, votes were cast for parties, not individual candidates. Parties drew up lists of candidates for each electoral district (equivalent in area to the Nazi Gau) and for every 60,000 votes the party received another candidate was elected. Thus those at the top of the list had the safer spots. Any surplus votes from the individual districts were applied to the national lists. Thus, to be placed on the national list meant virtual assurance of election. See F. A. Hermans, "Proportional Representation and the Breakdown of German Democracy", *Social Research*, Vol. III (1936), pp. 411–433.

the revolutionary struggle onc burned one's bridges, especially those leading back to people whom you were constantly attacking because of their allegedly weak willingness to compromise.

Nothing whatsoever came from Forster's election. He was inactive within the Nazi Reichstag caucus and therefore had no effect upon practical social legislation. Since he had no ambition in this direction at all, he never responded to the various requests and suggestions from the DHV. In 1932 he was expelled from the union for his wild attacks on President von Hindenburg. In 1934, as Gauleiter of Danzig, he made a few ineffectual gestures toward saving the DHV from submersion into the German Labor Front. Since, however, he had no clear conception of how unions were to fit into the Nazi system, he was easily dispatched by Dr. Robert Ley.[18]

After the September 1930 Reichstag elections the new policy which Habermann had first mentioned to me early in the summer began to reveal itself in broad outlines. On September 19, 20, and 21, I was in Munich, Berchtesgaden, and Berlin to prepare the way for an interview between Hitler and Brüning. The request came via Habermann, from whom I was referred on to Treviranus.[19] This was not a coalition negotiation but rather a personal meeting by which Brüning simply hoped to become acquainted with Hitler. At a second conversation, which took place a few weeks later, Brüning attempted to explain to Hitler what role a constructive and responsible opposition could play in his foreign policy plans.

According to Habermann (who, to be sure, inclined toward optimistic judgments), both discussions went relatively well.[20] To begin with, Hitler was said to have not simply spoken but actually listened and above all immediately comprehended what it was that Brüning wanted of him. On the other hand, according to reports from the party, Brüning made a strong impression on Hitler. "That is a real man!" Hitler was supposed to have said after the first conversation. To be sure, the consequences for the future were

[18] Subsequent head of the German Labor Front, a Nazi party subsidiary, which took over the role of all unions in 1933.

[19] This episode is described in greater detail in Chapter 5.

[20] Brüning, in his posthumously published memoirs, mentions only the second meeting, at which he says Hitler gave an hour-long speech, which Brüning thought resembled Mussolini's style.

that Brüning was viewed as the one really dangerous adversary who blocked the path to power. Therefore, the struggle against him grew ever sharper until in the end Brüning appeared to be the Evil One Himself to the average fanatical Nazi.

But this emerged later. In the year 1931 views and verdicts shifted back and forth; the DHV leaders were still inclined to see the polemics against Brüning in the Nazi newspapers and mass meetings as analogous to the practices of other parties and thus not to be taken seriously. Despite these attacks they still believed in the possibility of arranging connections. Then occasionally they would again become disinclined to foster any closer relations. When I reread my diary pages, which record conversations with Habermann and Ziegler over this whole complex question, there emerges a confusing picture of moves, countermoves, and rapidly changing estimates of the situation.

When the 107-man Nazi delegation marched out of the Reichstag in February 1931 and proclaimed to the masses that their withdrawal was a revolutionary deed, Habermann talked about hollow demonstrations and a manifest inability to deal effectively in politics. In truth, since no revolutionary deeds followed the withdrawal, it remained without practical consequences. After a few weeks the Nazis secretly tiptoed back into the Reichstag. In the ensuing months the dominant mood inside the DHV was that the internal attrition of the Nazi party had already commenced and would proceed at a rapid pace once Brüning's policies demonstrated their expected success. This mood was based on the good results which they thought he had obtained through the use of emergency decrees.[21] Brüning was so sure of himself, they said, that he brushed aside the proposal of Otto Braun and some of the generals that a dictatorship should be established as a defense against the Nazi threat.[22] Furthermore, the slow but undeniable

[21] Beginning in 1930, Brüning issued decrees through the constitution's Emergency Clause (Article 48) instead of having laws passed by the legislature. This violated the spirit of the constitution by making his cabinet independent of the Reichstag.

[22] Otto Braun was a major leader of the Social Democrats and head of the state government of Prussia, which constituted three-fifths of Germany. Neither his nor Brüning's memoirs mention Braun offering to support a dictatorship; on the contrary, Braun persuasively details his logical and ideological

internal strengthening of the DHV seemed to indicate an abatement of the Nazi power drive. The political agitation within the Local Groups lessened. At my sessions with Nazi DHV members during 1931, criticism against the union declined while that against the party increased. Since it was primarily younger members who reacted in this way, this was justifiably viewed as a success for the Circle of Young DHV Members and its fine magazine, *State and Estate*. Beyond that, there were similar experiences in the universities, where the fraternities showed themselves far more capable of resisting the Nazi Student League than were the unaffiliated students or those in political organizations. This too fostered the conclusion that the mature associations had risen from the nadir of their susceptibility and that it was now only the masses from the spiritually and organizationally anchorless lower middle classes who were streaming into the Nazi party.

While there was much to be said for this idea, the hopes that were linked to it were far too optimistic in the face of the then clearly visible election trends. The extent to which judgment could become divorced from concrete events was demonstrated at the time of the great bank crisis at the end of July 1931.[23] The Nazis expected not just the fall of Brüning but of the whole Weimar Republic, and they prepared themselves to inherit everything. Habermann viewed the twilight of the banks as the end of the whole previous reparations policy and thus the first great international success of Brüning. His assumption was doubtless correct. But this success was primarily a theoretical and abstract matter from which the man in the street could hardly perceive any advantage. On the contrary, unemployment and distress would increase considerably before the inevitable economic effects of the success

opposition to the whole notion. This apparent rumor perhaps derived from Braun's offer to resign and let Brüning combine the offices of Reich chancellor and Prussian minister-president through personal union, an idea Braun had espoused since 1927. See Otto Braun, *Von Weimar zu Hitler* (New York, 1940), pp. 354–370.

[23] A run on Germany's banks led the government to declare a temporary bank holiday, after which the banks reopened with no further trouble. But this incident led President Herbert Hoover to declare a one-year "moratorium" on international debts, including reparations. A few months later Brüning unilaterally declared that Germany would never pay reparations again. He had previously exaggerated their harm to Germany.

in ending reparations would begin to bear fruit. Furthermore, none of Brüning's collaborators were skillful enough propagandists to make this success meaningful to the people. The entire "state-supporting" press failed miserably. Even in the eleventh hour of the republic they did nothing but recite their same worn-out political clichés filled with partisan phrases and spitefulness.

Brüning's friends, nevertheless, were well satisfied in those August days. Within the DHV the politics of national concern receded before the politics of trade union concern. These arose from attacks by the Nazis, or by certain Nazi groups such as the Nazi League of Physicians, upon the medical insurance fund or the independence of the employee insurance. The bigger the Nazi party became, the more it inclined toward standardizing and leveling, or *Gleichschaltung* as it was later called. The ideological similarity to Marxist attitudes, which had long been apparent to perceptive observers despite (or perhaps precisely because of) the bitter mutual enmity between the two, now began to manifest itself also in overt measures. It was still possible to uphold one's own position through argumentation in the press and simultaneous representations before the Nazi leadership. But in the long run it proved impossible to maintain the complete self-administration of the medical fund and employee insurance. Of course, this did not come until after the Nazi seizure of power.

One factor that contributed to the temporary frustration of these dangerous trends in social policy was the financial link that existed since autumn 1930 between the Nazi Insurance Plan and the Deutsche Ring. Yet neither the extent nor the effect of this connection should be overestimated, since none of the partners on the Nazi side (Schwarz, Dr. Wagener, Pfeffer von Salomon[24]) had any extensive influence on political decisions.

On the national level the situation rapidly changed again. The formation of the Harzburg Front,[25] though it demonstrated that

---

[24] Supreme commander of the Stormtroopers, 1926–30, and subsequently head of the Stormtrooper Quartermaster's Department. The Nazis required every Stormtrooper to insure himself against injury from street fighting. This was then reinsured with the Deutsche Ring, an insurance group associated with the DHV. Pfeffer is described in Chapter 10.

[25] A temporary alliance between the Nazis, the Steel Helmets, and the German Nationalist party.

Hitler, in pursuing the "legal road to power," had become ready to seek allies, showed also that he sought them from decidedly social-reactionary and capitalistic circles. Though the former fact could be viewed as indicating Hitler's progress toward an understanding of practical politics, his turning to Hugenburg, Schacht, and their reactionary friends was like an alarm signal to the DHV leadership. Beyond that, the resignation of Curtius[26] at the beginning of October 1931 required Brüning to reshuffle his cabinet, an apparently difficult task. It was even more difficult for the chancellor to obtain a vote of confidence from the Reichstag. When he finally did, on October 16, his margin came to exactly twenty-four votes.

Under the influence of all these events, Habermann wrote an article, "Brüning and Hitler," which had the goal of leading the two men together. The article appeared in the DHV's *Handelswacht* and was reprinted in a number of major newspapers: *Der Deutscher, Die Tägliche Rundschau, Germania,* and others. We also printed it in the *Hamburger Tageblatt,*[27] where it was given a lightly critical introduction by the political editor, Wolf Meyer-Christian, and where it caused great displeasure on the part of the Gauleiter and a considerable number of our readers.

The first effect was satisfactory: There was an uproar in the Nationalist party press and in the newspapers of heavy industry. Gregor Strasser gave a speech in which he embraced socialism, and this was beyond doubt taken as an answer to Habermann's article. Beyond that, he wrote a personal letter to Habermann in which he invited closer contact. Ultimately, after initial hesitations, Strasser arranged a conference between Bechly, Habermann, Hitler, Hess, and himself.

This meeting took place in Munich on November 6, 1931. Hitler's participation, according to Habermann, was disappointing and produced virtually no results. Bechly and Habermann between them had about fifteen minutes' opportunity to speak and then were treated to a three-quarter-hour monologue in which Hitler said nothing at all about the current political situation but simply set forth his fundamental positions. Contained in these was at

[26] Foreign minister and representative of the People's party.
[27] Krebs' Nazi newspaper for Hamburg, described in Chapter 4.

least the promise that unions, wage agreements, and the state arbitration system would be preserved in a Nazi Reich.[28]

Following the "audience" with Hitler there was a conversation with Rudolf Hess that was at least quite useful in clarifying attitudes on both sides. Hess listened carefully and took great pains to grasp the opinions of others. But as far as political results were concerned, Hess was valueless, since, in accordance with his custom, he reserved all decisions for Hitler.

The actual theme of the visit—"Brüning and Hitler"—could be discussed in a fundamental way only with Gregor Strasser. Habermann later reported that he had been very frank with Strasser. He told him that he was trying to promote cooperation between Hitler and Brüning solely in the belief that Brüning was the last and only German politician who might still be able to control the force of Nazism and put it to work for Germany's future. After Brüning there was no one. The middle-class parties, except for the Catholic Center, which was not strong enough to take over responsibility by itself alone, were intellectually and numerically bankrupt. The Social Democrats still had most of their voting strength, thanks primarily to the Free Unions, but they were as intellectually sterile in confronting the driving new ideas as the bourgeois parties were. Thus sooner or later, unless the Army could be used against him under some pretext, Hitler would actually come to power legally. His opponents would be so weak that none of them would be able to prevent him from establishing a total dictatorship. In Habermann's view such a dictatorship would be a catastrophe for Germany.

Strasser agreed partially with Habermann's analysis but had no confidence in a successful collaboration between Brüning and Hitler. Nevertheless, from the time of that conversation on, the political relationship between Strasser and Habermann grew ever closer. It outlasted the overthrow of Brüning, Strasser's resignation from his party offices, General von Schleicher's plans, and Hitler's victory on January 30, 1933. It ended only with the assassination of Strasser on June 30, 1934.

It soon became apparent that Strasser could not further the hopes Habermann had expressed in his article. Already by mid-

[28] All these promises were, of course, later broken.

November I heard from Habermann's secretary that the Strasser-Hitler-Brüning connection was collapsing. On November 27 I visited Hitler and Hess and learned myself that they saw little value in any closer relationship with Brüning. Even without him and against him they were sure of coming into the government. Habermann's efforts appeared to have been wholly in vain.

The DHV now turned its attention to the forthcoming presidential election, which it thought would be decisive for Germany. During my above mentioned visit to Munich I tried, at Habermann's request, to get some intimation from Hitler or Hess as to Nazi intentions for the presidential election. I got none, obviously because they had not given the matter any thought. Hitler said he was depending on God, who hopefully would let the "old fogey who can't pee any more" (Hindenburg) die before the election. He also depended on his own intuition, which would show him the right way at the right moment. Hess was depending on Hitler. My suggestion, inspired by Habermann, that Hitler should endorse Hindenburg as the Nazi candidate, was not favorably received. They did not intend to make any long-term plans or commitments.

The uncertainty over Nazi intentions for the presidential campaign lasted for many weeks. By mid-January 1932 it had at least become clear that the Nazis would refuse to endorse Hindenburg again.[29] Brüning had wanted to prevent a national campaign by letting the Reichstag reelect Hindenburg.[30] His confidential soundings of the parties over this met with refusal, first from Hugenberg and then from Hitler. At the same time Dr. Wilhelm Frick[31] began to speak publicly against a Hindenburg candidacy.

For the DHV this was a most difficult situation. It was impossible to avoid taking a position on this vital question of German politics. Logically, the union's previous support for Brüning necessitated support for Hindenburg, since Brüning's political position

[29] When Hindenburg was first elected Reich president in 1925 he had been endorsed by the Nazis and opposed by the Catholic Center and Social Democratic parties. In 1932 the exact opposite occurred.

[30] Actually he tried to get the Reichstag to extend Hindenburg's term by two years, which would have required a two-thirds majority.

[31] Nazi minister of the interior for the state of Thuringia, 1930–31, and Reich minister of the interior after 1933.

and effectiveness depended on Hindenburg's confidence. Should Hindenburg be nominated, the DHV would have no choice unless it wished to shift its political position completely: It had to endorse his nomination. On February 3, 1932, Bechly signed the Sahm committee's appeal calling for Hindenburg's reelection. He did so at first only as an individual and not as chairman of the DHV, but a few days later the union also signed.

This decision put an end to the temporary armistice of 1931 between the DHV and the Nazi party. Though the Nazis waited for two weeks to announce Hitler's candidacy, bitter attacks on the DHV by the Nazi press and by speakers began the moment Bechly joined the Sahm committee. With the first heat of the campaign, clashes grew sharper and led again to numerous expulsions of Nazis from the union. Albert Forster, as noted above, was one of those expelled, as was Friedrich Stanick, the Nazi country leader of Hamburg.

In consequence there were no further attempts to resolve differences and renew contacts between the party and the union, even though Brüning's overthrow removed one cause of conflict. Nazi politics were henceforth so clearly aimed toward a total seizure of power that the DHV hardly saw an opening. The only remaining link was that between Max Habermann and Gregor Strasser. This took on a new significance in the second half of 1932 because of the various hopes and maneuvers of General von Schleicher.[32] However, the goal was no longer to incorporate the entire Nazi party into a politically reorganized Reich. Now the goal was to split the Nazis into a constructive (not "moderate") half under Gregor Strasser and a radical, nihilistic half under Hitler. In this plan it was agreed that the influence of the parties—all parties— would be rigidly curtailed in the future to the benefit of corporate professional organizations and a legislative upper house.

I cannot report the details of the various political events and moves during these last months before Hitler took power, since I was severely ill, unable to work, and hardly in contact with the outer world. When I finally returned to the DHV office in May 1933 there was little left of the union except its name, and the

[32] Minister of defense from June to November 1932 and then chancellor in December and January 1933, Kurt von Schleicher was the decisive political figure in the death throes of the Weimar Republic.

Nazis wanted to change even that. They did so by forcing the fusion of all the various white-collar unions: the DHV, the Christian Union, and the Socialist ZdA. The "coordinated" result bore the designation "German Office Workerhood" for about a year thereafter, when it too was incorporated into the Labor Front, which was organized, in the Marxian manner, by industries.

The old administration was disbanded; most of its members plus almost all the section directors were fired—some of them without notice and, furthermore, forbidden to enter the offices, while the employees were told not to have any further contact with them. Director Winter, as a consequence of the false and malicious charges against him by the new "union leaders," committed suicide. This new leadership of the union was primarily composed of people whose credentials consisted of little more than a Nazi membership card, a desire for recognition, and a questionable character.

But even these people had no wish, once the smoke of victory had blown away, to sacrifice the entire tradition and property of the DHV to the pretensions of Dr. Ley and his Labor Front. Until autumn 1934 I was able to observe their fierce and (in view of the atmosphere) courageous struggle to maintain themselves. But before I can describe this I must return to some of the factors involving my own position in the period between summer 1930 and May 1932.

The preparations for the Reichstag elections late in the summer of 1930 gave new importance to the Hamburg Nazi newspaper, the weekly *Hansische Warte*, whose editor I had been since 1929. The DHV therefore decided to lighten my working load somewhat and to give the newspaper (which was privately owned by the former business manager of the Nazi party in Hamburg, Edgar Brinkmann) a subsidy of a few thousand marks. This was due to the new attitude described above, which the DHV had developed toward the Nazi party, but it was also in accordance with the union's usual practice. In addition to its economic function, the DHV was involved in a variety of enterprises, some political, some not. In this case it was not actually a subsidy that was given but rather a loan (which, like all others, was eventually later repaid) or, as was later the case with the *Hamburger Tageblatt*, the frequent purchase of advertising space for Deutsche Ring insurance.

Nevertheless, the loan, which naturally could not be kept a secret in the long run, was used by the Gauleiter as a reason or pretext for constant attacks on the newspaper and on me as its editor. The course of this struggle need not be described in detail here[33] except to note that at its climax higher offices intervened. In the summer of 1931, when Munich still valued the friendly attitude of the DHV and had just as little fear of tiny subventions from union treasuries as they had of crass gifts from capitalists, this intervention was beneficial for the newspaper. The *Tageblatt* became the property of the Nazi publishing firm Eher *Verlag*, but Brinkmann and I remained in our positions with a relatively large amount of independence. In May 1932, the Gau finally had its victory and I was fired, mainly because Hitler and Goebbels wanted to give the whole Brüning-DHV-Strasser tendency something to think about.

The newspaper's attitude toward Brüning's policies had been determined by the following considerations (which were a subject of constant and passionate debate among its editors): If the Nazi party really wanted to come to power as part of a coalition, then the only meaningful and possible partner would be Brüning. This was recognized even by those of my colleagues who did not share my mistrust toward the party and its leadership—a mistrust that had been growing since 1930. We were all strongly opposed to collaboration with the "patriotic bourgeoisie" of the right-wing parties, but for different reasons. My colleagues feared a "watering down of the goal" through the infiltration of reactionary attitudes and capitalistic forces. In their view the "goal" was a completely formed spiritual fact that the party and its leaders were going to turn into a political and constitutional reality. For me, Nazism was an intellectual and spiritual current but hardly conceptually complete or sufficient as the basis for a practical and permanent political structure. But above all I could no longer visualize or accept the Nazi party as the instrument, nor its leadership with Hitler at the head, as the honest servants of this "goal," whether the goal was clear or not. I saw only a power bloc consisting of and driven by idealistic and demonic forces. This bloc would have pulverized any "patriotic bourgeoisie" in a coalition. The result would be the total dictatorship of Hitler which, by the way, would also be a "watering down of the goal." Those were my fears, for since 1931 at the very latest I no longer wanted to see a complete victory of

[33] It is covered fully in Chapter 4.

the party with its inevitable consequence of an unlimited dictatorship.

Obviously I could not explain this clearly to my colleagues. But neither was this necessary, since we were united in the conclusion: prevent every alliance with the "patriotic right," hold open the possibility of a coalition with Brüning, and, finally, maintain and continue the original anti-parliamentary revolutionary attitude of the Nazi movement. Even conservatives could be won over by the argument that a real revolution would not only eliminate the Weimar Republic but would also cleanse and purify the Nazi party, the paramilitary forces, the trade unions, and all the other big and little groups.

My expulsion from the party in May 1932 put an end to the attempted development and promulgation of a separate political line in the newspaper. It did not put an end to the consequences of this attempt or to my peculiar position between the union and the party. Even though I was no longer a Nazi, my prior membership was a headache to the DHV's new masters. At first they tried to rid themselves of it by a very simple method. Three days after I resumed work in May 1933 I received telegraphic notice of my immediate dismissal without any explanation. I raised objections, but before they could be dealt with, orders from Hess and Karl Kaufmann[34] rescinded my dismissal. Two former members of my editorial staff had secured these orders without my having asked them.

Now new methods were used to remove me. Neither an office nor duties were given to me, but I acquired both without worrying too much about the objections of my immediate superior, Herr Schneider from Nuremberg. That was not difficult since he hardly understood what the work was all about. So then they tried to draw me into ensnaring conversations in order to use some unguarded remark of mine as a weapon against me. That failed too, since I was forewarned by the secretary of the union's new chairman. (The secretary had participated in one of my indoctrination workshops.) Finally I was told to produce a statement that I was not in touch with Max Habermann and would make no attempt to meet him in the future. I could only state truthfully

---

[34] Krebs' successor as the Gauleiter of Hamburg.

that our families had been friendly for years and that I had no intention of changing this, especially since I owed a debt of gratitude to Max Habermann for many things. This declaration was duly noted as were my continued visits to Habermann, which were surely reported by the spies posted before Habermann's house. But ultimately they let me alone because they needed me again.

This was because the situation in some of the union's offices had been rapidly clarified and reconstituted. After autumn 1933, for example, a change in directors for Section 17 led to an orderly resumption of work through conferences of the section members. It was "orderly" only in the sense of method, external organization, and the routine production of informative material. The meaning and objective of our work had either been lost or had never been rethought and reformulated. This was not our fault but rather that of the entire situation the union found itself in. As long as there were doubts about its future role, or for that matter about its continued existence, educational work functioned in a vacuum.

Unfortunately, the union's leadership had produced little in the way of new ideas or proposals to influence its future status. It is surely false to assume that the Nazi leadership had already worked out the future form of the "Labor Front" by the time they came to power. Naturally all the centralizing, totalitarian, authoritarian currents within the party pointed in the direction of such a mass organization, just as similar tendencies in Marxism desire an all-comprehensive and unitary trade union. But given the prevailing contradictory currents and tendencies in Nazism, developments in the initial months of the Third Reich were doubtless still fluid. All that was needed was to have the responsible people produce a clearly thought-out scheme, couched in the appropriate Nazi terminology, in order to maintain at least some independence and freedom of action for the German Office Workerhood.

But despite the goodwill of some men, such a conception was totally lacking. No one even grasped the usefulness, in a defensive campaign against an overpowering centralism, of geographic separation. Despite all warnings, Dr. Ley's request in the spring of 1934 that the union's administrative offices be moved from Hamburg to Berlin was blithely and speedily granted.

The Education sections also had to move. They were housed in the office building of the former Socialist white-collar-workers union, beautifully situated in a large park on the edge of the Zehlendorf section of Berlin. For a few weeks it almost seemed as though there could be a new beginning in the spirit of the best DHV tradition. The comradeship, which included the few remaining representatives of the Socialist union as well as the newly employed technical assistants, the zeal for the work, the freedom and breadth of the discussions, the desire to push into new realms of knowledge and create new patterns, all these reminded me of those first months in St. John's Lutheran Institute.

These hopes rapidly evaporated once we had been discovered in our island. While some still believed that by christening our institution the Albert Forster School its new namesake, the Gauleiter of Danzig, would be forced to become our protector, it was precisely this christening ceremony with its attendant inspection of our building by prominent Nazi leaders that touched off the process of infiltrating outsiders into our ranks and undermining our work. Party and Labor Front officials became observant, suspicious, covetous. Soon an attempt was made to limit our work to business training alone and to transfer the cultural and political aspects to the appropriate party offices. They began to supervise us and to read things into the material that we sent out. Forster gave us no support at all. For him it was enough that the school should bear his name; what went on in it was of no concern to him. When the Office Workerhood was submerged into the Labor Front, his whole assistance consisted of one or two weak remonstrances to Hitler.

By the summer of 1934 it had become quite clear to me that fruitful or effective work could no longer be done in this situation. I gave notice and resigned on August 31, 1934. It was easy to give up work that had become meaningless. It was harder to leave my comrades and my memories.

CHAPTER 2

Editor's note: *In the 1930 elections the Nazi party shot from obscurity into a decisive national force. In 1928 the Nazis received only 810,000 votes throughout Germany, but in 1930 they received 6,400,000, which made them Germany's second largest party. From there they were to increase their vote in a steady and alarming fashion. This was reflected in Hamburg where the Nazis received 2.6 percent of the votes in 1928, 19.2 percent in 1930, and 33.7 percent in the summer of 1932.*

The onslaught of the depression and other objective factors contributed to the initial Nazi victory, but Hitler's party could never have exploited these factors without an effective cadre organization in the various areas of Germany. This organization was built up in the years 1926–30. During this period local Nazi organizations developed attitudes, structures, and techniques that were to carry them through the years of Hitler's successful drive for power and were also to influence the nature of the Third Reich. This is thus a crucial phase in the history of Nazism, though more needs to be known about it. Albert Krebs' recollections provide us with valuable information about this period as it was experienced in one local organization, that of the city-state of Hamburg.

In the summer of 1926 the Education sections of the DHV, and I with them, moved from Berlin to Hamburg. Since I had rejoined the Nazi party shortly before this, I reported to the Hamburg party headquarters. It was located in the Grindelallee in the back rooms of a cigar store operated by the Gauleiter, Josef Klant. The furnishings were the simplest imaginable: one or two file cases, a cigar box for the treasury, and a bulletin board plastered with old leaflets and yellowed special issues of the *Völkischer Beobachter*. The Gauleiter's appearance was equally simple and odd. The looks and accent of this small squat man with the round graying head proclaimed instantly that he came from the Silesian hill country and from limited circumstances.

For reasons I could hardly comprehend, since they arose from circumstances of which I had no knowledge, he began by refusing all of my wishes and offers, even my wholly technical request that I be listed on his membership rolls and assigned to a section or Local Group. He didn't want any new members, he scolded softly, since even the old ones were traitors. And above all he didn't want college graduates. And as for my ideas about simply coming from Berlin to Hamburg and right away giving big speeches . . . (I had offered to deliver a lecture on social policy or on a historical theme for a members' meeting).

But all the while he was grumbling he was also filling out a provisional Hamburg membership card for me which assigned me to the District Group of St. Pauli (the section where I was living until my family arrived), accepting my dues for three months, and writing up a notice to the St. Pauli group that I would be the speaker at the meeting after next. Not until he had finished these obviously unpleasant, and for him superfluous, chores did he become somewhat more approachable. He told me of bygone mass meetings and assured me that he and Hitler would yet speak before 20,000 people on the Moor Meadows. At the moment, he had to admit, it seemed perhaps, that the party was standing still in Hamburg, even slipping backward. The blame for this lay upon those "corrupted bums and traitors" who were trying to remove him, the Gauleiter, from his post. He threw out some names that meant nothing to me, since I knew little of conditions in Hamburg. Then he declared that since he was an old fighter from the Christian Social Movement,[1] he had known ups and downs before and would never be shaken by such contemptible opponents. The opposition would be removed and this would pave the way to new growth.

[1] An anti-Semitic party founded in the 1870s in Germany. Though it never attracted any significant numerical backing, some of the welfarist ideas promoted by its leader, Adolf Stöcker, influenced Wilhelm II, and the party may be considered a precursor to Hitler's movement.

To crown this little scene of self-encouragement, Klant then showed me his "famous" cat trick. He laid half a herring in the feeding dish of his fat tomcat. As the cat was about to gobble it down, Klant said: "Don't eat it! It's from the Jews! It's from the Jews! Whoever feeds from Jews, dies!" The cat actually held back until, after the trick had been repeated a couple of times, the herring was finally declared to be suitably Aryan and was speedily gulped down.

Gauleiter Klant was already sick at that time (with hardening of the brain arteries) so that a part of his oddities and eccentricities may be chalked up to his decrepitude. But aside from these symptoms of illness he embodied almost completely the characteristics that marked most of the followers and lower level leaders of the early Nazi movement. These were men from the bottom ranks of the middle class; they acted on the basis of emotional drives originating in pre-World War I attitudes. For them Nazism was not something new but rather a continuation of the old anti-Semitic and national-social parties and groups. Their political methods were also those of the prewar period. It was only slowly and with much internal resistance that they accustomed themselves to strict organization, prompt payment of dues, and constant, driving propaganda and recruitment work, even beyond electioneering. Naturally, despite their call for a "strong man," they also had no intention of giving up their accustomed democratic rights and playing rules written down in their "club" constitution. As I was soon to learn, Klant was especially zealous and skillful in using these rules to maintain himself in his struggle with the internal opposition. At the same time his opponents made no attempt to suspend the rules to force Klant out. In this respect Gau Hamburg was still operating in a democratic manner in 1926.

Little by little I began to perceive these conditions since I was asked to speak at the different district meetings. As far as I can recall there were seven effectively functioning District Groups at that time: Barmbeck, Eilbeck, Eimsbüttel, Hohenfelde, Rothenbaum, St. Georg, and St. Pauli. There were rarely more than thirty people at these meetings. Guests were hardly ever invited in those months since the fight over Klant came up for discussion after almost every speech. They preferred not to have outsiders listen.

Most of the members were of the lower middle classes, primarily artisans or in retail trade. There were also many white-collar workers from businesses, though by no means as many as was assumed in the DHV national office. "Real" workers were as rare as civil servant or academicians. Former professional soldiers or Free Corps people were also only occasionally within the Nazi party; they were overwhelmingly to be found within the Steel Helmets, the Young Germanic Order, the Werewolves, the veterans' clubs, or similar societies.[2] You met very few jobless or otherwise uprooted persons; they were to flow into the party in greater numbers only after 1928–29. There was a small group of career women who were highly active. The two most important District Groups were Eimsbüttel and Rothenbaum. Eimsbüttel, under the leadership of the master chimney sweeper Penzhorn, had the most members and the fullest treasury. Rothenbaum, under the cargo supervisor and later Nazi county leader Walter Gloy, exercised a great influence in the whole Hamburg organization through a number of able members who were active as speakers.

The age of the members ranged from twenty-five to seventy-five, though the generation twenty-five to forty predominated. Many of the younger people still belonged to smaller paramilitary leagues in those days. Ideologically, they were close to Nazism, and in case of need, they supplied us with hall guards and propagandized for us, but they were not regular members.

The most important of these paramilitary societies was the Blücher Gymnastic League under the leadership of police officer Arthur Böckenhauer. This was originally a cover organization of the Stormtroopers, made necessary by the repeated prohibitions of the party and its affiliates in Hamburg since 1922, but over the years it had become so accustomed to its organizational independence that one could hardly speak of it as part of the party any more. Very few members of the Blücher League were also members of the party. Böckenhauer himself belonged but took no orders from the party for the Blücher League. It would have been completely unthinkable to dismiss him from his position of leadership: the Blücher people followed him, not the party.

---

[2] *Stahlhelm, Jung deutsche Orden, Werwolfe,* etc., were all right-wing organizations, which grew up in the wake of World War I. Of these the Steel Helmets was to prove of continuing importance, since it constituted a paramilitary group associated with the Nationalist party. The Nazis incorporated it into the Stormtroopers in 1933.

In the first autumn months of 1926 the party deteriorated rapidly because of the growing strife over its Gauleiter. The complete derangement of party finances and the growing burden of debts finally moved the Munich party leadership to intervene, as had been so often requested in letters from Hamburg. A notice from the Reich Organization leader, Lieutenant General (Ret.) Bruno Heinemann, dissolved the State-of-Hamburg Nazi Association. Klant thus lost his post. A membership meeting, which would be attended by Gregor Strasser as representative of the Reich leadership, was supposed to pick a new executive committee.

The removal, or hounding out, of Klant led Hamburg into that second period of development in the history of the Nazi party, whose beginning was to be seen in all the other Gaue and under similar circumstances about this time. Characteristic of this period was the rapid or slow disappearance of all those leaders and subleaders, except for a few parliamentary representatives, whose attitudes and political methods were still rooted in the prewar era. In their place now stood the young men of the so-called "front lines generation," aged twenty-five to thirty-five.

The significance of this changing of the guard can hardly be overestimated. The unquestioning quality of their feelings and judgments, the unweakened power of their belief, the purely physical energy and combativeness of these young men gave the Nazi party a striking power that had to be met sooner or later, especially by the middle-class parties. The assaults of youth are seldom bogged down in the barbed wire of gray experience or the minefields of bitter skepticism. Such things were, for the youth of the '20s, little more than a new excuse to demonstrate their obstinacy and revolutionary exuberance. The first to learn this were the racialist groups and parties whose leadership still represented the bypassed conservative, or more properly, reactionary attitudes of the past. Within two short years, by about 1928, they were utterly insignificant in politics, even those which, like the German Offensive and Defensive Alliance (*Schutz-und-Trutzbund*), had once had a few hundred thousand members and followers. Even in Hamburg, where the Nazi party developed rather slowly, the Racial Freedom party was in full dissolution within a year. "Without youth you can't organize," one of their representatives told me; "you can't even distribute leaflets."

The members' meeting, called by the Nazi national leadership, took place (under the chairmanship of Gregor Strasser) on November 4, 1926, in the Heusshof. It elected me the new chairman of what had now been degraded to "Local Group" Hamburg. They chose me purely as the lesser evil since no one else was available. Dr. Helmuth Schranz and Helmuth Reinke, nominated by District Group Rothenbaum, had made so many enemies during the fight over Klant that they would have had to reckon with a strong opposition from their first day in office. They both, therefore, declined the nomination. Böckenhauer also refused to serve; he wanted to stay with the newly regathered Stormtroopers. He probably was loath to use up his influence prematurely and preferred to work in a less apparent way from behind the scenes, as was his custom.

Thus they followed the proposal of District Group St. Pauli, to which I belonged, and elected me. No one was particularly enthused about it. Gregor Strasser, as a representative of the national leadership, made no secret of his misgivings. Most of the members shook their heads dubiously, and I myself had no sense of satisfaction even though I could not at that moment foresee all the difficulties to come. One, at least, was immediately apparent to me via my own ears. The District Group leader of St. Pauli, the gigantic milk dealer Mundt, spoke low German in nominating me so that I could only understand about half the things he said in my favor. Today I am really not certain why, despite my misgivings, I accepted the position. Probably the reasons came out in simple phrases: "Things can't go on the way they've been going . . . some one has to stick his neck out . . . what others have done, you can do, too." Beyond that I was twenty-seven years old and filled with that age's joy of testing one's own strength. Finally, and this was probably the prime reason, I believed in the cause at stake.

What sort of people were in the Hamburg Nazi party at that time? Where did they come from? What motivated them to act? Were they frustrated adventurers and conspirators or upright citizens, average human beings, no better nor worse than the rest of us, filled with the same hopes, desires, yearnings, and inclinations as all men? To understand a historical movement it is indispensable to know the men who composed it. I want to try to describe these men of the beginning, as I met them in Hamburg, by using a few examples.

The vice chairman was Helmuth Reinke, "Worker" Reinke as we used to call him. Actually Reinke was not a worker either in the orientation of his consciousness or in the sociological sense; he was an artisan, trained as a blacksmith in the village where he was born in West Prussia.[3] He still felt himself to be such, even though he had to find employment in Hamburg as a factory worker. He neither wanted nor was able to disavow his origins from a frontier peasant family. He possessed no trace of that adaptability and cocksure attitude of the true big-city worker. At first impression he appeared clumsy and slow. But once he had painfully struggled his way to a decision, then he was sure of himself and his ideas and ready to fight for his views. He strove with great tenacity to overcome his lack of formal education with the result that he came remarkably far toward grasping the intellectual essence of problems, but had less success in eradicating formal errors. His articles were clear and almost impeccable stylistically but full of spelling and grammatical mistakes. The purity and honesty of his disposition contributed essentially to the recognition of his authority by people who were his social and educational betters.

The war and the loss of his homeland drove Reinke to Hamburg, though the working and living conditions of the big city displeased him. But the social demands of Nazism were not as essential to him as its nationalistic side, as his speeches showed. The defeat must be overcome, the Treaty of Versailles undone, the lost territories won back again. . . . Reinke was much concerned with the question of Freemasonry. It was to this movement that he looked to find those responsible for the defeat of 1918. This was not an unnatural quest for a man of the people who was trying to comprehend how things fit together and who still lived emotionally in his own wartime army service. Unconsciously he was attempting to restore the lost order and to reconstruct an intellectual and spiritual sphere in which he could continue his life.

As for the party's treasurer and business manager, Edgar Brinkmann, not even I, who worked closely with him for many years,

---

[3] The "Polish Corridor" of the interwar era.

was told why he joined the Nazi party. To be sure I never asked him since intimacies of this sort were not customary between us; they would have seemed out of place to Brinkmann. He was not a wordy man, especially not about himself. Thus it was not until 1927, when he had to write a short autobiography for the City Council Directory, that I learned a few details of his past, especially of his years in America. I had known that he had been over there, but until he asked me to proofread his little autobiography I had no conception of how much he must have struggled as a cabin boy, cook, and police trooper until he had fought his way into a respectable business position. After he returned from America he became a ship's broker with his own small firm.

Brinkmann's years of travel and learning in America gave him the typical qualities of a self-made man or, more correctly, developed those natural attitudes in him. Brusque, sometimes even gruff, he was undeterred by any practical difficulties. He applied his rapid and hardworking pace to both professional and party activity. When it came to purely political decisions, on the other hand, he showed considerable uncertainty since he had little understanding for delicate problems and was probably even secretly contemptuous of them. Since he generally left purely political problems alone, as a good business manager should, our relationship was only occasionally distrubed by this. Other Nazis held him in respect and recognized his authority precisely because of his organizational and business competence. It was only with Böckenhauer that he had repeated clashes, and that was due to a conflict in personalities. Bluntness fits poorly with bluntness, especially in the narrow confines of one office.

Brinkmann's path to Nazism, in my estimation, led via America. I know that he brought his anti-Semitism back with him from there. I suspect, furthermore, that a young German who had to live abroad through the intense anti-German propaganda of the war years, and who was even watched by the police after 1917, probably had his sense of nationalism awakened and sharpened by that very propaganda. Finally, some of his remarks led me to believe that Brinkmann was trying to make up, through his work with the Nazi party, for his failure, owing to his absence from Germany, to fight in the war. I never noticed any material or social motives apart from a certain discontent with the constrictions of his life stemming from his family and professional milieu. Such dissatisfactions were common in his generation, especially among those who had seen the breadths of foreign lands and continents.

Brinkmann was not the only Nazi leader in Hamburg, incidentally, who owned his own small business and thus suffered no immediate economic distress. Four of the District Group leaders enjoyed a relatively secure position as artisans or retail businessmen. Even those party officers who were in a dependent position hardly saw their economic situation as a reason to become Nazis. None of them had such a hard time that the only hope open to them was to fight for the victory of a radical party. They could all have fit into one or the other of the existing parties, excepting the Communists, whose annihilation was their special hope. As good bourgeois people, they chose radicalism because the real bourgeois parties seemed too cowardly and prone to concessions in defending bourgeois values and because none of the other parties seemed to have recognized the causes of the prevailing unsatisfactory situation.

For the convinced Nazi of the year 1926 the world looked something like this: Germany lost the war in 1918, despite the greatest soldierly achievements and a series of magnificent victories, because the "German" parties, led by Jews and other supranational powers, had stabbed the army in the back. At Versailles the same supranational forces converted Wilson's concept of a peace through understanding into a dictated treaty whose annexations were strangling the still powerful German nation. To insure this annihilation still further, the leaders of international Jewry simultaneously created the Communist party which, operating out of a Russia yoked down by the Bolshevik revolution, became the shock troops of chaos. At the same time the parties of fulfillment functioned internally (either because of their own weakness, or also because of secret higher directives) to increase the misery of the masses. Thus they were agents of the eastern and western enemies. No matter what a Nazi fought against, whether Versailles, capitalism, the Red Front, the department stores, or the democratic parties of fulfillment, it was always one and the same enemy. To destroy him meant to destroy the causes of Germany's misery with one stroke. Therefore, it was a mistake to be overly concerned with any single problem, such as socialism. That only turned you away from the real goal of the struggle. "What is socialism?" Hitler screamed at me in 1930. "A Jewish invention to incense the German folk against itself!"

All these men had experienced the overwhelming enthusiasm of the German people in August 1914 when, for practically the first time in their history, destiny called the Germans to action as a unified nation. They rushed to the colors as volunteers; they were wounded and decorated; they still believed in victory in autumn 1918. The defeat that came despite their tremendous efforts and sacrifices was thus not just a defeat for their nation but a terribly personal blow. This defeat had to be overcome. That meant that in the years 1926–27, even in Hamburg, they were more counter-revolutionary than revolutionary. It is true that the concept "national revolution" was already heard here and there as a slogan to indicate the future, but linked with it was the loose conception of a "strong man," the elimination of partisan strife and corruption, and above all the suspension of the Treaty of Versailles and the pacts that followed from it.

The distinction between Nazism and the old nationalist parties lay less in ideological differences than in the divergent methods, ages, and social origins of the respective leaders. These differences also conditioned my fellow party members' strange relationship to the class struggle. In theory it was strictly rejected. In practice, however, they were by no means free of the emotions of class struggle. Throughout the whole of these years every attack upon capitalists and plutocrats received the warmest applause from these lower-middle-class officials, while those who had come over from the Marxist camp were much more skeptical about such slogans and looked for new attitudes.

In short it can be concluded that the majority of the Nazi leadership of Hamburg in the years 1926–27 derived from the middle and lower middle classes and still lived by values and goals that had been formed in the prewar era. This vision of order became a conscious force to them in August 1914 when the individual fused with the struggling and sacrificing community of the nation. At that point they undertook responsibility for this community in addition to sharing its honor and dignity. During the war they acted in accordance with this consciousness, but autumn of 1918 brought with it defeat and thus shattered or at least negated the

newly achieved values and visions. They were not prepared, however, to accept such a shattering or negation. They protested, they
prepared for a counter stroke, and when they searched for the
causes of the catastrophe, they discovered the nation.

At first this movement was diffuse: Concepts were confused and
contradictory, the quest found no satisfactory answers and above
all no goal to which all could pledge themselves. Then came Nazism—Hitler and his slogans, which, with grandiosely simplified formulations, provided an answer for every question, a certainty for
every doubt, an enemy for every hatred, a goal for every impulse to
action, an interest for every self-seeker, a flag and an enlightening
word for every idealist. At last the younger burghers knew where
they stood. Unburdened with the experience and misgivings of age,
trained by the war to quick, tough decisions, they could throw
themselves into the task.

This stratum of party officers was to provide a large number of
the Local Group and County leaders, the functionaries of the Nazi
Welfare Organization and the Labor Front, the leaders of the
Hitler Youth, the Stormtroopers, and the Labor Service, throughout the whole of the Third Reich. As a type they predominated in
the early years of the Nazi movement; yet even then there
appeared a second type who, as the years went by, was to play an
even greater role. A representative of this more intellectual sort,
noted for their strongly individualistic traits, was the first leader of
the Hamburg Stormtroopers, Arthur Böckenhauer. The tension
between emotion, will, and reason led him, after reason had
triumphed, to exactly the same worship of force and power as
could be seen in Bruno von Salomon. But it was not this alone
that indicated this spiritual relationship; it could be seen also in
the way in which Böckenhauer substantiated his opinions, in his
method of subtly and pitilessly dispatching his opponents, in the
way in which he was driven by a constant restlessness, the real
motive for which was often unclear, and which he tried to justify or
to hide by calling it other names. At such times he spoke of his
"duties," which left him no time for a private life. In fact his duties
were his private life. This life denied him entry into certain middle-class circles, just as he prevented himself from giving in to certain middle-class emotions.

It was remarkable how much Böckenhauer, who certainly knew

nothing of the theories of nihilism or those of the fate-conscious superman, incorporated those theories in his attitude. Within the bounds of his effectiveness he was the complete representative of that breed of man who finds only in politics the opportunity to acquire and exercise power. In this connection he was never troubled for an instant by the question of the moral justification of power, as far as I could see.

Full of primal vitality, this product of a small artisan family and the noncommissioned officers' school grasped for power in order to satisfy his burning but wholly egotistical ambition. To him Nazism meant little more than a chance to develop and use his own powers and abilities. Once, when Hitler refused to accede to his wishes, Böckenhauer made the following significant statement in a public meeting: "What right has this man from Munich to give us orders in Hamburg?" But at the same time he resembled Hitler in his ability to inspire a fanatical following and in his daredevil courage, which was partly a matter of temperament, partly the result of the sober reflection that nothing ventured means nothing gained.

Naturally these characteristics did not make Böckenhauer a comfortable party member. It was his ambition, rather than any ideological doubts or reservations, that led to his repeated quarrels with officials of the civilian sector of the party and to consequent disciplinary measures against him. I had to expel him from the party once myself. Nevertheless, he always found his way back into the party again and in increasingly higher positions, even though he was not looked on with any particular favor by the national leadership. Rudolf Hess, for example, believed Böckenhauer to have Jewish blood in his veins, because of his physiognomy.

Böckenhauer died in an auto accident in 1943 or 1944 as an officer in the army, not as an SA leader. Whether there were particular reasons that led him, as an SA *Gruppenführer*,[4] to join the army, or whether he had simply been ordered to do so, I cannot say. Neither do I know of his attitude during the Roehm conflict.[5] I

[4] A rank equivalent to lieutenant general in the army. "SA" stands for *Sturmabteilung* or Storm Section—i.e., the brown-shirted Stormtroopers.

[5] *I.e.*, the struggle that culminated in Hitler's purge of the SA, June 30, 1934.

did hear that he was arrested for a few days in Berlin after June 30, 1934, and then, because of an incompletely conducted purge, had been temporarily demoted to the SA quartermaster's store.

When I first came to Hamburg, in 1926, Böckenhauer was still an officer in the Hamburg police. He had even worn his police uniform while commanding the Stormtroopers at a few meetings. Naturally, this was in violation of the Hamburg Senate's prohibition against city employees being members of the Nazi party. He was probably indifferent to the threats of expulsion from police service or else felt protected by the supposed practice of the Hamburg police of always maintaining a certain percentage of officers who were obvious anti-Communists and nationalists from rightist organizations. In any event, Böckenhauer was dismissed from the police in March 1926, though he continued to wear his uniform pending an unsuccessful appeal of this decision. Together with a friend he was then active in business until (about 1930) he finally acquired a paid position in the Stormtroops.

Less complicated personalities than Böckenhauer were Dr. Schranz and Arnold Peters, who were practically the first and the only ones among the leadership in those early years whose socialism went beyond practical considerations. To be sure, they came to their socialism from diverse directions.

Dr. Schranz was the descendant of a middle-class family from Weilburg in Hessia. He had received, except during his wartime service, the customary education from Gymnasium through the university, where he earned a doctorate in political science. As a soldier he had come in contact with fellow soldiers from the working class. This led him to consider social questions and still more to notice the effect of the social order upon human destinies. For the first time he began to doubt the desirability of the traditional social structure. His doubts were reinforced by Germany's defeat, which he, unlike so many of his class, attributed not only to the treason of the "November criminals" but also to the criminal incompetence of the powers who had ruled the now shattered Reich.

On the basis of his studies after the war and of his experience in various businesses, Dr. Schranz came to the conclusion that traditional economic liberalism was socially unjust and economically outmoded both in theory and in practice, because it hindered productive forces and increased the costs of the distributive system.

Like many reformers of those years he saw the cure in combating finance capitalism, a retreat from the gold standard, and the establishment of the fundamental thesis that all value is created by labor.

In any event, there was less favor in the Hamburg party in those days for unambiguously clear formulations than there was acceptance of a revolutionary socialism. Thus Dr. Schranz played an essential role in the determination of the Hamburg party's development. Unfortunately, he soon moved from Hamburg to Rüsselsheim to become an executive in the Opel factory there. After 1933 Dr. Schranz became lord mayor of Offenbach-on-the-Main.

What for Dr. Schranz had been the result of an intellectual blending of experience and systematic study was for Arnold Peters an emotion formed from youthful adventures. When I first met him, he was a lad of seventeen years whose appearance and personality were a joy to behold. He came from a Hamburg working-class family in which adherence to the Marxist-Socialist labor movement was taken as a matter of course. Thus Peters had become a member of the Red Falcons and later of the Young Socialist Workers. Exactly what impelled him to leave these organizations I was never able to discover. From the point of view of social attitudes, Peters still lived completely in the world in which he had been brought up. He considered himself passionately and unqualifiedly as a National *Socialist* without troubling himself too much about the theoretical differences between that and Marxism, apart from those which centered about the antithesis "national vs. international."

Because he was only seventeen, Peters was too young to belong to the party. Since he pressed for activity, however, and since the new leadership had a great need for people of his type if it was to achieve its goals, I was happy to approve his suggestion that he organize a "League of Young German Workers." This league was not to be a direct sub-organization of the party. Our common attitude, deriving from the experience of the Youth Movement, saw little to approve of in a party-youth. On the other hand, the old form of the completely free and unpolitical youth group struck us as out of tune with the times. Thus we agreed to follow the example of the Traveling Journeymen of the DHV, that is, while maintaining the organizational independence of the League as a whole, to train its individual members for ultimate work for the party. Entry into the party would then be on a voluntary basis and would come first when age eighteen had been reached.

Peters began to build up his league in the spring of 1927. Within a short time he had gathered a rather large group of fine boys, when his work was disturbed by orders from Munich to organize the Hitler Youth. Peters refused decisively to follow these orders. He wanted neither to give up the name of his group, which signified both commitment and goal to him, nor to transform the group itself from a free youth organization into a "Young Army" or "Young Stormtroopers," as the orders (later changed, incidentally) envisaged. Since I understood and agreed with his reasons, I argued for them orally and in writing to the national leadership. This culminated in a discussion of almost two hours' length with Hess, von Pfeffer, and Gruber[6] representing the national headquarters. Hess seemed to be disposed toward my conceptions with respect to organizational and working methods, but he was insistent on the name "Hitler Youth." In the end he turned the decision on the whole question over to Gruber and von Pfeffer. With that my case was lost. These two lived in a very narrow and intellectually long since obsolete world; they had no conception of what I was talking about. They wanted their "Army Youth," which von Pfeffer could command and to which Gruber could sell the brown shirts, the pipings, the drums, and the canteens from his sporting goods store in Plauen. They ordered me, as Local Group leader of Hamburg, either to incorporate the League of Young German Workers into the Hitler Youth or to dissolve it. I tried to win Arnold Peters over to the idea of incorporation by appealing to discipline and by suggesting that he might be able to have his ideas triumph by working within the Hitler Youth. He stuck to his refusal, however, so that his league had to be dissolved.

It was not until later that Peters was willing to cooperate actively again and in this he remained true to his social inclinations. He ultimately wound up in the youth office of the Labor Front, which brought him into contact with the work of the Hitler Youth again. In the Second World War Peters fell, as a member of the Armed SS, in the East.

[6] Krebs means Franz Pfeffer von Salomon, leader of the SA, 1926–30 (profiled in Chapter 10). Kurt Gruber was Hitler Youth leader until 1931.

Similar to him in attitude and in happy nature, though less temperamental, was Wilhelm Kohlmeyer, who became District leader of the Hamburg Hitler Youth after 1933. He also came to the party when he was still a young lad. To overcome his awkwardness and bashfulness and to extend his knowledge, he worked his way through the courses at the Fichte-Academy. During his term of office he emphasized social work and vocational training within the Hitler Youth. He, too, died on the Eastern Front.

Among the district chairmen, Hugo Hank, leader of District Group Rothenburgsort (which had been founded in 1927), considered himself a convinced socialist. To be sure, his socialism had less to do with theory than with practical efforts to protect and improve the position of artisans. His whole appearance showed that Hank was a peasant transplanted to the big city. He was simple, straightforward, blunt, and reliable. He managed somehow to bring off the trick of holding office both in the Nazi party and the (Social Democratic) Free Unions. "And why not?" he told me. "When you consider it properly, it's all one. It's just that most people don't consider it properly. . . ." After 1933 Hank became a Hamburg city councilman. When we met once or twice later, he told me of his dissatisfaction and disappointment in the party's development.

A few more names could be mentioned, a few more personalities from those early days could be described, but no new aspects of the general picture would emerge from them. Let me return, therefore, to the events.

After the election of the new executive committee of Local Group Hamburg on November 4, 1926, the Local Group held the traditional memorial ceremony[7] on November 9 in the Wilhelm Gymnasium. At my request, Klant made the speech in order that he might have a decent departure from his office. Contrary to the predictions of his personal foes, Klant understood the intention and fulfilled it in a short, calm address. That ended the history of the state organization of the Nazi party in Hamburg; the newly decreed Local Group could begin with reconstruction.

The very first organizational conference with the District Group

[7] In commemoration of the Nazis who had been killed on that date in 1923 in Hitler's Munich Putsch.

leaders disclosed that the number of active members had shrunk in the previous months to approximately 135 persons. On the other hand, the debts had increased to a few hundred marks, though only a part of this, insofar as private persons were the creditors, had to be paid back in the near future. Thus it was decided, despite the debts, to open our own business office on December 1 in the same building as Brinkmann's office. Districts Eimsbüttel and Rothenbaum contributed the first rent payment. Dues collections were regulated with the requirement that most of the sums collected this way were to go to the Local Group until its finances were sound. Pamphlets and posters, which had to be ordered from Munich, were only to be purchased when we could pay cash. Stormtrooper Leader Böckenhauer promised to take responsibility for the gradual enrollment of all SA members in the party. In return the SA was provided with a modest subsidy. The District Groups were required to hold at least one monthly membership meeting and to submit regular financial and activity reports. Beyond that they were to make a special monthly report on the increase in membership.

These demands of the new executive committee caused lively discussion. The District Groups felt that their financial and organizational independence was being curtailed and many of the officials felt that the creation of a stricter organization with supervision, reports, and centralized directives was completely unneeded. But in the end the new executive prevailed, though not without threatening to resign a few times. These experiences awakened or strengthened authoritarian tendencies, which usually slumber beneath the surface in young men anyway, so that in the following years the application of democratic rules within the Local Group fell increasingly out of practice. The general discussion developed into a sort of order-receiving session. There was always the chance to ask questions and express opinions, but decisions were not reached by a vote any more—they were simply handed down from above. The system of a free and secret election also atrophied bit by bit until it came to a visible end in the spring of 1929 when Munich appointed Kaufmann Gauleiter. Long before this, though, its use had become rare. At first we did away with the secret nomination and posting of candidates' names, the passing out of ballots, the election of a tabulating committee, etc. In place of this, elections were held by spoken nominations and voting by raised hands. This was thought to be worthier and more proper for a true popular movement, precisely because of its openness. But since this frequently led to bad choices through the pressures of a loudmouthed minority, the Local Group executive not only reserved the right of approval but step by step asserted the right to name District Group officials directly. In practice this right was used only two or three times, as far as I can recollect, down to 1928. But it contributed considerably to the acceptance by the members of an authoritarian system in which ultimately there were no more elections but only appointments.

The party's first headquarters office was located in Kajen, in the harbor sector. When that was no longer sufficient it was moved a few hundred meters, to Dovenfleth. From a point of view of public transportation, both offices were very unsatisfactory; but this disadvantage was the price we paid for a propaganda goal. This goal had two aspects. The first was to speak directly to the workers who passed by the office in great numbers on their way to and from work. (To make the office readily visible it was plastered over with placards and posters.) And secondly this was to make clear to the party members themselves where, in the future, the direction of the party's work would be: not just externally in the struggle to win the working class, but also internally in efforts toward a true socialism. In my view the offices in Kajen and Dovenfleth did promote the intended purposes.

There were some worried people who feared that in this neighborhood we would not be able to hold out against the Communist and Socialist terror, but this proved illusory. There never were any serious attacks on our headquarters or upon the party members working there, even though some of us rapidly became well known to the neighbors. Nor was I personally ever set upon when I made my way home late at night, even though most of the surrounding *Reichsbanner*[8] families knew me as the "Nazi Doctor" and although the dark, lonely streets of the district in which I then lived offered a splendid opportunity for a little assault and battery.

The work of the party in the first months of the year 1927 was

[8] The *Reichsbanner* was a paramilitary society for the defense of the republic which was founded in 1924. Almost all of its members were Socialists and militantly anti-Nazi. See Roger P. Chickering, "The Reichsbanner and the Weimar Republic, 1924–26," *Journal of Modern History* (December 1968), pp. 524–534.

limited to the strengthening and development of the organization, the regular holding of membership meetings, spurring the members on to personal recruitment, and local propaganda activities such as distributing leaflets and pasting up posters. Since it was propaganda activity above all which claimed the energies of almost every member of the District Groups, it was possible for the party, in individual sections of the city, not only to be heard but to appear far stronger than it actually was. Anyone who found a Nazi leaflet in his mailbox every Sunday might justifiably assume that there were numerous distributors. Even the two representatives of the Hamburg political police, Quidde and Prechlin, who visited me from time to time and drew me into harmless small talk, overestimated our numerical strength by tenfold. In actuality, however, the District Groups grew very slowly. Also to be taken into account was the regular attrition of membership: sectarians, cranks, and those who were expelled for nonpayment of dues or nonparticipation in party work. Those District Groups with an average membership of thirty to forty generally did not increase in size at all. That had two prime causes. With thirty to forty people the usual tavern meeting place was full, whereupon clubbish considerations stifled the political ones: The members sat cozy and close to one another; they had gotten to know each other well and felt no need for new faces, and the stimulus of the half-empty room was lacking. A second factor was that many of the District Group leaders lacked the energy, the perspective, and the training to activate and control larger numbers.

In such cases the only remedy was to break up the District Group into two or sometimes even three new groups, which stimulated new growth forces immediately and also promoted previously passive members into active work as chairmen, treasurers, secretaries, propaganda directors, and so on. Beyond that our organization of strongpoints throughout the city could be more tightly knit together by such measures. Nevertheless the party membership in Hamburg remained extraordinarily small for years and was nothing compared to that of the Communists and Socialists. In the fall of 1927 we had about three hundred members. In May 1928, when Brinkmann and I resigned, there were about six hundred, not counting a considerable part of the SA who were still not yet party members.

The refusal of SA members to join the party was not just due to financial considerations on their part; there was also an ideological factor involved, especially in the case of those who were former members of the paramilitary organizations. There were "fundamentalist Putsch-makers" who swore exclusively by hand grenades and machine guns and. viewed the party's political-parliamentary struggle with disgust and thinly disguised contempt. There were passionate devotees of General Ludendorff who hoped for his return to the political spotlight and naturally expected Hitler to subordinate himself at that time to the General's orders. There were even already atheists, theists, and Wotan worshipers who took issue with the plank in the Nazi program that called for "an acceptance of positive Christianity." I encountered all this already in the spring of 1927 when I negotiated with the leaders of the Hindenburg League for their entry into the party or SA. Since I made no concessions to them, the result was that barely half of the league (about forty men) came into the SA under the leadership of Ellerhusen. Even that probably would not have occurred if Ellerhusen had not been made commander of Standarte II of our SA.

In that spring of 1927, even though Hamburg's Nazi Executive Committee doubted that conditions were really ripe yet, it nevertheless decided to sponsor a few mass meetings. In the long run we could not simply continue our previous organizational work and keep morale high unless the reasons for and the results of this work became visible in corresponding action. The members' drive for activity was not satisfied with the mere holding of party meetings, leaflet distribution, and the nocturnal pasting up of posters—especially since individual members could not see the cumulative effect of these efforts. Beyond that, individual Nazis periodically needed the stimulus of a mass meeting in which their secret wishes, hopes, and dreams would be openly expressed and their courage, sense of comradeship, and willingness to sacrifice would be enhanced. They gave little thought to the purely financial and organizational problems created in preparing for such a mass meeting. Just to come near filling the larger halls and providing protection against disturbances, we had to gather together the entire Nazi membership of Hamburg, Altona, Wandsbek, and the suburbs. Since our funds were still very limited we had to arrange an advance sale of tickets in order to rent the hall. We did this by requiring that every member sell five tickets and turn the money over to Local Group Hamburg. It was only rarely that we could accept any unsold tickets back, nor did members often try this. The old lesson was again proved that you can get pretty far with demands when the necessity for them is obvious.

Our first three mass meetings were held at the end of March 1927. The very first, sponsored solely by Hamburg, was held in the Banz Society Building and the speaker was Otto Telschow from Harburg (who later became Gauleiter of Eastern Hanover). It was relatively peaceful. But the other two, held in the Holsatia Hall in Wandsbek and the Toska Hall in Altona, and sponsored by Gau Schleswig-Holstein with Hamburg participating only as a neighbor, led to pitched battles with Communist harassment squads under the leadership of Westphal and Edgar André. The Nazi speakers were Joseph Goebbels and Gottfried Feder.[9]

There is no doubt that the Communists intended from the beginning to break up these meetings; that was clear from their heckling and from Westphal's speech from the floor in Wandsbek.

In the ensuing battle the Hamburg SS went into action for the first time and its members henceforth felt themselves to be more or less marked men. Some of them had to change their addresses repeatedly to escape persecution. The difference between the behavior of the two Communist leaders was striking. While Westphal slugged away with the best of them, André hopped out of the way quickly as soon as the blows began to fall.

After these rather decisive defeats for the Communists, I can remember no further large scale disturbances of our meetings until spring 1928. On the other hand we had to terminate our 1927 May Festival in Wedel because of the women and children there, when a constantly increasing crowd of political opponents gathered outside the beer garden where we were holding the party. At first the police gave us no assistance but after energetic appeals they held the turbulent crowd a stone's throw away from us while we

[9] Gottfried Feder was the chief Nazi economic theorist prior to 1933. When Hitler came to power he completely ignored the somewhat cranky ideas of Feder and gave Feder no role in the Third Reich. Up to 1933, however, Feder was thought of as being as important as Goebbels; hence the Communist raid on his meeting. Feder is described in Chapter 10.

marched to the railroad station. Then, while the SA made a propaganda march through Vierlande, we drove three trucks filled with the noncombatant remainder of the Hamburg group (mostly women, children, and old men) through the parts of the city east of the Alster. Since everything went well, we finally decided to brave the working-class district of Rothenburgsort where within a few minutes the sight of our trucks brought the entire neighborhood to the brink of a riot. They threw rocks at us and dropped flowerpots and bottles down on us. For a while our drivers held off a direct storming of the trucks by backfiring their motors, which sounded like pistolshots, but the trucks could barely inch their way through the crowd. Finally, just as the workers were preparing to block off the street completely with pushcarts, two police cars appeared and escorted us back to the more peaceful district of Hammerbrook. A businessman who was sympathetic to Nazism, or at least an enemy of the Communists, had telephoned the police. The police were justifiably furious about our frivolity and our failure to keep the regulation requiring prior notice for propaganda parades.

At that same May Festival a Nazi Women's Auxiliary had been founded under the leadership of Frieda Koenig. She owned a dressmaker's shop, and at that particular stage this was rather important. One of the chief duties of the Women's Auxiliary was to repair the clothing and linen of young Stormtroopers who had no family or whose families had expelled them from the home for political reasons (such cases were frequent). Beyond that the Women's Auxiliary devoted itself primarily to charity work, though this by no means excluded political activity. Though our opponents often claimed that Nazis wanted to keep women out of politics, the party never espoused this particular crudeness. In those early days of Nazism, when women were our most zealous agitators, such a position would have been utterly impossible.

In addition to the Women's Auxiliary which was partly in the tradition of the patriotic women's clubs, there was formed—albeit unofficially—a girls' group. It followed the form of the Youth Movement and emphasized singing, hiking, and dancing. Frau Zideck was its chosen leader and there were other young women who joined the girls' group too. What distinguished it from similar groups in the German Youth Movement (apart from its political connection) was its emphasis upon practical activity. As a beginning there was a course in first aid.

Local Group Hamburg held its summer solstice celebration for 1927 in a forest meadow near Duvenstedt. As opposed to earlier years we ruled out the brass band and concluding visit to a tavern, which was heartily applauded by most of the participants. On the other hand the applause was pretty thin for a choral recitation of Kleist's poem "Germania to Her Children." This was not only because of the quality of the performance, which despite much practice sounded rather pitiful, but was due also and primarily to the lack of intellectual preconditions in the audience. In retrospect, therefore, my efforts with the choral recitations seem rather ludicrous to me. I should have learned what was really near to the hearts of most Hamburg Nazis from a collection taken up within the SA for an enormous glockenspiel. It began early in the summer and piled up coin after coin for this clanking, shiny instrument.

The Hamburg SA wanted the glockenspiel in order to make a big impression, despite their still limited numbers, at the first Nuremberg party rally, which was to be held in August. They were almost unable to do this, since using an instrument of this sort was permissible only with a large marching band. In the end, however, the national commander of the SA, von Pfeffer, overlooked the regulations, in order not to upset Böckenhauer, and permitted the Hamburg and Schleswig-Holstein SA contingents to be led by their glockenspiel.

If I remember correctly, a good half of the Hamburg Nazi party members went to the Nuremberg rally of 1927. This is rather remarkable since everyone had to pay the costs from his own pocket (the only subsidy given out by the Local Group was a very small one to the SA). It was worth the expense, nevertheless, since the party rally was a powerful experience for most of the participants and gave them renewed vigor just from meeting the masses of fellow Nazis from all parts of the fatherland. They became aware of the whole and felt themselves lifted up and strengthened through the realization that they were not alone in isolated outposts. Beyond that, the actual preparation for and organization of the party rallies as well as the propagandistically oriented stage direction left hardly anything to be desired, while Hitler showed himself especially on these days to be the master magician of mass manipulation.

Thus it was no miracle that by the end of the rally all of the participants, simultaneously exhausted and overstimulated, found themselves in a giddy ecstasy of enthusiasm that precluded every critical property—even to the extent of considering anyone who had not also lost his critical faculties as a disgrace. When, during the return trip from this party rally of 1927, I remarked to a close circle of friends that it was not thirty thousand but at the most fifteen thousand Stormtroopers who had marched past Hitler (Brinkmann, Otto Strasser, and I had counted carefully), I engendered rage, disgust, denial, and deep suspicion even among these Nazis with whom I had thought I had developed a personal relationship.

At the beginning of September 1927 Joseph Klant died of a stroke. He had at least lived to see his repeated efforts finally succeed in obtaining a suspension of the prohibition against Hitler's speaking in Hamburg—in view of the impending elections in the city-state. The Local Group provided a large honor guard for Klant's funeral, and then hurled itself with astounding confidence and hardly imaginable self-sacrifice into electioneering.

The Hamburg Senate had (in order to exclude so-called splinter groups) stipulated that all parties not previously represented would have to gather the signatures of four thousand qualified voters and post a bond of RM 3,000 in order to be placed on the ballot. The bond money would be returned if at least one city councilman was elected by the new party. Klant had been elected as the representative of the *Völkisch-sozialer Block*[10] and thus this law, in addition to affecting a few other small parties, primarily hit the Nazis.

The law violated both the letter and spirit of the Weimar constitution and we intended to challenge it before the Supreme Court. Still this did not relieve the Local Group's executive from the need to decide whether or not to participate in the election. From the Racial Freedom party we received a proposal that would have provided a tactical way around the law. We could join with them to run candidates under the former title: *Völkisch-sozialer Block*. With Reventlow and Gregor Strasser present we negotiated with representatives of the Racial Freedom party but without coming to an agreement. Reventlow and Strasser then gave us permission

[10] A proto-Nazi racist group that the Nazis used as a cover when they were outlawed following the Munich Putsch of 1923.

to work out our own decision and Local Group Hamburg decided to refuse the Racialists' offer. This was because we felt that our previous link with them had obscured the particularly nonbourgeois (if not anti-bourgeois) social goals of our politics for almost four years. If we were going to go into the election campaign at all we wanted to do so as National Socialists.

After these negotiations, which, incidentally, spelled the end of the political effectiveness of the Racial Freedom party in Hamburg (they put up no candidates and their former councilman ran on the Nationalist party ticket), those of us on the Hamburg Nazi Executive Committee spent about two more weeks considering what we should do. Just collecting four thousand valid petition signatures with barely three hundred party members appeared an exceedingly difficult task. In fact we were barely able to accomplish it since the City Registration Office challenged so many of our signatures (many actually were invalid) that ultimately almost five thousand had to be gathered.

But collecting the RM 3,000 to post bond, which at first gave us the greatest concern, above all since it might be lost by a poor election showing, was accomplished in the shortest period through the self-sacrifice of the membership. While we were still hesitating and vacillating, there were brought to us in the party headquarters and formally pressed upon us the first savings books and pawn tickets from Sunday suits, watches, and parlor furniture. For the moment, of course, this was only a loan. But it was clear to every contributor that, in view of the smallness and poverty of the Local Group, electoral failure would mean no return of the money or at best not for many years. And by that time the pawned items would surely have been sold, while no one who had just experienced the inflation and gradual deflation could predict what the value of the money would be in the future.

Nevertheless, they put the money at our disposal even though we felt our responsibility and at least our moral liability enough to indicate repeatedly the sober calculations that made electoral success doubtful. The party members were undisturbed by calculations. They believed in victory, but they were also ready to accept the consequences of defeat. This attitude was a factor in the Nazi movement for years to come. One had to have experienced it in concrete cases such as this before one could pass objective or moral judgments on it.

In September 1927, to be sure, the faith of the Hamburg Nazis rested on two real foundations. On the one hand they had frequently found in their signature-gathering that even people who were far from the party's position—some actually opponents of Nazism—had signed as a form of protest against the Senate's undemocratic election law. Many party members hoped that this attitude would continue to have an effect; they built their hopes not on our three hundred members but on the five thousand signatures, and with this bold counterargument against the Local Group executive they came to fantastic conclusions. A second hope felt by almost all members was in Hitler's appearance and in his skill in convincing people, since in the course of the campaign he would be speaking in Hamburg for the first time. In fact this first speech by Hitler, held at Sagebiel in the beginning of October, turned into a significant political event. The admission tickets, even the expensive ones for the first rows, were immediately sold out despite the extensive and conscious exclusion of our usual "customers." The hall was filled to the brim with two to three thousand people from every class and profession, though the middle class predominated overwhelmingly. The upper classes were also strongly represented. Hitler avoided cheap demagogery but also avoided taking any position on the concrete political situation; he spoke on the fundamentals of the Nazi movement. It took him an hour to establish sufficient contact with his audience, so that bursts of applause began to interrupt him. Within another three-quarters of an hour he had whipped the two thousand separate individuals into an exulting, cheering mass. In view of the conscious reserve and decidedly mistrustful and critical attitude of the overwhelming majority of those present, this was undoubtedly a great success. On the other hand, many Nazis were not satisfied. They had been much more pleased by Goebbels' speech of a few days earlier in which political enemies had been hacked and ground through the usual Goebbels rhetoric mill.

It is impossible to guess the extent to which the Hitler meeting had a direct influence on the election results. My personal opinion is that its unique composition indicated less effect than other meetings attended by those who had already felt drawn to Nazism for a long time. In any event the approximately nine thousand votes that we received could not be analyzed as to how and where they had been garnered. These nine thousand votes elected two

senators for us: Brinkmann and Reinke. I myself refused to be a
candidate since the peculiar structure of the Nazi party and the—
at that point—still controversial question of how far we should
engage in parliamentary tactics necessitated, in my opinion, the
maintenance of a free and independent position by the head of a
Nazi state organization. The public was to be shown, particularly
by my absence from the candidate lists, that the election had not
meant a shift of the party's emphasis into the parliamentary arena.

The income that the election (especially the mass meetings)
had brought us made our Local Group solvent. After paying all
debts we had enough of a reserve to begin, after a two-week rest, a
winter program much broader than the previous year's. Instead of
ten thousand leaflets, we could now distribute a hundred thousand.
This also vindicated the distribution methods worked out by the
Local Group's two propaganda experts, Schwiesow and Matusick,
though the members had previously criticized them. Furthermore,
we began to hold, in addition to the regular discussion evenings in
each district, one or two city-wide meetings every month. If possible we held one in Sagebiel and the other in one of the smaller
rooms of the Heusshof, the Banz-Society Building, the Eilbeck
Community House, and so on. The favorite speakers in Hamburg
were Gregor Strasser, Goebbels, and Count Reventlow. Apart from
them we had in those years, as far as I can recall, Feder, Dr. Frick,
Hildebrand from Mecklenburg, Dr. Ley, Lohse, and Streicher for
our mass meetings. Often these were sponsored jointly with Local
Groups Altona and Wandsbek, which belonged to Gau Schleswig-
Holstein. In December Hitler came again to speak for a meeting in
the Circus Busch, which drew primarily peasants from Dithmarschen and Holstein[11] who came into the city in great droves.

At the end of November our Local Group held its annual business meeting in the Heusshof. In accordance with the statutes and
the democratic playing rules, the executive committee gave a
report on the preceding year. The treasurer's report was presented
and affirmed by the auditors. The chairman and vice-chairman
were reelected, though by acclamation rather than formal ballot-

---

[11] *I.e.*, from Schleswig-Holstein. For an analysis of why this district went
Nazi so strongly and so early, see Rudolf Heberle's *From Democracy to
Nazism* (Baton Rouge, La., 1945).

ing. There were no sensations. The biggest impression on the party members was made by Brinkmann's report that all debts had been paid and that a few hundred marks were in the treasury. The number of members had more than doubled, although that was hardly saying much since it had started out with only about 130 and was still fairly insignificant with 300, though since the election a rapid increase was clearly noticeable. It should also be mentioned that then, as before, failure to pay dues for three consecutive months meant automatic expulsion.

The number of meetings had increased considerably, including those within the District Groups. That meant that it was no longer hundreds but rather thousands who attended the meetings and were addressed directly. There was an astonishingly large number of leaflets, stickers, and special numbers of the *Völkischer Beobachter* that had been distributed. In some parts of the city they had been able occasionally to shift from the time-consuming stuffing of letter boxes to the easier but more extravagant method of distributing literature in the streets. For mass meetings the Local Group had even been able to permit itself proper billboard advertising. And they could pride themselves on doing all this out of their means. No contributions had been accepted from any interest groups whatsoever—to be sure, none had been offered. Thus the party moved with considerable self-assurance into the year 1928, which was to confront it immediately with a series of demands.

The Supreme Court had declared the Hamburg election law of the summer of 1927 to be unconstitutional. It was thus nullified and the September elections had to be held over again. The new elections were set for February 19 and thus our propaganda activity and mass meetings were stepped up as soon as the new year began. Our organizations had, in the interim, gained enough experience so that though the campaign claimed all of the strength of the party and SA to the utmost, still it ran much more smoothly than in the previous autumn. Shortly before the election Hitler spoke again, this time in the great double hall of the Sagebiel. It was at this meeting, if I recollect correctly, that the SA and SS first wore uniformly the brown or black shirts. Some units were even fully equipped with leather shoulder straps, buckles, and uniform trousers. The Local Group had provided a small subsidy for this equipment. The "Heil Hitler" salute was already used, I think, at the Nuremburg rally of 1927, but at first it was strongly opposed in Hamburg—in fact all over North Germany.

On the Nazi list of candidates Reinke had given up his place as second candidate to Wilhelm Hüttmann and had asked to be nominated to the third position. This arrangement, so characteristic of Reinke's selflessness, was brought to my attention for approval only after it had been done. I was instinctively dubious about it but could find few arguments to oppose those presented by Reinke and other members. Hüttman had made a name for himself and won a considerable following among the members within a short time, thanks to his various talents. He had a vigorous tongue, which no inhibitions or serious considerations could keep behind his teeth.

He also made many persons morally indebted to him by his little favors and bits of advice as a lawyer and knew how to show himself a jolly mixer in long-winded drinking bouts. In short, he appeared at least to broad segments of the middle class to be just the right parliamentary representative. He was hardly stupid and was experienced in many areas of life. Beyond that he had done a good job with his District Group, Hohenfelde: The membership was steadily increasing and his cooperation with the Local Group's business office was quite valuable in some respects.

Despite that, it soon developed that my doubts were well grounded. Hüttman's behavior in the city council was crudely and unnecessarily provocative. In the difficulties with the SA that broke out shortly after the elections, Hüttman intrigued and agitated here and there for his own personal advantage until he finally got himself made business manager and deputy Gauleiter. His rich knowledge of life showed itself, upon investigation, to have been gained in rather questionable activities. There soon were no doubts that having shifted rapidly through a number of professions he had now seized on Nazism as a new business. In this sense he was a Hamburg forerunner of that drove of bandwagoners, self-seekers, and wheeler-dealers that grew so rapidly in the Nazi movement especially after 1930.

Hüttmann's departure from Hamburg occurred under unpleasant and hardly glorious circumstances. The party business office in Neustädter Street, which he administered, was broken into and a few thousand marks were stolen. Since, remarkably, the alleged thief also took the account books with him, some of the members began to suspect that it was an inside job. Hüttman was unable to dispel these suspicions. An opposition group within the party led by "Talmud" Schmidt (Schmidt, an office worker, got this nickname because he held lectures for any and every group on the "secrets" of the Talmud) demanded with increasing vigor that Munich remove Hüttmann. Finally the party leadership acquiesced. But Hüttmann did not vanish into obscurity; he was transferred to the post of *Untergauleiter* in Upper Silesia. According to Munich's way of looking at things, a little suspicion of theft and embezzlement was hardly justification for the complete dismissal of such a vigorous person. In Upper Silesia there was said to have occurred a similar affair, so that Hüttmann had to take leave of this area also. Again he fell upstairs. this time as expert for the Nazi businessmen's organization in the Saxon *Gauleitung*. Later he was transferred to Berlin where he held a post with one of the half-party, half-governmental organizations.

In the weeks before the election, party-comrade Hans Hesse suggested that in view of his own experience and the availability of funds we ought to found a weekly party newspaper. We had felt the lack of a party newspaper very keenly during the autumn elections of 1927: The assertions of some of our opponents could not be countered or weakened in any way. Thus the Local Group's executive seized immediately on the suggestion without giving the man or his financial proposals a thorough examination. For some reason and in view of the inability of any of us from the executive to pay close attention to the newspaper during the election campaign, we insisted that the paper would have to be connected with an existing party newspaper. And thus there appeared the *Hamburger Volksblatt*[12] (we turned down all emotionalisms such as "The Fore-Fighter" or "The Storm Signal"), which was editorially a local insert of the Berlin *Combat Press*, founded and directed by Gregor Strasser. The party members viewed the appearance of a weekly newspaper as a sign of our steady growth and were very pleased; the favorable propaganda effect could hardly be denied, either.

The election of February 19, 1928, brought the Nazi party an

[12] Literally, "People's Sheet"—a very common name among German Social Democratic newspapers.

increase of about six thousand votes and thus a third seat in the
city council. This was hardly an overwhelming success, but it was
seen as a great victory within the ranks of the party. The outside
world began to pay more attention to the Nazis, too. Applications
for membership multiplied. Attendance at the discussion evenings
began to be more than we could fit into the small district meeting
places. Our propaganda literature was increasingly in demand
among nonmembers. The first representatives of the upper bourgeoisie and intellectual circles now sought in private conversations
a cautious, nonbinding contact with Nazis.

Munich also obviously considered our increase in votes a success.
Hitler sent a congratulatory telegram and raised the Local Group
to the status of Gau, which hardly changed our position within the
party, since we had always been immediate to the national leadership, but certainly increased our dignity. Since this increase in
esteem unavoidably benefited some individuals, it also led to the
outbreak of a conflict that had been brewing for a long time
between Brinkmann and Böckenhauer. The conflict ultimately
broadened into a fundamental struggle between the Hamburg
Gauleitung and the SA, which ended with the reciprocal removal
of all of the protagonists.

In the crowded rooms of the party's business office there had
been tension from the very beginning between Böckenhauer and
Brinkmann. Gradually this developed into an almost unbearable
situation of mutual bitterness and enmity. Now, after the election,
an open fight broke out because the results of the election not
only wounded Böckenhauer's personal ambition but also painfully
affected his attitudes and political claims as an SA leader.

Back in 1926 the work of the Local Group could hardly have
been carried out at all without the support of the SA, which gave
the SA leader considerable significance in the political sector, too.
At certain moments he played the role of a secret dictator in the
Hamburg movement. Then, with growth and with the organizational extension and development of the civilian side of the movement, the center of gravity shifted. In terms of numbers alone the
District Groups achieved preponderance over the Stormtrooper
units and could increasingly conduct action without the aid of the
SA. Financially the SA even slipped into extensive dependence
upon the Local Group. Above all, most of the Stormtroopers who

had joined the party after 1926–27 began to think of the political struggle of Nazism as more important than other ideologies. They no longer felt themselves to be "political soldiers" who only temporarily put themselves at the disposal of the party while maintaining their own attitudes and decisions, but rather considered themselves to be party-comrades who happened to serve in the party's defense organization. Thus the natural developmental tendencies within the SA coincided with the views of the political leadership. The Stormtroops became the obedient instrument of the political struggle and maintained a certain independence only in internal service matters.

To be sure this development did not unfold without resistance. Above all, that segment of SA leaders who derived from the *Freikorps*[13] era persisted in a latent inclination to mutiny. The deep mistrust of the professional soldier against the politician, who so often frivolously gambles his blood in wars and then wastes the victory, had been re-strengthened by the experiences of World War I and the postwar years. They were thus no longer willing to risk their necks for the murky plans and goals of some boss or interest group who hid only abominations behind the words "Nation" and "Fatherland." But unless they were willing to withdraw into a resigned inactivity, then the only logical alternative was to demand that political power be turned over to the soldiers. Thus there arose the concept of the "political soldier" such as was painted so clearly by Ernst Roehm[14] in his *Memoirs* and was outlined, however sketchily, in many other writings of those years: in Gilbert, Heinz Killinger, Schauwecker, Ernst von Salomon, Bronnen, and even in General Hans von Seeckt's publications.[15]

[13] The *Freikorps* were volunteer military units that sprang up in 1918–19. They were involved in border wars against the Poles and Bolsheviks, were used to suppress proletarian uprisings inside Germany, attempted to seize power in Germany in 1920, were dissolved, and thereafter engaged in ultra-rightist underground terrorism against Jews, Socialists, and democratic leaders. Most of them ultimately ended up in Hitler's Stormtrooper organizations. See Robert Waite's *Vanguard of Nazism* (Cambridge, Mass., 1952; also in paperback).

[14] Ernst Roehm was head of the SA, 1922–26, and then again, 1930–1934, when he was murdered by Hitler. On the concept of "political soldiers," see Waite, p. 265 ff.

[15] Available in English are von Salomon's *The Outlaws* and *The Questionnaire*, and Seeckt's *Memoirs*.

The hopes and aspirations of the political soldiers were doubt-less predominant in Böckenhauer's approach, though probably more in the form of a vague emotion than as a conscious concept and vision. His autocratic nature and drive for power made intoler-able for him the slow but irresistible development toward reduced influence for the SA and thus for his own person. The elevation of the Local Group to a Gau and the "promotion" of his enemy Brinkmann to Gau business manager and treasurer filled his cup with bitterness, since Böckenhauer had a great weakness for honors such as these. When Brinkmann was elected city councilman while Böckenhauer had turned down a nomination out of impure modesty, the cup overflowed. He absolutely had to remove Brink-mann in order to assure the SA and himself their prior position of strength.

Böckenhauer found his excuse in some wholly proper expense accounts (which he copied out of the account books with the bad manners of a policeman) and in an unfortunate attempt by Brink-mann and myself to add to the party treasury by renting part of the business office to a book dealer. After one short week our book dealer disappeared, returning to his South German home and leav-ing considerable debts behind him. Although he knew exactly what was involved, Böckenhauer proceeded to claim that the expense accounts and the book dealer's debts were scandalous. By spreading these accusations among the members, he managed to unleash a considerable storm of protest against the "revelries and mismanagement" of the "party bosses." When the storm reached its scheduled intensity, he demanded that I immediately dismiss the responsible business manager, Brinkmann, from all of his posts. Naturally I refused and made it clear to Böckenhauer that his job was not to make demands but rather to use the SA and SS to support the authority of the political leadership. Thereupon the conflict reached the point where the SA refused to provide protec-tion for our meetings and in some District Groups also refused to pay any further dues. And now the fears expressed by Gregor Stras-ser at the time of my election—that I would suffer as an outsider who had not come out of the Hamburg movement—were borne out by events. Most of the members adhered to Böckenhauer, whom they had known for many years and whom they respected as a fanatical fighter. I, on the other hand, had hardly been able in the few months since I had taken office to establish and nourish personal relationships.

Furthermore I made a series of mistakes during the development of the conflict. Instead of patiently allowing the artificially inflamed indignation to burn out by itself, I repeatedly fanned it up again through my own vigorous reactions. Thus the reciprocal bitterness developed to such a measure that fistfights threatened to break out at any moment in the business office. Finally, when only great efforts prevented a general battle at a members' meeting in the Wilhelm Gymnasium, which was supposed to prepare for the upcoming Reichstag elections, I announced my decision to resign, effective May 1. Brinkmann had quit his post as business manager and treasurer of the Gau the day before.

There were various reasons for my decision. To begin with and quite simply, I'd had a bellyful. After a year and a half of exhausting and not quite wholly ineffective efforts, I hardly appreciated, by way of gratitude, being shouted at by my own party comrades and having clenched fists waved around under my nose. Should such things occur, however, it is understandable to feel the need for peace and aesthetic distance. Yet even this need would probably have proved insufficient for my own self-justification had it not come on top of a series of experiences and considerations of a more general nature.

Already before the meeting in the Wilhelm Gymnasium Munich had dispatched Pfeffer[16] to Hamburg. He told me, however, that he thought of himself as an observer for the national leadership but not as its representative in the sense of having a mandate to intervene. He had added remarks about the discipline within the SA which were exactly the opposite of my own conception. What Pfeffer understood by discipline was solely obedience to one's superior but not an inner discipline affecting the entire man. After he actually refrained from any intervention during the meeting and visibly beamed upon his growling Stormtroopers ("That's the way we like to see 'em!"), I could no longer believe that this was simply his private opinion. That cast a different light upon the entire behavior of the party's national leadership during the conflict. It was not that they had simply fumbled my request

[16] Head of the SA, 1926–30. For a sketch of him, see Chapter 10.

for intervention; on the contrary, they acted according to principles that Hitler liked to apply to any power struggles within the Gaue or other party units.

These principles can be formulated approximately as follows: Power struggles on the lower level are the best hindrance to the formation of a common and united opposition against the national leadership. They are therefore more useful than damaging and should be left to develop by themselves or in some cases even be covertly promoted. Insofar as exceptional circumstances make that impossible, then judgment is to be made, irrespective of the claims of justice, in favor of the stronger—in other words, in favor of the man with the tougher elbows and the more calloused conscience.[17]

These principles, whose effectiveness I now experienced for the first time, but which I could observe repeatedly in subsequent years, were as repugnant to me as Pfeffer's (and obviously the party's official) views on discipline. With them one could neither select and train a true leadership elite nor create a national and state order such as I had previously envisaged. Nor did they arise from necessity, such as might have been present under certain internal and external circumstances. The worst of the confusion of the initial postwar era had already been overcome and by means which I had already learned and experienced in the work of the DHV. It appeared senseless to me to try to attack the remaining tasks by maintaining and encouraging destructive elements rather than by directing efforts toward the formation of true counterforces. Thus the first serious doubts came to me in the spring of 1928, not about National Socialism as a movement but definitely about its leaders. During the election campaign there was a short, unannounced visit to our business offices by Hitler and this had left me with some unpleasant impressions, too.[18] Thus I withdrew from active participation in order to have the peace to observe, for a while, how things would develop in Hamburg and in the Reich.

[17] For parallel observations see Alan Bullock, *Hitler, A Study in Tyranny* (New York, 1964), p. 381. For a theoretical explanation see Joseph Nyomarky, *Charisma and Factionalism in the Nazi Party* (Minneapolis, 1967). Internal struggles of this sort became, in the Third Reich, the prime characteristic of the Nazi regime.

[18] See Chapter 5.

Since I had pursued no personal ambitions, at least I had no need to be upset about their miscarriage.

This exit caused some consternation in Munich. Precisely because the Nazi leaders had calculated on personal ambitions they were not able to comprehend a voluntary withdrawal. Therefore they also refused to accept my resignation but instead inaugurated wearisome negotiations with me to get me to resume my activity. Probably in order to stimulate an inclination toward this, they now expelled Böckenhauer from the party, as I had previously asked them to, on the charge of "mutiny" during the conflict. But now the reason given for his expulsion was disobedience against Hitler's order prohibiting the SA from possessing weapons.

This matter dated back to more than a half year before. I had cited it in a conversation with Pfeffer as evidence of Böckenhauer's autocratic methods. The old Blücher League had possessed a small store of weapons in Hamburg, which dated from the 1923 days. When Böckenhauer told me of this I asked him, for political reasons, to turn in the weapons. He promised to do so, but did not keep his promise. I pressed him no further on the matter because I had complete understanding for his pleasure in possessing weapons.[19] Then the location of the weapons was betrayed to the police, but simultaneously Böckenhauer learned of this betrayal. He was quicker and turned the weapons over to the army. The guns were already gone when the police conducted their raid and thus they came away empty-handed. There was no damage to either the party or the Hamburg SA, so that Böckenhauer's belated expulsion could only be justified on the grounds of principles which would probably not have been applied in other circumstances. Beyond this, Böckenhauer had informed me completely about the end of the affair and I had supported his measures. One could not blame him and his friends, then, if they viewed his expulsion as a rather dirty act of revenge on my part. Munich must have been quite clear on this effect too, so that I assumed that a consciously malicious intent lay behind their whole move. They wanted to keep a few "moral" trumps against me in their hand in order to continue into the future their game of divide and rule. Here lay

---

[19] On the psychology of having arms, see Waite, p. 222. It was a dominant trait of the Free Corps movement in postwar Germany.

the beginnings of methods that were later to have fateful results in the political affairs of the Third Reich.

Consequently, I protested immediately to Munich, not against Böckenhauer's expulsion but against the grounds given for it, and at the same time declared that this would not lead me to resume the office of Gauleiter: it was not past events that had to be regulated but rather the future arrangement of the Gau. For this I demanded the removal of Hüttmann from his new position as deputy Gauleiter and business manager. The party leadership refused to accede, since what I saw as Hüttmann's failings were in their eyes virtues.

Thus the negotiations collapsed and in September 1928 the party leadership accepted my resignation and gave notice of it in the *Völkischer Beobachter*. My provisional successor was Hinrich Lohse, the Gauleiter of Schleswig-Holstein, who in view of his own multifarious tasks obviously would have to, and did, turn the actual work over to Hüttmann. The members of the party in Hamburg were not too happy with this solution, the objective insufficiencies of which were soon apparent. On the other hand, this provisional situation lasted exactly one year until Hitler appointed Karl Kaufmann as the new Gauleiter of Hamburg.

CHAPTER 3

The Nazi Shop-Cell Organization in Hamburg, 1930–1931

Editor's note: *The formal title of the Nazi party, National Social-ist German Workers party, suggests one of the major attractions of Hitler's movement to Germans: it promised a new synthesis that would end the extreme class distinctions and ideological divisions that had plagued German politics since the beginning of indus-trialization. Many followers of Nazism took the party's "socialist" slogans seriously. Consequently, an attempt was made to recruit workers, through the NSBO, the Nazi Shop-Cell Organization. Though this had some success among white-collar workers, it was an abysmal failure in the factories. Even if we accept the NSBO's most extreme claim, that it had 400,000 members by January 1933, that still represented only 6 percent of the number of workers in the Socialist Free Unions—and the vast majority of the NSBO's members were not blue collar. In short, the German working class remained loyal to their socialist-dominated unions and voted over-whelmingly for the Social Democrats or Communists. After Hitler came to power the NSBO was shouldered aside in favor of the Labor Front (DAF), which was run not by workers but by the Nazi party bureaucracy. Nevertheless, the NSBO and other "social-istic" aspects of Nazism were extremely important in convincing the true backers of Hitlerism—the lower middle classes and farm-ers—that Nazism was capable of bridging class cleavages. The fail-ure of the Nazis to win working-class support is largely attributable to the peculiar strength of Marxist appeal in Germany and to the very intensity of class division, but it was also associated with the problems and ambiguities of the NSBO itself and its role in the Nazi party. Krebs' experience as NSBO leader in Hamburg helps explain why "national socialism" remained a chimera.*

It would be a grave mistake to judge the phrase "workers of hand and brain" as nothing more than propaganda. Without a doubt the National Socialists actually hoped to replace the concepts of "labor" and "worker," as they had developed through class-war ideology, with an awakened recognition of the equal value and mutual interdependence of intellectual and physical labor. To demand a "folk community" meant trying to eliminate the opposition between worker and bourgeois by establishing common values. Such common values could not be represented by the concepts of "folk" and "folk community" during those years when the masses of workers believed passionately in the International. Instead, these concepts provided a goal to be fought for and it was precisely for their common recognition that there was struggle between the so-called "nationalist bourgeoisie" and the so-called "internationalist proletariat." Here and there people worked against this split.

But as soon as one succeeded in showing both sides their mutual interdependence and simultaneous bonds in work itself—and even a mediocre speaker or propagandist could manage that—you could take that commonality as a given factor, and even more important, have it generally accepted as such. That produced a further advantage: The more you propagated "work as a basic value," the farther you disassociated yourself visibly from capitalism. And beyond that you could, in the process of developing a substitute religion, use "work as a basic value" as a pillar of the Nazi temple.

Thus far these considerations (whose propagandistic formulation "workers of hand and brain" was probably Hitler's own doing[1]) were quite logical both in point of departure and in the goals set. Nevertheless it was not to add up that way by the end of the party's history—or, more accurately, not even at the beginning. The worker was shown a "Labor State" (portrayed, naturally, in strongly collectivist and materialist terms), but he wouldn't buy it. Even in the public meetings he was hardly to be seen amid the mass of lower-middle-class, artisan, and white-collar employees, except when he showed up as a part of the heckling squads organized by both Marxist parties. And among the actual party membership, workers played no role at all down to 1930–31, except for a few rare instances.

[1] Actually the slogan originated among English Socialists before World War I.

To avoid error or contradictions the term "workers" needs more precise definition. Naturally there were many Nazis who made a living by working with their hands and who were listed on the tax rolls as non-independent wage-earners. These "workers, too," who were mostly very young or were forced in the postwar years to become factory workers (for example, because they had to give up a professional army career), are not what is meant here. What I mean are the politically and union-organized "class-conscious" workers who acknowledged their social and economic status and played an active role in the life of the nation on the basis of that recognition. To win them over, to convert them from "international Marxism," seemed a most noble assignment to most Nazi activists, at least in the early years of the movement.

Hitler personally may well have thought from the very beginning only about winning over "the broad masses," especially since his knowledge of the structure and mentality of the German labor movement was hardly profound. But since the worker necessarily formed a part of "the broad masses," this meant at first more difference in the point of attack than in ultimate goals; in other words, even Hitler had to concern himself with agitation directed toward factory workers. But in accordance with his basic position, which was strictly opposed to any differentiated propaganda appealing to individual groups, he was disinclined to adopt any special methods. In his view the worker had to be won and could be won by the usual methods: mass meetings, ecstatic demonstrations with flags, drums, and uniforms, poster and leaflet propaganda. The special circumstances in southern Germany where social and class contradictions were less developed and where the populace was more easily aroused by external glitter and visible power (Swabians must be excepted from this judgment) fit in well with Hitler's approach and even substantiated it in some places. In my view he always adhered to this approach and never acquired a taste for the shop-cell work which Gregor Strasser's circle later developed. Hitler disliked plodding, day-to-day, detail work and especially any that threatened to pin him down ideologically or practically or could widen the conflicts between employers and employees. But he drew the obvious conclusions from the failure, in the spring of 1928, of that direct attack upon the unions (and especially the DHV) mounted by Kube, Goebbels, and other Nazi leaders. Despite the explicit publicity support given by the *Völk-*

ischer Beobachter, this was just about totally ineffective except for stirring up a lot of dust.

The reassessment of tactics came at the Munich Conference in autumn 1928, as I described above in the chapter on my experiences in the DHV. Henceforth the unions were to be tolerated as representatives of social-interest groups and attacked only when they mixed into general politics. Moreover, the struggle for the worker was henceforth not just to be fought out in mass meetings but rather was to be brought into the shops. It was hoped that there, where the worker could be found in his immediate sphere of life, he could be spoken to more easily and effectively.

The decisions of this conference laid the theoretical foundation for the construction of the Nazi Shop-Cell[2] Organization. But its practical realization encountered many delays and difficulties. Furthermore, one cannot speak at all of a full success. Down to 1933 bridgeheads were made only in a small segment at the great industrial shops and even there they were very weakly held. And the Labor Front set up after 1933 was so far removed from the theoretical basis of the original NSBO that it cannot be considered as a legitimate continuation of the NSBO and by no means a culmination.

At the beginning of the work it was apparent that the most important precondition in the shops was lacking: people to do the job. Since they couldn't be conjured up, one had to wait until they would emerge bit by bit with the slow growth of the party, which took many months. First the depression with its radicalizing effects and then the great electoral success of 1930 brought forth a stream of capable and willing party members for work in the shops.

However, this betterment in the technical-organizational sphere did not vanquish problems, since in the interim conflicts had developed over goals and methods. Their origins lay partly in opposing opinions and partly in the old rivalry between Goebbels and Strasser. In Gau Berlin shopwork consisted almost exclusively

---

2 *Nationalsozialistische Betriebszellen Organization. Betrieb* is impossible to translate directly since it encompasses any enterprise: a bank, a hardware store. a government office, a factory—all are *Betriebe.* The word "shop," with its ambiguity, comes closest in English but the reader should remember that "shop-cells" were formed in almost all places employees could be found except on farms, in schools, or in the army.

of propaganda, which necessarily led to radicalization. They wanted to win the masses by stirring up mass instincts; they wanted, for example, visible numerical successes in the Shop-Council elections[3] without any concrete social successes. The result was that instead of any inroads into the Marxist Free Union Movement there was mostly a jostling about with the Christian-National unions over one or two seats. In the course of this all efforts were limited to struggles over immediate issues. Even when it led to the gain of a few seats here and there, especially among the salaried employees, hardly anything was gained toward the special goal of the party, namely overthrowing the Marxists. On the other hand political groups were thrust into irreconcilable enmity, which had originally not been so disposed at all. The consequences were what one would expect: They were expressed even later in the resistance. Responsible for this form of "the struggle in the shops" was the Secretariat for Labor Affairs of the Berlin *Gauleitung*. The head of this was party-comrade Johannes Engel, by profession, as far as I remember, a foreman at Knorr Brake Works. In the background was, as I have suggested, Dr. Goebbels. His goal was to upset the work and the plans of Gregor Strasser's NSBO and, if possible, to weaken it in Hitler's eyes by showing it to be ineffective or even harmful.

What drove Goebbels to these efforts was not just his long-standing hatred for Strasser but also some not wholly unjustified defensive considerations. It is very probable that Strasser set up the Reich headquarters of the NSBO in Berlin (against all party traditions) in order to attack and weaken Goebbels from this position.[4]

---

[3] The Weimar Constitution required regular election of shop-councils, whose members were empowered to deal with grievances and working conditions. The candidates were nominated by ideological groupings, however: Communist, Catholic unions, etc. Throughout the Weimar Republic the Socialists (Free Unions) won these elections by 90 percent majorities, on the basis of effective bread-and-butter negotiations, with the other ideological slates dividing the other 10 percent of the vote.

[4] Goebbels, in addition to being Reich propaganda leader, was Gauleiter of Berlin from 1926 on, with vastly more autonomous powers than the usual Gauleiter. Also, the shop-cell movement had begun in Berlin, under his direction. See Dietrich Orlow, *The History of the Nazi Party, 1919–1933* (Pittsburgh, 1969), pp. 92–94, 169, 196–97. The usual location for Nazi national organizations was Munich.

According to the statutes of the Shop-Cell Organization, as officially founded in March 1931 (originally it was called *RBA*: Reich Shop-Cell Section), the individual Gau chairmen were not appointed by the local Nazi Gauleiter but by the national headquarters of the NSBO. This alone was at least a threat to Goebbels' dictatorial position in Berlin. But Strasser's plans went well beyond this tactical consideration. In his basic view the winning of the workers, including white-collar employees, was not just the most pressing and noblest task of the party; he also calculated that these two groups would one day form the core of the party, while the majority of the middle-class people who were currently flooding into the party would gradually trickle out again. At that point of development the party office that specialized in labor affairs and workers' problems would logically achieve the greatest influence and power over against the specialists in demagoguery and propaganda. Thus the conflict between Goebbels and Strasser and perhaps even Strasser's differences with Hitler, apparent since 1929, would be resolved in Strasser's favor. To be sure, this office must not allow itself to be mired down in propaganda and demagoguery any more than it should be allowed to locate itself in Munich, where the atmosphere was so unfavorable to a thorough mastery of these kinds of problems.

In point of fact the Reich leaders of the NSBO tried very seriously to produce constructive and formative achievements with the shop-cells. Although Engel in Berlin, like many other functionaries throughout the Reich, viewed the shop-cells primarily as party recruitment bureaus, Walter Schuhmann, Reinhold Muchow, and their co-workers wanted to make them into catalytic agents for a future social system. Naturally, to accomplish this you could not duck real and essential social problems by lazily pretending that they would take care of themselves "after the victory." You had to take a position on questions such as profit-sharing, co-ownership, uniform insurance, moonlighting, and old-age pensions. You also had to have the courage, at times, to push through unpopular measures such as coalitions with other unions for shop council elections. It cannot be denied that the national leadership of the NSBO recognized this assignment very clearly and made an attempt to carry it out, at least at the onset. The NSBO's newspaper (*Workerdom*, edited by Muchow) also concerned itself above all with seriously coming to grips with Marxism and the other tendencies and currents in the labor movement down to 1933.

In Hamburg the shop-cell work stood under the immediate and long-range influence of both factions, which produced some intolerable and contradictory situations. At first party-comrade Reinke, who was assigned in autumn 1929 by Gauleiter Kaufmann to prepare for the formation of shop-cells, and party-comrade Ingwersen, who set up the unemployed cells, followed the model of the Berlin Secretariat for Labor Affairs. Accordingly, cell-work chiefly served propaganda and recruitment. It was from this viewpoint that a mass meeting was called, with Engel from Berlin as speaker, in January 1930. But this was prevented when the Communists occupied the meeting hall, located in the Red neighborhood of Barmbek.

In the summer of 1930, at Kaufmann's request, I took over the leadership of the Shop-Cell Organization with Reinke as my deputy. I now oriented the work in accordance with my own views and my connections with Gregor Strasser and his circle, following the guidelines of the RBA. That led to difficulties within the organization itself, because several of the previous cell leaders refused to go along with it. There were also conflicts with the *Gauleitung*, which did not wish to recognize the guidelines of the RBA and above all not its power to appoint leaders. The then Gau organization leader, Dr. Hans Nieland, who belonged to the national reactionary wing of the party, found the entire tendency unpalatable. In less than a year I was twice fired and then, through pressure from the NSBO national headquarters, twice reinstated. Finally in August 1931 I gave up the office for good. But the evolution of the NSBO in Hamburg was conditioned far less by these internal altercations than it was by external objective circumstances.

When Reinke set out to approach his assignment in autumn 1929, he quickly ascertained that here, too, suitable people were lacking. The number of "real" workers in the Hamburg Nazi organization was, as mentioned before, still very small. And of these few there were even fewer who were capable of any successful shop-cell agitation.

In those excited times, so suspicious and touchy about all efforts at political persuasion, you could not win significant influence in a factory or other industry without rather considerable human, professional, and political qualities and capabilities. Usually it was also necessary to have been part of the shop community for quite a while already. Among the younger twenty- to thirty-year-old party members there were very few who had all these qualifications. As for the older ones, they were loath to risk their jobs in those months of increasing unemployment. Nazis were not liked in the shops anyway, and both employers and the shop councils used every opportunity to get rid of them.

So in the first months Reinke had to limit his activity almost exclusively to working up files. There were only two real cells founded: one by Thoma at HAPAG,[5] composed solely of office workers, and the second, as I later discovered indirectly and to my displeasure, a secret one in the DHV headquarters. The latter was to make life difficult for the "Jew-dominated" officials, but it did not dare show itself publicly until the spring of 1933. Apart from that, contacts were established with some officials at the German Union League[6] who, as Hamburg Protestants, disagreed with its connections to the Catholic Center party or who used this method to express some personal grievance against their superiors or the national board members. Though these were at first very loose contacts they later became extremely significant.

Better than the Shop-Cell Organization was the development of the unemployed movement under Ingerwersen. It is true that entrance into it came almost automatically, given the circumstances of those years, but still it took considerable courage to propagandize for Nazism at the Employment Offices and sell or distribute (at the Gau's expense) the newspaper *The Unemployed*, which was published irregularly.

It was only seldom that the success of this propaganda work could be gauged in detail. But generally favorable results were indicated by the powerful opposition (which often mounted to open terror and the expulsion of Nazis from the employment offices), the increasing circulation of *The Unemployed*, and the growth of the cells. It is definite that the unemployed cells brought a number of former Communists into the Nazi party, who rapidly showed themselves to be eager and convinced activists. Here and there

[5] One of the biggest shipping firms in Germany.
[6] Krebs means the Christian trade unions.

among them may also have been a double agent. But this hardly constituted any danger, given the morale and mental condition of the Nazi movement at that time. Subversion by some radical element or by a conspirator is generally a serious threat only for unstable and decaying organizations.

What was more important was that these mostly young Communists, whether they were agents or trustworthy adherents, working class or uprooted bourgeoisie or intellectuals, were, sociologically speaking, in the fallow fields of the labor movement. Therefore they were of little use as shock troops against the fully molded, self-conscious "workerdom." In this respect they were hardly different from the young locksmiths, joiners, waiters, plumbers, mechanics. As the sons of artisans they had made their apprenticeship in little shops but did not think of themselves as "workers." On the contrary, they were conscious of their bourgeois origins. Still, because of the depression they had to make their way to the employment offices as "unemployed." There were a great number of these types in the unemployed cells. But the majority of the members were white-collar workers, including many older people and a number of women. Many belonged to a union—the DHV, GDA, and VWWA[7]—which both benefited the organizational buildup of the cells and counteracted excessive radicalization. The Gau chairman of the unemployed, Ingwersen, was also an office worker who could no longer find a job, despite a considerable speaking knowledge of his profession. In time he fell victim to the usual fate of the long-term unemployed: he was unable to work in a concentrated way any more and lost discipline over himself and his life.

By early summer of 1930 the situation in Hamburg for shop-cell work began to get better. The influx of party members brought new collaborators for the shop-cells. In addition, the contacts with functionaries in the German Union League, mentioned above, took on a concrete significance through the formation of agreements for common action in the shop council elections and similar mutual assistance ventures. A number of these functionaries also

[7] The GDA was another non-socialist white-collar-workers' union, though smaller than the DHV. The VWWA was an association of salaried women employees.

joined the party, though it was only partly out of true acceptance
of the goals of Nazism. Their hope of recruiting new members for
the German Union League among Nazis who were not yet members of any union played a role as strong as political convictions,
since the Union League was rather underdeveloped in Hamburg.
Nevertheless, the Hamburg Shop-Cell Organization acquired an
excellent number of capable, organizationally trained collaborators.
From among them I chose, in autumn 1930, my deputy, Dickszas.
Reinke had resigned, since his work in Bergedorf-Vierlanden
County called for all his energies and also suited him better.

The undesirable aspect of these new collaborators was that they
formed primarily professional groups and not shop-cells. Thus
within a short period there emerged, with rather considerable
memberships, groups for bank workers, sailors, butchers, railroad
men, restaurant workers, chauffeurs, and so on. These professional
groups included both employers and employees. In shop-cells, that
would not have been propagandistically advantageous, but still it
would have been barely tolerable. In the professional groups this
composition very rapidly led to massive tensions and hefty conflicts. These were not just conflicts of interest or of personality but
were also based on the serious and difficult question of reaching a
proper accommodation between the two elements. On the one
hand they all rejected the idea of class conflict and wanted to
bring entrepreneur and laborer together under "the banner of
work." But on the other hand the economic situation at the time
required a particular stress on the social interests of the economically weaker and dependent elements of the nation. Also, under no
circumstances did we want to give the appearance of being a
"yellow" organization—one bought out by the employers. And so
the employees produced some rather extreme demands, which then
engendered natural reactions from employers in the professional
groups and beyond that in other party sub-organizations, such as
the Economic Policy Section. In any event this led to endless
mediation and arbitration without ever producing any objective
compromise or synthesis. The attempted solution later undertaken
by the Labor Front, that is, turning the state (or party) into a reg-
ulative command authority for all social questions, was hardly yet
mentioned at that time. At most it was implicitly presaged in such
generally employed phrases as "After the victory there won't be

any more social problems!" or simply "Later everything will be different!" On the other hand there were energetic discussions over profit-sharing and co-determination. As was typical in general for the early days of the NSBO, these discussions were conducted under highly democratic procedures. Specific themes were proposed for debate, speakers were recognized by the chair, votes were taken. Also the executive committees in the professional groups were still partly chosen by free and secret elections. On the other hand it was amazing how swiftly some of the newly elected executive committees and former functionaries from the German Union League got used to issuing orders and exceeded, in this art, some of the old-time Nazis. Quite frequently I had to explain to certain cell and professional group leaders that the members were not subjects and they themselves were not Caesars or satraps.

Another unpleasant aspect was that not a few of the NSBO functionaries inclined toward petty corruption, like falsifying expense accounts, pocketing parts of contributions, and other disreputable practices. Since such doings were not very widespread in the party, at least as far as I could observe it in the years down to 1933, I have never quite understood the reason for their frequent appearance in the NSBO (here I speak only of Hamburg). Perhaps it was the close contact with the deranged economic and social circumstances of those times that also deranged the moral values of those men who, far more often than the political leaders, had to cope directly with the victims and objects of this dislocation and sometimes were even victims themselves. It is hard to wade through a swamp and keep yourself clean. Men who had known hunger through unemployment were tempted to make up for hungry days with the money of others, especially since money and the value of money had become subject to question.

Perhaps the greater susceptibility of NSBO functionaries to the temptations of their offices occurred because they were more special interest advocates than political representatives. Special interest does not fight for a cause; it seeks an advantage. That can lead only too easily to a result where advantage is ultimately viewed from a purely personal angle. What argues for this analysis is that petty embezzlement occurred far less frequently in the true shop-cells than in the trade groups. The cells were relatively undistorted communities with definite political goals operating in an environment that was still orderly and healthy. Special interest could not be promoted in a cell; on the contrary, it was considerably endangered. This danger from employers, or from political opponents who were fellow employees, enforced a selectivity and comradeship which, while it did not completely rule out corruption, held it down to a minimum. Admittedly, true shop-cells were, as I have pointed out, rare in the beginning. The biggest cell was in the Hamburg Elevated Railway; there were salaried employee cells in several banks. The municipal slaughterhouse had a cell; I already mentioned the one in HAPAG. On the other hand the NSBO could hardly get a toehold on the docks any more than it could in the other big industrial shops. But several ships carried Nazi cells aboard them, mostly made up of men from the SA Maritime Squads.

That was the state of the Nazi shop-cell work in Hamburg when I left it in the summer of 1931. As far as I could determine, nothing was essentially changed up to the "seizure of power," except that under Dickszas' and Habedank's leadership there was a return to propaganda again and an eschewal of "social politics"—now viewed as an intellectual aberration. Naturally the number of members increased and there may have been a few more shop-cells and professional groups established down to 1933. There were no overwhelming accomplishments or successes, but in the end what there was sufficed to supply people ready for the take-over of the unions and the establishment of the Labor Front when it came to that, in the spring of 1933.

CHAPTER 4

Editor's note: *The Great Depression swelled the Nazi party from a fringe organization to a mass movement. Krebs observed this from the vantage point of the editorship of a major Nazi newspaper. This position also involved him in the organizational and political struggles that were characteristic of the internal history of Nazism. Hitler was committed to social Darwinism in practice as well as in theory, and the intraparty power contests that typified this period were to become a major trait of the Third Reich. Superimposed upon this internal dynamic was a ruthless centralization, which also progressively broadened the scope of the Darwinian process in Nazism.*

All this characterized the general history of the Nazi press, too. Though important to the movement, its growth was never commensurate with the size of the party until after Hitler became dictator. In 1932, for example, when the Nazi vote reached almost 14 million, the party had 59 dailies in Germany with a combined circulation of only 782,000. By comparison there were some 4,700 other dailies and weeklies published in Germany that year; Krebs' paper was one of ten daily papers in Hamburg. The Nazi press arose from local initiative and everywhere it was a shoestring operation. In 1932, for example, Krebs' editorial staff consisted of six men, only three of them paid. Down to 1933 the Nazi press remained decentralized in ownership and control, but there were ceaseless efforts to impose uniformity and centralized direction. Krebs' experiences thus were typical of almost all Nazi newspapers. Their general history is surveyed by Oren Hale, The Captive Press in the Third Reich *(Princeton, 1964), Ch. II. More information on Hamburg is available in Roland V. Layton, "The Early Years of the Nazi Press in Hamburg,"* University of Virginia Essays in History, *Vol. VII (1961–62), pp. 20–36.*

The first Nazi newspaper in Hamburg, the weekly *Hamburger Volksblatt*, was founded shortly before the city council elections of February 19, 1928. Journalistically speaking, it was a local edition of Gregor Strasser's Combat Press, with one page inserted for news from Hamburg, edited by party-comrade Hans Hesse. From a legal point of view things were the other way around. Hesse, as owner and publisher of the *Volksblatt*, purchased from the Combat Press the requisite pages (from the weekly *Der nationale Sozialist*) and Gau Hamburg guaranteed to cover any deficit.

Outwardly the evolution of the *Hamburger Volksblatt* was fairly satisfactory in the first weeks. To be sure, income did not cover expenditures, especially since there were hardly any advertisements. But the deficit was relatively small, so that the guarantee, which the Gau had to pay at the beginning of May, for example, came to only about six hundred marks. Less satisfactory were the editorial skills of Hans Hesse. I can no longer remember whether Hesse's claim that he was a trained journalist had any factual evidence behind it. His abilities certainly provided no proof of it. It was hard to imagine how, under his leadership and responsibility, the newspaper would ever work itself away from the all too close connection with the Combat Press and become an independent Hamburg publication.

The necessity for this emerged more quickly than we had anticipated. After the resignation of the old *Gauleitung* (Krebs, Reinke, Brinkmann, Gloy) at the end of April 1928, the new Deputy Gauleiter, Wilhelm Hüttmann, refused to recognize the guarantee to the Combat Press, whereupon they cancelled their contract with the *Volksblatt* as of May 3. This forced Hesse to consider whether he should or could continue with the *Volksblatt* as a private undertaking or whether he would have to give it up. He decided to go on publishing it; probably he hoped that a continued growth of the party would automatically promote the prosperity of his newspaper.

The result was disappointing. Hesse turned his weekly into something halfway between the *Stürmer* and the *Nachtpost*.[1] If

---

[1] The *Stürmer*, edited by Julius Streicher in Nuremberg, was the most noto-

you called that to Hesse's attention he tried to excuse it by saying that he had no choice: The loss of subscribers, which he blamed on adverse word-of-mouth publicity from the new *Gauleitung* (which was opposed to him), supposedly forced him to drive up his street sales by stressing sensational news and articles. Such excuses and explanations sounded rather hollow. The loss of subscribers was much more simply explained by the obvious decline in the paper's quality. Also it was difficult to see why he was proffering criminal and sexual senationalisms rather than political ones, since he was publishing a political newspaper. The truth of the matter was that Hesse understood little of his craft and hardly anything at all of politics.

Personally, I was hardly concerned with the *Volksblatt* in the first weeks after my resignation as Gauleiter. To begin with, I had my own concerns. A considerable component of these was a conflict with my temporary successor, Hüttmann—even though this was basically a foolish and needless conflict, considering the insignificance of its content and my opponent. In the course of this conflict I came to the recognition that I really was not fitted to be a Nazi Gauleiter and that, therefore, any reoccupation of that post —which was a notion I had toyed with for a while—was out of the question. My style and my views corresponded neither to the conceptions and wishes of the membership nor to those of the national leadership. Furthermore, I had become acquainted, here and there, with attitudes and methods with which I neither wanted nor was able to conform. If there was going to be any possibility at all for me to continue working with Nazism, I would have to seek out areas where, at least for a while, there would still be room permitted for the play of free opinions.

These considerations led me, once my resignation as Gauleiter was finally accepted by the national leadership and published in the *Völkischer Beobachter* (in September 1928), to concern myself again more strongly with the *Hamburger Volksblatt*. I wrote a regular column, "Politics of the Week," and produced several commentaries on political and cultural affairs. I also tried to get friends and acquaintances to join me in this. It didn't change

rious, pornographic, sadistically anti-Semitic example of Nazi gutter journalism. The *Nachtpost* was a commercial venture in sensationalism, specializing in crime and sex exposés.

much, since our contributions did not fit into the main framework of the paper and since Hesse, despite good advice and warnings, continued to show himself recalcitrant and contrary. So the paper made its troubled way through the year 1928, and every week we were amazed again to see that it was still being published.

On January 1, 1929, the situation of the *Hamburger Volksblatt* reached a dangerous crisis, for from that day on there was published a second Gau newspaper, the *Hansische Warte*. Its publisher was Hüttmann, the editor was C. G. Harke, the advertising director was Plasberg. The only thing that saved the *Volksblatt* from immediate liquidation was that the *Hansische Warte* was a privately owned venture too, owing to the financial weakness of the Gau.

In those days most of the party-comrades held the view, in unconscious dependence upon Marxist conceptions, that the Nazi slogan "common good precedes private interest" excluded any private property in party affairs. A considerable role in this attitude was also played by the belief—which was wrong, at least in those early days of Nazism—that you could earn a pile of money by publishing a newspaper. The party leadership promoted such views as strongly as it could. To be sure, they were less concerned about "the common good" than they were about producing intellectual uniformity and "coordination."[2] In accordance with the saying "he who pays the piper calls the tune," they wanted to turn the editors of the party press into paid functionaries, or to put it more harshly, into hired opinion-mongers. To this end they were concerned to choke off every private publishing venture in which personal independence of opinion might find shelter and convert it into party property. In every Gau there developed, because of this intention, massive conflicts that were ultimately won, in almost every case, by the doctrinaires or the clever *Apparatchiks*.

In Hamburg this conflict remained undecided at first. But as weeks went by, the *Hamburger Volksblatt* went further downhill. In the eyes of most of the party's members and followers the *Hansische Warte* gained the reputation of being the legitimate organ of the Gau, because of the official party position held by its pub-

[2] In German, *Gleichschaltung*, the term used in the Third Reich to denote the destruction or subordination of all centers of independence.

lisher. In mid-February 1929, Hesse came to me and reported that unless he got immediate and effective assistance, he would be unable to continue publication. As a consequence, Brinkmann and I decided to buy the *Volksblatt* from him.

This decision was portrayed to the mass of party members in Hamburg as an attempt to make things difficult for the then *Gauleitung*. But the matter wasn't quite that simple. Among other things, the purchase required several thousand marks, which we had to borrow, pay interest on, and someday repay. We would not have taken on a risk like that just to give ourselves wicked pleasure. On the contrary, there were other considerations, political ones, that were decisive for us.

As I described in the chapter "Between Nazism and Trade Unionism," once I had resigned from the office of Gauleiter I began to concern myself increasingly with the whole complex of social policy within the Nazi party, especially relationships between the party and unionism. Naturally it became a keen desire of mine to communicate my newly won conceptions to the public. The purchase of the *Volksblatt* gave me an opportunity to do this —with an additional advantage in the financial independence of the paper from party funds.

But the explication of social questions by no means exhausted the assignments set for the *Hamburger Volksblatt*. In the course of 1928 the National Socialist Student League had established itself at the University of Hamburg and the National Socialist Pupils League, led predominantly by the "Geusen,"[3] had gotten a firm footing in the academies and professional schools of the city. I had worked closely with both groups from the day of their foundation. Therefore I knew how much they longed for an organ in which they could promote their cause and simultaneously argue about it without limitations being imposed by doctrinaire party directives. The demand for discussion was strong among young people, even when they only wanted to use their discussions to prove the political impotence of a discussion era.

---

[3] A racialist youth movement organization that was extremely close to the Nazis, though organizationally independent. It particularly favored the Strasser wing of Nazism and many of its members belonged to the DHV. Hence Krebs' close collaboration with them.

Generally speaking, the Nazi students of those early days did not include the kind of crude types who tried to cover up or counterblance limited intellectual talents through political daredeviltry. On the contrary, most of them were decidedly smart kids. Some were true intellectuals who were trying to save themselves from their own intellectualism by moving into what they believed was the clear, clean, simple world of Nazism. For example, among the first active members of the Pupils League were a considerable number of pupils from the Lichtwark School. The Lichtwark School in Hamburg was operated according to the most modern pedagogical principles and methods. Theoretically this should have immunized its pupils against all radical influences. Since this was not the case—Communism had even more adherents in the school than Nazism did—it would appear that theory and practice were not fully in accord. In any event the boys from the Lichtwark School wanted nothing more to do with such modernisms as student councils and so on. "Freedom"—all kinds of freedoms—were highly suspicious to them, in view of the way "freedom" had been misused in the instances they had observed. They had chosen themselves new gods and ideals, admittedly not without outside influence, for example, the writings on "the new nationalism" and the lectures of the national political school of the Fichte Society.[4] Now they wanted to bear witness in print to these new idols. We gave them one page in the *Hamburger Volksblatt*, which was entitled "Youth in Upheaval" and was edited by a leader of the "Geusen," Ludwig Schmidt. We also provided a page for the students, called "The Academic Watch," which was edited by K. Massmann. Now and then there was yet another insert, edited by Wolf Meyer-Christian, called "German Soldierdom."

From a journalistic standpoint it was burdensome to have three pages committed in a weekly paper only eight—sometimes only six —pages long. It limited unduly the scant space allotted to the general part designed for all readers. Still, these inserts pretty well saved the life of the *Volksblatt* in its situation at that time. They

---

[4] The Fichte Society grew out of an unsuccessful attempt to unite all racialist groups before World War I. When this failed it became an educational organization for the general promotion of racialist ideas. See Nelson Edmondson, "The Fichte Society: A Chapter in Germany's Conservative Revolution," *Journal of Modern History* (June 1966), pp. 161–180.

brought us a crowd of subscribers, who thenceforth viewed the *Volksblatt* as their own personal newspaper. Furthermore, their undoctrinaire attitude also recruited us friends in circles that were more sympathetic to the idea of national socialism than they were to the National Socialist party. Thus the crisis threatening the paper in February 1929 was overcome within about ten weeks after it passed into the control of the Brinkmann Publishing Co. That is, it was still losing money but the losses steadily declined. We could calculate that the existing capital would suffice to carry us to that point in time where income would match expenditures.

This calculation and supplying the means to make such a calculation was the work of Edgar Brinkmann, who straightened out the *Volksblatt*'s finances just as he had reorganized the finances of Local Group Hamburg in 1926. Admittedly, it would not have succeeded without the greatest frugality, occasional irritations, and general unpleasantness. We ourselves carried the paper to the wholesale dealers and to a number of stationery stores, whose owners occasionally sold it door to door. Sometimes we even hawked it on the streets ourselves. This was actually against the law, but on the other hand it gave us useful insights into the psychology of our readers. The only thing was that at the DHV people were not especially charmed over this kind of spare-time activity by me.

The total independence of our newspaper from the party organization lasted only a few months. On April 15, 1929, Hitler appointed Karl Kaufmann as Gauleiter of Hamburg. He arrived in Hamburg on May 1 and began his activity by trying to end the press duality, with the hope of acquiring as property of the *Gauleitung* the single newspaper that would emerge from an agreement. A merger was swiftly effected since it was objectively justified. Apart from that, the Hüttmann Publishing Co. was on the brink of financial collapse. By June 1, I was able to take over the editorship of the *Hansische Warte*, newly merged with the *Hamburger Volksblatt*.

Kaufmann had less luck with his further goal, since the Gau did not have the money to publish a newspaper and since Brinkmann and I persistently refused to give up the legally private character of our paper. After extensive and not particularly enjoyable negotiations, we finally reached an agreement, in September, according to which Brinkmann and I remained in unlimited possession of the newspaper but the Gau was to receive 50 percent of its future profits. I was to continue as managing editor but was to pay heed to the suggestions and desires of the Gauleiter. Naturally the *Hansische Warte* was to publish official notices of the Gau and its subsidiaries promptly and in full, as far as space permitted.

External it was all settled. The problem itself, however, which could be briefly summarized under the title "Apparat vs. Personality," remained unsolved. Down to my extrusion from the newspaper and the party I constantly had to be on the defense against attempts by the *Gauleitung* to reduce my fellow editors and me from the status of free journalists writing from conviction to the status of paid functionaries writing for money.

It was a dispute based fundamentally on principles. Real differences of opinion, such as could have gone beyond tactical viewpoints to encompass the basic political attitudes of the editors, appeared quite rarely, actually not until Hitler ran for the Reich presidency in 1932. To be sure, one group of party officials constantly grumbled over the lack of radicalism in the Gau press, while we were too radical for another segment because of our position toward the middle-class parties and the nationalistic paramilitary organizations. Still others considered us too intellectual or were opposed to our "modernistic" views on art. But all this almost always concerned single issues of peripheral significance.

In the little shop where our paper was printed (Hubenthal's) there was also printed the Communist weekly, *The Unemployed*. That produced an amusing and simultaneously thought-provoking situation: Two representatives of opposing armies sat across from one another at one narrow table, proofreading and getting along quite well with each other. It was not exactly a relationship of hearty friendship, but we exchanged the time of day, spoke a few words about the weather, prices, world politics, and in farewell waved Hitler salutes and clenched fists at each other. Occasionally the Communist editor questioned the "Nazi-Doctor" about grammatical or spelling rules, whereupon the latter dusted off his stale schoolmaster wisdom and gave a quarter hour's worth of German lessons. The Communist indicated his gratitude by very decisively opposing the intentions of the Red Front leader, Edgar André, who showed up one morning with a couple of young bullyboys and a loudly expressed desire to give the Nazi-Doctor "a proletarian rubdown." Shortly thereafter *The Unemployed* took its business to another printing shop. This pinched Hubenthal financially to the point where he could no longer let us dawdle in paying our bills. Once again we had to come up with money and at the same time cut our own expenses to the bare bone, since the weekly circulation at that time was still quite small. As I remember, it came to about 3,000 at the end of 1929, with about a third going to regular subscribers. The advertising was pretty miserable, too; as far as I recall, it never even brought in as much as a thousand marks a month.

But our editorial work was hardly touched by these economic difficulties. Apart from the young assistant editor, Richard Bülk, none of us was dependent on the newspaper's income and even he could accept with composure the constant delays and installment-type payments of his salary, since he lived with his parents in a thoroughly modest, Spartan style. Beyond that we were all in those days much too filled with righteous contempt for money, that Phoenician-Semitic discovery, to get gray hairs over financial troubles. At most we lamented the lack of enough "filthy lucre" to build up our newspaper with proper generosity.

After some experimentation the *Hansische Warte* acquired something like a profile. The profile was not wholly what we might have wished, but it showed, among the many party papers, its own idiosyncratic traits. Perhaps the profile, with pedagogical wrinkles in its brow, was too introspective, looked too much at the party instead of growling and flashing its eyes at the opponents. In any event, fundamental expositions, aimed at broader contexts, overshadowed the uninhibited attacks that were customary in most of the party's "fighting press." So the complaint of some party-comrades that the *Hansische Warte* lacked a cutting edge was not wholly unfounded.

Of the inserts in the *Hamburger Volksblatt* only two were taken over into the *Hansische Warte*: "Youth in Upheaval" and "Academic Watch." The insert "German Soldierdom" was abandoned. The theme was no longer supportable for the Nazi party. Instead, we published an insert for the SA: "The Storm-Column." In it Hermann Okrass earned his spurs as a reporter. The editor of the *Hansische Warte* from Hüttmann's days, C. G. Harke, handled a page called "Hanseatic World" in which there appeared primarily historical and geopolitical articles. The idea of making a specifically "Hanseatic" contribution to German politics by developing connections with England, Scandinavia, the Lowlands, Flanders, and the Baltic States played a considerable role in Hamburg—and not just in Nazi circles.

An expression of the aforementioned pedagogical desire of our paper, aimed at "dressing up the ranks" of the membership intellectually, was, in addition to my own editorials, a fluent and witty column by Meyer-Christian: "1000 National Socialist Words." In these "1000 words," which appeared for many weeks, theoretical concepts as well as objective organizational problems were discussed. The column also contained guidance for the personal behavior of individual party members and SA men toward their fellow party-comrades and other "Folk-comrades." These "etiquette guides" certainly had no intention of promoting outmoded bourgeois virtues, nor did they aim to educate roughnecks and thugs. Their goal was rather men of a new, hardened type, free of sentimentality and illusions, suited for an era between war and revolution. Not for nothing was their author an admirer of Ernst Jünger and his views on the emergence of a new world.[5]

Most readers preferred a column called, in dialect, "Shut Your Traps and Listen to Fietje." This "Fietje" was a cousin of "Orje" in Goebbels' *Angriff* and just as the latter incorporated the Berlin type and the particular style of the movement in that city, so Fietje spoke for the Hamburger in general and the Hamburger Nazi and SA man in particular. Actually Fietje was somewhat closer to the people than Orje, who often did not speak to the people from the heart but consciously and determinedly spoke from the trap. Fietje had a healthy sense of humor which put things in their proper place and for all his scourging of the deeds and misdeeds of opponents seldom banished them from humanity. In the process he showed himself amazingly well read and dis-

[5] Ernst Jünger (b. 1895) was a significant neo-conservative of the Weimar era. A highly decorated officer; he wrote books glorifying the hardening experience of World War I, especially *Storm of Steel* and *Battle as an Inner Experience*, and eventually called for a complete militarization of society and the regeneration of humanity through warriors. By 1939 he had turned anti-Nazi (he was never a party member) in *On the Marble Cliffs* and other books.

played an astonishing ability to synthesize what he'd read and apply it objectively. I say "astonishing" because "Fietje" was not a trained intellectual but a trained butcher, who at that time worked as a salesman in a packing house in the city. He wrote his column of observations in Low German and experts repeatedly assured me that it was a goodly and fluent *Plattdeutsch*.

My personal contribution, apart from editorials with various, generally "fundamental themes, was a continuation of the regular "Politics of the Week." In it I was primarily concerned with foreign policy and, frankly, the result was that probably only a tenth of the readers, at most, took note of my expositions.

Domestic politics was handled in the *Hansische Warte* under the heading "From Colonial Germany." This title was supposed to remind the reader constantly that though Germany was not *de jure* a colony, the Treaty of Versailles, the acceptance of the Dawes and Young plans, and the occupation of the Rhineland[6] gave her that status *de facto*. In line with the purpose of the newspaper, this section was where we fired off the heavy artillery. Nevertheless, even here we tried not just to "finish off" our opponents but to refute them, perhaps even convince them. Admittedly, this intention was inhibited somewhat by our lack of space, which forced us to employ short commentaries and thus pretty well precluded basic factual analyses.

Lack of space also hindered the development of an adequate section on amusements and the arts. It was only through occasional, coincidental reviews of plays, books, and films that we could indicate our intentions in this direction. We were never in a position to realize them. That was particularly galling to me personally since artistic criticism was not only thoroughly neglected in the Nazi press but extraordinarily so in the so-called national and bourgeois newspapers.

As far as I can recall it was in the early summer of 1930 that the number of subscribers first began to climb strongly. The street

[6] Under the terms of the Treaty of Versailles French troops occupied the western side of the Rhineland, though this remained German territory. They were withdrawn in 1930, five years ahead of schedule. The Dawes and Young plans were reschedulings of reparations, 1924 and 1929 respectively, and thus involved a tacit German recognition of the reparations idea, which German nationalists found abhorrent.

sales also began to increase and, what was very important, so did the advertising income. The newspaper now brought in so much that it became possible to move to a roomier office, buy some furniture, and occasionally hire some part-time help. It was the growing domestic and foreign crisis above all that led numerous readers to the *Hansische Warte*, people who were not yet ready to join the party but who increasingly wanted to examine its views and opinions. The dissolution of the Reichstag on July 18, the immediately ensuing fierce election campaign, and the prohibition of the wearing of brown shirts in Prussia, Bavaria, and Hamburg (which we gratefully used for a little publicity trick by printing the newspaper on brown paper—though actually it was more yellow than brown) produced a sudden upward surge. The great success of the party in the September elections[7] finally freed us completely from all economic concerns. We were able to increase the size from eight to ten to fourteen pages. We could publish promotional issues and advertising posters, and we could supply the street salesmen more generously because an abnormal return of unsold papers would no longer threaten to bankrupt us. We could even, thanks to the favorable development of advertising space sold, build up a considerable reserve fund—at least as measured by our modest standards. For us, 5,000 marks was a lot of money.

In this situation Brinkmann and I decided that as of January 1, 1931, we would convert from a weekly to a daily paper and that we would begin immediately to build up the editorial and business staff. We calculated that with about 140,000 Nazi voters in Hamburg we could easily find enough readers to support a daily newspaper. On the other hand, what with our youthful lack of understanding being unencumbered by any practical experience, we did not calculate on having any objective difficulties in the technical or editorial realm. We imagined that changing from a weekly to a daily signified only a quantitative alteration and therefore would require only an increase in the amount of work. Within ten weeks we were to acknowledge how much we had deceived ourselves.

The first difficulties, to be sure, were those created by the *Gauleitung*. We had hardly communicated our decision to them when their resistance commenced, on all sorts of different grounds. Inso-

[7] On September 14, 1930, the Nazis went from 12 Reichstag seats to 107.

far as these concerned doubts based on financial or technical qualms, we treated them seriously and discussed them. Unfortunately, such concerns were subsidiary, when they were not simply used as excuses to cover up the real goals of the *Gauleitung*. These were, just as in the previous year's struggle over the legal possession of the *Hansische Warte*, a desire for the total power of command over the planned newspaper. Beyond that, it was not just the Gauleiter who claimed such power, but also the Gau business manager, the propaganda leader, and the organization leader, each for himself. All of them wanted to be able to give binding orders to the editorial and business directors of the paper in all their activities.

The dispute with the *Gauleitung* lasted for weeks. For a while they pursued a plan to buy up the *Hamburger Nachrichten* with money that would be donated from National Club circles.[8] It was not until the beginning of December, after the intervention of Gregor Strasser, Rudolf Hess, and Max Amann,[9] that the question was settled, but again, only provisionally.

The content of the agreement was approximately the same as had been reached the year before over the *Hansische Warte*. The planned daily newspaper would remain our private property. (To bolster our claims we invented an aunt in South America with RM 70,000.) But 50 percent of the profits were to go to the Gau. The paper was to adhere to the general political line of the Gauleiter and publish all official party news. From a formal viewpoint it thus appeared that the Gau's claims had been mostly warded off, since the owners of the newspaper kept decisive say in every instance. But given the structure of the party and the attitudes of the overwhelming majority of Hamburg's party members, the actual weight of the *Gauleitung* was far greater than the agreement indicated. A Nazi newspaper (unless it had extraordinary financial resources) could neither be founded nor kept alive in a Gau against the will of or without the acquiescence of the Gauleiter. You always had to try to reach agreement, even on isolated ques-

---

[8] *I.e.*, upper-class reactionaries. The *Nachrichten* was a conservative paper close to the monarchistic Nationalist party.

[9] At that time, respectively, National Organization leader, Deputy *Führer*, and head of the party publishing house.

tions. The *Gauleitung* could not only cut off sales promotion inside the party, it could also, drawing on the higher authority of the party, order the Nazis who worked for the newspaper not to obey the publisher and editor. At the very least this would cause a severe crisis of conscience. Therefore, we could only consider this agreement as an armistice, which was why we took the precaution of securing Gregor Strasser as arbitrator for any future dissension arising over the terms of the agreement. How much this precaution was justified was to be proven within a few months.

All this gets ahead of the sequence of events, though. Already in early October, without waiting for a clarification of the *Gauleitung*'s attitude toward our plan, we began to initiate all the steps required for its realization. We assured ourselves space for editorial offices and presses in the as yet uncompleted Gotenhof Building. At the same time we attacked the problem of finding increased personnel for the editorial and business staff. We hardly lacked for applicants. As everywhere after the elections of September 1930 there was a press of people, exceeding all expectations, who "had always secretly supported and secretly worked for the Nazi cause." Regrettably, most of these people smelled too much like the bandwagon to make them suitable for our purpose. There were also whole ranks of professional journalists among them, whose technical competence we could have sorely used. But the personal impression their interviews left did not recommend their engagement. Routine competence without character or human decency was something which, given our particular situation, we could not make use of.

Already in the previous summer we had made a mistake regarding this. Therefore I undertook to inquire more closely than before after the origins, education, and history of the applicants and to pay as much attention to their character as to their talents. But above all in the future, the first, instinctive impression was to be determinative.

By mid-December 1930, after we had moved the business and editorial staffs and the printers into the Gotenhof, we were able to put out the first experimental and promotional issues of the new Nazi daily newspaper in Hamburg, the *Hamburger Tageblatt*. In the weeks beforehand the public had been suitably informed of the forthcoming event through the *Hansische Warte* and the party's propaganda office.

The product in no wise justified all the fanfare. The mountains heaved and brought forth a little mouse that was not only rather small and ugly but also hardly looked as though it would live. Under normal circumstances the enterprise would not have gone beyond these experimental issues. The peculiar mentality of Nazis and their friends produced, however, exceptional circumstances that assured opportunities for even a second-rate or third-rate achievement. And so within a few days the experimental issue brought, against our own expectations, some five thousand regular subscriptions and along with them hundreds of letters with vigorous criticisms and unambiguous declarations of intent to cancel in case the tiny gazette failed to turn into a real newspaper within the next few months.

These letters were really not needed to convince the editors and the publisher of the inadequacy of the experimental issues. None of us was satisfied, but none of us was capable of producing real improvement within a day or two—or even within the foreseeable future. Contrary to the convictions of most of the letter writers, the cause of the imperfect accomplishment lay far less with the editors and writers than it did with the compositors and printers.

In the printing plant there was not one man in those first three weeks who had even been present when a daily newspaper had been printed. Both bosses, Hubenthal and Büring, plus all their journeymen, stood helpless before the great new machines that had been acquired on the advice of a few professional colleagues and the factory representative. Naturally they were able to learn the purely technical operation of them in a few days, though even in this respect there were a few unpleasant and expensive blunders. But when it came to the organization and coordination of production, there were no directions printed on the box. They had to learn from experience.

In those first weeks of January 1931 there was hardly an employee who got away from the building or out of his workclothes. It was not till then that you could count on the paper appearing promptly and no longer had to worry about finding the weather map in the middle of a movie review, the editorial replaced by the masthead, and the place for party notices filled up with unpaid and spurious want ads. It still took a long time before we put the paper to bed in halfway decent shape, according to the editors' wishes. For months to come an unconscionably great part of almost every editorial conference was taken up with a discussion of technical questions: page-proofs, proofreading, composition of individual pages, where the late-breaking news should go, how headlines should fit, and so on.

In general we retained the inserts from the *Hansische Warte*, partly under a broader title, for example, "Academia and Folk." Some pages were also new creations, such as "Folk and Soil," "Survey of Social Politics," "German Crisis—Border Crisis." The latter insert alternated with special sections on racialist organizations and parties outside of Germany, in which we gave preference to the Hanseatic area. There were especially close connections with racialist groups in Flanders, Holland, Denmark, and Sweden. Most of them were linked with the "Geusen" and there was not, let it be explicitly stressed, any German diplomatic or imperialistic character to them.

When we were putting out the *Hansische Warte* it had been our pride to write the newspaper by ourselves, down to the last line, independently and without any press-release material. Learning to give up this inappropriate pride was difficult in the early days of our work for the *Tageblatt*. It was even harder to learn how to use press releases and wire service material properly, with scissors and paste. That was primarily because reports from the official and semiofficial wire services were not compatible with the goals of a Nazi newspaper.[10] We felt ourselves, therefore, duty-bound to interweave commentaries in the headline stories, which thus generally became so lengthy that they robbed us of space for secondary news stories. Gradually we learned to adapt wire service news to our purposes by cuts, headlines, and comments. Nevertheless, as a news organ we were always behind the aspirations of our more discerning readers, especially since at that time we could neither find nor pay for special correspondents such as the other papers had. Hardly a day went by without every editor having to produce two or three pages of news collations and commentaries, which in the long run was doubtless too much to demand.

[10] In the Weimar Republic most of the wire services were connected with particular parties or with newspapers associated with a particular political stance. It was not until after the establishment of the Third Reich that the Nazis set up their own wire service.

There was yet another difficulty. In the *Hansische Warte* we had developed the national socialist viewpoint in all its basic and theoretical breadth. No matter how unconditionally these theories and fundamentals were presented, they were connected with something indefinite. You could move across vast areas with them without feeling the need to prove their correctness and realizability every minute. It was like addressing a mass meeting where you could limit yourself to "setting forth the idea" and could select your own examples out of anything that fit from real life.

In a daily newspaper you had to take a stand on every significant event; that is, you had to descend from general theories and fundamental formulas into iron-clad individual judgments. That was much harder than we had originally assumed, at least for some of our writers. The programs previously developed by the party left unreflective persons without any guidelines on practically all concrete issues. As for party members who were capable of thinking things out themselves, they were likely to produce highly arbitrary interpretations and conclusions. It required quite a number of conferences and discussions to attain a more or less unified course for at least the chief matters before the editorial staff. By no means was this achieved everywhere; for example, the review section was a regular *enfant terrible* for many months because of the reactionary attitudes of some of its contributors toward art.

The development and reorganization of news material was more than just an internal editorial problem. We also had to take into account the attitudes of the various party offices from Hamburg to Munich. Fundamentally they were opposed to any variegated, independent press activity within the party. Even as late as the occasion of my expulsion from the party in May 1932, Hitler accused me of using the paper to express my own opinions more than those of the party. He went on to say that Gau newspapers were not supposed to have their own opinions at all. It would be completely sufficient if they limited themselves to reprinting the opinions of the *Völkischer Beobachter* and filled up the rest of their paper with party news, explications of the party program, and either unambiguously polemical or completely comment-free repetitions of the most important news events.

Yet remarkably, despite these basic views, the number of altercations with party offices over the contents of the newspaper and its evaluation of political occurrences remained relatively small. And this was even though we seldom lacked for idiosyncracies and personal judgments. Already at the beginning of February 1931, in order to test the limits and possibilities of what was permitted, I wrote an editorial on "Fascism and National Socialism," which in conscious contrast to Munich's evaluation, sharply differentiated between the two movements. The Harzburg Front[11] got very bad publicity in our paper. The discussion over that political approach also touched off a ferocious press feud over circumstances in Hamburg, between us and the *Stahlhelm* and *Hamburger Nachrichten*, which we started with an editorial entitled "Clear Fronts." Eight days after Dr. Walther Funk[12] joined the Nazi party we attacked him as a prototypical economic liberal. In book reviews and in my column, "Politics of the Week," certain official party views and methods were criticized openly and between the lines—from racial theory to the South Tyrolean Question.[13] In all these cases there were either no rebukes from the party or else only mild complaints. The only time the *Gauleitung's* criticism became sharp was whenever the paper allegedly handled Reich Chancellor Brüning or the DHV too benevolently. This stemmed from the ineradicable mistrust against me as the "secret agent" of the DHV.

From the party's national office in Munich I can remember not a single judgment on our work, either positive or negative. Max Amann, to be sure, mentioned Brinkmann favorably a couple of times but also immediately added that Brinkmann had nothing to do with the contents of the paper. The properly qualified officials, Rosenberg, Hess, and Otto Dietrich,[14] kept their peace. There

11 This was a loose, uneasy coalition between the Nazis and the conservative Nationalists. It was inaugurated in October 1931, broke up the following summer, and then was reconstituted in the Hitler cabinet of January 1933. "Left-wing" Nazis like Krebs and Gregor Strasser found it repugnant to associate with reactionaries.

12 Walther Funk was a professional economic commentator, used by Hitler as a liaison to industrial and banking circles. In 1938 he replaced Schacht as minister of economics and for his role in preparing for World War II was condemned at Nuremberg to life imprisonment.

13 "South Tyrol" was a German-speaking area of Austria, just below the Brenner Pass, which was given to Italy in 1919. Hitler was against agitation about this violation of nationalism because he hoped to make Mussolini his ally.

14 Otto Dietrich was press chief for the Nazi national office. Alfred Rosen-

were some things they probably overlooked, some ambiguous phrases they did not understand. But in view of Hitler's accusations, mentioned above (that I had always presented only my own opinions in the newspaper), I believe it safe to assume that the office of the Reich press chief had painstakingly combed out and collected all of the deviations perpetrated by the *Tageblatt* in order to have damning material on hand for the decisive moment. According to the information I acquired about the prehistory of my expulsion, it is probable that a similar collection of material was maintained by some officials in the Hamburg *Gauleitung*. It should also be noted that beginning late in 1930 the internal party surveillance and counterespionage organization was built up. I still don't know who initated this; probably various party offices began the buildup simultaneously. What speaks for this are my observations of how quickly things got massively confused and mutually antagonistic. Some of the spies gathered information for the Gauleiter, others against him; certain ones followed the old secret agent tradition and played both sides. Even women were active in this specialty. You had to be particularly careful about them since either they acted out of sincere fanaticism or because of erotic connections, and generally they could hide their activity better than the men. Naturally there were true fanatics among the men, too. But mostly they were the kind who liked the game or the adventure and had the weakness that afflicts that type of personality. So usually they quickly gave themselves away. In any event we generally saw through our cloak and dagger men on the newspaper rapidly and behaved accordingly. The good comradeship that united all the staff in the business, editorial, and printing departments made it relatively easy for us to defend ourselves. In the years after 1933, when there was created a uniform, strictly regulated organization, trained and led by specialists—the SD[15]—things were to become much harder.

Incidentally, I did meet one trained and competent secret serv-

---

berg, in addition to being editor of the *Völkischer Beobachter*, was supposed to oversee all ideological matters. Hess, as Hitler's deputy, was in charge of routine political decisions.

[15] Krebs follows the usual loose terminology here. What he means is the *Gestapo*. Despite its repute, the SD was a general research organization concerned with the ideological foes of Nazism, not an internal party spy unit. In these early days Hitler could depend on personal hostilities as checking devices.

ice man in those days. He was an allegedly retired Bavarian major, B. That he was gathering information on the Nazi party in Hamburg was something he himself admitted. What I never could find out in many long conversations with this clever, witty, well-read, and widely experienced man—he had spent many years abroad—was whom he was working for. At first I took him to be commissioned by the Nazi national headquarters, especially since Hess and Frick mentioned that they knew him.

During World War II, I encountered B again and spoke with him. Since then, I believe that he belonged to an official intelligence unit of either the Reich government or the Army, charged with surveillance of the Nazi party. In that event his particular concern—observing the SA and SS—would indicate a faulty judgment of conditions by his employer. After the September 1930 elections the SA and SS had only a second-rank significance next to the party. Naturally the party required their support for propaganda demonstrations and mass meetings. But since the decisive arena was doubtless to be sought on the political-parliamentary level—and, after the 1930 election results, was also found there—this need was no longer a vital necessity. It seemed that the goal would be reached without either organization.

What was completely misguided was to think that the SA and SS constituted something like a potential civil war army. Despite all their willingness to fight and be sacrificed, their combat power would have been utterly insignificant in a military showdown against really trained troops, such as the Army or the police. To determine this required no special surveillance. It sufficed to compare an SA unit from 1923 with one from 1931. Earlier 90 percent of the Stormtroopers were former front-line soldiers and Free Corps people, and of these practically everyone was a specialist in the use of the customary street-fighting weapons. But by 1931, on the other hand, especially in northern Germany, 80 percent of the SA consisted of young people who had never served in the Army. Furthermore, a considerable number of them had been physically and morally debilitated by their long unemployment. Whole ranks of these young fellows used to faint during big parades! You could fight meeting-hall battles with them but not an armed uprising. Yet it was remarkable how officials and high ministers seemed to have believed in such a danger, as evidenced by the alternating prohibitions of the organizations and their uniforms.

In the editorial offices we often shook our heads while discussing these measures, which struck us as utterly senseless even from the viewpoint of their originators. In the prevailing situation they only strengthened determination and radicalism and provided the party's press and speakers with welcome and effective propaganda material—as we knew from our own work. A new prohibition and we were assured of headlines, editorials, and a half-dozen commentaries for our next issue. Even "Fietje" didn't have to scratch his head over the contents of his next Saturday's ruminations. The authorities had delivered him the text and in doing so they had simultaneously undercut their own foundation: respect for the authority of the state could hardly be sustained through falsely directed and, furthermore, purely negative half-measures. I do not doubt that it still would have been possible, even in 1931 and 1932, to eliminate the Nazis as a party organization. But it would have required, in addition to the power of the state, a spiritual and political leadership that pointed toward a future. That was not forthcoming or else, like Chancellor Brüning, found no backing among the narrow-minded German politicians.

We argued heatedly about such things both freely and frequently within our small group of editors. But in general we hardly got to serious and fundamental discussions. Routine work ate up our time and our energies. For example, it took weeks alone to eradicate the typographical errors that popped up like weeds in our news columns. Without the zealous cooperation of newly hired proofreader, Goltz, we probably would not have brought it off even over a longer period.

Goltz, who looked like an ex-schoolmaster, was one of the strangest creatures ever to cross my path. He was tall, awkward, and heavy, with a round and kindly child's face, and somehow came out of the fairy tale history of the German people. He was a volunteer in World War I who became a Communist after 1918 and in the mid-'20s traveled to Moscow with some likeminded fellow teachers from Hamburg. There, according to his own testimony, he felt like a lost child in the dark woods and returned to Germany deeply disappointed. His disillusionment, however, did not keep him from being told that Hamburg no longer required his services as a teacher. He then tried to find employment here and there. Occasionally he succeeded, but most of the time after 1928 he was unemployed and had, with his large family, a miserable enough household. Nevertheless he found the strength—and this is what was most amazing about this remarkable man—to cover his desk with manuscripts and drafts of plays. And they were not doggerel or the imitative and derivative efforts of a Sunday-afternoon poet, but serious works in which the surrealism and existentialism of our day was already anticipated. Naturally, in the beginning he tried to interest theater producers and publishers in his work. But like almost all those in the last thirty or forty years who have tried this without the support of cliques, wealthy patrons, or politicians, and have also had the bad luck to be born in Germany, he failed. Like all of them he kept on working, possessed and hopeless, struggling over the destiny of mankind "between the devil and the dear God."

Goltz came to us not as a follower of the Nazi movement but simply as a man looking for a job. He had learned of the opening from one of our typesetters who was likewise an ex-Communist. As I mentioned, he helped us very much: partly by his own trustworthy proofreading, partly by the spelling lessons he gave to the second proofreader and even, for a while, to the make-up editor. Ultimately he extended the field of his pedagogical talents to the composition of headlines, corrected stylistic awkwardnesses and grammatical bloopers here and there, and made proposals for the development of the review section. Most of what he did was well done. We regretted it, therefore, when he left us all too soon. He had joined the party in the interim and got a job (I can't remember how anymore) with the Düsseldorf Branch of the Reich Quartermaster's Store.[16] There I visited him once, but found that a modest bourgeois living style was not suited to him. Having stilled his physical hunger, he apparently found that his spiritual hunger was beginning to vanish, too. Behind his humanitarian attitude, which embraced all men fraternally, there began to appear a certain Babbitry, which sought harmony because it did not feel quite up to the disharmony required by struggle.

After this visit we still exchanged a few letters. After I left the party our correspondence fell off and I neither saw nor heard from him again. His manuscripts have probably long since been lost or burned.

[16] Official retailer of Nazi party uniforms, insignia, etc.

Eccentrics like Goltz were encountered rather frequently in those days, though usually the encounter tended to be less enjoyable. Large segments of the party membership regarded the newspaper as a collective possession. This led them to the conclusion that the people who worked on the newspaper should stand ready to supply the true bearers of the collective with information and a chance to ventilate views of every sort, at every length, at every moment. Legally considered, this position had no justification as long as the *Hamburger Tageblatt* remained under private ownership. Still, we neither wanted nor were able to reject this attitude on the part of party members. For one thing, we had to avoid any appearance of bureaucratic behavior. Secondly, and above all, there was hidden within their claims an honest democratic desire to collaborate and share in the decision-making. This was something that especially we could not afford to reject since we constantly represented the same argument to the regular party officials. The editors therefore made it their duty to answer every letter and entertain every visitor. Regrettably, this openness was massively misused by approximately half the letter writers.

They came with memorandums, with pamphlets published at their own expense, with fat files of material gathered over years, as prophets, reformers, inventors, sectarians, and modern Kohlhaases[17] who yearned to expurgate some real or supposed injustice of the times. They spoke for hours on end and generally were unreceptive to any objections or instruction. One particularly determined economic reformer even brought suit against the newspaper because it had rejected a pamphlet he had written and characterized its contents as not national socialist.

But apart from such personal unpleasantnesses it was really quite instructive to determine how many utopian dreamers still existed—even in a cosmopolitan city famed for the sober common sense of its inhabitants. Whether you took this utopian proclivity as an indication of how the existing spiritual system was destroying itself, as a sign of the depth of dissatisfaction with existing conditions, or simply as evidence of the unweakened power of human imagination, it was impossible to ignore its inner connection with

---

[17] Michael Kohlhaas, hero of Kleist's novella, relentlessly sought the rectification of injustice done him—even at the cost of upsetting the entire world.

the political events of the times. Extraordinarily significant in this respect was that all these utopias—their themes encompassed all areas of life from "the new marriage" to "the new church," from "the general brotherhood of man" to "the selective brotherhood of racial or spiritual leadership elites"—all of them were basically characterized by a thorough optimism, even when they no longer held to that faith in progress that had flourished in the early years of the century.

Only this basic optimism explains the happy confidence with which people of the most diverse, even antagonistic, views came to us in hopes of finding a loudspeaker for their desires and opinions. The sign of the times was optimism, which set itself no limits to a general quest for something "new" and a general readiness to accord trust to something "new." Not only simple or unstable natures, such as were most of the visitors just described, behaved this way. Even intellectuals capable of independent judgment believed they had found in the party a "place of fulfillment" for their frequently wholly incompatible ideas and ideals. Thus there met in front of my desk one day the two Hamburg writers Albert Petersen and Robert Walter, with the petition that I arbitrate their personal and substantive differences. The substantive differences, however, consisted of nothing less than each man's claim that his particular creative style represented the essence of national socialism and therefore the future of the nation.

In fact each writer represented, apart from the question of his abilities, a position diametrically opposed to the other's. One lived in the Bismarckian Reich of the past, the restoration of which he expected from Nazism. Furthermore, he viewed the past completely through the eyes of a stalwart bourgeois. The other one saw in Nazism an attempt to bring together all the modern revolutionary currents in order to overcome the decadent bourgeois social order and build a new world. The one heard only the nationalist, the other only the social slogans, and each found in them his whole personal viewpoint. In this attitude they anticipated that phenomenon which gave particular cachet to the period immediately following the Nazi seizure of power. By espousing Hitler and the Nazis as agents for their own goals these two managed to give themselves the agreeable impression that they had actually already won over Hitler and his movement by some sort of tacit conspiracy.

After 1933 it was just the same. Freethinkers saw Hitler as their ally in the struggle against clerical rule and religious obscurantism; old-Lutherans saluted him as the culmination of the Reformation, while conservatives, even Catholic priests, placed their hopes on him as the man who would overcome a rationalistic and materialistic era. All of these expectations, viewpoints, and spiritual faith offerings were explicable only through the passionate conviction of the broadest popular circles that the hour of the great change had arrived.

To condemn such convictions morally or rationally after the fact is cheap. If there is something to be condemned, then it ought to be only the hidden dishonesty and peasant slyness that lurked behind all this hope, faith, and confidence. Men and their thoughts were schizoid. On the one hand they put their hopes in Hitler. On the other hand they wanted to see him as nothing more than the tool of their own plans and ideals. But it is my view that this dishonest, reserved halfheartedness was exactly what was fatal. Hitler's talent was precisely the ability to play the song "beautiful dreamer" to all the anticlerics, reformationists, anti-materialists, to one at a time and all at once. He could make it sound like other seductive arias, too, such as the great hymn of peace or the ancient anthem of German yearnings: the "Thousand Year Reich of Brotherhood and Justice." The melody appears to have completely stolen from Germans the power of soberly reflecting upon men and circumstances.

In any case these two authors were rather upset when I tried, with gentle reservations (I was much younger than either of them), to clarify the ways in which both of them were in error concerning many points of their conceptions of the essence of Nazism. Because of this I had to respectfully decline any judgment over the degree of their inner connection to the party. Beyond that, considering the party's total structure, recognition as a national socialist author could surely be accorded only to those who somehow participated in the political struggle.

At this Robert Walter immediately withdrew. Albert Peterson made a start with participation by writing a column for the paper called "Hamburg Chatter." In it he tried, like Rumpelstiltskin, to survey all political and especially cultural events in Hamburg through his magic telescope. But it was just the bias revealed in his "chatter" that indicated how he actually didn't belong to us. Since

he had no desire to change either his mode of judgment and composition, nor was capable of doing this, there was no way to avoid
separating him from the paper. We seized upon an ostensible justification that spared us embarrassment: The Hamburg Senate suppressed the newspaper for several weeks in the spring of 1931
because the SA had shot a Communist member of the city council, Henning.

This suppression inaugurated a whole series of prohibitions,
effectively augmented by numerous other indictments against me
as editor, plus special indictments against individual sub-editors in
other cases. To my recollection I had to appear in court at least
twice a month in the year and a half during which I worked with
the *Tageblatt*. Apart from some libel suits, which were hardly
avoidable in those days of immoderate political excitement and
exceptional personal sensitivity, this was a matter of purely political trials, mostly involving violations of the "Law for the Protection of the Republic."[18]

Our assumption at that time, that the district attorney or State
Press Office had assigned someone to the principal task of handling our "sins," seems to me in retrospect as no exaggeration. His
work was, admittedly, unprofitable, since the Hamburg courts were
exclusively and painstakingly committed to passing judgments on a
nonpartisan, objective basis. Even Jewish or half-Jewish judges
were not exceptions to this; it was even noticeable how much the
prosecuting attorneys disliked this assignment.[19] Once when a very
young lawyer felt obliged to deliver a politically colored summa-
tion for the prosecution, replete with moralistic value judgments,

[18] This law actually did abridge freedom of the press and therefore was
passed with a two-thirds (constitutional) majority in 1922, following a wave of
assassinations, which culminated in the murder of Walther Rathenau, the
republic's foreign minister, by a right-wing assassination gang. These murders
were preceded by extensive vilification of the victims in the nationalist press;
hence the law assumed that terrorism was stimulated by newspaper polemics.
In the period covered by Krebs, the law, supplemented by Emergency Decrees,
was applied most severely against rightist extremists: of 284 newspaper suspensions during Brüning's chancellorship, 99 were against Nazi papers, 43 against
other radical rightist journals, and 77 against Communist ones. See Hale, pp.
11–12.

[19] For an analysis of the right-wing proclivities of Weimar courts, see A. J.
Nicholls, *Weimar and the Rise of Hitler* (New York, 1968), pp. 46–48.

the presiding judge invited him to restrain himself because "Neither the accused nor his counsel have spoken as though they were addressing a mass meeting." (Our defense attorney was the respected lawyer Dr. Droege, whom I had met through the Fichte Society.) The court's decision was frequently an acquittal and, where that was impossible, a relatively minor fine. Considering the paper's economic situation, the most nominal fine was always too much though, especially when attorney's fees and court costs were reckoned in. Brinkmann, the publisher, wrung his hands in pain, which indicated that the purpose pursued by the prosecuting attorney was at least partially achieved after all.

Doubtless the frequent suppressions were aimed less toward the maintenance of "law and order" and more toward the destruction or at least the undermining of the economic foundations of the paper. Whoever was in charge of harassing us must have known how weak we were financially. But the result was by no means that which was expected. On the contrary, we actually benefited from a prohibition under certain circumstances. In the first place, given the prevailing situation, every prohibition of the newspaper constituted free publicity. Our subscribers neither quit us nor demanded compensation for the missing issues. Many of them felt moved by a prohibition to an increased promotion of the paper, even when they had previously been somewhat critical toward it. In the same way street sales of the newspaper went soaring upward when it was issued again. Secondly, the money saved through a suspension was temporarily more than the loss of income. Naturally this depended on how long and when the prohibition occurred: at the beginning, middle, or end of the month. There were a couple of times when a prohibition virtually rescued us from bankruptcy by giving us time to negotiate a temporary loan. But when we reached a similar state again and actually tried to provoke a prohibition by vigorous attacks, we failed to achieve our purpose. Whoever was in charge of monitoring the *Hamburger Tageblatt* was either asleep on the job or else saw through our intentions.

Naturally harm was done to our political propaganda by these suppressions, though even that should not be overestimated. The special sort of propaganda produced by Nazism had its members and followers so convinced of the basic errors and mistakes of the enemies, even of the fundamental wickedness of their goals, that a daily disputation with them was not unconditionally required. What the "system's" government and parties did in domestic and foreign policies was wrong and bad in any case, just as every action of the Nazis was right and good. To express that every day in the newspaper appeared desirable but not an absolute necessity. Even those fellow Germans who were wavering or opposed to Nazism would one day be converted to the correctness of this viewpoint (excepting, naturally, the wire-pullers and exploiters of the "system"), and it was of little consequence whether the conversion took place three or four weeks later. The only time the suppressions were really unpleasant was when they coincided with an election campaign. It is only when you are fighting an election that the press becomes really indispensable and even ever so many pamphlets and posters are only inadequate substitutes.

But one harm done by these suspensions and court indictments, with their dubious legal justification, went beyond the period of their effectiveness. They stimulated the urge for retaliation, gave it an apparent justification, and strengthened many Nazis in the conviction that all the democratic talk about justice and liberty was just so much talk and hypocrisy. They might be barbarians, they said, to accept the position that "might makes right" or "freedom of expression is nonsense," but at least they were honest barbarians.

I already mentioned how much Brinkmann was concerned by having to pay the fines, court costs, and attorney's fees. The financial situation of the newspaper, which was difficult, even worrisome, from the very beginning, got worse with every month and gradually became the dominant problem for all our work.

There were various causes for this. To begin with, it was a penalty we paid for having gone at the founding of the newspaper so frivolously. Our own limited capital was quickly consumed, while the income remained very modest and increased only slowly and by installments. Apart from that we continued to have losses because we still had much to learn from experience about organizing the sales and soliciting advertisements. That meant that we could not avoid unfavorable and costly experiences with unreliable or incompetent companies or individual promoters. We gained some improvement by contracting all the distribution and promotion of the newspaper with the firm of Neckel. The circulation slowly but steadily grew. Street sales were satisfactory, on some days even pretty good. Advertising grew and began to bring in notable sums.

But despite all this the crisis still could not be resolved since our paper continuously had to cover the printer's obligations. The print shop was so undercapitalized that it could make neither the monthly installment payments for the machinery nor pay for the purchase of newsprint and other necessities of production. Very often they even lacked the money for the weekly wages of the typesetters and compositors. The publishers of the *Hamburger Tageblatt*, therefore, far from enjoying the usual period of grace in paying the printer, had to empty its own cash drawers almost every day to keep the print shop going. And beyond that, practically every other week a deputation of printers would show up at noon on Friday, payday, and threaten to down tools because they had not gotten their pay. Then, to assure that the paper would come out, Brinkmann would have to rush around in a taxi and beg up the necessary eight or twelve hundred marks. Usually those who helped out were private persons, party members, or personal acquaintances. Two or three times, at my request, the DHV (or, to be precise, the Deutsche Ring) made us a short-term loan, as a rule on a thirty-day note, of a sum that never exceeded RM 3,000. Thus we struggled on from week to week and month to month. The situation became increasingly untenable and the race between slowly rising income and unpostponable expenditure obligations threatened to resolve itself unfavorably for us. While we were still mulling over the most diverse plans to get out from under the crisis, in stepped the *Gauleitung* in July 1931, and we were forced to act.

Despite the agreement negotiated in December 1930 with Gregor Strasser participating and expressly approving the results, the *Gauleitung*, in February, already began to put forth its former demand for the foundation of a publishing company to be controlled by the Gau. Since there still were no financial resources behind this demand, not even the firm intention or capability of effectively utilizing the party apparatus to build up the newspaper (many functionaries were practically sabotaging the *Tageblatt*), we rejected all the ensuing proposals, which were alternatively accompanied by threats and by protestations of friendship. We adhered to the agreed upon arrangement: that we were to serve the party politically, respect the wishes of the Gauleiter, and turn over 50 percent of any forthcoming profits to the Gau, but that the publishing firm was to remain private property with all the risks and rights pertaining thereto. In the following period there was unceasing dispute over this unhappy matter with pinpricks and bodythrusts by both sides. No one gained an advantage in either direction as long as the situation remained unchanged on either side. But when the *Gauleitung* finally got wind of our growing financial weakness and thereupon decided to take direct action, things began to happen fast.

The action began while I was on an extended vacation trip and could not be immediately contacted. They engaged one of the editors, Humbert, with winning over the other editors, by promising him the post of editor-in-chief. At the same time they presented Brinkmann with an ultimatum: Either he must agree, within a set period of time, to the foundation of a new company according to the wishes of the *Gauleitung* or, if he refused, they would boycott the paper. In other words, they would no longer recognize it as an official party organ and would create a competitor in the form of a Gau newspaper actually owned by the party. The situation was unpleasantly dangerous as we all agreed after my return from vacation.

What worried us about a boycott was less a loss in circulation than the loss of future loans. Even those "financiers" with whom we had the best personal relationships were interested in supporting a party newspaper not a private publishing venture by Brinkmann and Krebs. That was also and decidedly true of the DHV whose interest in the *Hamburger Tageblatt* was based on the possibility that my activities would affect the development of Nazi attitudes toward social policies. If this possibility ceased through a cessation of the official party character of the newspaper, then that was the end of their interest, too—especially since in those months the DHV acquired, in the *Tägliche Rundschau*, a megaphone that was always available to disseminate their opinions. *Der Deutscher*, the organ of the Christian trade unions, was also readily available ever since Stegerwald had taken over its direction and Brüning had become chancellor.

And so we decided to offer the *Tageblatt* for sale to the Eher

Verlag.[20] Our terms were that Amann should take over our obligations, should keep Brinkmann and me on as managing director and managing editor of the *Tageblatt*, and should pay an appropriate purchase price. If we could no longer maintain freedom and autonomy because of the miserable financial situation, then we preferred coming under the direction of the Munich rather than the Hamburg party offices. Munich was far away and simply on this ground would be unable to be constantly interfering with our work. Organizational and business malpractices, such as bleeding our managerial resources for the party apparatus, were not to be feared from the well-directed and well-funded Eher *Verlag*. Also it seemed that I could hope for somewhat more understanding for the political stance and activities of our editorial staff in Munich, where my connections to Strasser, Hess, and Rosenberg were not bad, than in Hamburg.

After we had clarified for ourselves what had to be done, I took the train to Munich to make the necessary negotiations. Since Gauleiter Kaufmann, accompanied by Humbert and Dr. Nieland, followed a day and a half later, there ensued a highly dramatic turmoil, into which were eventually drawn, bit by bit, Amann, Hess, Schwarz,[21] Director Winter of the DHV, and finally also Hitler. But in the end everything turned out tolerably satisfactory for us. The *Hamburger Tageblatt* with all its obligations and all its employees was taken over by the Eher *Verlag*. Brinkmann and I were confirmed in our positions. The only thing was—no purchase price was paid. In other words the authority of the party was used for a sort of confiscation, such as was to be done on a broader scale after 1933. On the other hand, they acceded to the demand of the DHV, which had been infuriated over the action of the *Gauleitung* and over some of the statements and actions during the negotiations, and repaid the short-term loans due to the DHV and also

---

[20] The Eher *Verlag*, located in Munich, was the official publishing house of the Nazi party and was a profitable business. It owned several Nazi papers, the chief national paper of Nazism (the *Völkischer Beobachter*), and handled *Mein Kampf*. Sales of all these soared after Nazism became a mass movement. In 1932, for example, the *Völkischer Beobachter* contributed close to four million marks to Nazi election funds. Max Amann was the director of the Eher *Verlag*. See Hale, pp. 31–32.

[21] Franz Xaver Schwarz was treasurer of the Nazi party.

agreed for the future to assume exactly half my salary. The relationship between the newspaper and the Gau was to follow the previous agreement except that there was no longer any talk about dividing up profits. Of course profits were inconceivable anyway.

Amann did not provide larger sums for the development of the paper or for better salaries for the editors and staff. Henceforth we got only the exact amount of money needed to cover the difference between our income and our obligations. Amann's position, which was actually a sound one, was that the business ought to take care of itself and that too generous a supply of capital would weaken the will to achievement and encourage superfluous expenditures.

The offer of a loan from the DHV in the amount of about forty thousand marks was turned down by Amann, or rather he had to because Hitler's office desired it to be refused. This refusal would have been more understandable if the national leaders had been similarly steadfast against corresponding proposals from business circles. But that was not the case. We were permitted to accept any sums from "private persons" so long as no expressed political conditions were attached to them. And this permission was not simply of theoretical import. The transfer of the *Tageblatt* to the Eher *Verlag* so strengthened its political and economic credit rating that we actually did receive private loans and subsidies in large and small amounts. Their total never exceeded ten thousand marks, but that was enough to make up for Amann's stinginess and to permit a modest expansion of our shop. We increased the size of the editorial staff. The number of subscribers grew very slowly, but the street sales increased considerably. Above all the advertising business grew to such an extent that it seriously bothered the editors because we had to vacate new half pages repeatedly from our scanty space.

The change in ownership left the editorial staff wholly unaffected since the Eher *Verlag* had no chief editor for the various party newspapers it owned. Rosenberg, who would have been the first in line for such an office possessed neither the necessary confidence of Amann and Hitler nor the human and objective qualifications. The Reich press chief,[22] however, whose origins out of the camp of heavy industry made him somewhat suspect among many

[22] Otto Dietrich.

party members, was no energetically active man. His ambitions obviously were satiated by simply moving in Hitler's closest surroundings and being photographed with him. During the time of my association with the *Tageblatt* we never had any direct dealings with him. That he was concerned with us at all was something I never knew until I was expelled from the party and inferred it from Hitler's remarks on that occasion, as mentioned earlier.

On the other hand, certain groups of Gau officials were all the more zealous in their attention to us. The hopes of some of our staff, that the absorption of our paper into the Eher *Verlag* would ameliorate the previous tensions, were rapidly proven erroneous. The *Gauleitung* was nowhere near as interested in the fulfillment of the theoretical demand (with which they had associated themselves propagandistically) that "the party press must be party owned," as they were with the practical desire of bringing the *Tageblatt* under their own ownership. The solution found in Munich was viewed by them as such a severe defeat that at first the Gauleiter thought he would have to resign. But by the year 1931 a Gauleiter could neither voluntarily resign without thereby earning the permanent anger of Hitler nor could he be forced to resign by any democratic method. The demand was therefore voiced, with increasing vehemence, that to restore the Gauleiter's dignity I should disappear from the paper's staff, and if necessary, Brinkmann should too.

The editorial staff constantly felt the effect of this group, which gave rise to some peculiar political situations. Thus the *Tageblatt* had expressed itself rather unambiguously as opposed to the "Harzburg Front." We believed ourselves in full accord with Gauleiter Kaufmann on this since, as a follower of Gregor Strasser, he was always opposed to collaboration with social-reactionary groups. Beyond that he had shortly before assured me of his desire for a clearly social, even socialistic, policy. To our vast amazement, however, shortly after the appearance of our comments we received a reprimand from the Gau office stating that our article had strongly offended the Gauleiter. When we thereupon defended ourselves, the ensuing discussion revealed that it was not so much the content of the editorial that was being recorded and censured as it was the therein newly redemonstrated "willfulness" of the *Tageblatt* under the leadership of Dr. Krebs.

It occurs to me that this attitude manifested one indicative feature, not just of Nazism, but of every doctrinaire, dogmatic movement that strives for total power. In the core of the totalistic, monistic thinking lies a tormenting doubt about the truth of their own thought-constructs, and simultaneously a certainty that should this doubt ever become visible, it would mean the end. Just the slightest deviation from the prescribed dogma, the softest criticism from within their own ranks appears as a deadly danger. That is why they live in constant fear of heretics and lone wolves and why it is worthier to discover and destroy these than it is to convert a half-dozen open enemies. It was such considerations, probably only semiconsciously held, that promoted the attacks on our editorial staff. As an ostensible cause it was ever more frequently and more sharply asserted that the *Tageblatt* obviously promoted policies friendly to Brüning and the DHV. To emphasize and substantiate this assertion the *Gauleitung* repeatedly sent us over articles directed against the DHV with the demand that they be printed in a prominent place, preferably on page one. If we did not comply, or if we attached to the article a correction or clarification, then there was a simultaneously triumphant and disgusted: "See, just as we always said!"

When, in October 1931, along with the *Tägliche Rundschau* and *Der Deutscher*, we printed Habermann's article "Brüning and Hitler," which urged their cooperation, we set off a flood tide of recriminations from the *Gauleitung*. In this instance we had an easy time justifying it. The article had been jointly approved for publication by Habermann and Gregor Strasser. Therefore it found, with some reservations, favorable echo in the *Völkischer Beobachter* and a number of other party papers. So the *Gauleitung* had to draw in its horns, without, however, abandoning its charge of "pro-Brüning policy" against the *Tageblatt*. That Hitler, who was happy to see the article as the first sign of a willingness to accept him and the Nazis as capable of governing but by no means wanted any true partnership with Brüning, refused within a few weeks to continue the negotiations with Brüning served to justify the *Gauleitung*'s stance.

In fairness I must admit that on both these questions—our attitude toward Reich Chancellor Brüning and toward the DHV—there was in fact a considerable difference between the opinions of the Gauleiter and the Gau newspaper. In accordance with my basic formulation of the functionally conditioned relationship between party and trade union, I thought the constant attacks against the DHV (mostly with highly foolish arguments) were wrong. Therefore I was not prepared to give them space in the paper, apart from the individual cases in which measures taken by the DHV or statements made by certain of its officials obviously transgressed the political neutrality of the union. Whether or not such transgressions had taken place was something that we determined in editorial conferences on a purely objective basis and without any consideration for my professional connections with the DHV.

As for our attitude toward Brüning, there was no unified judgment among the editorial staff. In my view it was possible to expect that Brüning, given enough time, would free Germany from the shackles of the Treaty of Versailles. In domestic politics he would remove the excrescences of parliamentary democracy and thus create the basis for a thoroughgoing reform of the Reich. My colleagues were considerably more skeptical. They mistrusted Brüning from the very beginning because of his origins in the Catholic Center party, which they considered (following the Nazi conception) as rooted in enmity to the Reich.[23] They also judged his limited ability to address the masses and win them for his goals —in actuality, Brüning consciously renounced all demagoguery—as signs of insufficient energy and determination. Objectively these two opposing views were irreconcilable. Since, however, we had to present the public with a more or less unified handling of the subject of Brüning, we finally agreed on the following method: We toned down our articles and commentaries that dealt with Brüning or his policies in order to avoid too glaring contradictions among ourselves. Fundamentally excluded were criticisms that would lessen respect for the chancellor in ways injurious to the vital interests of the Reich. On this issue there was no disagreement among the editors. When I refused in early January 1932 to publish an

[23] The term Krebs employs is *Reichsfeindlich*, which was Bismarck's expression for such apparently supranational parties as the Catholics, the Socialists, the national minority groups, etc. Though the accusation was largely unfounded even in Bismarck's era, and though times changed, the label abided, especially in Protestant areas.

irresponsible article on Brüning (probably written by Hitler himself), which would have weakened his position in the reparations and disarmament negotiations, I had the support of all my colleagues. The only factors mentioned in mitigation were tactical ones, which in those months I was no longer disposed to permit as influences on my actions. My internal dissociation from the party leadership had already progressed too far.

The not wholly unjustified displeasure of the *Gauleitung* over the independent-minded political attitude of the *Tageblatt* was increased by the fact that it was noted and discussed by the public. It even led to certain speculations and differentiations. Though we neither intended nor could prevent people from drawing such conclusions, the fact was held against us. It was asserted that we wanted to diminish respect for the *Gauleitung*, to form an opposition, to destroy unity within the Gau, even to win the leading positions in the Gau for ourselves. In reality we desired only to develop the newspaper in form and substance as a megaphone for our conceptions and opinions as to what the essence and tasks of national socialism should be. Given this goal we had no reason, admittedly, to reject any sympathy or even indications of interest shown us.

On the contrary, we took every opportunity to make closer contact with people who approached us because of our particular way of looking at things or of handling questions. Out of this there developed an extensive correspondence and far-ranging discussions, which brought us into contact with numerous persons and circles outside of the party. As individual discussions began to take up too much of our time, we organized discussion evenings to which we invited people in the name of the newspaper and sometimes in our own name. Now and again we ourselves were invited, in those months of the growing significance of the Nazi party, to lecture to closed groups and in private homes.

At most of these discussion evenings we met with business people, bankers, and industrialists. These gentlemen wished to inform themselves as to whether there were hidden behind the official economic program of the party, which the majority of them opposed as addlepated and dangerous, any more sensible and clearer conceptions and goals. These encounters remained, apart from the value of personal acquaintances, not very profitable. Frequently we talked right past each other for half the evening; in fact, it might appear that we were speaking two different languages. The difficulty was intensified by the primary interest of our discussion partners in concrete individual questions, in the "practical," while we made an attempt to build up a general picture out of the basic theoretical concepts of national socialism.

Naturally there were exceptions, among whom I could mention, next to Kurt Woermann who belonged to the closest circle of collaborators with the *Tageblatt* anyway, especially Philipp Reemtsma.[24] Reemtsma did not come to our discussion evenings, but instead invited Brinkmann, Dr. Schlotterer (our financial editor), and me to a little dinner party. It was prompted by the hefty attacks on his company's business practices undertaken by a segment of the German press, especially the Nazi newspapers. His refutation of these attacks did not fully convince me, perhaps because I had no practical business experience and therefore could not comprehend the context. But they also played only a subordinate role in a very broad discussion. The actual purpose of our host was obviously to give us a glimpse into the world of a modern business leader so that we would thereby reexamine our own theoretical and doctrinaire views and possibly revise them. As far as the first part of his intention is concerned, he succeeded in an absolutely glittering way. Beginning with the consciously Prussian simplicity of the dinner to the description of construction plans in Othmarschen and prognoses for the development of international politics, we became acquainted with the range of Reemtsma's holdings, the social measures in his factories, the method of his trade relationships with Greece and Bulgaria, his political cross connections, and the particular intellectual interests he cultivated. It was a very impressive picture that we were shown, though frankly not wholly without excessive highlighting in some spots. Also impressive was the style of presentation, which was not in the form of a monologue but rather appeared to flow quite accidentally out of the conversation and out of his responses to our questions and objections.

Reemtsma was certainly no Nazi and made no pretense of being one. On the contrary he freely expressed his concern over the goals

[24] One of the biggest cigarette producers in Germany, one brand of which bears his family name.

and methods of the party and Hitler himself. But like many of his peers, he lived in the conviction that true power no longer lay with the politicians but with the masters of the economy. Therefore even dangerous and dynamic political movements could be tied down by economic methods. Probably his invitation to us derived from this belief. Already in this instance his error was evident, for our admiration for him and his accomplishments could not shake our conviction that his world and his views were not ours. He also failed to recognize that the Nazi movement, like all great mass movements, lived from elemental drives which could neither be steered nor shaped by rationally calculated economic measures. Nevertheless, that evening in the house on the Palmaille in Altona remained in good memory with me as an evening of encounter with a man who, unlike so many of his class, did not depend upon inherited prejudices, but contended freely and openly, in theory and in practice, with the problems of the present day.

Similarly pleasant in human terms was another meeting, this one with representatives of the opposite camp, the Marxist one. A working committee of Young Socialists had invited me to a discussion on the Young Plan and reparation policy, held in the trade union house on Besenbinderhof. Since the "old officials" were not supposed to learn of this outrageous conversation with a Nazi chieftain, I was secretly snuck up the back stairs to the third or fourth story, where the working committee, with a good dozen male and female participants, was in session. I was not able to discover the professional composition of the group; my impression was that most of them were office workers. Anyway, one of the main speakers and the prime promoter of the reparations policy hitherto pursued by the Weimar Republic was, as I recall, a bank clerk. That his arguments rested mainly on the ideology of the efficiency of an internationally applicable and binding economic rationality, and to this extent could have won the applause of any bank director belonging to the *Staatspartei* or the DVP,[25] was something that impressed me and remained in my memory. It struck me as corroborating certain Nazi views on how the power of international finance capitalism overshadowed all party boundaries.

[25] Respectively, the left and right parties of classical liberalism in the Weimar Republic. The DVP was Stresemann's People's party.

The discussion did not limit itself to the question of reparation policy, which meant that the envisioned single evening's talk was insufficient. The starting points in our discussion were so far apart from one another that we first had to work out an agenda to find room for a thorough discussion and possibly the desired achievement of agreement. Beyond that we were young people and German ones to boot. We could not possibly have been satisfied without setting forth the fundamental concepts and basic problems of all political, economic, and social areas of humanity. That took time. So ultimately we talked ourselves hoarse for a half-dozen evenings. Admittedly, we hardly ever thereby came close to substantive agreement. Personally I learned, through my discussion partners, to recognize the advantages and disadvantages of a conceptually complete intellectual system: dialectical superiority on the one hand and dogmatic rigidity and narrowness on the other. The actual profit in the encounter lay in the fact that at a time when political struggle usually consisted of fistfights rather than arguments, we succeeded in carrying on a true discussion over so many hours. To be sure, the expression "true discussion" must be understood more in terms of its spirit than its form. Sticking to the rules and dictates of customary courtesy was no special achievement in such a small circle. But not denying to your opponent, despite all the sharpness of the objective oppositions, the honesty and purity of his convictions, not listing him in one of the categories of traitor, subhuman, sellout, warmonger, and so on was, as a deviation from the mass psychosis that ruled those times, remarkable and enjoyable. We probably amazed ourselves sometimes with the degree of our deviation: Here, up above, we tried to understand each other and even to convince each other; we actually shook hands at the beginning and end of each session. There, down below in the streets, the different political emblems alone were enough to start people punching each other.

This "Nazi brawling" seems to have stood in the foreground of most people's opinions. When we made an attempt to extend the newspaper's discussion evenings into the sphere of cultural policy, that attitude manifested itself in a way that was as obvious as it was amusing. Our invitation to those writers and poets whose work made us think they might be interested in political matters, produced from at least half of those invited a refusal couched mostly in terms that were more evasive than explanatory. Only Hans Friedrich Blunck declared, in rather bathetic language, that as an intellectual he was obliged to reject any traffic with us, the representatives of a crude, barbaric movement, as insulting to his personal dignity and his poetic talent. At that time Blunck was still legal adviser to the University of Hamburg; some two years later he was less harsh in his thoughts.[26]

Nevertheless, we did not lack personal contacts with writers and artists. As the months went by, numerous fiction writers, poets, critics, and also academicians introduced themselves to us either in person or in writing. Among them were capable people and incompetents. We were not interested in the incompetent and generally could not pay the competent or else could not use their services in the long run because they insisted on preserving their anonymity at all costs. Of course we knew how dangerous it was, for example, for a young university instructor to be known publicly as a contributor to a Nazi newspaper.[27] Yet after a certain period we had to insist upon such an open acknowledgment. The simple party members and SA men, who put their own heads on the block practically every day, found it all too difficult to understand why some-

[26] Krebs' scorn requires some background information: Blunck (b. 1888) was a minor but prolific poet and writer of stories drawn from Germanic mythology and North German folk themes. In his youth he associated with various racialist groups, though the major American historian of these movements, George Mosse, insists that Blunck was never racially anti-Semitic and never at ease with the Nazis (*The Crisis of German Ideology*, pp. 79–80). When Hitler was named chancellor in January 1933, however, Blunck wrote a poem commemorating the event. Four months later the Nazi minister of culture promoted Blunck to the Prussian Academy of Arts and in October 1933 Blunck was one of eighty-eight German writers whose names appeared as signators of a declaration of loyalty and praise for Adolf Hitler. That same year Blunck was named president of the Reich Chamber of Writers, one of Goebbels' cultural control organs, which post he held until 1935. In 1938 Hitler awarded Blunck the Goethe Medal and as late as 1942 Blunck was writing poems in honor of Nazi victories. In his postwar autobiography Blunck claims to have always been opposed to Nazi excesses.

[27] Actually the universities were strongholds of Nazism but Krebs' "university instructor" could still have hurt his career by being known as a Nazi since in several states (including Hamburg) state employees were forbidden to belong to the Nazi party. All university instructors were state employees. See Frederic Lilge, *The Abuse of Learning: The Failure of the German Universities* (New York, 1948).

body else's head was more important than theirs and so had to be protected. This problem caused us to terminate working relations with some writers, though it did not thereby affect our personal relationship with them.

The attraction that communism held for many artists in the years between 1918 and 1933 was something Nazism never exercised. *Inter arma silent musae*[28]—Nazism was always a decidedly militant movement in which there was little room for the sometimes excessive individualism and intellectualism of many artists. Furthermore, the astonishingly Babbit-like views on the essence and purpose of art held by most Nazi leaders contained little that could tempt or convince (to say nothing of enthusing) any artist involved in the contemporary intellectual concerns and problems of form. Nevertheless, in time, there were gathered into the party small groups of talented and capable people—some because they agreed with the party's reactionary doctrines (for example, in architecture); others because they considered the general political line of the movement more important than its opinions on artistic or cultural policy; a third group, finally, because they considered the attitudes of Rosenberg and even Hitler as preliminary and inconsequential. "Today what is elemental, essential, and indicative of the future in the movement cannot yet be expressed, in an artistic sense; the true appearance of national socialism is something we will first recognize and make visible tomorrow." This, approximately, was the formulation of one representative of this third group: Fritz Hoeger, the designer and builder of the Chile House, the Sprinkenhof, and many other buildings and churches in Hamburg and northwestern Germany.

We made his acquaintance in a rather odd way. The art critic of the *Hamburger Tageblatt*, Dr. Harald Busch, wrote an article strongly attacking him and his buildings as artistically false and artificial. Hoeger thereupon invited us to a discussion, which brought no substantive agreement, but which led to a firm personal relationship between him and me. Henceforth I often sat in his office in the Sprinkenhof and let him tell me about his plans, his artistic views, and the chemical techniques that went into the firing of his colorful bricks and tiles.

As for Nazism, Hoeger was not much interested in its political

[28] "The muses are silent in the presence of weapons."

foreground, which was what most professional politicians used to be eager about. On the other hand, this Low German farmer's son believed that he saw in the movement as such the beginning of something related to his own creations: a primarily healthy and powerful folk renaissance. In our conversations his thoughts often touched on the related spirit of statesmen and builders. Then he would thrust one of his hard-baked, sometimes blue–dark–red bricks under my nose: "That'll last centuries! That's been burnt in a hot fire; mass meetings are still not hot fires." He shared passionately in the party's fight against the Treaty of Versailles and reparations. Here he felt himself very personally affected, since whatever way he turned his great plans were hindered by the scarcity of money. And in general a good part of his artistry was tied to a peasant's sense of reality and business acuity.

A type completely different from the broad rural vitality of Hoeger was the violin professor and privy councillor Burmester. He was a delicately limbed old gentleman, sensitive in all senses of the word, and lived in a world that belonged not even to yesterday but to the day before that. He was a monarchist with some small romantic inclination toward being a heroic revolutionary, which fit well with his admiration for Hitler. Insofar as he hoped that Hitler would destroy the "November Republic,"[29] he hoped simultaneously for the restoration of all the big and little princes, whose capitals and courts he could never praise enough as centers for the patronage of scholarship and the fine arts. Furthermore, this privy councillor's appearance, but even more his gestures and bearing, seemed themselves to be a part of the Biedermeier Era[30] in the best and most charming sense. Admittedly, his strong and alert national consciousness did not fit into this picture, unless one thought of the *Burschenschaften* and the Paulskirche.[31] But probably it was not historical recollections that awakened and sharpened his national consciousness, but rather the experience of his many trips abroad.

[29] The Weimar Republic, having been proclaimed in November 1918, which was also the month that the Kaiser and lesser German princes abdicated was often referred to by its opponents as the "November Republic."

[30] The period 1820–40 in Germany.

[31] *Burschenschaften* were patriotic student fraternities formed in Germany after the Napoleonic Wars; the Paulskirche was the meeting place of the all-German parliament during the Revolution of 1848.

I think Privy Councillor Burmester was born in Hamburg; but he visited the town only for a few days or a week at a time. He would stay at Streit's Hotel. Usually he invited Brinkmann or me to come see him, so that we could tell him of the status of the party. Sometimes he had little commissions for us: the formulation of a letter to Hitler or an election appeal to artists. In gratitude he would supply us with free tickets for one of his violin concerts.

Though Professor Burmester let his relationship to the party be influenced mainly by emotional factors and stood aloof from a more rational concern with political issues, practices, and methods, he did not lack an instinct for the true essence of certain incidents and persons as symbolically revealed. Thus I met him in autumn 1931 in an express train going from Munich to Stuttgart and found him quite depressed over the impressions he had just had upon visiting Hitler in the "Brown House." Having been accustomed to the reserved courtesy of well-trained butlers and chamberlains at former palaces, he was confronted with the raw Bavarian crudity of the SA guards who asked him who he was and what he wanted there. Then they passed him from vestibule to vestibule, making him wait too long in each. Finally, and this was the worst of all, he had recognized behind Hitler's effusive cordiality, the insincerity, the theatricality and the propagandistic intentions. Though he tried to explain it all, and thus console himself, by saying that he was an old man who measured the new, young world with an outmoded yardstick, nevertheless I gained the impression that he could not surmount his disappointment.

In any event, after this meeting he never sought any political discussions with us and also, as far as I could determine, never made any more statements in the Nazi press. I recall that Professor Burmester died in the mid-'30s without ever having received any particular recognition from the party. I am certain that he never sought such, since in general there was hardly any connection between his artistic endeavors and his political sympathies. Without denying the national roots of art, he believed, as a practicing artist, that he had to value art on its own terms. For instance, he gave preeminence to the Italian sonatas from the beginning of the eighteenth century as better than the German ones. His pride as a German consisted in perfecting every work to its utmost.

While art and politics hardly touched each other in Professor Burmester, the specific reason for my encounter with Karl Wüstenhagen, who was later to become state councillor and general director of the Hamburg Theater, was Wüstenhagen's hope of securing understanding and support from our newspaper and the party for his artistic plans and goals.

The Hamburg Theater was in a severe financial crisis at the turn of the year 1931–32. There were two different causes. On the one hand the depression robbed the theater of a part of its audience, who could no longer permit themselves the "luxury" of the admission price. Secondly, the selection of plays and a not always very tasteful experimental direction of them drove certain segments of the audience away from the theater. To overcome the crisis, therefore, it was necessary to inaugurate serious artistic changes as well as financial ones and to synchronize them with the critically minded public.

To promote such a coordination, Wüstenhagen invited me to come talk with him in December 1931. After explaining to me that he had been picked to succeed Röbbeling as the director, he set forth his intended organizational and personnel measures. Along with issues of lesser significance, he went into the problem, raised now and again in "the newspaper," of employing Jewish artists. He declared that he would not feel it necessary to remove them on racial grounds alone. On the other hand, he would no longer permit any objectively unjustifiable promotion of Jewish ladies and gentlemen. Then he turned to an outline of his artistic goals as an expression of his expectation that a young generation of actors would be linked with the rise of Nazism.

There were two key terms that Wüstenhagen wanted to apply to his future work with the Hamburg Theater: "Popular Education" and "Manly." Three desires were bound up with the concept of a theater of "popular education." Through a carefully conceived table of admission prices, the theater should be available to the broadest circles. Along with this Wüstenhagen hoped to collaborate with existing ticket clubs in a major promotional drive to win back audiences from the cinemas, the variety houses, and the amusement parks. But in pursuit of this goal the theater was not to turn itself into an amusement park for so-called "popular" plays. On the contrary, Wüstenhagen followed Lessing and Schiller in seeing the stage as a place to present the highest values of the nation. What he understood by this were the great dramatic works of German literature, especially those of the eighteenth and nineteenth centuries, but including also all those works of world literature that the German spirit had made its own and had thus grown and evolved new ways in the process. And out of such considerations there came the third and highest goal of Wüstenhagen's intentions. The theater, which had originally started as a place of holy, religious purpose, was now in the twentieth century to become a place of popular national education in the sense that it was here that the *Volk*, by perceiving all comprehensible verbal and spiritual images, all binding, engaging ones, would finally achieve form for itself and would see itself as a fraternal community.

It was harder to comprehend what Wüstenhagen had in mind with the term "manly" theater. Apparently this was primarily a polemical term as he conceived it and there were united in his concept quite a varied number of negative and positive opinions. "Unmanly" was in Wüstenhagen's view, the theater of revues, or works that were directed as an art-craft, or the exalted expressionists: "I am screaming, screaming, screaming!" But it was also "unmanly" when a production of Schiller's *Don Carlos* deemphasized the role of the man, Phillip, and emphasized the adolescents Posa and Carlos. "Manly" theater, according to him, was that in which preeminence was given to the great political tragedies, serious problem works, and naturally also the true comedies: *Der zerbrochene Krug, Tartuffe, Minna von Barnhelm, Der Revisor, A Midsummer Night's Dream,* and so on. Wüstenhagen wanted especially to take up the works of Hebbel, Grabbe, and Schiller, who in those years was enjoying a sort of revival anyway, as a "political poet." He, spoke little of the modern writers, whether out of caution or out of indifferent interest, I cannot say.

The presidential election campaign that commenced in January 1932 marked the first time that the entire Nazi press was subjected to central direction. Day after day the office of the Reich press chief sent out or phoned in reports on Hitler's flights over Germany,[32] prepared articles on "the fundamentals and goals of Nazism," and excerpts from the campaign speeches of prominent leaders—in every instance with directions to print them promi-

---

[32] For reasons of propaganda and efficiency, Hitler used a chartered airplane in this campaign, the first time any German politician had done so.

nently and in full. At the same time we had to give due consideration to the local election campaign with its proclamations and
reports from the *Gauleitung*, the SA leaders, and the various sub-
organizations of the party. Gradually the entire structure of the
newspaper, from deadlines to layouts and subject divisions, became
thoroughly disorganized. The independent work of the editorial
staff came to an end; in its place we plagued ourselves with editing
and correcting the reports that came in over the telephone in a gar-
bled condition and the barely readable sections of the prepared
articles. That was hardly satisfying, but in view of the election
campaign it simply had to be.

Much worse and more depressing was the uniformity and super-
ficiality that emerged in these reports and articles. The organization and propaganda techniques were extravagantly and consciously modeled on the example of American advertising, and
they revealed with cold brutality the demonic and violent simplification in Hitler's character. Most people may not have noticed
this. They saw only the surging wave of the "folk-soul" whipped
up by the propaganda storm from Königsberg to Freiburg, from
Passau to Emden. We, however, saw the shoals and sandbars of
superficial, cynical, foolish directives, written in bad German, over
which the wave was sweeping. In the brief pauses permitted us by
the turmoil, we shook our heads while passing page-proof corrections back and forth and asked ourselves: "What is to come of
this?" We thought that now everything would have to move very
rapidly toward an attempt at a resolution through violence, or otherwise the waters would have to subside again. Remarkably, the
prevailing opinion was that the party had reached the crest of
the wave, and unless totally different methods were employed in the
future, would rapidly sink back into the trough of insignificance.
Hardly anyone on our editorial staff still trusted Hitler to have
enough determination for a revolution and surely no one expected
any lasting success from such an action. This did not keep the disappointments of the last months from reawakening revolutionary
plans and convictions in some.

Naturally there were some differences among the individual editors as to the strength and sharpness of pessimistic mistrust. In
general, a decidedly depressed mood was dominant inside the

newspaper, especially after Hitler lost the second election, too.[33] For most members it was a completely new experience to suffer defeat despite great exertions, and initially they had to work it out and master it in their own minds. That did not happen without frictions and personal tensions, which also caused our work to suffer, especially since at first we could not agree among ourselves as to what the next alignment ought to be. Some believed we ought to redouble efforts to keep the masses in motion with the radical slogans of the election campaign. A second group, including mc, put their hopes in a new course indicated by Gregor Strasser in a Reichstag speech and an article in the journal *Die Tat*. Before either of these views triumphed or a compromise was reached, the ground was knocked out from under our reflections and disputations by the intervention of the *Gauleitung* which, when joined by Göbbels and Hitler, led to my expulsion.

The background, occasion, and causes of my expulsion, from a perspective of the entire situation in the party, are things I will go into later, in the chapter on Adolf Hitler. Those aspects that derived from circumstances in Hamburg, and especially from the party's development there, can be briefly explained here.

When Karl Kaufmann was appointed the new Gauleiter in April 1929, he was received in Hamburg with rather limited enthusiasm. There was still enough life in the democratic feelings of the Hamburg membership so that they were upset by the party leadership sticking another outsider under their noses (and a Catholic one to boot) without having asked them or even informed them beforehand. Furthermore, there was so much mutual distrust stored up from the conflicts of the previous months that the strength and will to confidence was practically completely choked up.

In the beginning Kaufmann tried to win party comrades over by initiating a campaign to straighten things out and conciliate people. In this he was only moderately successful, since at first he could not find a stance above the contesting groups. So he generally

[33] Since Hindenburg failed to receive an absolute majority in the presidential election of March 13, 1932, a runoff election was held on April 10. Hitler got 30 percent the first time and 37 percent the second (when Hindenburg was elected with 53 percent of the vote).

left the organizational reins in the hands of his capable business manager, Burat, whom he had brought with him from Elberfeld, and quietly began to gather around him a circle of officials who appeared trustworthy. His goal was to renew the party apparatus from within through them. The center of his efforts was less to be found in the Gau business office than in the home of the physician Dr. Friedrich Lauerbach, where he succeeded, in this private atmosphere, in establishing a number of alliances and personal relationships. To this inner cicle there then attached itself, in looser form, further circles. After a year or eighteen months of operating with such patient and skillful tactics, Kaufmann had gathered to himself a "corps of leaders" who cannot exactly be described as an elite group but was certainly a rather long-term community of interest.

Despite occasional tensions, frictions, and antagonisms, its firmness was proven by the fact that no opposition attempts within the Gau were effective. To be sure, such attempts were undertaken on inadequate personal and factual bases. Someone who had embezzeled party funds should not consider himself legitimized as a judge of morality. Someone who was aiming for a religious revival should not have tried to work through the Nazi party, since already at the party convention of 1927 it had been declared that any discussion of religious questions was harmful to the party's cause. Someone who was convinced of the corrupt nature of certain personalities and institutions within the party should not step forward first in the moment of his personal anger over the rejection of his own ambitious desires. All the oppositional initiatives of the years 1929–31, therefore, never got beyond the composition of letters of complaint or memoranda or the exchange of opinions within very small groups, who usually overestimated their own capabilities.

Theoretically Gauleiters held practically dictatorial powers over their "corps of leaders." If they simply adhered to the party directives their regime was subordinated to no limits of a constitutional nature on the Gau level. The prevailing rule was total power of command downward and total duty of obedience upward.

Nevertheless, things looked different in reality. Just the existence of the numerous party sub-organizations, with their staffs and central command posts, narrowed the power position of a Gauleiter considerably. Even a Dr. Goebbels could not make his directives prevail against the resistance of the SA.[34] And even the women's organization, the shop-cell organization, or the motorized corps (NSKK) could make great difficulties for an autocratic Gauleiter who relied upon his deputized authority. For example, during an election campaign the party was dependent upon the cheerful cooperation of all elements. Independent of these general factors a special situation had developed in Hamburg that would not have allowed the Gauleiter to maintain a regime of personal absolutism. His relationship with the narrow circle of collaborators, which he had personally recruited, did not permit the application of dictatorial methods, which were foreign to Kaufmann's nature anyway. That he occasionally conducted himself like a dictator was nothing more than rhetorical behavior, in keeping with the style of the times and the party. As long as he wanted to maintain himself as the central figure in his circle, as first among equals, Kaufmann had to stick to using political tactics, political persuasion, and patient political endeavor—the methods with which he had begun his activities.

The result was that in Hamburg it was not the Gauleiter who ruled but rather the *Gauleitung*, a team, a collective of a dozen men under his chairmanship. And thus it was not always the chairman who set goals and directions. On the contrary, under certain circumstances other members of the team—Ahrens, Allwörden, Dr. Nieland—stepped into the foreground as the instigators and impellers of certain actions.

The political behavior of the *Gauleitung* as it was composed in spring 1932 was mostly set by the relatively numerous members who had joined the party since the election of September 1930. The attitude of these "new men" was distinguished by a concrete personal ambition that saw its realization as imminent, by an uncritical acceptance of certain developments in the party, such as the exclusion of all democratic forms, the *Führer*-cult, the growing fascistification, and finally by an awareness of the significance of their mutually supportive and protective clique for their own advancement. Out of this attitude there grew a very conscious per-

---

[34] Krebs refers here to the mutiny in the Berlin SA on the eve of the 1930 elections. Goebbels was Gauleiter of Berlin, but the mutiny was quelled only by Hitler's on-the-spot intervention. See Chapter 6.

sonnel policy that operated in two ways. On the one hand only members of the *Gauleitung* and its circle of friends and clients were marked out for future positions in the party and the state—which, of course, was customary in other parties too, but precisely for that reason had previously been stalwartly combated in the Nazi party. On the other hand, individual party members were appointed to the *Gauleitung* irrespective of their previous accomplishments for the party and their human behavior, if they were needed for some particular business and should therefore first be clothed with the authority of the title "Member of the Gauleitung."

And so, at the beginning of April 1932, when the former editor of the *Hamburger Correspondent*, Hans Jacobi, was suddenly named press officer in the *Gauleitung*, we immediately recognized at the paper that with his appointment the struggle over the newspaper had reached a new, dangerous, possibly decisive stage. At last the Gau had something it had lacked in its previous actions against me and against the relative spiritual independence of the *Hamburger Tageblatt*. This was a successor who could be presented to the national leadership and the members with hopes of winning agreement and approval. Jacobi was a trained journalist, he knew the situation in Hamburg, and he had good connections with those circles of the upper bourgeoisie with whom at just that time they were seeking an alliance and to whom I had always been a thorn in the side. To be sure, Jacobi was a very recent party-comrade, but this "blemish" was balanced out by his fame at having been the youngest volunteer soldier in World War I. Beyond that, in a few years, even the members who had joined in 1931 would count as part of the "old guard."[35] And so it was only necessary to create a favorable opportunity in order to put Jacobi into the spot selected for him.

Attempts by the *Gauleitung* to arrange the opportunity indirectly failed because our guard was up. I declined, on the basis of the original agreement, to recognize the *Gauleitung*'s press officer as my superior. Brinkmann regretted that Amann had expressly

---

[35] As in most millennialist movements, the early Nazis were contemptuous of later converts. In fact, the only reward these "Old Fighters" received in the Third Reich was a special golden lapel pin.

forbidden him to create any new editorial posts. And so the Gau had to wait until, with an article against General von Schleicher, we ourselves put the opportunity into their hands. Then they moved with surprisingly eager decisiveness and speed; probably they were also better informed than we were about events behind the scenes. Immediately upon the publication of the issue of the *Tageblatt* with the incriminating article, a delegation of the *Gauleitung*—Kaufmann himself was not even informed—took the train to Berlin to lay the *corpus delicti* before Dr. Goebbels with a list of the older sins of Dr. Krebs attached. I had to go; Jacobi became managing editor of the *Hamburger Tageblatt*.

My expulsion, which ended some ten years' membership in the Nazi party, left me with split emotions. I felt as much disappointed and embittered as I did liberated from what had become, in the end, an unbearable physical and psychic burden. The reaction was a severe nervous collapse, whose effects lasted for months. It was only three-quarters of a year later that I could slowly return to normal life and work.

In the interim the German world had changed with Hitler's seizure of power. I had to get myself back on my feet and find a job. That was not easy—in a time of high-tension activity by true believers—for a young man who was an ex-Nazi. But I managed and it was considerably easier thanks to the comradeship that bound me then as before to my former colleagues at the newspaper and which I also experienced from some former opponents in the *Gauleitung*. I learned to grasp the necessity of cleansing one's political activity from negative emotion and sickly imagination and to make a clean, sharp distinction between human categories and political obligations. To put it simply and clearly, I did not find any conflict in being humanly grateful to the now Reich commissar of Hamburg, Kaufmann, for his offer of assistance toward helping me find a job after 1933 and at the same time being obliged, as a member of the resistance, to combat him because he was an official of the Hitler-State. Had I been persecuted after 1933, which almost happened, perhaps I too would have fallen heir to the persecution-retribution complex after 1945. The comradeship shown to me saved me from that. For the sake of truth and justice let this be here expressed.

PART TWO
ENCOUNTERS

CHAPTER 5

Adolf Hitler

In the first years that I was a member of the Nazi party I neither saw Hitler nor heard him speak. My entry into the party had more to do with the substance of national socialism than with the personality of its drummer. Nevertheless, Hitler's personality naturally had its long-range effects on me, too.

After I came home from World War I, I shared the experience of many others in seeing the nationalistic movement, despite the greatest self-sacrifice by its individual followers, repeatedly foiled in its political struggle for control of the state. The reason for failure was twofold: ideological and programmatic confusion plus the unremitting egoistic pretensions of its individual leaders. Leagues and organizations sprang up. Each made a name for itself by its role in the border battles and the civil war against the Communists.[1] Then young men and activist veterans flowed into them. The leagues became big and powerful. But within a short time they began to atrophy again because, after their initial success, they simply did not know what to do next. All their actions, no matter how revolutionary they might appear, were basically only reactions to undertakings by the other side—defensive maneuvers rather than chess moves on the grand political board.

Up to November 9, 1918, nationalist Germany had an obvious natural focal point in the monarchy. After the rather unheroic collapse of this institution, what was left was a spiritual and organizational void, which could not be refilled, in a few short years, with contents of equal value. The older generation dreamed of a restora-

---

[1] Krebs is referring to the *Freikorps*: ephemeral, hypernationalist, nihilistic volunteer fighting units that emerged during the chaos following World War I. See the note on them in Chapter 2.

tion of the monarchy; young people sought new ideals, such as were offered in racialist concepts, the corporate state, fascism. Accordingly, they also conflicted with each other over the correct method of conducting the struggle. Those whose origins lay in the constitutional monarchy approved of parliamentarism and parties and opposed only the degeneration of these institutions. For most young people, on the other hand, parties and parliaments were simply the outgrowths of a system which itself was degenerate. Their ideal was the Free Corps in which leaders and followers interrelated through soldierly discipline and mutual loyalty. In such leagues one lived with the hope that a Communist uprising would finally provide the opportunity for a vast counteroffensive that would cleanse everything. Following which, the state would be reconstructed on the model of the Free Corps.

Of course this analysis is all understanding after the fact. In the early '20s members of the nationalistic movement were not yet aware of this: They saw only the general confusion and its consequences, but not its causes. They saw the tremendous outlay of faith, goodwill, readiness for sacrifice, will to action, and at the same time they experienced the useless and senseless squandering of it all. Perhaps to the good burghers it seemed a great success when the Spartacist Uprising[2] was smashed, but members of the Free Corps were left with a vague sense of having been misused for an alien purpose. Signs of lassitude appeared. Here and there members began to be indifferent about their duties or simply gave up. And therefore they listened attentively when the first reports emerged from Munich about the activities of a new party led by a certain Adolf Hitler—a party in which apparently, or at least in intent, the previous deficiencies of the racialist-nationalist movement had been attacked and overcome.

Just by deciding to call itself a "party" and to be active as a true party, Nazism appeared to have taken a significant step toward realistic political effectiveness. At the same time its establishment

[2] In January 1919 tensions between the revolutionary government of moderate socialists and the newly formed Communist party led to armed clashes in which government-backed Free Corps won a bloody victory. The predecessor of the Communist party was the *Spartakus Bund*; hence that name was given to this and generally to all the leftist upheavals of the spring of 1919. See Eric Waldman's *The Spartacist Uprising of 1919* (Milwaukee, 1958).

of a "Storm Section" (the SA) took up and carried forth the tradition of the military leagues—not for the sake of tradition, but rather as a political instrument. Furthermore the program of the new party, no matter how disputable this or that individual point might be, finally provided an opportunity for grappling with the enemies in the Marxist parties. Its formulations were also communicable to the common man and sketched a picture of the future that could attract him. The leader of the party, Hitler, may have been a "new man" whose background nobody really knew, but on the other hand he belonged to the "generation of the trenches," and it was precisely his independence from traditional political and social modes that seemed to assure his followers that he would not let himself march under false flags for anonymous interests. Beyond that, this Hitler was said to have oratorical talents such as had never previously been experienced in the nationalistic movement and he was said to use them to express ruthlessly all that had burned to be uttered within the souls of tens of thousands since that gray November of 1918. And finally, people praised him as a fearless man who at last dared to stand up against the terrorism of the Marxist parties and reconquer the freedom of assembly guaranteed on paper by the constitution. All over South Germany people spoke of how he had, with barely a hundred of his Munich Stormtroopers, smashed the rampaging Communist disruption squads out of the town of Coburg on the occasion of the Germanic Convention there, and thus assured its completion after the actual sponsors (the United Patriotic Associations) had given up.[3]

This and similar stories indicated that this man and his party possessed the uncompromising, unhesitating approach that had so long been desired for the nationalist movement. Given that, it was easy to do without a program distinguished by sophisticated formulations, such as was demanded by the intellectuals—who were not

[3] This refers to the first widespread street battle between the Communists and the Nazis, in Coburg, Bavaria, in October 1922. Krebs' description follows Hitler's, who portrayed the incident in *Mein Kampf* as "breaking the Communist terror." Actually Hitler had some eight hundred SA men with him and provoked fights with workers for calculated propaganda reasons. See Werner Maser's *Die Frühgeschichte der NSDAP. Hitlers Weg bis 1924* (Bonn, 1965), pp. 357–358.

overly valued anyway. Admittedly, there were aspects of the party that caused others besides intellectuals to pause and ponder. A number of the closest and apparently most trusted of Hitler's collaborators made rather unpleasant impressions by their political origins and their personal and public behavior. Yet it was clearly impossible to get rid of these people despite their bad reputations. It was explained that Hitler himself protected them because he was loyal to everyone who did not break faith with him. Since this explanation corresponded exactly with the emotional attitude of the nationalistic movement, it was accepted even though it constituted a safe-conduct pass for Julius Streicher, Hermann Esser, Christian Weber, and so on.[4]

Also, the radical statements of some of the party's speakers, and even Hitler, produced even in those early days a certain sense of uneasiness. If brought to fruition, they could only lead to the destruction of the enduring values that are inalienable to every state form and social order. The danger emerged of a pseudoscientific racial materialism. Like every materialism, it would ultimately end in a form of Bolshevism or nihilism. This danger soon came under discussion, especially in student circles, but for the moment people calmed or anesthetized themselves with the phrases that are usually applied to politics: "The Devil can only be driven out by Beelzebub"; or "The sauce is never eaten as hot as it's cooked." After all, the movement was just beginning and it seemed unnecessary at this early point to worry about future possibilities. Beyond that, one shouldn't overestimate statements uttered in the heat of a mass meeting. Taken as a whole, anyway, the advantages of the new party outweighed its disadvantages even in the eyes of its critical adherents.

But there were certain other incidents that might possibly have led to an unfavorable judgment on the party, except that they were still obscure in their causes and contexts. During the uprising in Upper Silesia, Hitler strongly forbade his followers to participate in the German resistance that culminated in the storming of

---

[4] Julius Streicher, Gauleiter of Nuremberg, was a pornographer; Hermann Esser, a member of Hitler's "shadow cabinet" from 1919 on, lived from the earnings of his various mistresses; Christian Weber, a former horse dealer, used to horsewhip recalcitrant party members at the Nazi headquarters.

the Annaberg.[5] He even accused *Freikorps Oberland*, led by
Beppo Römer, of showing Bolshevist tendencies because it elected
its own officers.[6] Hitler took the same attitude toward the Ruhr
struggle, being opposed to both the active and passive resistance.[7]
It was not until the death of Schlageter, which caused extraordinarily strong repercussions among wide circles of German youth,
that Hitler felt forced to give way somewhat. He still adhered to
his basic rejection of all actions by the "system" no matter how
pure their objectives. This he justified by saying that because of
the "system's" secret connections with supranational forces and its
consequent weakness, a true success would be unobtainable and
probably was not even desired. His slogan ran: "National actions
by the system are internally false and mendacious actions; the
idealistic fighter who participates in them is being betrayed and
will constantly be betrayed!"

Hitler's attitude doubtless showed a certain logical consistency.
Since he had sworn irreconcilable enmity against the "system" he
had to act in a manner similar to the Social Democrats, who
before 1914 had conducted politics for decades under the watch-
word "Not one man and not one penny for this system." Beyond
that, it was a tactical necessity for him, just as it is for any opposition leader, to differentiate as sharply and clearly as possible
between his own goals and methods and those of the ruling
powers. And even beyond that, Hitler had to set himself off just as
sharply against the other nationalistic associations in order to justify the separate existence of his party, to maintain his reputation

[5] In 1921, before the question of what parts of Silesia should go to Poland
had been resolved by diplomatic interpretation of a plebiscite, Polish irregular
troops attempted to seize the whole area. German Free Corps flooded into
Upper Silesia in response and, by storming the heights of Annaberg, drove the
Poles out. See F. Gregory Campbell, "The Struggle for Upper Silesia, 1919–
22," *Journal of Modern History* (December 1970), pp. 361–385.

[6] This Free Corps declared the old army commissions dissolved; positions of
leadership had to be won by achievement and trust; thus sergeants gave orders
to officers (*Krebs' note—W.S.A.*).

[7] When the French occupied the Ruhr in 1923 the Germans resisted non-
violently through a general strike and massive noncooperation. But Free Corps
units soon infiltrated the area and undertook sabotage. In May 1923 Albert
Leo Schlageter, a Nazi member of *Freikorps Heinz*, was executed by the
French for dynamiting a railroad bridge.

as an uncompromising man, and to stake out his claims to future leadership. All that made the radicalism of his demands and refusals explicable and understandable.

Nevertheless, I am convinced that it would be false to see Hitler's attitude as having been only a matter of tactics and to cite, as proof of this, the actual active participation of Nazis in actions that he had condemned. It is true that especially in the Ruhr struggle local Nazi units were vigorously involved and consequently made many sacrifices. Still, the reason was not because they had gotten some secret order from Hitler contravening his official stance but rather because they simply didn't bother themselves about his official position. In those early days Hitler's authority was much too limited to permit him to command or forbid his very self-willed original followers against their own opinions.

Therefore, one may surely assume that quite apart from tactical considerations, Hitler's attitude, even in those early years, already contained the germ of the view: "Germany and I are one" or "If I do not save Germany, then it does not need to be saved." Whether he was already aware of this attitude, whether therefore his self-characterization as the drummer, the path-breaker, the temporary place-holder was only rhetoric can hardly be clearly determined. It is probable that in those early years of the struggle his psyche was constantly in a state of spiritual-intellectual division between honest assertion and egocentric self-portrayal and self-enhancement. The latter must be accorded the greater significance, however. What speaks for that was Hitler's behavior in a matter in which consideration for public reaction or other tactical viewpoints was largely excluded.

In autumn of 1922 Paris began to issue increasingly blatant threats that they would occupy a section of western Germany in retaliation against Germany's alleged nonfulfillment of the Treaty of Versailles. Because of this, organizational preparations were made for a guerrilla war against the invading French troops. What sort of political and military plans stood behind these preparations and what their prospects were cannot be discussed here. What was unambiguous was their, so to say, "official" character. That was evident to the participants simply from the precision with which the work was carried out and the high quality of the human and technical material employed. Beyond that, the "recruiters" made no secret of the fact that official agencies were behind it, even though they naturally named no names. The organization itself did not employ the usual sort of stirring title but simply called itself, according to the region involved, by the name (or cover name) of whoever was the local leader. Recruited were primarily foresters, young peasants' sons who had distinguished themselves in the war, technically talented artisans, and a few teachers and academicians. The number of participants was, accordingly, small; there was strict selectivity. Entry into the organization involved a promise of silence about what was being asked of the individual member and how he was to carry it out.

In terms of numbers this organization in no way constituted competition for the Nazi party. Nor was it any threat from a political or military-political viewpoint since it was completely neutral toward all domestic disputes. This distinguished it expressly and decisively from the regular army, which despite all its political neutrality, was committed to intervene in the event of a state emergency. Thus Hitler had no reason to fear that this organization, about whose goals he had been sufficiently instructed in writing and orally, would be opposing him in the event of a revolutionary action by his party. Nevertheless, already in autumn 1922, he refused it any support and prohibited Nazis from joining it.[7a] The reason he gave was that he wanted to put an end to the nuisance of multiple membership within the nationalistic movement (there were people in those days who belonged to five organizations simultaneously). But this was not a valid argument. The guerrilla organization was not a part of the nationalistic movement but rather a covert segment of the state defense organization. Thus in substance Hitler's refusal amounted to a refusal to bear arms. If he consciously realized that, then that would prove that even in those early years he, as a legitimate heir of Jacobinism, accepted only a

[7a] Krebs' account of the existence of this guerrilla organization is corroborated in F. L. Carsten, The Reichswehr and Politics, 1918 to 1933 (Oxford, 1966), pp. 155–161. But its composition and goals varied considerably in the different parts of Germany and in some places it definitely had goals directed toward internal politics and involved rivals to Hitler's movement. Thus Krebs' conclusions, while perhaps true for the segment he writes about, are not necessarily valid for the situation as a whole, as perceived by Hitler.

state formed according to his own ideology as worthy of his duty and his defense. From this conception it was only a short step to the sentences: "Germany will be national socialist or it will not be at all." Or: "If the German people leave me in the lurch in this war, then they have earned their downfall."[8]

While no clear answer may be found to the question of Hitler's inner motives for his attitudes and actions during the so-called "first years of struggle," a perusal and evaluation of his more visible methods and reactions leads one to clear conclusions. They clarify the extent to which the Hitler of those early years already resembled the pigheaded, uninstructable captive of delusions of infallibility that was Hitler at the height of power. Two episodes out of the prehistory of the November Putsch of 1923 may serve as examples.

Late in the summer of 1923 I received orders to attach all the men capable of bearing arms in my Local Group of the Nazi party (located in the Odenwald) to the SA regiment in Bamberg. According to the message from Munich, this regiment was supposed to be several hundred strong, recruited from Bamberg itself and from the neighboring rural counties. The orders seemed to me to make little sense and, as far as the assertions about Bamberg were concerned, to be rather unbelievable. In case of need how were we Oldenwalders supposed to get to Bamberg quickly[9] if the railroad connections, which were poor anyway, were interrupted by some counteraction? Furthermore, I could not believe that Bamberg had an even halfway powerful Nazi organization, since up to then the only military leagues able to establish themselves there were those friendly to the Bavarian People's party.[10] Therefore I

---

[8] This quotation is a paraphrase from General Halder's memoirs, *Hitler als Feldherr* (Munich, 1949), p. 62. The essence of it is corroborated independently in Percy E. Schramm, *Hitler the Man and the Military Leader*, edited and translated by Donald S. Detwiler (Chicago, 1971), p. 176, and in H. R. Trevor-Roper's *The Last Days of Hitler*, 3rd ed., paperback (New York, 1962), p. 111.

[9] The distance between these two localities is close to 100 miles.

[10] Bavarian wing of the then anti-Nazi Catholic Center party. For the attitude of the Bavarian People's party toward the Nazis, see Geoffrey Pridham, *Hitler's Rise to Power: The Nazi Movement in Bavaria, 1923 to 1933* (London, 1973).

inquired with some friends who had connections in the army and the state police and learned that the Bamberg Regiment existed only on paper. Some swindling freebooter chieftain who commanded a bunch of perhaps thirty to forty personal followers had sniffed business possibilities in the revolutionary bull market. Since the party's leadership needed troops for the intended action and obviously had sizable funds to recruit and maintain them, he opened up a business office, demanded a subsidy for his phantom soldiers, and got it. Those were the facts that I reported to Munich along with my concerns about the distance and transportation difficulties. But the only result of my report was that the original order was repeated without any mention of my objections. At that time I believed, after I got the answer (which I think was signed by Alfred Rosenberg), that the party leadership had acted that way to assert its authority, but would quietly clear up the abuses in Bamberg. Today I am convinced that my critical report had disturbed Hitler's illusions and therefore was simply ignored.

A second episode from those months left a more lasting impression. The communist disorders in Thuringia and the growing tension between the Reich government and Bavarian General Commissioner Gustav von Kahr drew the most diverse nationalistic leagues into the Bavarian border area around Coberg. While the members of these leagues had rather common ideas and feelings in their conception as to who was friend and foe and in their political hopes, their leaders pursued quite divergent goals. That is, they all had similar vocabularies, but what a leader of the Young Germanic Order[11] meant by the words "national revolution" bore very slight resemblance to what an SA leader understood by them. Therefore, the prevailing atmosphere was quite troubled and murky, and tensions were increased even more when Captain Hermann Erhardt showed up with the people of his brigade.[12] No one knew exactly

[11] *Jungdeutsche Orden*: a hypernationalistic organization of former Free Corps members, which nevertheless eventually supported the Weimar Republic.

[12] Hermann Erhardt was the most famous of the Free Corps leaders; he also organized the assassination gangs called Organization Consul, which murdered Erzberger, Rathenau, and many other "traitors" to German nationalism. See Howard Stern, "The Organization 'Consul,' " *Journal of Modern History* (March 1963), pp. 20–32.

what party Erhardt was backing, probably not even his own followers. Nevertheless, his vast authority within the nationalistic movement and his superiority in military and political matters quickly
won him the position of supreme commander over the assembled
leagues. That did not put an end to the jealousies, personal frictions, and political differences, but at least the military preparations became more uniform. Yet within a short time it became
noticeable that the SA units, which admittedly were not very
strong in numbers, were the only ones to gain no advantage from
this. They regularly came out short at the distribution of equipment and arms, which were supplied from some depot of the state
police or the *Orgesch*.[13] Therefore, the political leader of the
Franconian Nazis sent a warning to the party leadership that it
should not view the leagues assembled around Coburg as allies.
But the warning was ignored. At the end of October the Bavarian
state police supplied a few light armored cars. Again the SA was
passed over, though they immediately put in a claim. Thereupon
the Coburg Nazi delegate, Hans Dietrich (who was a friend of
mine and told me about this at that time and reconfirmed it later;
he died in the last months of the war), drove to Munich to repeat
and explain directly to Hitler the warnings that had previously
been put only in writing. Dietrich said he openly told Hitler in
this conversation that in his view probably a part of the leagues
and definitely the Erhardt people and the state police would resist
an action by the Nazi party. Thus the assumption by the party
leaders that they already had the allegiance of the whole nationalistic movement in Bavaria securely in hand was an error. The circle
around von Kahr and the Bavarian District Army Command were
pursuing fundamentally different goals in their struggle with Berlin
than the party was. He concluded, therefore, that Hitler should not
let himself be deceived by the similar tone in the Kahr government's pronouncements and proclamations.

Hitler took Delegate Dietrich's warning no more seriously than
he had the other warnings; he hardly paid attention to them. He

---

[13] Short name for *Organization Escherisch*, a nationwide organization of
local paramilitary units led by ex-Major Georg Escherisch, which flourished in
the period 1920–23. They had at least two hundred thousand rifles in secret
depots, mostly in Bavaria. See Waite, pp. 198–202.

felt that the world of his illusions was being disturbed. In his exaggerated self-confidence, he could not bear to have any opponent described to him as dangerous. In his imagination he was already the universally recognized leader of nationalistic Germany, which was only awaiting his signal for an uprising. Whoever dared to dispel this image by asserting that a significant segment of this nationalistic Germany not only followed other leaders but would even oppose Hitler's call—such a person must be thrust aside as a defeatist, a fault-finder, a stupid know-it-all, or even an agent of the enemy. Hitler needed such self-deception in order to be able to act. Had he viewed matters and men with sober realism, he would never have found in his whole nature the strength to make decisions.

The course of November 9, 1923,[14] showed that even at that point Hitler found himself in the same state of self-deception. Only this explains his neglect of the most elementary security measures with respect to Kahr, Lossow, and Seisser after the oath of loyalty was extorted from them in the Bürgerbräu-Keller. Then when the Putsch was put down, this self-deception logically engendered the accusation of betrayal. Hitler was undoubtedly honestly convinced that he had been the victim of a shameless betrayal on November 9. He needed this belief in order not to lose faith in himself. Therefore, it surely never occurred to him that he had provoked the "betrayal" himself through his own blind unwillingness to be taught anything.

The first time I met Hitler personally was at the beginning of October 1927. At that time he visited Hamburg for the city election campaign. Just shortly beforehand the Senate's prohibition against his speaking there had been lifted. Edgar Brinkmann (the party's local business manager) and I met him at the railroad station. He was accompanied by Rudolf Hess. On the way to the Phoenix Hotel Hitler asked a few questions about the preparations

[14] The date of Hitler's "Beer Hall" Putsch. After kidnapping von Kahr, head of the Bavarian government, Otto von Lossow, the district army commander, and Hans Ritter von Seisser, chief of the state police, Hitler promised them posts in his revolutionary government and let them go—whereupon they promptly organized the police and army resistance that defeated Hitler's attempted coup. The best account is Harold J. Gordon's *Hitler and the Beer Hall Putsch* (Princeton, 1972).

and prospects of the mass meeting and rather nervously inquired about the mentality of Hamburgers. It was obvious that he was suffering, in anticipation of this first appearance in Hamburg, from stage fright. At the hotel Hitler immediately went to his room. Hess quickly followed him after instructing us to have twenty bottles of distilled water placed on the podium. He explained that Hitler sweated mightily during his major speeches and lost up to five pounds through dehydration. The loss had to be made up as rapidly as possible to prevent severe damage to his health.

Our plan to bring Hitler and Hess by car to the Sagebiel Auditorium about a half hour before the beginning of the meeting was not approved. Hess explained that Hitler wished to enter the hall only after it was full or at least after the influx of people had ceased. Protracted waiting on the platform during the noisy preparations for a mass meeting disturbed his concentration. Also there were to be no lengthy introductory speeches with greetings to the guests and discussions of local politics. It would be best if no more than five or at most ten minutes elapsed between the time Hitler entered the hall and his first words.

Hitler had prepared carefully for his speech as was indicated by a multi-paged outline manuscript. Since I sat next to him I could see by his turning of the individual pages that he also stuck to his outline. Whole phrases and sentences, which seemed to come out spontaneously in his speech, had been written down in the manuscript. Hitler was not an emotional orator, as so many people (especially among his opponents) believed. He constructed his speeches systematically and always knew exactly what he was saying and what effect he intended with his words. Even his refusal to discuss immediate issues, his apparent development of theses out of "fundamental values" divorced from political realities did not derive from some visionary fantasy. On the contrary, he clearly understood that he could only win the attention of the masses by avoiding customary terminology and by working with new words and new concepts. The ideas he developed in this way were of such a generally acceptable nature that people of the most diverse political tendencies could approve of them.

Thus he was able, at that first appearance in Hamburg, after about an hour's worth of his speech, to move his initially quite mistrustful and reserved audience to slowly increasing bursts of applause, which mounted in the end to a great acclamation. Even the soberest of his audience, men who before and after the speech were opposed to Hitler and his party, stated in subsequent conversations that Hitler was obviously far more sensible than they had assumed.

It is such judgments that form the basis of the legend that still exists that the crimes and errors of the party were committed by Hitler's subordinates against his will and without his knowledge.

Immediately following the meeting Hitler drove back to his hotel and was available for conversation only for a few moments before his departure the next day when he was given the morning newspapers from Hamburg. Then he limited the conversation to a few exchanges indicated by the situation. He was interested in neither the factual nor the personal aspects of conditions within the party in Hamburg. His gestures toward comradely unity, which he occasionally made by shaking hands and looking "deeply" into the eyes of some functionary or favorite SA man, were mostly little more than gestures. I never heard him express praise or even approval of part-comrades. Two or three times he said in my presence: "I don't like that guy!" He did not explain why. In my estimation such statements were not so much an evaluation of character and achievement as they were a fixing of an instinctive impression derived from his whole personal relationship with the "guy." With an animal-like acuteness of perception he differentiated between people who gave him unconditional loyalty and an almost religious faith and those who viewed and judged him from a critical distance according to standards of reason.[15] Such people he did not like, though admittedly he usually first gave utterance to his distaste only after deciding that he could not use them any longer for himself and his cause.

My next encounter with Hitler was again occasioned by his coming to give a speech and followed a course similar to his first visit. Before and after the meeting Hitler shut himself off from any close association with party-comrades and was stoutly supported in

[15] This same quality was also noted by Percy Schramm (*op. cit.*, p. 34) in almost the same words.

this by his entourage. The reason for this was never clear to me. Perhaps it was to conceal a certain gaucherie or the gaps in his education, which were then still quite noticeable. But perhaps he also wanted to create a nimbus of inaccessibility. I can remember only one instance when Hitler was willing to converse at length with a small group of party-comrades. At that time he had spent several days in Hamburg and Schleswig-Holstein. Thus he could not evade the pressure of many party-comrades to meet and speak with him by the excuse that he had to prepare a speech. So he left his room for an hour and sat in the hotel restaurant.

Admittedly, there was no real conversation on this occasion either—in the sense of alternating exchanges among all those present. At first Hitler answered a question of mine by painting a rough picture of what Nazi laws and constitutional reforms would be like. To the accompaniment of vigorous and not wholly unjustifiable attacks upon lawyers and bureaucrats, he put forth the view that the lawgiver should create only a framework but not statutes and paragraphs in which everything was spelled out specifically. Life must not be bogged down in ink; organic evolution must not be rendered impossible. Hitler expressly cited the example of England, though he neither understood nor portrayed the essence of it correctly, either because of conscious, doctrinaire misinterpretation or insufficient knowledge. For him England's lack of a written constitution and precise codes of law was not the consequence of centuries of development but an intentional decision by wily sly-dog politicians. He could not understand (or did not want to) that the force of a slowly developed tradition and a thoroughly integrated society had created such strong ties that they could dispense with printed parchment. He only saw that the lack of specific regulations made it possible to behave arbitrarily at any time according to monetary needs. This "law of arbitrariness" that he thought had been set up by English "sly dogs" pleased him and he made no bones about his desire to imitate it.

Following this political exposition, Hitler spent about twenty minutes describing how Mathilde Ludendorff, before she married the General, had tried to infatuate Hitler into marrying her. Whether this was a true story, or was only an attempt to ascribe personal motives to the attacks on the Nazi party that the Tannenberg League[16] had just initiated, is neither here nor there. In any case it disclosed Hitler's ability to put things both wittily and maliciously. He peeled off, so to speak, all the high lady's priestly, philosophical, scholarly, erotic, and other skins until all that was left was an evil, sharp onion. Anyone who shared in this peeling process was in all probability immune for all times to any enticements from the House of Ludendorff. And maybe that was the real reason for this ostensibly personal and confidential chitchat.

In February 1928 Hitler suddenly showed up at the Hamburg party headquarters on Dovenfleet Street without prior notice. I was not told what had occasioned his visit to the city. Later I heard that he had been (unsuccessfully) trying to raise funds in Hamburg business circles, but I have no evidence for this rumor. Still, Hitler's remarkable behavior during this visit, which is why I describe it, argues for its accuracy.

To begin with, Hitler's clothes were enough to cause most of the party-comrades present to shake their heads. He and his escorts wore business suits with soft, elegant felt hats, light raincoats, brown leather spats, and short riding whips. Perhaps this was wholly suitable to advertise him and his followers as goon squads against "Red terrorism," but it did not exactly fit into our impoverished party headquarters. Hitler hardly took any notice of the party-comrades, though they crowded happily around him full of things to tell him. With obvious reluctance he let me introduce my fellow workers who were on hand. Nor was he interested in the business and the equipment of the headquarters. On the other hand, he found the location in the harbor area propagandistically disadvantageous and refused to accept the reasons we gave him for having chosen just this location. Either he was much less interested than we Hamburgers in winning over workers, or else the

16 Mathilde Ludendorff was the driving force behind this nationalistic religious cult and veterans' organization named for her husband's most famous victory in World War I. It competed with Nazism and in 1926–27 actually recruited ex-Free Corps members away from Hitler's party, especially in northern Germany. Its lack of political action and wild anti-Catholic paranoia (for example, Ludendorff accused Hitler of being an agent of the Pope) eventually condemned it to insignificance, especially after the General went insane in 1928.

people he had just unsuccessfully approached had told him that the Hamburg Nazis ought to adopt a less "socialistic" pose. In any event, he unloaded his bad temper on us and with all sorts of pointed remarks made us responsible for the fact that his expectations for quicker success had up to then not been fulfilled. Since we were right in the middle of a strenuous election campaign, and furthermore in our opinion the last two years had shown quite good progress, and above all had no notion of what the causes were for Hitler's bad mood, we were all pretty angry over this kind of "gratitude." Unless my memory deceives me, we let him know it, too. Perhaps that is why he compensated by sending us, about ten days later, a real "thank-you telegram" in which as reward for our success in the city election he raised us to the status of Gau again.

In this he revealed two of his characteristics: one, burdening others with the guilt for failures and, two, rewarding others with honors that mostly enhanced and honored him himself in his own self-consciousness. The inflation of medals and honorifics of all sorts during the Third Reich sprang from the same impulse: With every award of a medal or a title, a certificate or banner of honor, the grantor elevates himself over the recipient and thus enhances his own dignity, his own authority.

After my resignation as Gauleiter in February 1928 I did not speak with Hitler for about two years, or at least not about anything important. But there were various occasions when I was able to observe him at close hand. His gestures and bearing, his individual reactions, in general his entire behavior and also that of his constant escort and collaborators showed his personal characteristics and peculiarities at least as clearly as his words. Even when he was dissimulating and play-acting he revealed himself, especially since his acting was bereft of humor or that playful light touch that fools people easier than heroic pathos. Still, it would be a mistake to ascribe crudity to him. He didn't play his roles all that poorly. A few examples illustrate this.

When I resigned as Gauleiter, Hitler at first refused to accept my resignation. Instead he withheld his final decision until a conference that was to be held early in autumn. The conference took place in September 1928. However, Hitler did not involve himself personally in adjusting the matter, but left it to Hess. Even that was not without its reasons. Hitler wanted to avoid having to

accept a refusal from me in any form. In his eyes it was an honor
to be allowed to be Hitler's Gauleiter. Therefore, he considered a
rejection of this honor as an insult to which he did not want to
subject himself and which, if it were done face to face, he could
not have left unpunished. Thus Hess had to be the one to try to
tame the unruly. When Hess was unable to do this in a protracted
discussion, in which Hinrich Lohse and for a while also Gregor
Strasser participated, and informed Hitler of this, plus suggesting
that Lohse be made provisional Gauleiter, there followed a second
significant gesture. Hitler had Lohse brought to his office in order
to tell him that the suggestion would be effected. I had to wait
outside and beyond that was informed by Hess that Herr Hitler
was very displeased over my refusal. Next there appeared in the
Völkischer Beobachter a day or so later, under the heading "News
of the Movement," the notice that Hitler had regretfully accepted
my resignation, caused by bad health, and had conveyed his gratitude to me for the work I had accomplished. That was not a con-
tradiction of his previous behavior but the final consistent step of a
rather exaggerated, complicated, but well-thought-out ceremony.
Its purpose, apart from the immediately obvious gestures of a
claim to sovereign power, is assuredly comprehensible only if one
understands Hitler's position in the Nazi party in the year 1928.

For the mass of party members, Hitler was doubtless already
then the *"Führer,"* whose decisions were accepted as final and
binding. But among the sub-leadership there were still influential
circles who more or less vigorously contested a Hitler dictatorship
on the fascist model. These circles could base their opposition on
the still valid laws of association, which did not permit a party
"registered as an association" to be organized in a hierarchical
authoritarian manner.[17] Gauleiters and Local Group leaders were
to be elected by the members, if things were to be legal. When
Hitler appointed, furloughed, and dismissed them, he was violating
the law. Thus Hitler was smart enough not to announce his claim
to appoint party officials through a party directive and base it on
that. Instead, he acted at every possible opportunity according to
this claim in order thus to create a sort of customary law within the

---

[17] For various legal advantages the Nazi party was registered as an association (*eingetragener Verein*), which, according to German law, required intra-
organizational democracy.

party. For this, in turn, it was necessary to have an impressive demonstration that would instruct all participants of the *"Führer's"* will and opinion. Such a demonstration was what I had just experienced.

And it really was impressive if one considers further that I had given as the reason for my resignation the obvious lack of confidence in me felt by the members of the party in Hamburg. Now I was instructed that it was not the members' confidence but the *"Führer's"* that counted. Furthermore, one must not disappoint this confidence lest it change into mistrust and displeasure. For its part, the party had seen that the *"Führer"* alone appoints and dismisses Gauleiters, that he recognizes services and is not grudging with his gratitude; in short, that every political ambition within the Nazi party could be satisfied only through Hitler's will and concurrence. For the future development of the party such instruction was of great significance since it created the psychological precondition for the acceptance of Hitler's demand for unconditional obedience. Even ambitious people who rejected this demand internally complied with it externally, since cleverness dictated this. In connection with this it can be noted that this kind of cleverness was less to be found among the "old fighters" than among the opportunists who put their "abilities and skills" at Hitler's disposal after his victory.

Hitler showed himself less clever and thoughtful in another instance. In October 1928[18] there was a conference in Munich to clarify a number of political questions, which were important in our conflicts with opponents but which the party leadership had not yet dealt with decisively. Probably because of Gregor Strasser's urging, the conference did not take the form of an order-receiving session but instead involved open discussion. Nor were the initial briefings delivered by people from the national headquarters or well-known and prominent party orators. On the contrary, the speakers were lesser known party-comrades with expert knowledge in various subjects. (I gave the lecture on "Party and Union" described earlier in Chapter 1.) Thus the external form and the approach of this conference was like any other customary party or club meeting where attempts are made to solve problems by an exchange of opinions.

[18] Actually in August. See Orlow, I, p. 139.

This conference in Munich was not a success. The reason was that though the participants spoke up freely and openly, they always waited in the end for a concluding statement from Hitler that was to bring the solution and the decision. That indicates the extent to which they had become accustomed to accepting his directives and decisions as correct and final. But Hitler did not fulfill their expectations. Once or twice he nodded or shook his head; most of the time he wore a bored or contemptuous expression; it was only very rarely that he opened his mouth. It was obvious that he expected nothing out of the "chatter." By this means he also achieved, after a while, an atmosphere in which all the participants were infused with a crippling apathy. The conference petered out in a feeling of purposelessness.

Surely it can be assumed that Hitler wanted it that way. It is also probable that he only permitted the conference to be held in order to use it to demonstrate the correctness of his opposition to all forms of democratic participation: Men do not want to decide for themselves and bear responsibility; they want to be given orders. They wait for orders. They are grateful for them. He succeeded in demonstrating this. In fact, he succeeded so well that I know of no conferences having been held after that with open expression. Even at the technical sessions of the Reich Party Convention of 1929, the sessions on organizational questions, union matters, press factors, and so on, there was no longer any true discussion. On the other hand, the pure negativism of Hitler's demonstration had a vexatious and exasperating effect upon the participants, with some exceptions. Even the most willing follower takes it amiss when his leader will not take him seriously.

But in general Hitler knew well how to avoid mistakes of this sort. After all, his great success with the masses depended on his art of addressing them—that is, of awakening in them the impression that they were being taken completely seriously. This was probably a very consciously developed art with him. It achieved its surety of method precisely because there was no inner conviction or sympathy involved. It was solely a matter of cool calculation. The high point of this art was reached at the Reich party conventions. I had personal experience only of the conventions held prior to the seizure of power, and at these Hitler had to operate within limitations imposed by financial factors. Still, even then, he showed himself as a protean wizard of constantly changing forms.

There is no doubt that as far as the intellectual preparation and plans are concerned, the party conventions were Hitler's personal work. Just as when the SA was being built up Hitler concerned himself with the tiniest details of the proposed uniforms down to what color should be used on the shirt emblems of regionally organized *Standarten,* so he let himself be taken up in the planning of the party conventions with such matters as what the seating order for the guests of honor should be and how the Congress Hall should be decorated with boughs and flowers. Here he followed not only the instinctive baroque preferences of a southeastern German; he was also fully clear and rational about its effect upon the masses. In this respect this fallen-away son of the Catholic Church had learned enough of its methods, tested over the centuries, and had no qualms about using them for his own purpose. To be sure, he did this in a way similar to the imitation of the English constitutional model described above. He only saw the external forms and not their spiritual causes, their inner motivation. Probably he also had no desire to see deeper at all since for a mass leader and mass propagandist it would destroy the necessary lack of consideration and inhibitions to recognize the diversity and many-sidedness of phenomena. It was quite characteristic that at the just mentioned conference in autumn 1928 he spoke passionately against the party using propaganda methods that would take into account regional and social differences. Later he was always very displeased when I explained the special stance of the party press in Hamburg by referring to the special mentality of Hamburgers. He did not want anything to be unique; he wanted everything homogenized.

Nevertheless, he was utterly capable of adapting himself to diverse people and groups. He would run down the steps of the Brown House to grasp Count Ernst zu Reventlow's[19] hands in both of his and greet him with "My dear Count!" while his voice tremoloed with benevolent friendship. Everyone watching this knew that Hitler's true feelings toward the Count had nothing to

[19] Ernst zu Reventlow was a leader of the rival Racial Freedom party recruited over to the Nazis in 1927 and thenceforth the second most prominent Nazi Reichstag delegate after Goering. The Brown House was the Nazi headquarters in Munich. On Reventlow see Chapter 10.

do with dear benevolence. He wept tears before the mutinous SA men in the Veterans' Hall in Berlin to lead them back to obedient loyalty. He could be a charming conversationalist who kissed the ladies' hands, a friendly uncle who gave children chocolates, a folksy fellow who shook the calloused hands of workingmen and peasants. Once again it was at the party conventions that Hitler reached the pinnacle of his promotional arts and efforts. When he met the trains at the Nuremberg railroad station and greeted party-comrades from all parts of the Reich, when he visited the quarters of the SA and the Hitler Youth in the middle of the night, when just a few hours later he saluted the marching SA columns with his arm raised for hours on end, when in addition to the big words of the convention speeches he also found kind little words for the women of the party, then he was celebrating true triumphs as the victorious, inexhaustible, omnipresent, solicitous *Führer*, comrade, fatherly friend and protector, future savior. To the simple party-comrade it must have appeared that the Hitler of the Nuremberg Conventions, who seemed never to sleep (and probably did sleep only for a few hours), was a miracle of ability and eager initiative. To be sure, the party-comrades did not know that Hitler had prepared himself for Nuremberg by a week-long vacation during which he was unavailable for any party business, that he had brought himself to the highest form, and that afterward he took another vacation. But even if they had known that their admiration would doubtless have been diminished only slightly.

Actually, it is one of the arts of the superior politician to bring himself into shape for extraordinary efforts by taking enough relaxation to gather his creative powers. Without doubt Hitler had mastered this art and applied it quite systematically for more than just the party conventions, as Hess repeatedly told me. His superior striking power and swiftness of decision at crucial moments, as opposed to that of his opponents, had this as not the least of its causes.

As far as his applied methods of propagandistic self-portrayal are concerned, perhaps one can take the view that they were of a rather superficial nature. Theoretically it was in fact not all that difficult to divine and fulfill the expectations that the Storm-trooper, the Hitler Youth, the Womenhood Leader held for the form of their *Führer*. But that they really were divined and fulfilled also required Hitler's superior capabilities. On the other hand, it remains an open question as to whether or not Hitler also had any understanding or intuitive capabilities when it came to more complicated and more profound forms of thought.

I know that Friedrich Wilhelm Heinz[20] tried to prevent the introduction of the "Heil Hitler" salute borrowed from fascism by characterizing it, in contrast to the Prussian service salute, as an expression of an extravagant exaltation that violated the bounds of spiritual discipline. But he was unsuccessful in this. On the one hand Hitler was basically against repealing decisions once he had made and announced them. Secondly, Heinz probably was not even able to get Hitler to understand what he was talking about.

What were the actual limits of his insight? There really were considerable gaps in his education even though he read many books, especially on history. On the other hand, despite these gaps he was smart enough to comprehend the hesitations and objections that came from balanced, judgmental reasoning. But perhaps he didn't want to comprehend them because in them he recognized impediments to his intentions, and this last was for him still an expression for his nonrational inspiration and sense of mission This opens up a glimpse into the domain of the demonic, which can neither be described nor explained by the use of reason.

In all this one must not forget, as I have already repeatedly emphasized, Hitler's way of masking and disguising himself. It made it difficult to fathom the essence of his nature.

There have been many reports of his elemental rages, of his "carpet-biting." Men have seen these outbursts as evidence of Hitler's pathological mentality. But were not these seizures of rage also partly play-acting in order to impress some people in the desired direction by awakening fear or cold shivers in them? In my presence Hitler never bit the carpet either literally or metaphorically. Even during the last conversation between him and me, in which he announced my expulsion from the party and I called him an Oriental despot, he was thoroughly controlled in bearing, gesture,

[20] Local leader in Hanover and editor of the Nazi newspaper there in 1928–29. He belonged to the northern, social revolutionary wing of Nazism and had been recruited out of the *Stahlhelm*.

and speech, though pale with fury. On the other hand he once cursed and raged like a whirling dervish before an assemblage of Hamburg political leaders (I recall it as having taken place between the first and second presidential campaigns of 1932): The functionaries were at fault for his defeat because they had believed too little, done too little, sacrificed too little. Admittedly, this glimpse of the cursing Hitler was not very pretty, and for a few of those present, not very impressive. The spittle literally dribbled out of the corners of Hitler's mouth over his jerking chin. But even on this occasion one cannot speak of an actual pathological attack of rage. A person truly trembling with fury loses control over speech; he can only stammer and spew out words without clearly intelligible connections. Hitler, on the contrary, never for a moment interrupted the best form of propaganda and psychological mass manipulation in his exhortation, though this must have demanded strong mental concentration. I believe that in this instance, too, Hitler was playing the role of a furious thunderbolt-hurling Wotan, rather than that he was driven into fury by bitter disappointment over a defeat of rather customary dimensions. Perhaps in the course of his act a goodly portion of Bavarian temperament led him to overdo it somewhat. But in any event, even on this occasion, he never lost his self-control, but rather stayed within the bounds of his self-chosen role.

There was only one time when I personally saw him step out of this role and that, actually, was not over political matters. During the presidential election I brought Hitler, in the "Atlantik" Hotel, a fresh copy of the morning newspaper with the speech he had delivered the night before printed in it. The situation I encountered there, amidst the plush and plaster of the oversized rooms, was like a scene from a French comedy movie. Already in the corridor I began to hear rhythmic cries, in various tones, of "M'soup! M'zoup!" Then, in the suite of rooms where Hitler and his entourage were staying I ran into the members of his entourage—adjutants, chauffeur, personal photographer, personal journalist—dancing around the vestibule with contemptuous grins on their faces and bouncing back and forth among them, like a football, the cry: "M'soup! Hizzoup! Another bowl of soup . . . he wants hizzoup!" It was apparent that this was about Hitler's breakfast soup. It was equally obvious that among his entourage this soup did not quite fit into the image that the followers of the *Führer* and would-be Reich president had made of him.

Hitler himself had thus unconsciously drawn a few corrective lines on the propaganda picture of the unshakable racial hero with no human weaknesses or defects. In the farthest room I found him, alone, hunched over a round table, looking melancholic and weary, slowly slurping his vegetable soup. I had to sit down next to him; the special edition I had brought along was shoved aside unnoticed (usually he always read them through very critically: ever since I had once, when our press stenographer could not keep up with him, filled out his speech from my own memory and in the process, as Hitler upon later reading the account maintained, corrected his sentences like a schoolmarm), and Hitler began to question me urgently and with obvious anxiety about my views on vegetarian diets.

Even though in those years I myself lived extensively on a vegetarian diet, I was so amazed at the unexpected questioning that at first I hardly knew how to answer. To be sure, Hitler had not seriously expected answers—in this respect he remained the same even at this moment—but instead immediately launched into a lengthy and detailed lecture on the views and objectives of the health food movement.

It was not particularly surprising that he employed in his lecture that sectarian one-sidedness that seeks mentally to overwhelm others rather than to convince them. But what did make the scene unforgettable for me was that he should so lightly, almost without inhibitions, betray his hypochondria expressly to me, with whom he had never had personal dealings but solely political ones. Since, in view of our relationship, I could not take this as the sign of a sudden outburst of confidence, I had to take it as evidence for the existence of an internal instability that found a rather unpleasant form of expression. This revelation of weakness in an unguarded moment threatened to expose the hidden truth: that his "strength" was only an overcompensation in quest of measureless power to shore up weakness, which is what almost always distinguishes the despot from the true ruler.

Beyond that, his hypochondria contained a second danger. Among the ills that Hitler listed as having led him to take up a health food diet (outbreaks of sweating, extreme nervousness, physical trembling, and so on) there were also stomach cramps.

These cramps he saw as the harbinger of cancer and thus he believed that he had only a few years left in which to complete his work.[21] "I have no time to wait!" he explained to me over his soup bowl. "If I had time, I would never have run for the presidency at all. The old man [Hindenburg] won't last much longer anyway. But I can't lose a single year more. I *must* come to power soon to be able to finish the gigantic tasks in the time left to me. I must! I must!" In the face of such a really sick mixture of death fears and missionary obsessions, any advice pressing for patience and moderation was bound to be ineffective. Whoever plans grandiosely but simultaneously expects to be dead at fifty cannot move slowly until the goal draws nearer of itself and the fruits ripen. He will leap forward; he will artificially force a premature ripening. It was this approach, this method, that was the basis of Hitler's political system, especially his foreign policy. Oppressed by a terror of time he wanted to compress a century's development into two decades.

With the words "gigantic tasks," Hitler had given himself the cue for a termination of the conversation. One could even say he called himself to order, which immediately showed itself in a changed posture, facial expression, and tone of voice. The depression was overcome; Hitler the human being had changed back into the *Führer*. He now began, without objective necessity but to prove himself before me and himself, to criticize the special edition of his speech and finally to get his entourage moving again. Telephone calls were announced, conferences and visits were planned, dictation taken down. The homely morning soup atmosphere had vanished as I left the hotel.

With the beginning of 1930 I once again came into more frequent contact with Hitler than in the two previous years. As editor of the Nazi newspaper in Hamburg I took part in various party conferences and beyond that often had other official reasons to visit Munich. Furthermore, certain assignments given me by Max Habermann either led me directly to Hitler or to his headquarters. This all occasioned numerous observations and personal conversations that provided considerable insight into Hitler's goals and

[21] Hitler's premonition of a premature death is independently corroborated in Joachim C. Fest's *The Face of the Third Reich* (New York, paperback, 1970), p. 79.

methods. But they could not produce a complete picture of his personality. Hence, the individual encounters will simply be described in their approximate order of occurrence.

Near the end of June 1930 the Nazi press was invited to a conference in Munich, which began with a tour of the recently completed "Brown House." On the second floor of the undoubtedly tastefully designed and furnished building there was a room, called the Hall of Senators, with twenty-four red-leather armchairs. This hall became the point of departure for the speech with which Hitler concluded the conference. It was a speech whose range and content made it one of the most impressive I had heard from Hitler.

He began by developing in clear, sharply drawn strokes, a picture of the external organization of the Catholic Church and its hierarchy. On the other hand he gave his audience only a vague or propagandistically distorted picture of the internal moral forces that had built the structure of Catholicism and that held it together—though this was surely noticed by only a few of those present. To what extent this distortion, which took cognizance only of the church's temporal power and authority but not its spiritual origins and objectives, derived from Hitler's rational consciousness and not from the custom of all fanatics of seeing in every matter only their own concerns, cannot be determined. Probably both factors were at work in Hitler at that time and were so intermingled that even had he striven with the greatest self-honesty to sort them out, he could not have interdistinguished. Beyond that, the purpose of his presentation was not historical accuracy but political application. The Nazi party was to be built upon the model of the Catholic Church. Upon a broad pediment of preachers and "political pastors" living and working among the people, the structure should ascend the leadership pyramid of the party from the county leaders over the Gauleiter to the senators and ultimately to the *Führer*-Pope. Hitler did not shrink from a comparison between Gauleiter and bishop, future senators and cardinals, no more than he was concerned about shifting the concepts of authority, obedience, and faith out of the realm of the spiritual into the temporal without even indicating how those concepts changed in the process. And apart from Count Reventlow, who whispered in my ear a mocking comment about "His Eminence and Holiness, Dr. Josef Goebbels," most of Hitler's audience seemed wholly taken in.

They did not remark that this presentation signified the victory of the "fascistic tendency" within the party and the ultimate exclusion of all democratic elements and methods. They did not notice that Hitler's speech threatened to justify the old accusation of Hitler's diehard racialist critics that he was "Romish," insofar as this accusation implied an intellectual and not just a financial or organizational dependency. In fact, his audience was so caught up by Hitler that, as I later established, most of them did not even take in his concluding words at all. Just as the average participant in a mass meeting ultimately can give no useful summary of the contents of the great speeches he has just heard, but only has the reverberations of the grand and shimmering words in his ears, so also the participants of that press conference, though there were quite clever and critical minds among them, were unable to repeat to me the content of Hitler's concluding sentences, which they had just heard and enthusiastically applauded.

These concluding sentences ran about as follows: "Since despite the incitings of some of our so-called friends [Hitler meant by this Arthur Dinter's followers[22]], I have no ambitions to become a religious reformer, I will not contest the claims of the Holy Father in Rome toward spiritual—or is it clerical?—infallibility in matters of faith. I don't understand much about this. But all the more do I believe that I understand politics. Therefore I hope that the Holy Father will also henceforth not contest my claims. And thus I now proclaim for myself and my successors in the leadership of the National Socialist German Workers Party the claim to political infallibility. I hope that the world will as rapidly and uncontestably accept this, as it has accepted the claim of the Holy Father."

As I said, Hitler's declaration was either not comprehended or not perceived at all by his listeners. It caused, therefore, no reverberations in the Nazi press at that time. That may be regretted by those who believe that a storm could have been aroused by an appeal to reason or a warning of the threatening danger. But in actuality the situation of the year 1930 was such that a publication of this bold self-exposure by Hitler would have prevented nothing and would not have hindered developments for a single day. The

---

[22] Krebs refers to Arthur Dinter, erstwhile Gauleiter of Thuringia, who wanted to establish a Germanic religion with himself as leader. He was expelled from the party in October 1928, after accusing Hitler of being a tool of the Roman Catholic Church. See Orlow, I, pp. 96 and 139–143.

revolutionary masses in the Nazi party would not have seen Hitler's claim for the infallibility of his political decisions as an individual one at all; not, therefore, as one indicating a claim toward personal despotism, but rather as as collective claim by the party as a whole for leadership and unlimited power. In my view Hitler understood with full clarity that his speech would have such an effect. In his perception of and contempt for humanity he saw both the need of mass man, grossly and crudely interpeted, to have his potentialities exaggerated, to be willing to identify himself with the demands of his spokesman, and to give his all for their fulfillment. And therefore I also do not believe, as was said to me then and partly still, even now, when I relate this episode, that Hitler was probably carried away by his own rhetoric into making such an immoderate proclamation. To my observation, Hitler very seldomly let himself be carried away into unreflected statements, even during excited flights of oratory. In general he always knew what he was saying. In the incident just described, that was undoubtedly the case. It was a speech before a closed circle, which gave no occasion for particular outbursts of temperament. The speech was so clearly and consciously conceived and constructed that it admitted no possibility of an arbitrary formulation of the concluding sentences. And finally, the conclusion given was also the logical culmination of everything said before. If the equation between the two hierarchies was to be valid, then the *Führer*-Popc must claim political infallibility. Hitler did claim it.[23]

After the elections of September 1930, wherein the great success of the Nazi party led to a considerable redistribution of political power in Germany, especially in the Reichstag, Habermann asked me to deliver an invitation from Reich Chancellor Brüning to Hitler, requesting a personal meeting. As to what Brüning intended by this invitation, Habermann gave me only some vague indications; I was supposed to acquire more intimate details from Minister Gottfried Treviranus,[24] whom I was to seek out for

[23] In a speech delivered in 1934, Goering used virtually the same words to claim "political infallibility" for Hitler, comparing him directly to the Pope. See Joachim Remak, *The Nazi Years: A Documentary History* (Englewood Cliffs, N.J., 1969), pp. 68 ff.

[24] Gottfried Treviranus, a leader of the Popular Conservatives; he narrowly escaped being killed by the Nazis in the purge of 1934, emigrated to the United States, and has since written his own account of the Brüning regime.

instructions in Berlin before traveling to Munich. In Berlin I met with Treviranus under rather adventuresome circumstances, designed to maintain secrecy, and received the promised explanation. Apart from a series of technical-organizational proposals for dates, cover names, cover addresses, and secret telephone numbers, I was told primarily that the proposed discussions were in no way aimed toward introducing coalition negotiations. On the contrary, the Reich Chancellor was initially concerned only with personally getting acquainted with the leader of the largest nationalist opposition party and perhaps learning something about his latest plans and intentions. If the impression turned out somewhat favorably, then Brüning hoped to try to obtain a certain amount of cooperation between the government and the opposition with regard to the forthcoming international negotiations on reparations and disarmament. These negotiations would undoubtedly be both long-winded and difficult. To bring them to a successful conclusion, it would be highly desirable if the opposition would strengthen the hand of the negotiators in Geneva, or wherever, by a clear and sharp exposition of the German demands and also by simultaneously exercising a certain amount of self-imposed restraint in the domestic political struggle. Furthermore, such restraint would be of advantage to the opposition in due course. After the last remnants of the evil heritage of Versailles had been done away with, a Hitler given power and responsibility could devote himself with full strength to the tasks of the future.

Whether these explanations of Treviranus fully and honestly reflected the ideas and intentions of the Reich Chancellor, or only his own,[25] may be set aside. Perhaps he only wanted to make the mission more attractive to me, since I was after all myself a member of the Nazi party; he could thus convert the bearer of the message into a promoter of its contents. In any event he urgently pressed me not to speak of these matters to Hitler but to confine myself to delivering the invitation and, should I be permitted, to advising its acceptance. Apart from that, he underlined, in taking leave from me, Brüning's urgent wish that the action be kept wholly secret. The meeting could only take place if Hitler gave binding assurances in this respect.

[25] They did not exactly, but in general are corroborated by Brüning's account in his posthumously published memoirs.

The meeting did take place, was repeated, and, as was reported to me, initially also led to some positive results. Brüning was said at first to have had a not unfavorable impression of Hitler. Hitler for his part, as I was told by Hess and Strasser, was so strongly taken by the appearance and behavior of the Reich Chancellor that he was only able to free himself from a feeling of inferiority toward Brüning by forming a hate complex against him. These feelings were gradually transferred to the entire party and produced peculiar imaginings about the hidden evil intentions of the Chancellor. These notions no longer had anything to do with politics; rather they fit into the category of mass delusions in which phantoms float about—sometimes called the Junkers, the Militarists, the Ruhr Barons and other times the Jews, the Jesuits, the Freemasons. Brüning, too, became such a phantom, whose defeat appeared the precondition for the final victory. *Führer* and follower in the Nazi party were united in this attitude. Peculiarly, the elements and beginnings of this were already recognizable in the conversation that I had with Hitler in connection with the delivery of the Chancellor's invitation.

In Munich I did not find Hitler, nor were Strasser and Hess there. Philip Bouhler,[26] who appeared after I had waited a while, did not want to reveal where Hitler could be found (he was resting up from the exertions of the election campaign). As to the message, to whose contents I only alluded at first, he rather arrogantly belittled both its significance and the danger of committing it to paper. He suggested that the Reich Chancellor ought to write a letter and convey his requests to the "boss" that way. But at my urging he finally telephoned Hess in his apartment and informed him of my arrival and my request. Hess came very quickly to the headquarters, just as quickly grasped the significance of the invitation, and was only visibly disappointed that it did not contain an offer for a coalition. Obviously, the party headquarters at that moment would have been ready to agree to such an offer. Bouhler was instructed to drive me to Hitler, while Hess, in the interim, would report our impending arrival.

Bouhler first told me where we were going after we had been on our way through the autumn landscape for more than an hour. In

[26] Executive secretary of the NSDAP, a self-effacing bureaucrat. Krebs describes him in detail in Chapter 10.

doing so he emphasized expressly that the house on Obersalzburg belonged neither to Hitler personally nor to the party, but had been placed at Hitler's disposal by a North German family so that he could have a hideaway. There could be no question, therefore, of some sort of corruption on the model of other party big shots. And, in fact, the mountain house at that time was still a simple structure both in size and furnishings without any sort of ostentation, yet fitted out with solid taste.

Hitler received us on a little terrace in front of the house accompanied by his two German shepherd dogs. In a sort of hall, which formed the main room of the house, a tea had been laid. There, also, we met the two ladies who kept house for him. Hitler introduced them to us as his aunt and his niece,[27] which as far as the girl is concerned sounded a bit improbable. According to proper contemporary usage he should have said "cousin." Both women were tall and stately, true Alpine types of the best breed. They bore hardly any resemblance to Hitler; on a basis of pure physiognomy, they made a much better human impression.

Immediately after greeting me, Hitler had me relay the contents of my message without expressing himself about it. Also during our half-hour at the tea table the talk was not of the invitation but of organizational matters and the new SA insignia. In the course of this it became apparent how much Hitler fussed over the smallest details and kept decisions in his own hands. During the conversation he repeatedly muttered: "That Pfeffer[28] should ask! . . . When will that Pfeffer finally learn that he can't do things on his own hook. . . . Basically it doesn't matter how it's done, but they mustn't get the idea that they can do anything they want!"

I myself took no part in this, which pleased me considerably in view of the many meals I had missed in the last forty-eight hours. Hitler and Bouhler ate little; what was noticeable about Bouhler was that as often as he was spoken to, or spoke himself, he made a

[27] Angela Raubal, Hitler's widowed half-sister, and her daughter, Geli, who became Hitler's mistress. Geli Raubal committed suicide in September 1931, causing a scandal and a great emotional shock to Hitler. See Alan Bullock, *Hitler, A Study in Tyranny*, rev. ed. (New York, 1964), pp. 134 and 393 ff. For a photograph of her see Frederic V. Grunfeld, *The Hitler File: A Social History of Germany and the Nazis, 1918–1945* (New York, 1974), p. 130.

[28] Franz Pfeffer von Salomon, SA commander, who was replaced about this time by Ernst Roehm. Pfeffer is described in Chapter 10.

respectful little bow. At the end of the tea Hitler asked me how I happened to be playing mailman for Herr Brüning. I explained the matter to him, to which he made no reply. But I got the clear impression that his old mistrust of me had become greater. Also, following this I was sent into an adjoining room with his niece, because Hitler, as he said, wished to think the situation over. That he surely did; he undoubtedly also had several long telephone conversations with Munich, as I could clearly hear.

My attempts at conducting a real conversation with the companion assigned to me were unsuccessful as long as I tried to talk about politics and party matters. The young girl gave evasive or annoyed answers. She first opened up and became natural and jolly when we discovered our mutual appreciation for art, music, and the theater. She herself was a music student and was shortly to take her final examination. Allegedly because she failed that examination she committed suicide a few months later. According to my own personal impression of this life-loving young human being I never found this official party explanation very believable. Equally unconvincing, though, was Otto Strasser's report, which made out of Geli Raubal a dumb and frivolous thing who ultimately found no way out of her various love affairs except through death. Personally I assume that Hitler's relationship with his "niece" was closer than that usual between relatives and that its demands were ultimately more than the girl was equal to.

After about an hour, Bouhler called me back into the main room again. Hitler had not yet come to a decision, paced uneasily about the room, and looked, with his lock of hair hanging over his wrinkled forehead and suddenly puffy face, as though he had just finished some severely strenuous activity or extravagant debauchery. Bouhler sat at the window with an expression suggesting that he hadn't a clue and was depressed about it; he shot me angry glances because it was my message that had reduced the "boss" to such confusion. Finally Hitler stopped, turned to me, and did what he seldom had done; he asked me: "What do you think? Should I accept the invitation or not?"

I did not dare to answer with a simple "yes," for fear that Hitler would then do the exact opposite. So at first I tried to evade the question by saying that I was only the mailman and had no opinion on the matter. Hitler would not allow me to escape via this classical citation. Thereupon I clothed my answer in a conditional sentence: If he negotiated with Alfred Hugenberg,[29] he could also negotiate with Brüning.

From this sentence Hitler heard at first and primarily only the criticism. In a fervent voice, therefore, he praised Hugenberg as an outstanding economic leader and a true nationalist who already had had dealings with him, Hitler, when the Nazi party was small and insignificant. Now, to be sure, all the others came running, not just rich Germans, but Americans, Frenchmen, even Jews. Then Hitler asked me what I had against Hugenberg. When I expressed doubts about the good nationalist attitude of Hugenberg because it had no culmination in social attitudes, Hitler caught me up: "Socialism! What is Socialism, then? When the people have enough to eat and their pleasure, then they have their Socialism. That's just what Hugenberg thinks!" My objection that it had less to do with food and pleasure than with the development and uplifting of the talented and healthy hereditary core of the nation, he dismissed with a few remarks about trade union ideology. He said no more about Brüning's invitation but sent me back into the adjoining room again. This time I had the feeling that I was being sent away above all as an expression of Hitler's anger over my remarks and to make me clearly conscious of my role as "just the mailman."

After the shortest time, Bouhler brought me back. Hitler now stood in the middle of the room with his arms folded; he had obviously stepped out of his previous uncertainty and into the role and self-consciousness of the future statesman. "Tell Minister Treviranus," he declared, "that I have determined to accept the Reich Chancellor's invitation. In a short while I will be negotiating with the French minister-president or with Stalin. So I can also deal with Herr Brüning!"

In this declaration every word, in my opinion, had been calculated: whether or not to use the word "Herr," the inclusion of

---

[29] Alfred Hugenberg, Germany's greatest newspaper magnate, was the reactionary leader of the DNVP. He had collaborated with Hitler in the Young Plan plebiscite, as described above, and within a year of the incident described here was to join Hitler in the Harzburg Front, a confederation of rightist parties. When Hitler took office in 1933 it was actually in coalition with Hugenberg's party.

Brüning among the leaders of foreign states that for Hitler were primarily "enemy" states.

In conclusion, Hitler expressed a few requests about the way the planned meeting was to occur. Their chief purpose was to make certain that I, or the DHV, would be excluded from any further negotiations. Then Bouhler and I were dismissed and drove back to Munich in the late evening hours.

In connection with the Pfeffer affair, I again came into contact with Hitler. Even before the end of my visit to Hitler in Berchtesgaden, I had dictated an affidavit for Hess, Walter Buch,[30] and Franz Schwarz concerning the payment of a 30,000-mark election contribution from the DHV for Albert Forster's campaign. The money had been given to Captain Pfeffer, but it had never been passed on by him to the party treasury. Whether he used it for SA purposes or for something else I never found out. Following my accusations, Pfeffer was demoted from the leadership of the SA to the Reich quartermaster's store and was generally removed from the upper echelons, but formal proceedings against him were never initiated. Beyond that, it remained unclear whether the measures taken were actually a result of the money matter or stemmed from Pfeffer's questionable attitude in the Stennes-Goebbels conflict.[31] In any case the DHV leadership wanted the question of the use of its contribution clarified. Therefore, on my next trip to Munich I asked Hess what had become of the matter. Hess shrugged his shoulders and went into Hitler's office. After a few minutes I was summoned to follow him. Hitler received me in the worst possible mood. He would not let himself be pressured by the DHV, he declared. He had the impression that the 30,000 marks was given less as an election contribution than to incite strife and disunity.

---

[30] Major Walter Buch was head of the *Uschla*, the internal party court. Hess and Schwarz were, as will be recalled, respectively, deputy leader and treasurer of the Nazi party. Buch is further described in Chapter 10.

[31] Shortly before the September 1930 elections there was a mutiny of the SA in Berlin caused by disagreement over financial questions between Walter Stennes, the SA leader for Berlin and East Germany, and Goebbels, the party's Gauleiter of Berlin. Hitler had to intervene locally, and personally, by assuming the office of commander of the SA (*Osaf*). The following spring Stennes rebelled outright against Hitler and was expelled from the party. See Orlow, I, pp. 210–12 and 217–20. The sequence of events indicates that Krebs' accusation against Pfeffer of money mismanagement played no role at all in Pfeffer's demotion, despite the chronological proximity of the two events.

He accused me of having lent myself, as a member of the party, to a purpose harmful to the party. To my objection that in my view Pfeffer's failure to deliver the money was more harmful to the party than my demand for cleanliness, Hitler responded that I should spare him such petty bourgeois views. What was 30,000 marks to the filthy rich DHV? Did anyone believe that for such a trifle he would let himself be separated from a true comrade-in-arms who daily risked his life for him? The marshals of Napoleon had received duchies for their services!

That Hitler should cite Napoleon might be taken as a sign of his bad conscience, which needed to call upon a great name for self-justification. But at the same time the phrase "marshals of Napoleon" reveals with great clarity Hitler's image-world in those months.

Yet a third time I heard from Hitler a sentence that served equally his self-enhancement and testified to the images—wishful visions, daydreams—that determined his thoughts and actions. In autumn 1931 I was supposed to bring Hitler a message from Captain Erhardt, which was primarily concerned with the possibility of a Franco-German understanding. What Erhardt intended with his message I did not completely understand. It is irrelevant, anyway, since Hitler hardly heard me out on the grounds that since Erhardt was one of his worst enemies his sole goal was to injure Hitler. What is relevant, however, was that on this occasion I was witness to a conversation between Hitler and SA Chief of Staff Roehm.

I was not present for the beginning of the conversation, but from its further course it could be concluded that Hitler's request for closer collaboration between the SA-SS and the army had been turned down by the army high command. In any event, Hitler, who was rather upset, unloaded onto the army leadership and its conception of professional soldiers in a small highly mobile professional army, such uncomplimentary terms as idiots, boneheads, sillies, traitors, and so on. Also Hans von Seecket[32] received an

[32] General Hans von Seeckt was chief of the general staff, 1919–26, architect of Weimar's 100,000-man professional army, and a proponent of the army's political neutrality—in accordance with which he refused to support Hitler in the Munich Putsch of 1923 and thus was instrumental in its failure. See the chapter on him in Gordon Craig's *Politics of the Prussian Army, 1656–1945* (New York, paperback, 1964), p. 382 ff.

equally bad testimonial, both politically and militarily, whereby it became clear that Hitler had neither forgotten nor forgiven Seecket's behavior on November 9, 1923.

In front of Hitler there hung a huge map of Europe on which he sought to demonstrate, with his index finger nervously pointing here and there, that a mass era naturally also required mass armies, that soldiers must not become toys for super-shrewd general-staffers, that limiting oneself to a small professional army meant limiting oneself to a petty, cowardly, narrowly confined foreign policy. In speaking, Hitler was gripped by a sort of ecstasy: His exegesis became prophecy: "One day we shall command colossal spaces, shall have to be concerned with the security of colossal areas. Can that be done with a hundred thousand men? With three hundred thousand men? *Millions* will we mobilize! . . ."

In contrast to other utterances and speeches of Hitler, which only seemed improvised but actually were well thought out and prepared, this time I had the impression of a direct outburst of true conviction and passion. The rejection from the army high command had not only hurt and angered Hitler, it had shaken his self-image, in its sensitive insecurity. To restore this self-image, it was not enough for him to refute the opposition objectively and establish a logical basis for his own opinion; no, he had to dream himself into the position of the great men of power, the world movers of historical significance. Only thus could he become fully conscious of the difference between his own greatness and the nothingness of the "dwarfs" opposing him. He needed this image in order to dull or shout down his own fear. Like so many tyrants, for Hitler, too, the words and deeds of his delusions of grandeur were defense mechanisms against the fear that he was, in the last analysis, unequal to his self-chosen tasks. To be a true ruler one must be born for it and singled out. Surely Hitler was no born ruler, no matter how fanatically he tried to convince himself of it or, with the wild and bloody deeds of a Tamerlane, tried to make himself one.

It must be remarked that Roehm by no means agreed compliantly and without reservation with the views of his lord and master. Though Hitler became increasingly agitated, Roehm continued to advance his opposing opinion calmly, definitely, and with objective emphasis. I was able to observe Roehm closely only twice; both times the impression was not unfavorable. He was a capable man, at least in his own area of expertise, and in his external bearing he was no disgrace to the school of the officer corps. Furthermore, he was the only one I know of in the upper echelon of the Nazi party with whom Hitler was on a "*Du*" basis.[33] This relationship stemmed, so far as I have been told, from the beginnings of the movement when Roehm was still liaison officer in the Munich Army Corps District and gave more or less binding directives to the "patriotic associations." Hitler also began his political career after 1918 as "special propaganda leader" in the remnants of the old army while it was being changed into the cadre-army, and thus took orders from Roehm. To me it seems probable that it was primarily this that cost Roehm his head on June 30, 1934. It was a heavy burden for Hitler that anyone was living who knew only too well about Hitler's first tottering ventures into politics. And when this person then also developed political ambitions, he was forfeiting his right to live.

This leads me to believe that the "mystery" of June 30, 1934,[34] can be solved without great difficulty simply by employing psychological considerations. Seen from Hitler's viewpoint, it was not so important whether a conspiracy against him actually existed. But it was of existential importance to Hitler that there existed people who did not view him as the culmination of the German revolution and the infallible leader into the glorious future. Undoubtedly many of the SA leaders were people of this sort: either because, like Roehm, they had been looking behind the scenes too long, or because they were used to looking at everything from a different viewpoint and their experience and instincts filled them with skepticism and mistrust. Especially the former soldiers and Free Corps leaders among them frequently possessed amazingly keen insights into people and the interconnection of events. This was true despite their lack of bourgeois virtues and skills and their inclination to depravity.

Thus, they also recognized the dangers posed for the future by

---

[33] The familiar form of address, as opposed to the formal, respectful "*Sie*."

[34] On this date Hitler murdered Roehm and many of the other top leaders of the Stormtroopers, on the spurious grounds that they were planning a Putsch against him.

the "petty bourgeois Babbitts run amok" much more quickly and clearly than most of Germany's professional politicians. To be sure, their nihilistic frivolity and indifference kept them from drawing the necessary conclusions from their perception. They criticized, mocked, and at most played a bit at conspiracy and private revolution in their own command areas until they stood before the rifles of the firing squads. Somehow they too were what they fought and cursed at in others: spiritually rootless. Thus they lacked what the "petty bourgeois run amok" had in excess—a realistic and crudely grasping will to power. They talked about the breakneck methods of modern revolutions; they were splendid theoreticians of civil war and, if they received the necessary orders, preeminent practitioners of it. But in the decisive moment it was Hitler who shot first, and the "political soldiers" became the victims of the civilians.

Even prior to 1933 Hitler liked to talk about his calculations and plans, which would inevitably assure victory for the party. I cannot say whether he himself believed these assertions or only meant them as propaganda. In any event, I observed little in Hitler of premeditated planning and calculation. He was a tactician but not a strategist of political struggle, with a possible exception in the area of propaganda. Yet even in propaganda it was less long-range goals that led to success than it was day-to-day brilliant inspirations plus the constant repetition of basic themes. Suppleness, quickness of response, ruthlessness, and a daredevil approach were the essence of Hitlerian politics, to which must be added, despite all his Bohemianism, a goodly portion of pedantry. What was totally lacking were truly creative ideas and the well-thought-out preparation for and formulation of problems. On the other hand, Hitler possessed an amazing perspicuity for all factors in his environment which he could employ, with some hocus-pocus, for his own purposes and objectives. Where he sensed that something could be harnessed and driven for his own needs, he could also force himself into sustained receptivity. Thus I repeatedly had to supply him with detailed descriptions of the organizational structures, the leadership techniques, the financial system, and the cultural work and vacation excursions of the DHV. What interested him especially were the professional contests developed by the DHV, whose purpose in educating highly qualified specialists seemed to accord with Hitler's own ideas. He also approved of the vigorous construction program of the union, which aimed toward building a meeting hall for white-collar workers in every major city. He showed understanding for the idea behind this: that the association should have a visible symbol expressed in its buildings.

The publishing activities at the DHV also impressed Hitler considerably, as I discovered during our various conversations. To be sure, he saw their significance primarily in the creation of a power position for cultural measures, a counter to the great influence of the Jews in the Weimar era upon the publishing business. As far as the actual publications of the DHV press were concerned, Hitler took cognizance only of the political and military literature. The artistic and scholarly publications, on the other hand, especially those of the Langen-Müller and Filser publishing houses, by no means coincided with the views of Hitler and the Nazi party. This immediately became apparent after the seizure of power through the open and covert measures taken against the editors and a number of prominent authors such as Grimm, Stapel, Holbenheyer, and so on. What was bothersome here were the Christian, philosophical, problematic, esthetic elements; in other words, anything that did not lend itself to an immediately applicable propaganda (that is, whatever was not portrayable in back-white terms). Of Hans Grimm's great novel *Volk ohne Raum* (*People without Space*),[35] Hess once remarked contemptuously that the best thing about it was the title. Since Hess rarely uttered such judgments without authorization, it may be assumed that Hitler thought the same, if the judgment did not actually derive from Hitler himself.

Hess, by the way, always had to take careful notes, at Hitler's nod, whenever we engaged in such informative discussions. I am convinced that they ultimately found employment, though there is no way to prove it. But some things in the German Labor Front are clearly recognizable as having been based on the DHV model, such as the Strength-through-Joy excursions, professional contests, and after-hours assemblies.[36]

[35] On this novel see Francis L. Carsten, " 'Volk ohne Raum.' A Note on Hans Grimm," *Journal of Contemporary History*, Vol. II, No. 2 (1967), pp. 221–227.

[36] Others have seen the "Strength-through-Joy" organization as modeled on Mussolini's "Doppo Lavoro" movement.

Nevertheless, in my opinion, Hitler had no plan, no clear concept of the objective he was working toward and the path he would tread but rather only visions. In February 1933 he summoned Max Habermann and tried to persuade him to undertake a peace mission to the Christian Trade Unions of France. On this occasion he stated that he planned to visit Stalin on the eve of the forthcoming Reichstag elections. From Moscow there should issue forth a peace manifesto to the world. The nations would learn that it was not the rule of the so-called dictators but rather that of the anonymous forces in the democracies that caused misery, distress, anarchy, and war. "We will provide Europe with a century of peace," he told Habermann. And Habermann had the impression that at least at that moment Hitler meant it sincerely.

To me it seems that this episode substantiates my analysis. For Hitler, vastly different, even totally opposing options were open, because his goal was a purely egoistic one without any fixed objective substance. But it was precisely that which put him in a position to seize every possibility with swiftly striking force and smash the surprised opponent from the battlefield. Of course he was also a master of deception, but in my opinion only within limits sharply defined by time. To mount a major political campaign requiring long-range perseverance, such as was done by Metternich, Talleyrand, Disraeli, or even Bismarck, was beyond Hitler's competence.

For this assertion there is a plentitude of evidence, even from the years prior to 1933. Hitler's inability to think constructively, comprehensively, and authoritatively over longer periods of time emerged primarily before 1933 in the sometimes grotesque confusion of varied and contradictory opinions inside the party. Even those who had little use for programs and opposed any premature fixing of the party's development through rigid, possibly written, individual demands were convinced of the necessity of at least sketching an outline of the movement's path and objectives. But whenever this conviction led to a serious attempt at such an effort, it ran into disagreement and opposition from Hitler.

Naturally, what initially determined Hitler's attitude in this instance, too, was the tactician's fear of undesirable and hasty commitments. However, this fear was not always because there existed some secret plans that had to be kept from the public for the moment, but often because there were no plans on hand, and even because of an inability to create them.

In the year 1931 I had a discussion with Rudolf Hess about the future of the Reichstag and the states' parliaments after the "total" victory of the party. Hess was unable to give me any answer to the question of what was to become of these institutions and what a Nazi constitution would look like. "For a few years there won't be any elections," he opined; "the Communist party will naturally be outlawed! The power of the government must be strengthened." He did not speak of the creation of a pure dictatorship. I am convinced that he was not silent in order to hide intentions of this sort but rather that the party leadership had no concrete constitutional plans. For example, Hess concluded the conversation with something like the following words: "In the decisive moment the correct idea will come to the Führer. Providence has always inspired him to do the right thing!"

Trust in Providence, inspiration, instinct—that was doubtless also Hitler's conception of his own task, because he did not feel equal to the conscious intellectual creation of a systematic formulation. That did not exclude, as already suggested, Hitler's zealous willingness to learn, his hunger for education. But to begin with he only retained lessons that appeared useful to him in strengthening opinions he already held, and secondly his quest for knowledge was limited to certain individual areas: political biographies, historical descriptions of a general nature, miltary history, defense policy, and so on.

Social and economic policy were scarcely of interest to him. When Hans Bechly and Max Habermann from the DHV wanted to discuss with Hitler the future of the unions and a few major problems in social policy they discovered that he knew pitifully little about even the basic facts. His ignorance in the area of economic policy led to his making Dr. Wagener the economic expert for the Nazi party on the basis of their having shared a fortnight's auto trip through Thuringia. That this man's views had nothing, and I mean absolutely nothing, to do with national socialism, was something that escaped Hitler despite his instinct and "unerring inspiration."

Of course a politician cannot be a specialist in all areas of knowledge. But he should have a general overview that will permit him to employ forces intelligently and to assess his own and oppositional strengths. Hitler possessed no such overview. Every attempt within the party to arrive at a theoretically clear formulation of the party's goals ran aground on this deficiency. To some extent a substitute was found in Hitler's tactical and propagandistic skills. Probably the party would have collapsed because of the vagueness of its goals very early except that it was rescued by a favorable situation, the stupidity of its opponents, and the stubbornness of the passionately enthusiastic masses once they had been set in motion.

From autumn 1930 on, Hitler's inability to make long-range strategic plans, even in the area of practical politics—excepting the field of mass propaganda action—became noticeable with increasing frequency and force. With his sizable Reichstag delegation and his rapidly growing representation in the states' legislatures Hitler could no longer avoid every concrete political decision, as he had previously done. Positions had to be taken on legislative proposals, cabinet formations, party alliances, and so on. Anyone with even a modicum of inside knowledge of conditions in the Brown House saw with amazement and shock the confusion and uncertainty that this necessity engendered for Hitler and most of his associates in the upper echelon. It is only a slight exaggeration to say that for the party leadership the entire period from September 1930 to January 1933 consisted of a perpetual crisis of confidence, and above all self-confidence, which was hidden from the general public and from themselves only by increasingly wild pounding on the big propaganda drums. After the Stennes Putsch the crisis also extended to the party collectively. As far as the "old fighters" were concerned, the Nazis who were pursuing ideals rather than personal advantage, strong doubts grew as to whether victory could still be won, and if won, whether it would be worth the sacrifices made. In the summer of 1932 the crisis of confidence reached its high point. I am convinced that a clever and courageous man could, at that time, have saved the Reich from the growing danger of Nazism by removing the incompetent leaders and winning over the men of goodwill in the party for a true national and social policy. Naturally, such a man would have had to make swift decisions and take hard, and perhaps also dangerous, measures. Furthermore, the decisions and measures would have had to derive from the clear insight that a revolutionary situation can only be mastered by combining the forces struggling with and against each other into a new current. Such a man was not there in the decisive months of 1932–33.

Reich Chancellor Brüning, who was the most likely one to accomplish such a task, though in my opinion even he lacked a proper understanding of the subsurface volcanic forces of Nazism and its leader—the imponderables—was toppled from office at the worst possible moment. Though Kurt von Schleicher and Franz von Papen may have been masters of the political salons and conference rooms in which, since 1920, the governments of the Weimar Republic had been managed, they were failures in the face of the furious revolutionary national movement and the wild will to power of its popular tribunes. Their wire-pulling tricks were inadequate. Thus, the hour of the great internal weakness of the party and the readiness of many subleaders to join Gregor Strasser and leave Hitler remained unused.

Hitler's uncertainty when faced with the problems and tasks posed by the election victory of September 1930 has already been mentioned. His reaction to Brüning's invitation demonstrates clearly how little he had thought about what political measures he ought to take next.

When the great German banks collapsed in the summer of 1931,[37] this led to a full scale alarm in the Brown House. The situation was totally misread; they expected Brüning's government to collapse immediately and they prepared themselves for the inheritance. That the Reich Chancellor could only be pleased by the effect the bank crisis would have on his policy of pushing for an end to reparations, that possibly he might even have contributed to the dramatization of the incident, such considerations did not even distantly dawn upon the party leadership.

During those days I had no conversations with Hitler, but only with Rosenberg and Hess. It was my experience, however, that

[37] The depression caused a run on the major banks in June 1931 and a government-declared bank holiday. After a few days the government guaranteed deposits and reopened the banks. Though this contributed to the "Hoover Moratorium" on international debt payments (including reparations), it was no more a fatal crisis than a similar occurrence in the United States two years later. See Chapter 1.

these two would have expressed no views, in such a tense situation, except those that reflected Hitler's in every essential point. The views they did express were grotesquely naïve; they imposed upon political events unreal, phantasmagoric imaginings, fantasies out of detective stories or spy thrillers. They made it clear that for them all the anti-Semitic, anti-Jesuit, anti-Masonic accusations were not propagandistic exaggerations but reflections of a political delusion that they had convinced themselves was reality itself. Brüning as the path-breaker of communism for the benefit of the Catholic Church, which in the distant future, after the eradication of Prussian Protestantism, would become heir to the communist dictatorship—whoever submitted to such contorted paths of thought was living outside the world of actuality and knew nothing of really essential matters. But in the realm of politics such ignorance ruled by delusion signified and was equivalent to an inability to act on the basis of calculated planning.

Thus in the Brown House no one knew what to do other than to wait to see if someone else would do something. But since Brüning neither voluntarily resigned nor was forced to resign by someone else, the trumpets that had so vigorously sounded the attack in the Nazi press squeaked into silence again. This whole petering out of the event resembles very much the bitter description given by Friedrich Wilhelm Heinz, in his book *Sprengstoff*, of the SA demonstration of May 1, 1923: "Hitler fastened on his helmet! . . . He took his helmet off . . . He put it on again . . . He took it off again . . . He marched home." Probably Hitler would have marched home again on January 30, 1933,[38] if Papen and his friends had not smoothed the way for him.

When, on the other hand, after eight or nine years, Hitler marched, not home but into Poland, France, and Russia, he did it out of the same internal situation, the same underestimation of the enemy's strength and overestimation of his own, which led him to misunderstand completely the real and actual situation. A few days before the silent mobilization of August 1939 Hitler spoke in Hamburg to a closed group of party officials and higher civil officials. He assured them that there could be no question of a real threat of war. Perhaps it would go so far as a punitive expedition

[38] Date of Hitler's appointment as Reich Chancellor.

against Poland, if that country was foolish enough to reject the demand for a reincorporation of Danzig. But a conflict with England and France was completely impossible. Neither country had proper armaments: One's was too weak, the other's too old. Above all, both nations were defeatist with leaders who were decadent through and through.

Hitler similarly had no plans or proposals for the Reich presidential elections. He was hoping that Hindenburg would die and when this hope was not fulfilled he let Dr. Goebbels force him into the role of a candidate, a role for which he had undoubtedly not originally planned. After his defeat in the first election a conference of press and propaganda specialists was called for on March 31, 1932, in the Kaiserhof Hotel, in Berlin. At this conference I was once again to experience all of Hitler's superior and weak qualities.

The mood of the conference participants was not good. After all, they were the intellectuals of the party and they could measure the significance of the defeat better than the ordinary SA man or party member. Beyond that, on the basis of their activities, they were well aware of the signs of what in some respects could be called a crisis inside the party and had themselves partly been infected with the counter ideas and slogans of the "Black Front,"[39] the Stennes-Opposition, and the "resistance circle." The obtrusive, gilded-plaster ostentation of the hotel in which Hitler had established his Berlin headquarters also engendered considerable vexation, which came out in contemptuous and rebellious words. Never before had I heard so much oppositional spirit, so openly expressed—not even the *Führer*'s person was immune.

Hitler immediately detected this mood among the assemblage and met it with his tested tricks of rhetoric, gesture, and dramatics. Entering the conference hall with a springy step and a face shining with self-confidence, he called out special greetings to a number of the participants: "*Heil* Franconia! *Heil* Ruhr! *Heil* Brunswick! *Heil* Kurmark!" Just with this entry he destroyed part of the displeasure and above all dissolved the unity of mistrust, doubt, and secret anger by winning over those he had just singled out for special honor. In their expressions and their whole attitudes one could

[39] Otto Strasser's anti-Hitler Nazi movement.

already discern how they had begun to feel ashamed of their previous feelings of aversion. Then Hitler delivered a speech that was a real masterpiece.

He began by describing the just completed election campaign and the motives that had led him to become a candidate. This description involved little that was news until he came to the assertion that his candidacy was something planned and prepared for months in advance. Since this assertion brought a general shaking of heads in response—all the press people knew the circular telegram of the party headquarters: "Dr. Goebbels proclaimed Hitler's candidacy for the office of Reich President in the *Sportpalast* without his knowledge or permission"—Hitler did not dwell on this but instead sought the approval and applause of his audience by extravagant praise for the determination and self-sacrifice shown by all elements in the party and its leaders in this the most gigantic election campaign of all times. He reminded them of the high points of the campaign, mass meetings from Königsberg to Ulm and again called upon some of those present as witnesses of the "victories" that they had fought for together—Napoleon before the veterans of Marengo, Austerlitz, Jena!

Then his intonation changed. After everything had been so well prepared and so promisingly begun, the reasons must now be found for the undoubted failure. The first cause Hitler saw in the person of his opponent. The ancient Hindenburg had become, so Hitler argued, a symbol to the German people. To destroy symbols could be ruinous for the destroyer. That is why the party had put certain limits upon itself in combating Hindenburg. As for himself, to be sure, Hitler proved by a series of drastic and cynical remarks how far he was removed from any reverence for symbols. For the runoff election campaign he supplied the following slogan: Only Hindenburg the man and ex-soldier will be spared; but Hindenburg the politician will be ruthlessly attacked.

A second cause Hitler saw in the failure of the intermediate and lower levels of the party. In contrast to the smirking flattery of his introductory sentences Hitler now insisted that only the decisions and actions of the party leadership were correct and had promised success. The individual elements of the party, on the other hand, the Gaue, the Local Groups, NSBO cells, Women's groups, and so on, let him down to a shameful extent. Everything that they did was stupid, petty-bourgeois, uninspired, small-time, clumsy, and therefore, of necessity, also useless. The party had left him, Hitler, in the lurch!

With these immoderately violent and unjustified accusations Hitler obviously wanted to achieve three things. The last remnants of any existing criticism of his decision to be a candidate in the runoff election, despite the defeat just suffered, were to be erradicated. His audience was to be so morally dispatched that they would never again feel justified in criticizing. And thirdly, they should have only one desire left: to make amends in the coming weeks by giving the last ounce of their strength and will for the party. It was my impression that Hitler achieved this goal with about two-thirds to three-quarters of the conference participants.

In the third part of his speech Hitler devoted himself to the Nazi press. Like all great orators he had little regard for the press. Apart from that, the Nazi press people had chiefly irritated him in past years by clinging so long to the bourgeois prejudice that one not only ought to have his own opinion but also ought to express it. The assembled press representatives were, therefore, extremely surprised when Hitler chided them not for taking journalistic excursions, but for being boring, uniform, unindependent, and tepidly passionless. The amazement turned into uneasiness when Hitler's attacks upon the party press culminated in the demand that the party press should incite the masses to revolutionary deeds.

Enough SA men, he said in essence, had been struck down in recent months and what had been made of their deaths? They had buried them with fife and drums, and the party's little newssheets had written bloated and plaintive sermons about them. Why didn't they exhibit the dead, with their smashed skulls and bloody knife-torn shirts, to the people—in the show windows of the party newspapers? Why hadn't these newspapers themselves drummed the people to uproar around the stretchers of the dead, whipped them into an uprising against the murderers and their backers, instead of delivering themselves of ridiculous political sophistries? The sailors on the cruiser *Potëmkin* turned bad grub into a revolution; but we were unable to take the death of comrades and turn it into a national struggle for liberation.

As far as I can recall not one of those present applauded this exposition. Most of them probably felt repelled by the suggestion that they should make political capital in this way out of the death of their comrades.

A few weeks later I had my last personal meeting with Hitler. The political situation had again undergone a basic change. Hindenburg had won the runoff election, too. Since the president's disinclination to accept the "Bohemian corporal" as Reich Chancellor had only increased as a consequence of the violent Nazi attacks during the election campaign, Hitler was going to have to seek his path to power through back doors. Negotiations began with the different groups, political circles, and individuals who for years had participated in the formation of the Weimar Republic's governments from behind the scenes. Among those individuals was General Kurt von Schleicher, who replaced General Wilhelm Groener as minister of war.

In the *Hamburger Tageblatt,* whose editors knew nothing about Hitler's change of policy, the new minister of war was attacked for his relationship with heavy industry and with certain financial circles. In doing this our political editor, Meyer-Christian, used terms and concepts that appeared to be taken from speeches and articles by Gregor Strasser, who had been sharply critical of the party leadership's policies in the past weeks. Out of this apparent connection there was constructed an actual connection, a conspiracy, a conscious disruptive action against Hitler's policies. The men behind these accusations operated from various motives. Those from Hamburg wanted to get rid of me as the disquieting editor of the *Hamburger Tageblatt;* Dr. Goebbels, to whom they turned for support, hoped to blacken the hated Strasser in Hitler's eyes as the inspirer of the articles and, if possible, to get him expelled from the party.

Goebbels succeeded in bringing the matter before Hitler and in depicting it as a dangerous and consciously malevolent attack on his policies and his authority. Thereupon I was summoned to an interview in the Hotel Baseler Hof in Frankfurt.

The interview began with Hitler's announcement that he intended to make an example and therefore had to expel me and all the editors of the *Hamburger Tageblatt* from the party. It ended with his assurances that he was very sorry about the expulsion. The intervening half hour was at first filled by an attempt on my part to clarify Goebbels' distorted portrayal. I had enough success with this so that Hitler at least rescinded the expulsion of the other editors. Also he saw quite clearly that he had deluded himself or had been deluded. And, therefore, he began to recapitulate my earlier "sins": my inclination to contrariness, my open opposition, my disobedience of received orders. These accusations led to a short, heated exchange over the concepts of obedience, loyalty, freedom. Hitler declared that what he demanded from party members was unconditional and speechless obedience. He was thankful for advice and instruction, but he alone determined the party's policies. As, in the course of this, he mentioned something about the loyalty of Germanic tribesmen, I responded that his demand was not for loyalty but for submission: The true Germanic leaders had not only always listened to advice, they had sought it out and had honored the adviser. He, Hitler, was therefore not a leader in the Germanic sense, but rather an Oriental despot.

This severe reproach must have had a disarming effect for a moment; Hitler sought to be reasonable and tried to move me to a gesture of subjection by reminding me of my long membership in the party. When he was unsuccessful in this I was quickly dismissed; all the while he repeatedly asserted that he was very sorry.

In actuality he was immoderately angry and in years to come his anger did not lessen. Only a few days after my expulsion Max Amann telephoned Brinkmann and told him that the whole matter could have been smoothed over if I had not constantly contradicted the *Führer*: "He's mad as a wet hen at the Doctor!"

In June 1934 my father sent word to me that for the past month my letters had obviously been subject to surveillance. Perhaps June 30, 1934, would have been fatal for me, too, if I had not shortly beforehand taken myself off to a small, remote Baltic seaside resort. In the summer of 1938, according to a report from Habermann, August Winnig[40] was ordered to report to Hitler. Hitler wanted to ask Winnig, probably at the suggestion of General Beck, his opinion as to how the working class would behave in the event of war. Winnig suggested that the confidence of the workers would be strengthened if reliable but also respected former trade union leaders were brought into the Labor Front. Hitler refused—

---

[40] A former trade-union official and Social Democratic leader who went over to the Nationalists in 1920. Though he was counted as part of the extreme right wing in Germany, he was actually not pro-Nazi.

for the representatives of the Free Unions[41] immediately, and, after some hesitation, for the Christian and nationalist unions. The Christians were priest-ridden, he said, and in the DHV there was that Dr. Krebs "who always wanted to schoolmarm me." Probably he assumed that the schoolmarming had been on the orders of the higher-ups.

Shortly before I was named *Senatsdirektor*[42] in the spring of 1940, Reich Commissar Karl Kaufmann made application for me to be readmitted into the party. I had nothing to do with this; it was because of a Hamburg ordinance which provided that every official had to be a member of the Nazi party. The application was rejected by the party headquarters by express direction from Hitler.

In 1943, again without my knowledge or initiative (Brinkmann told me the story much later), Amann tried to get Hitler's approval for my appointment as editor of one of the new German newspapers in southeastern Europe. Hitler growled at Amann: "What? Is that damned guy still living?"

Whether this story is accurate in all particulars I do not know. But it is undoubtedly correct in essence and is further evidence that Hitler could neither forgive nor forget, that his anger against his critics actually grew with time. The more he was surrounded by difficulties, so much the more did Hitler seek refuge in the delusion that his problems and failures were engendered by the contrariness of his opponents. But also the conviction in him increased that everyone who contradicted him must be extirpated—and especially anyone who, on the basis of facts, had correctly contradicted him. The former destroyed his success, but the latter destroyed faith in the "infallibility" of the *Führer*, not just the people's faith but also that of Hitler himself.

---

[41] I.e., the Socalist-oriented unions.
[42] Official in the Hamburg civil service.

CHAPTER 6

Dr. Joseph Goebbels

"We who were shot up in the World War . . ."—thus Dr. Goebbels began the first speech I heard him make. It was the winter of 1924–25 and I was a university student at Frankfurt. He was wearing an army fatigue shirt and the light gray dress trousers of an infantry officer. All of us in the audience were convinced that it was, in fact, a former officer from the front lines, wounded in the leg,[1] who was speaking to us. Some even claimed precise knowledge: Goebbels had been a fighter pilot. His lithe, supple figure seemed to underscore the correctness of this assertion so that for almost two years I passed this rumor along. My good faith in the "shot-up warrior" was not completely destroyed until Franz Schauwecker's "Open Letter" was published (I think it appeared around 1927 in one of the many short-lived newspapers of the national-revolutionary movement), which attacked Goebbels for his "Front Soldier Legend." But Schauwecker was probably wrong to assume that Goebbels was trying to dress himself up with soldierly glory. Apart from his physical defect, Goebbels did not suffer from feelings of inferiority. He was much too conscious of his own abilities for that, though admittedly he needed an audience to unfold them fully. For him, wearing an old uniform and referring to the deeds and sufferings of the World War soldiers was nothing more than a carefully calculated propaganda trick attuned to the situation.

In those years anyone who argued against fulfilling the Versailles Treaty had to cope with the charge of being a warmonger. The

---

[1] Goebbels never served in the German army—he was rejected for physical inadequacy; his crippled foot was a result of an attack of polio when he was four years old. For further information see Helmut Heiber, *Goebbels* (New York, 1972).

only ones who could evade this were those who had participated in the war and, specifically, had fought at the front themselves. Anyone else was shouted down at meetings. Since combating the Treaty of Versailles was one of the essential aspects of Nazism and brought the party its first and most durable gains, every party speaker bestirred himself to produce the required alibi. Goebbels had none; so with the unscrupulousness of an intellectual fanatic he invented one, as did others also in those turbulent times.

In that speech his subject was "Lenin or Hitler?" He had not yet become the great demagogue, the virtuoso of rhetoric that he was later to be, but rather gave a talk that, although effective, was almost an academic lecture. Nevertheless this speech, which he repeated almost a hundred times, influenced the early development and thrust of Nazism considerably by articulating the hopes and desires of its adherents, elevating the unconscious to the clear.

There were other fanatical anti-Bolsheviks, such as Alfred Rosenberg and the anti-Comintern people. Their anti-Bolshevism, however, was more or less a paper issue designed for the petty bourgeoisie and for covert circles of the semi-educated, who could be agitated into a hectic defensive determination by atrocity stories, revelations of Jewish machinations, and historical fantasies. Goebbels approached the question quite differently. He, who as late as 1919 was supposed to have belonged to a Communist student group in Heidelberg,[2] but in any case had intensively investigated events in mysterious Russia (which was a complete riddle for the average European), depicted Lenin to his audience as one of the greatest personalities of world history. "Lenin freed the Russian people from the chains of tsarist slavery and the medieval feudal system," he declared. But this liberation was unstable, since it rested upon a brittle basis—Marxism—which was flawed because of its spiritual roots in the Enlightenment and the French Revolu-

[2] Goebbels did not enroll at Heidelberg until 1920; none of the standard biographies confirm this rumor. Goebbels did have a close friend who toyed with Marxism for a while; also the hero of Goebbels' semi-autobiographical novel, *Michael*, was a "socialist" in the amorphous sense; this may have engendered the rumor. See Roger Manvell and Heinrich Fraenkel, *Dr. Goebbels, His Life and Death*, paperback (New York, 1960), pp. 12–29, for Goebbels' early life.

tion. The end product of Marxism and Western democracy could only be a mechanistic state. Behind its initial pseudoliberation loomed a new and now ultimate slavery.

Against this thesis of the democratic-Bolshevist compulsion state, Goebbels then presented the counterthesis: the racialist organic state. It had failed to develop out of early romanticism, the rebellion against Napoleon, and the Revolution of 1848 (which was debased, but only partially, by the Liberals). But now it must find ultimate creation in Germany through Adolf Hitler's movement.

Of course, these ideas were not original with Goebbels. But he made them comprehensible to the masses by personifying them in such well-known figures as Lenin and Hitler. At the same time he overcame the sterile and purely defensive attitude of many Nazis by setting thesis against thesis and naturally assigning to his own thesis the rights and forces of the future. Further, for him the birth of the German nation in the trenches of the World War was not just "an epochal but also a European precedent." What was happening today in Germany would have to happen tomorrow in all the European nations, though perhaps through variant forms. For all the peoples of Europe were equally threatened by Bolshevism. With this Goebbels articulated the supranational messianic feelings which, since the end of the war and especially in the youth of all classes, had awaited a summons. Though most Nazi speakers stressed the slogan of national self-focus for many years more, the moral justification for Nazi policy after 1938, for imperialist expansion, had already been prepared.

Goebbels' speech, despite its strong theoretical content and its overload of historical examples, was enthusiastically received by the majority of the audience. Only a small group of former racialists seemed disgruntled because the Jewish Question had been given only passing mention. We few students from the Youth Movement were also strongly impressed. Since 1919 this had been the first speech at a party meeting, and particularly at a meeting of the Nationalist Movement, in which the speaker had risen above the usual clichés, with their cursing of the enemy and their stinking self-praise, to attempt a grand survey illuminating the political-historical background of events.

My next encounter with Dr. Goebbels left a less attractive impression. I heard him speak in the north of Berlin[3] shortly after he had been named Gauleiter of Berlin early in the summer of 1926. Although in the interim he had learned much about oratory, the contents of his speech lacked basic intellectual substance. It glittered with brilliant, razor-sharp phraseology, but the core of it was demagogic claptrap, tailored to the place and the audience. Most of these were extremely unattractive types. They were truly uprooted proletarians, whether they wore the Soviet star or the swastika as an emblem. The only exception were the so-called *Frontbann* who were generally excellent people. This organization stemmed from the days of General Ludendorff's National Socialist Liberation Movement, and its members were almost all former combat veterans and Free Corps fighters. Their units were the cadres for the subsequent formation of the Berlin SA, though there was always a certain contrast in human behavior between the ex-*Frontbann* people and the young SA men. This contrast was evident also in the *Frontbann*'s reaction to their new Gauleiter. They were by no means pleased with him. They were unable to give many objective reasons for this but instinctively "didn't like that guy." In my opinion this rejection formed the underlying basis for the subsequent Stennes *Putsch*. Beyond that, the regular party members showed considerable initial opposition toward the "half-French Jesuit pupil" Goebbels.[4] But this opposition quickly disappeared or in any event became insignificant, as far as I recall.

During the time I was Local Group leader in Hamburg I often met Dr. Goebbels. Hamburgers had an extraordinarily high opinion of him as a speaker. This was probably because his slick dialectics, his Latin attitude and diction, his wit, and his icy irony were so totally foreign to their own deliberate, down-to-earth, or humorously sly natures. Among the party comrades in Hamburg the question was frequently discussed in those early years as to whether Hitler or Goebbels was the better speaker. Many voted for Goebbels, which was often the same as expressing a preference for

[3] One of the major slum areas of the city.

[4] Actually, Goebbels was Dutch (on his mother's side) rather than French, and though educated in Catholic schools, as customary in the Rhineland, he never studied under the Jesuits and renounced his Catholicism as a university student.

Goebbels as the better party leader. As in almost all the other parties, oratorical talents were equated with leadership qualities. Whether Goebbels ever noticed these sentiments I do not know. In any case I never heard of his trying to exploit them, no matter how independently he behaved in his own Gau, Berlin. I will try, later, to analyze the reasons for his "loyalty."

Goebbels' visits to Hamburg hardly provided opportunities for more intimate personal conversations. After what were usually very exhausting mass meetings, neither he nor we felt much like long sessions extending the night. Beyond that he inclined to be ascetic toward food and drink in those years, perhaps in imitation of Hitler. Thus I can only recall that he preferred to talk about cultural or artistic matters, mentioned politics only peripherally, and, in contrast to Gregor Strasser, cautiously avoided internal party questions and problems. Once, without any real occasion for it, he gave a little speech in praise of Hitler as a man, a speaker, and a politician. Precisely because there was no ostensible reason for this and because of vague premonitions, I avoided my usual habit and made no response. Afterward I suspected (and it still seems so to me today and thus worthy of mention as an example of the way Goebbels played politics) that this little intermezzo was a carefully planned chess move in Goebbels' great contest with Strasser. Perhaps Goebbels reckoned with a hesitant or critical response from me. Then he would have complained to Hitler: "See how Strasser's friends and followers think!" He knew, of course, that Strasser had confirmed me as Local Group leader for Hamburg and that the *Hamburger Volksblatt* was published through Strasser's *Kampf* publishing house. On the other hand, perhaps he hoped that I would sometime mention his "faith in Hitler" in Munich party circles and that it would be passed along. I cannot say with surety what Hitler thought of Goebbels in those early years. As for Hess, Rosenberg, Dr. Frick, Pfeffer, and Amann, I know for certain that for a wide variety of reasons they viewed the Gauleiter of Berlin dubiously or were openly opposed to him and his political methods. Sometime or other I heard him referred to in Munich as "the guy with the little, cold monkey hands," which had a certain correctness of characterization to it. Goebbels' hands did, in fact, have a malicious quality about them. But it would have caused all his personal enemies in the party to be cautious and reserved if they were to hear that even in private conversations Goebbels praised Hitler's valuable qualities and analyzed them individually. That bespoke a personal intimacy between Hitler and Goebbels which could lead to highly unpleasant consequences if one attacked the "little Doctor."

In connection with this I might add that even those in the highest circles of the party leadership never knew for sure who was Hitler's golden-haired boy at any given moment. From the earliest times Hitler used to enclose not just his feelings and thoughts but all his actions with a veil of secrecy. Sometimes he disappeared for weeks on end and only Hess knew his changing address and even he had no idea with whom Hitler was meeting and speaking. So whoever preferred not to cut himself off frivolously from Hitler's favor did well to make certain, before launching a massive attack on an enemy inside the party, that this person had not just finished spending a fortnight in the mountains or at the seaside with Hitler.

There was yet another little episode with Goebbels that etched itself into my memory. This was because at the moment of its occurrence it jolted me into wonder and disbelief, while later it seemed to me a sort of spotlight that suddenly illuminated the subterranean spiritual foundations of this strange man. After a meeting in Hamburg-Altona Dr. Goebbels wanted to walk a bit through the Reeperbahn,[5] which he claimed he had never seen before. Since at that time we never went out in the streets in uniform, but wore civilian clothes, and since furthermore there was as yet no reason to fear that we would be recognized (and certainly not by the frequenters of the Reeperbahn) we fulfilled Goebbels' request and strolled slowly from the Grosse Freiheit to the Millerntor. Along the way one of our group, a young SA man in whose face one could clearly read idealism, devotion, and a background in the Youth Movement, asked: "Doctor, after the victory, what will happen to streets like this?" Without hesitation Goebbels replied, "We will sweep them away like you sweep out garbage." And then, ignoring all the objections that were immediately raised, and speaking only to the boy, he spun a picture of an elite youth of such discipline, courage, purity, and power as had been dreamed of

---

[5] Hamburg's notorious red-light area on the waterfront.

since the days of the knightly and monastic orders by the greatest poets, teachers, and soldiers of German and Western history. As we climbed into our auto at the Millerntor, the young SA man gazed at "our Doctor" with glowing, enraptured eyes until the very second of our departure.

In the spring of 1931, shortly after founding the *Hamburger Tageblatt*, I went to Berlin to survey the operations of the *Angriff* and gather information that could possibly be applied in Hamburg. Upon applying to the editorial offices of *Angriff*, I was informed that Dr. Goebbels would personally await me and would supply me with the elucidation I desired. When I told Kaufmann this he declared ironically: "Well, then you won't learn anything at all, or else the little that you are told will be false. Whenever Goebbels opens his mouth he lies. I got to know him in Elberfeld."[6]

At the Berlin party headquarters I had to wait for a while in the anteroom, from which a door on the right hand led to the rooms of the SA, while the left-hand door led to those of the Gau. In the anteroom on that morning there was a tense atmosphere. In front of each door was a knot of young men: on the one side SA men and on the other, young party officials and especially distributors and street hawkers of the *Angriff*. Each group was taunting and swearing at the other. Obviously tensions between the party and the SA had reached dangerous levels. But the actual reasons for this could not be clearly discerned from the opposing verbal sallies. However, since some of the SA people used rather unamiable language about Goebbels' luxury apartment in the fashionable district of Berlin, one could conclude that his person played a significant role in the controversy. Yet from a sociological point of view the door guardians on the Gau side (and incidentally the door was very carefully re-locked after each use) obviously included more proletarians than the guards in front of the SA's door. The latter were noticeably of good middle-class, partly upper-middle-class, origin.

---

[6] Both Kaufmann and Goebbels had worked in the Nazi Gau for the Ruhr before becoming, respectively, Gauleiter of Hamburg and Berlin. The Ruhr city of Elberfeld was later fused with the city of Barmen and is now called Wüppertal.

After a while I was summoned and taken down a short corridor at the end of which was a second locked and guarded door. Beyond this we passed by a suite of offices with half-glass walls and ultimately came to a larger cross-room, which apparently was at the end of the building. But, in fact, it led into still another three large rooms, each one with locked and guarded doors, and in the last of these sat Goebbels behind his desk. The desk had been placed diagonally from the entrance against the far wall, without regard for the lighting arrangements. The room was otherwise almost bare. The Mussolini model was unmistakable, and though there was a vast difference between the size of a room in a Roman *Palazzo* and an office in the Berlin newspaper district, the visitor still had to take ten or twelve reverently trembling steps before he came to Goebbels' desk.

Be that as it may, my host did not subject me to such moral convulsions but met and greeted me halfway. Then, much to my surprise, he immediately began to talk about the difficulties between the party and SA leaders. Despite all his conciliatory efforts it threatened to develop into a vast mutiny. He had already been forced to dismiss his SA guards and replace them with party functionaries. Just two days previously, rampaging SA men had thrust their way into the business offices and had been removed only with great effort and trouble, so that he had been compelled to order that the doors be locked. The building's owner would terminate their lease immediately if fights or destruction should occur within the office rooms.

Though this explanation seemed credible, at the same time it was certainly insufficient. No doubt Goebbels also wanted to protect himself from a physical attack. He was definitely no coward, but he knew quite well that a Gauleiter who had been beaten up by his party-comrades would have to give up hope of playing his political role for quite a while, if not forever. Beyond that, the guards and the arrangement of the offices—the Gauleiter in the remotest, innermost room, the "inner sanctum"—expressed that need for the mystification of rank and value hierarchies, which is precisely strongest where externally the greatest skepticism, hard-headedness, and sober realism seem to rule. In this respect Goebbels knew his Berliners, just as the Nazi leaders in general had an excellent understanding of the psychology of the masses, especially in the years before the seizure of power. Later, in possession of power, they became more negligent or no longer thought it necessary to pay attention to popular sentiments.

I could not obtain from Dr. Goebbels a more precise explanation of the background and reasons for his conflict with the SA. He only indicated that it was more than a local matter, that Walter Stennes, in total misunderstanding of the task of the SA, had the notion that he could decisively determine party policy, and that he, Goebbels, thus saw himself forced to ask Hitler to intervene and decide matters within the next few days, though this ought to remain confidential. Then, on his own, he broke off discussion over this theme (I myself, out of ignorance over the situation, had said hardly anything) and proposed that we should drive out to the west end of Berlin for lunch. Beforehand, however, he wanted to show me through the business rooms of the office.

This tour was one of the strangest experiences I have had. Goebbels did not, as is customary, accompany me from room to room in order to point out the division of activity area by area and introduce me to the personnel. Instead he flitted along the corridor, opening here and there a door halfway or three-quarters, just long enough so that I could quickly glimpse the two or three people inside, while he made a couple of little waves with his hand, whispered a pleasantry, and flitted off again. The people in the offices hardly noticed the incident. Once I heard one say, "Oh, the Doctor." It did not sound very respectful.

There were only two offices that we actually went into. In these also I received no explanation nor was I introduced. All the officials working in these offices were typical of the organizational functionaries that could be found at the middle level of any of the parties and trade unions: healthy men with powerful elbows, powerful self-estimations, and powerful consciences; hardworking, reliable, and unreflective, they were actually not used to thinking. Again no one paid attention to us and I did not get the impression that this was in compliance with some office directive. What argued against this was the continuation of loud and unabashed conversations among the party employees and above all the behavior of two party comrades to whom Goebbels spoke. Both slowly began to rise with the first words spoken and thus ultimately after a few minutes stood towering over their Gauleiter and employer.

One can make all sorts of straightforward and sober explanations for this scene: the lack of an office manager who would assure the maintenance of customary forms of courtesy and decency; by-products of Gau Berlin's sharply emphasized revolutionary boorishness and informality, which certainly was not congruent with the ceremony of the Gauleiter's guarded and only distantly accessible office; Goebbels' disinterest in the work of filing, keeping accounts, and organizing in his headquarters, which led to insufficient personal relationships with those involved in this work. As I said, one can adduce all such explanations; but they are still not sufficient for me to elucidate these murky scenes. I had much more the impression that I was watching one of the slithering, weakly, sick wizards of E. T. A. Hoffmann's stories flitting among his artificial creatures, full of dread that they would recognize his weakness and hurl themselves upon him. And recognition would be the end, the unmasking, destitution. They would throw him on the dust heap. He shivered and the creatures noticed the shivers.

And actually one could hear through the thin walls the tumult in the anteroom. And, in fact, functionaries everywhere have a keen nose for shifting centers of power, for a change of bosses, and generally they put themselves quickly at the disposal of the coming man without suffering pangs of conscience over loyalty.

The tour scarcely lasted ten minutes and then we went down a back staircase into a courtyard where a Mercedes and a good fifty *Angriff* distributors were waiting. As the boys saw Dr. Goebbels they cheered him with loud calls of "Heil." In that same moment he transformed himself: Into his sallow face flowed blood; his body straightened up; his skin became taut. He was again the Gauleiter. From the running board of the auto he spoke a few words, a mixture of flattery and challenge: "You carry the truth, the German truth, into a city that today is ruled by Jews, Jew-associates, and political manipulators, but tomorrow will again be the capitol of the Reich, our Reich. Then you will be able to say that you were the *avant-garde*. . . ." What a contrast between that which I had just witnessed upstairs and what was now going on here below!

Under way, Goebbels asked me what I thought of his automobile. I could only respond that it was a very fine one. He had received it as a gift, Goebbels continued; naturally he had accepted it with gratitude. A modern movement required an automobile. The Gauleiter of Berlin required one that would make a good impression. It was contemptible to appear at a proletarian meeting without a collar and tie, like some Social Democratic leaders still did, though behind closed doors they could not get enough of bourgeois pleasures. Furthermore, it was not that the Gauleiter of Berlin should make a good impression for himself but rather as the representative of the movement. Or did I think otherwise?

I recalled the accusations of the SA men that I had heard an hour earlier and answered that he was undoubtedly correct but that the simple party member and the simple Volk-comrade whom we were trying to recruit as members often thought otherwise, and it was hard to persuade them to change their minds. Beyond that, when an automobile was a gift there was a further question as to whether the gift did not have some political strings attached to it.

"Well, Jakob Goldschmidt would hardly give me an automobile," he replied, slightly annoyed.

"You think it's completely out of the question?" I asked him back. But instead of an answer I got a not very explicit glance out of the side of his eyes.

We ate in a small restaurant on Kurfürstendamm, where, to judge by the kind of service given us, he was obviously well known. During and following the meal I tried finally to get into the actual purpose of my visit. But Kaufmann's prediction was borne out. Goebbels avoided answering my questions about Angriff's experiences. At the same time he did not want me to talk to the editorial staff personally. That is, he never said so, but I had unfortunately told him that I had an appointment at the DHV offices in the Kaiserallee, so he engaged me so long in conversation that a return trip to the center of the city became impossible for me.

As to the content of this conversation there is little of interest to report. In a mild way Goebbels expressed displeasure over our starting a newspaper in Hamburg and predicted probable failure, pointing to the large number of Angriff subscribers in Hamburg. He made no attempt to hide his desire for the Angriff to become the dominant Nazi newspaper for the whole of northern Germany. He approved only of weekly newspapers for the individual Gaue. In this connection he surprised me by making malicious though shrewd remarks about "Sergeant-Director" Amann and the "almost" Rosenberg. Rosenberg was almost adequate as a scholar, a journalist, a politician, but just almost. Naturally he added a bit of flattery to his criticism of our Hamburg doings by praising our former weekly, the *Hansische Warte*, for its avoidance of clichés and its unique characteristics.

That led to questions and problems of the Youth Movement, and especially the *Bündische* Youth Movement.[7] Since I knew more about these things than he did, I had to, whether or not I wanted to and whether or not the clock was ticking loudly in my ears, quench his thirst for knowledge. Then finally he wanted to pump me a bit about conditions in the DHV and inside the party in Hamburg. But then, fortunately, we had to rush so that I could keep my appointment in the Kaiserallee. In taking his leave, Goebbels uttered a sentence that I had heard almost word for word forty-eight hours before, though reversed: "Watch out for Kaufmann; whenever he opens his mouth he lies."

A few days after my visit the so-called Stennes revolt broke out. At first a large portion of the Berlin SA was involved, but then Hitler intervened personally and the mutiny was rather quickly suppressed. Only a small group remained loyal to Stennes and from them I later learned that Goebbels had repeated his Bamberg trick.[8] By their account, Goebbels had waited until the tension approached the breaking point and then met with Stennes to negotiate. (This must have been shortly before my visit to Berlin since Goebbels already spoke to me of his intention of going to see Hitler.) The meeting was said to have ended in an apparent full reconciliation and agreement. In reality, however, Goebbels wanted to draw out of the very open and forthright Stennes expressions of basic criticism against the party and Hitler. After succeeding in this, he took the evidence, in comparison to which Stennes' complaints about Goebbels' Gau leadership had now lost all weight, to Hitler and brought Hitler back to Berlin to help

[7] The *Bündische* Youth Movement, in contrast to religious youth groups, the Boy Scouts, etc., maintained the ideals of the original pre-1914 Youth Movement: mysticism, self-direction, charismatic leadership, etc. For a description of them see Walter Laqueur, *Young Germany* (New York, 1962).

[8] Goebbels shifted loyalties from Strasser to Hitler in 1926 at a conference in Bamberg and a subsequent visit to Munich. But at first he disguised his transference. See Orlow I, p. 69 ff.

him. Naturally I cannot attest to the accuracy of this account myself, but it does not seem improbable to me.

Personally I had no further dealings with Goebbels between my visit with him and the seizure of power except on two occasions, once directly, once indirectly. After Goebbels had proclaimed Hitler's candidacy for the presidential elections in the *Sportpalast*, we at the *Hamburger Tageblatt* received a telegram the following morning from the Munich party headquarters prohibiting us from disseminating the news since Goebbels had acted without Hitler's approval. A few hours later, around noon, a second telegram lifted the prohibition. Thus Hitler, despite proclaiming the political infallibility of his own decisons a year and a half before, had bowed to the intentions of his Gauleiter of Berlin. For his part Goebbels had not, as I see it, consciously acted over the head of the *Führer*, but rather was swept along by the mood of the mass meeting. He was expressing what ten thousand people expected and desired of him.

My view was supported by a remark Hitler made in my last interview with him. Hitler had declared that he would not let his editors write policy for him; therefore, my unauthorized behavior must be punished. To this I had replied that he had not equally punished Goebbels' unauthorized behavior in the Berlin *Sportpalast*. "Party-comrade Goebbels was standing before a gigantic meeting; you sat behind a writing desk—that's different!" was his answer.

Dr. Goebbels was also involved in working for my expulsion, which occasioned the final and direct contact with him mentioned above. Admittedly, it was only via the long distance telephone. On the day after the *Hamburger Tageblatt* attacked Schleicher's appointment as minister of defense and also made some unfriendly comments about Schleicher's links with financial and industrial circles, Goebbels called me up in our editorial offices. In an angry tone he told me that by taking this position we had injured the party's and the *Führer's* policies in the gravest way. Hitler was therefore ordering me to appear before him at the Baseler Hof in Frankfurt two days hence. When I objected that I had no notion of how a rejection of Schleicher could hurt the party and that the other editors had approved of the article, too, Goebbels replied: "Your attack on Schleicher has aroused considerable attention and satisfaction in all the ministries and among the party's enemies because it has been taken as the expression of a secret opposition group." I responded that even with the best will I could not accept this story from him for the simple reason that only very few copies of the *Hamburger Tageblatt* were delivered to Berlin and that it was also hardly ever quoted by correspondents. Naturally Goebbels did not let himself be persuaded. In fact, he even passed on to Hitler my statement that the other editors had also approved of the article in the distorted and damning form that "the entire editorial staff had declared their solidarity with me." He wanted me to be expelled, though certainly not because he had anything against me but because he viewed me as the political instrument of the DHV, Strasser, and Brüning. In his published diary he gave clear expression to these suspicions.[9]

After 1933 I no longer had any close contact with Dr. Goebbels. The ways in which his actions affected me in my job were experienced by thousands of others, too. Perhaps the delay of many months in approving my appointment to a special commission in the army may have been due to his influence. But I have no evidence to support this supposition and even if I did, it would not alter the portrait of him at all. The entire thrust of his work after 1933 was to snuff out any conceivable resistance while it was still a spark, a thought, and thus to sidetrack everyone holding independent ideas. Goebbels, the "beast with intelligence" knew what to expect of other "intelligent beasts."

Dr. Joseph Goebbels seemed to me to be first and foremost a typical intellectual of his times. Extraordinarily clever and with a many-sided education, he surpassed not only all the other Nazi politicians in intelligence, but also most of the rest of his contemporaries. Undoubtedly, he could also have attained a superior position outside of the political arena as a journalist, dramatic director, writer, and scholar. He was a complete rationalist who extended the phrase "I think, therefore I am" to read: "I am whatever I

---

[9] Joseph Goebbels, *Vom Kaiserhof zur Reichskanzlei* (Munich, 1934), p. 99 (May 19, 1932): "In the Hamburg party newspaper an extremely untimely attack is made against Schleicher. That's Strasser, in other words, the DHV, in other words, the unions, in other words, Brüning. Those responsible will be expelled from the party momentarily." (Krebs' note: this "diary" is available in translation as *My Part in Germany's Struggle*, London, 1935.)

think myself to be." This meant that he held open for himself all options, whether for good or for evil. But for him the "I" was always the middle point, the sun around which his thoughts orbited.

But to my way of thinking that also restricted him to the limitations of the type, no matter how brilliantly or startlingly he represented this type. The demonic, with which his personality was undoubtedly linked, was a property of the times and the type. At any moment, today or tomorrow, it could exist again. But what was, then, the relationship between Dr. Goebbels and the elemental forces with their murkiness, dangers, and demons? Goebbels possessed an infinitely acute sense of these forces and an equally vast ability to appeal to them as conscious factors and set them in motion with words. But since he himself, in my estimation was largely lacking in such vital elementary forces, he was not in a position to establish courses and goals for himself. On the contrary, he needed the force of others to be himself.

Goebbels' relationship with Hitler was fatefully determined, in my opinion, by Hitler's vast superiority over Goebbels in vital force. Goebbels had to be loyal to these forces even when that meant betraying not just his own comrades but his own convictions. His hatred for Strasser can also probably be explained easily on the basis of this psychological factor. It was the hatred of a highly talented functionary against a "real person." A functionary can never be more than the executor of an alien will or destiny, even when he has summoned it up himself, because he has neither the generally applicable standard of values nor the natural force to make a will and destiny of his own. A "real person," however, lives and acts from his own resources.

And that is why the life and death of Goebbels, despite the most powerful dramatic highlights, lacked true tragic characteristics. The revolver shot fired from his gloved hand only ended a heroic role, not a heroic life. The life and death of Strasser, on the other hand, cannot be dismissed as untragic, because in him the struggle of values within a human conscience became visible.

Jean Paul Sartre is said to have selected Goebbels as a "hero." Goebbels was history's first complete existentialist, thus also simultaneously an example of what possibilities of existence and action can be produced by the existentialist freedom of decision.

CHAPTER 7

Rudolf Hess

In the summer of 1930 Otto Strasser and most of his collaborators in the *Kampf* publishing house were expelled from the Nazi party. I had read only a few brief reports on this, since just at the time it was happening I was in Austria on a canoe trip. On the way back, therefore, I stopped off in Munich and sought out Hess[1] in order to learn the details.

Hess was amazed to see me. He had already assumed that I was one of the "apostates." He based his assumption on my occasional contributions to the *National Socialist Correspondence* and on the former organizational links between the *Hamburger Volksblatt* and the *Kampf* publishing house. But above all he asserted that my "intellectual inclination to criticism" of the party's measures would almost force me to align with the rebels. He used the exact words: "The boss also believes that you don't have proper respect for him."

In the ensuing discussion, and in response to my objection that I certainly did have respect for Hitler's abilities and his accomplishments up to now, it developed that what he meant by the term "respect" was actually "faith"; that is, unconditional faith, in an almost religious sense. Yet Hess's confession to this faith was based not so much on purely personal reverence for Hitler as primarily on a doctrinaire principle. The essence of this was: the era of monarchy and democracy is past in Europe; the era of Caesarism has arrived. One dare not wait for a leader, or call for one; one must *will* him. If all National Socialists and ultimately the entire nation honestly *will* Hitler to be the leader, and then are prepared to be

[1] The most recent life of Hess is Roger Manvell and Heinrich Fraenkel, *Hess: A Biography* (London, 1971).

completely loyal to him, then Hitler will actually *be* the leader that Germany needs.

Hess lent force to his view with the words: "I want to be the Hagen[2] of the party!" In saying this he was certainly not clear about the tragic perspective that he was opening up for the movement and the German people with this testimonial, though he surely understood what evaluation this implied for Hitler himself. Upon my remarking that along with Hagen you had to take King Gunther, who was known to have had some faults and weaknesses, Hess rejoined vigorously: "I know! I know! Hitler too, has faults and weaknesses. But if you had understood me correctly you would not have raised that objection. It depends upon us whether we show the world his merits or his faults. We must stand up for his faults. . . . I want to be Hagen," he repeated yet again.

For me this conversation has always been the key to Rudolf Hess's style and his political behavior. Hess was no silly, primitive, narrow-minded fanatic, as he has been portrayed by various people. He himself probably thought that fanaticism was a virtue, but in my opinion he was a man with a sensitivity and gentleness bordering on the pathological. He forced himself to behave with a "Roman simplicity" analogous to the statues in the monastery at Naumburg. Though he himself was a highly complicated person, he did not want to recognize complexity in people, things, or decisions, since this seemed decadent to him. How little of a born fanatic he was showed itself repeatedly in certain qualities and on several occasions. In contrast to Hitler he was capable of listening calmly to unfamiliar and divergent opinions, of actually suppressing his own opinions. Up to a certain point he even tried to present such opinions to Hitler, even at the risk of incurring Hitler's wrath. I personally experienced that in a variety of instances. And I also know, for example, that Hess joined Gregor Strasser in persuading Hitler, over his lengthy and bitter opposition, to receive Bechly and Habermann from the DHV for a basic discussion of trade union problems—though of course it had fruitless results.

---

[2] In the *Nibelungenlied*, "Hagen the grim" is the loyal retainer of King Gunther, determined and obstinate unto death, yet also the perpetrator of evil for his cause: he slew Siegfried and he occasioned the death of Gunther in order to hide forever the location of the treasure hoard of the Nibelung kings.

Hess was also something equally rarely found among fanatics, unless their fanaticism actually consists of a commitment to justice; he was honest and just both for himself and, as far as his influence stretched, for the party. When I was forced to levy accusations against SA Commander Pfeffer, in autumn 1930, because of his failure to pass on 30,000 marks of the party's money, I immediately found Hess's ear and his backing. In the conference involving Hess, Major Walter Buch (chairman of the *Uschla*), and me, he took the position unreservedly that transgressions must be punished without regard to rank or past services. In general and simply on the basis of his origins and education alone, he showed understanding for every attempt, no matter what group or personality was behind it, to cleanse the party's leadership corps of impure elements and to maintain a particularly strict discipline. Unfortunately, his theoretical insight rarely led to practical results —actually only in those instances that fell within his area of exclusive decision-making. Hitler himself had completely different ideas about the discipline and qualities of his subordinates. But Hess, with his "Hagen complex" was always willing to sacrifice his own views and attitudes. Therefore, he also ultimately tried to prove to me, when Hitler ordered the investigation against Pfeffer halted, that Hitler's maxims were correct: "One must not try to educate people but rather to make use of them according to their own characteristics and abilities. Even bums have certain abilities. A revolutionary movement like National Socialism cannot adhere to bourgeois virtues. What must be demanded is only unreflective faith and unconditional obedience."

It was obviously distasteful to Hess to have to make this effort, especially since I stuck to my original position and reminded him of his prior statements to the *Uschla*. He mortified his reason and his conscience for an entire hour because Hitler had ordered him to so instruct me and because he himself wanted to give me an example of exactly that kind of unconditional obedience. He was sincerely depressed when, at the end of the hour, he had to concede the futility of his efforts.

But such disappointments had no effect upon his commitment to Hitler's basic position and Hess's own consciously self-assigned function. Hess willed a *Führer* clothed with the glory of political infallibility and therefore did everything he could to present Hitler in this form to the nation. Thus, taking the whole political development into consideration, Hess must be accounted as the man chiefly responsible for the triumph of the fascist/totalitarian tendency within what was originally at least a halfway democratic popular movement. Despite his inadequate propaganda skills, he did more to engender and secure the myth of the *Führer*, that strange mixture of dream and doctrine, than, for example, Dr. Goebbels. With Goebbels you always recognized the propagandistic intention. But with Hess you believed his words, when he spoke of "our Führer," because everyone saw him as a believable personality. What was tragic in this was that he, who knew Hitler so well, actually did not believe in him but rather compelled himself to faith and, if need be, would hurl himself into the breach for Hitler.

This repeatedly produced schizophrenic situations. In 1933, after the seizure of power, leaders of the nationalistic trade unions intervened on behalf of the socialist trade unionists who had been mistreated and dragged off to concentration camps. Hess, who was always glad to help, willingly promised assistance in these cases, too, and was partially able to provide it. But he curtly rejected every request that Hitler be asked to make a fundamental decision on the illegality of such actions and arrests. His reasoning was significant. Hitler's vigor and decisiveness would be crippled if he learned of such infringements of the law. It was Hitler's pride that he had conducted the most bloodless and most disciplined revolution in history. (Information from Max Habermann.)

In connection with this I think it was no coincidence that Hess was seen with particular frequency in those photographs of Hitler depicting him as the friend of children, animals, and the common man. I am convinced that Hess never thought of such things as play-acting or propaganda. He revered King Frederick William I of Prussia and wanted Hitler, too, to be the strict but kindly father of his people.

Hess's split personality was probably intensified by his marriage. I became acquainted with his wife during two extensive visits at their home. This clear-sighted woman had a North German's repugnance for everything phony. She was hardly devoted to any

Führer myth and very definitely was no fanatical Hitler Youth. Already in the late 1920s she was making so many mockingly critical and sincerely disgusted remarks about incidents in the party and about Hitler himself that poor Hess was constantly giving her warning glances and even had to call her to task. Then later I heard that Frau Hess was rather actively involved together with Pfeffer, the former SA commander, in the so-called Stennes revolt. She was said to have inveigled Hitler into making an automobile trip into the countryside in order to make him inaccessible to Goebbels, who was seeking assistance, and in order to give Stennes time to exploit his initial success. According to this story Frau Hess was in Hitler's bad graces for years thereafter. Whether that is all true or not I do not know. In any event, it was noticeably the case that Frau Hess was never mentioned in official party announcements until the beginning of World War II. Not until then was her name mentioned in the party newspapers and even that article was worded in such a way that the uninitiated must have concluded that Hess had only recently married.

Hess's political and human destiny after 1933 devolved from his attitude with a logical inevitability. Hess became "Deputy Führer" because Hitler could depend unconditionally upon his loyalty and his obedience. Hess was probably also the only one in Hitler's intimate circle who never even thought of misusing his exalted position to satisfy his own ambition, and who also had no thought of pursuing politics of his own or for his own goals. And that is precisely why, given the particular circumstances in the Nazi party and the particular way Hitler operated, Hess was also unable to fulfill his duties and was increasingly shoved aside, primarily by the robust Martin Bormann. His flight to England was the appropriate conclusion of his political career—the ultimate sacrifice made by Hagen for King Gunther, and also for his people, in hopes of saving them both from destruction.

I know from trustworthy oral reports that certainly from the very beginning Hess was not an enthusiastic supporter of Hitler's war policy, even though it was presumably more the methods than the goals that he opposed. His concern grew and drove him to act when Hitler's aggressive intentions against Russia became increasingly clear. There were simple and comprehensible reasons for this. As a soldier in World War I Hess had himself learned how impossible it was to fight a two-front war successfully and had thus come to the same conclusions as Hitler had laid down in *Mein Kampf*.[3]

Secondly, Hess had drawn away from the "iron curtain" methods of the anti-Comintern circle and had kept his door open for anyone who brought him objective information on Soviet Russia. Through the intermediacy of Professor Haushofer, the geopolitician, he came into possession of documents showing that industrial construction had begun in and behind the Ural Mountains, that the Kasan and Kalmuck Steppes were being prepared for cultivation, that the railroad network east of Moscow was being developed. In general, he discovered a growing stabilization and strengthening of the Bolshevist system, which suggested that Russia had far stronger powers of resistance than Hitler wanted to recognize. Hess became convinced that war with the Soviets would become a life and death struggle. If there was to be even a minimal hope of success for Germany in this struggle then matters had to be terminated in the West. Given the situation, the initiative would have to come from Germany. Given Hitler's principled view that any sign of a willingness to negotiate was a sign of weakness, or at least would be interpreted as such, and given the undoubtedly stiffening attitude of England, it was obviously unthinkable that Germany would officially determine to make such a step. And so Hess did what Hitler and Foreign Minister von Ribbentrop were unwilling to do, and consciously took upon himself, in the event of an unsuccessful mission, the onus of treason or insanity. That he still thought of himself, in this self-chosen mission, as the completely loyal follower of Hitler is evidenced by the proposals he made to the English, insofar as they communicated them fully and correctly. Stripping away the threats and the

---

[3] In Chapter 4 Hitler argues that Germany must expand into Eastern Europe, seizing living space from Russia, and that this required an alliance with England. "With England alone was it possible, our rear protected, to begin the new Germanic march" (p. 140). In Chapter 7 Hitler describes what the two-front war meant from 1914–17: ". . . All this while the German had only his shield arm for defense, while his sword was obliged to strike, now in the East, now in the South" (pp. 195–196). Page citations are from the Ralph Mannheim translation, paperback (New York, 1962). Hitler dictated *Mein Kampf* to Hess while imprisoned in 1924; thus Hess was certainly familiar with its contents.

boasting, they boil down to the formula: "A guarantee for the Empire in return for a free hand in Eastern Europe." In other words, they were precisely the same terms Hitler had repeatedly uttered in public or to the party's leaders.[4]

Hess's peace action was bound to fail at that point in time. Churchill would have been foolish to agree, since a fight to the death between Germany and Russia would have taken pressure off the British Empire for decades to come anyway. Quite apart from that, Hess's inclination to view matters in the least complicated way and to deal with them like a woodchopper made him completely unsuitable for a diplomatic mission. I observed him in a telling example of this in Hamburg.

As I recall, it was after the Nazi Party Congress of 1929, which produced extensive debts, that Hess betook himself on a beggar's journey. He announced his intention to visit us, too, and asked Brinkmann and me[5] to assemble a group of interested businessmen so that he could speak to them. Fulfilling his request was pretty difficult. In those days Nazism had hardly any quotation value in the Hamburg stock exchange. But finally we were able to persuade five or six gentlemen to show up. They sat there with cold expressions on their faces and waited to hear what Herr Hess had to say.

But Hess had less to say than he had to show. He pulled two sets of photographs out of his pocket: One set consisted of turbulent revolutionary scenes (Red flags, mass demonstrations of Communists); the other showed marching Stormtroopers, SA men falling in for roll call, the SS with their select "human material"—in short, formations of "discipline and order."

He passed these two sets around among the assembled businessmen, waited patiently until they had all seen them, and then spoke. He uttered at most ten sentences, along the lines of: "Here, gentlemen, you have the forces of destruction, which are dangerous

---

[4] On Hess's flight to England see J. Bernard Hutton, *Hess, the Man and His Mission* (London, 1970) and James Leasor, *The Uninvited Envoy* (London 1962).

[5] Krebs' dating is probably off by one year here since he and Brinkmann resigned their positions around the time of the 1928 party congress and would hardly be asked to undertake this assignment later, when Kaufmann was leading the Nazi organization in Hamburg.

threats to your countinghouses, your factories, all your possessions. On the other hand, the forces of order are forming, with a fanatical will to root out the spirit of turmoil. Unfortunately, will alone is not enough, as long as all material preconditions are lacking. The SA man is poor; the party-comrades are poor; the whole organization is poor. Where will the uniforms come from? The boots, the flags, the drums? In short where will we get all the equipment that nowadays goes with the contemporary political style, if there is no money? Everyone who has must give lest he ultimately lose everything that he has!"

Unfortunately, the compelling logic of this presentation did not convince those assembled. They wanted to learn a bit more about the Nazis and tried to generate a discussion. But they were unable to do this by posing sarcastically provocative questions such as, "Surely you are not trying to say, Herr Hess, that your Nazis will be some sort of night-watchman service for big business?" Or: "We can hardly believe that your party-comrades and Stormtroopers agree completely with this role you have planned for them as deputy police and peacekeepers. As far as we've been informed, your supporters are overwhelmingly revolutionary and anti-capitalist." It was of no avail. Hess refused to be drawn into any further explanations or statements. The discussion ended without any result after a scant forty minutes.

Naturally Hess fully understood the extent of his failure and was also quite angry about it. But he was in no way prepared to accept the blame for it. He viewed his erstwhile audience as complete hypocrites who only wanted to avoid admitting that for capitalists the sum of politics consisted of protecting their property. When I objected that, firstly, he was fundamentally deluding himself with this analysis and, secondly, that even if he were right there were other means of protecting their possessions which might appear more effective to these gentlemen than financing the Nazi party, and that, thirdly, even the devil likes to be treated as a gentleman, Hess said that was just further evidence of my complicated intellectual ways. Yet I am convinced that he understood me quite well. He simply did not want to understand me. He refused to permit it because he viewed such ways of thinking as already backsliding into the impure and effeminate thought patterns of democracy. And he stated it openly: "If you look at everything from above and below and both sides, and you want to talk about it and discuss it that way, you will never reach a decision!" I could only reply: "And if you never consider and think about things, you will surely always make the wrong decisions!"

Despite these contradictions, we always maintained a mutual benevolence. Even today I refuse to view Hess as a "criminal," at least insofar as motives are weighed along with actions or failures to act.

CHAPTER 8

Alfred Rosenberg

My personal encounters with Alfred Rosenberg were rare. Furthermore, in view of his inability to engage in a proper conversation, which stemmed from his assumed arrogance and his actual insecurity, they were generally unproductive. Thus I have a precise recollection of only three conversations with him.

In 1929 or 1930 I wrote an editorial for the *Hansische Warte* in which I expressed doubts about the value of a foreign policy fundamentally opposed to Soviet Russia. Thereupon Rosenberg, who in those days before the emergence of Dr. Otto Dietrich was still the *Führer's* commissioner for the Coordination of the National Socialist Press, sent me a telegram ordering me to report to Munich and justify myself. As an employee of the DHV, and in order to protect my own independence, I neither wanted to nor was able to comply with this command immediately. So I did not report to the Schelling Strasse until about ten days later. Here I was at first told to wait in the anteroom with the explanation that Herr Rosenberg was still engaged in putting the *Völkischer Beobachter* to press. But after twenty minutes of waiting and after a printed copy of the newspaper had been delivered to the office, I told the secretary that the excuse given to me seemed to have lost credibility. She should inform Herr Rosenberg that because of previously made appointments with Rudolf Hess and Gregor Strasser I no longer had much time left. At this I was immediately admitted.

Rosenberg sat behind his desk but did not rise, did not look up, did not respond to my greeting with anything more than an incomprehensible growl, and made no signal to me to come closer or sit down. Obviously the "important man" wanted to follow up his punishment of making me wait outside by making me stand for a while in the doorway and obviously he wanted to deal with me while I was standing up. So I found a chair myself, moved it over next to his desk, seated myself, and began with a friendly smile: "You wished to speak with me?"

"Fourteen days ago," he grumbled.

"At that point I didn't have time."

"An employee of the party press *must* have time when I summon him."

"I am not an employee of the party press; I am an employee of the DHV," I answered.

He was silent for a moment and then he said, "Ah, so," and continued without transition: "For years the DHV has had remarkable politics; does it now favor an understanding with Bolshevism?"

"I did not write my article at the behest of the DHV."

"Well, then, it's Otto Strasser or Ernst Nieckisch[1] who's behind it!"

"Nobody's behind it except Dr. Krebs."

He shook his head in disbelief and grumbled: "Somebody's always behind it." Then suddenly he reached for his fountain pen and declared: "I have no more time! I have to write an article for tomorrow!"

Now that he had been unsuccessful in playing the role of Press Overlord, he obviously wanted to withdraw into the sheltering burrow of Overburdened Writer. But I was not going to let that happen. I had traveled all the way from Hamburg to Munich and now I wanted at least to learn the opinions of this man who was then viewed by most Nazis as the prospective foreign minister of Germany. I wanted his opinions firsthand, precisely, and with his supporting reasons. But I certainly had very incomplete success in this. That is, I got him talking again, but hardly learned anything more than I had already read a dozen times in his articles for the *Völkischer Beobachter* and the *Weltkampf*. What he added out of his own experiences of 1917 in Moscow was said with so little vividness and perceptual clarity that it produced the minimum effect and actually sounded unbelievable at several points. You could not shake off the suspicion: He's only telling me that now in order to provide supporting evidence for his assertions and theses.

[1] Promoter of an anti-Hitlerian ideology called National Bolshevism.

When questions or objections were raised he as good as ignored them. That is, when he came to the end of a monologue he let his discussion partner speak, too. But still one had the impression that he was not really listening at all. Now and then, at critical remarks, he would pinch his lips together or essay a calculated smile, which naturally earned him a reputation for arrogant surliness. Surely that was an unfair accusation as was the reproach that he wanted to exercise a dictatorship over ideas. It was simply that he was so rigid in acting out his imaginations and his egotistic daydreams of being the Baltic nobleman, the English lord, the scientific genius of Copernican dimensions, that this ultimately caused him completely to lose his already stunted capacity to relate to and converse with other human beings. In any event I returned to Hamburg after this "discussion" without Rosenberg's having even halfway convinced me that his "official party analysis" was capable of being proven. Basically he had not even made a serious attempt at it, since he was so wrapped up in his own opinions that he simply could not understand how anyone else could have different ones.

A second conversation took place in the summer of 1931 shortly after the banks collapsed. I was in Munich negotiating the takeover of the *Hamburger Tageblatt* by Eher Publishing Company. Rosenberg wanted me to tell him what people in Hamburg and in the DHV thought about the political consequences of the bank crisis. He himself hoped for an upsurge of political tensions that would lead to the rapid collapse of the Brüning government. My view, that the Chancellor was probably not at all distressed by the bank crisis, considering its effect on the reparations negotiations, and possibly might even have contributed to its inception, was a view which he absolutely refused to consider. But he was able to accept the notion of Brüning's responsibility, though from another viewpoint, as validating his own idea of what Brüning intended and was trying to accomplish. That is, he seriously believed that Brüning was an agent of the Vatican with the sole assignment of using his emergency decrees and their consequent impoverishment of ever increasing numbers of people to deliver Protestant North Germany into the hands of the Communists. Then the people, having been put through this purgatorial fire, would be ripe for a second Counter-Reformation through the restoration of the Catholic princely houses. We talked around and about this point for a

long time while I tried to refute Rosenberg's view by citing Brüning's record as a combat officer and his sharply anti-Communist
policy as business manger of the Catholic trade unions. However,
it was a complete failure. Rosenberg's political thoughts moved on
such rigid and well-worn tracks that you could not get around him
no matter how many concrete facts you produced. He simply
spoke of the camouflage and conscious deception with which world
Catholicism strove to conceal its secret plans and goals from the
eyes of the people.

The cause of our third conversation was again some remarks in
the *Hamburger Tageblatt*. On the occasion of the conflict over the
Hamburg Memorial we had expressed ourselves positively about
the works of Ernst Barlach.[2] Thereupon Rosenberg, who was particularly enraged by our having described Barlach as a "Nordic
artist," called me to account during one of my visits to Munich. I
tried to explain our position by pointing out the inner relationship
between Barlach and the masters of the Late Gothic style. As
Rosenberg was an admirer of Meister Eckhart, I assumed that he
would at least show understanding for the mystical spirit of Late
Gothic art. However, that was not the case. Rosenberg labeled
Late Gothic paintings and statues the decadent offsprings of styl-
ite-asceticism, hostile to life and the human body, and he denied
them any connection with the spiritualism of the mystics. Frankly,
I got the impression that he had never given serious thought up
to then to such a relationship. Though thanks to his excellent
memory and prodigious energy he had acquired an astounding
mass of individual facts, he completely lacked the aptitude to inte-
grate these facts and develop a proper understanding of the contexts and connections of historical events. Perhaps he did not even
want to because he could only uphold his theory by flight into the
world of schematic constructs.[3] Thus this conversation too

[2] Ernst Barlach (1870–1938) was Germany's foremost expressionist sculptor
and in general one of the twentieth century's most renowned artists. In the
Third Reich his works were condemned as decadent; in 1937 he was formally
forbidden to produce further art. For Rosenberg's view of why, see Joachim
Fest, *The Face of the Third Reich*, paperback (New York, 1970), p. 556, n.
30.
[3] Rosenberg authored the major historical exegis of Nazi doctrine, *Der
Mythus des 20. Jahrhunderts* (Munich, 1930), which explains all human his-

remained rather unfruitful, except for Rosenberg's parenthetical remark that he had studied Eckhart at the urging of Dr. Friedrich Weber. Weber was a member of the Munich Academic Guild, which in the winter semester of 1922–23 had thoroughly studied the writings of Eckhart, as published by Eugen Diederichs.[4] Obviously in the course of the political negotiations that began early in the summer of 1923 between Rosenberg and Dr. Weber, as leader of "Oberland" (in those months Rosenberg made his first contact with racialist academicians and Youth Movement people), the subject of Eckhart came up. Rosenberg, who was always looking for new "spiritual witnesses," followed it up. And actually one *could* see Meister Eckhart, the great preacher and teacher of mysticism, as a conscious rebel, a defender of the Germanic spirit against Rome and the Roman Church—if you followed the admittedly very controversial edition of his works by Eugen Diederichs. In any case Rosenberg took him as such and built him into his "Mythus."

And that was in general his way. As an untiring reader he took from every available writing anything that appeared useful as evidence for his own opinions. Thus he saw a reference in an unsigned article series in the *Völkischer Kurier*, the weekly newspaper of the Social Racialist Block in Bavaria, to the more than questionable book *Tusca*, by Albert Grünwedel; accepted this attempt at deciphering Etruscan texts as impeccable scholarship, and constructed his entire chapter on the Etruscans upon it.[5] And

tory by racial theory. This produced incredible feats of imagination: Egyptian civilization was inaugurated by Aryans from the "Lost Continent of Atlantis"; Rome fell because infected by blood-mixture with the Etruscans who were one of the "Twelve Lost Tribes of Israel"; etc. It was so turgid that even Hitler confessed that he had never been able to finish it.

   [4] An influential publisher, philosopher, and promoter of racialist ideas. His significance is discussed in George L. Mosse's *The Crisis of German Ideology*, paperback (New York, 1964), p. 52 ff.

   [5] Grünwedel was a respected scholar who, apparently as a result of senility, published the above mentioned book, which was so awful that his colleagues inserted notices in the scholarly reviews requesting that the book never be mentioned out of respect for Grünwedel's earlier accomplishments and reputation. Everyone complied except Rosenberg, who apparently knew nothing of this background. Thus the scandal reemerged when the *Mythus* was published. For details, see Reinhard Bollmus, *Das Amt Rosenberg und seine Gegner* (Stuttgart, 1970), p. 23.

thus, probably while he was still a student, Rosenberg took over
the view of the first generation of "free" Estonian historians
(Moora, Sild, Tallgren) that the invasion of German Christians
had caused the decline of a highly developed ancient Estonian culture, and applied it in his writings to the relationship between the
ancient Romans and Germans. Had he cited these and his numerous other "sources" from Gobineau to Chamberlain to Schemann
and the other race researchers, and had he further succeeded in
creating out of the little scraps of information he picked up everywhere a new pattern of ideas that was his own, then there would
have been little objection against his methods. Since, however, neither of these things happened, the *Mythus* was immediately subjected to vast criticism, even from the leadership ranks of the Nazi
party. The sharpest criticism came from Goebbels and the Strasser
brothers; somewhat milder criticism came from Hess and some of
the north German Gauleiters.

Hitler himself had a very clear idea of the value, or more accurately, the valuelessness of the book. A few weeks after it was published he asked me for my judgment but, without waiting for any
answer, threw a copy of it on his desk with a deprecating gesture
and said "Plagiarized, pasted together, nonsensical junk! Bad
Chamberlain with some trimmings!" Of course that did not prevent Hitler from making the author of the bad book the indoctrination leader of the party.[6] Perhaps it was just that which led him
to make the appointment: As a master of propaganda he knew,
after all, that it is precisely the incomprehensible and the nonsensical that has the greatest effect upon the masses.

One of Rosenberg's most vehement opponents was Max Amann,
his publisher. But undoubtedly this was not so much for intellectual reasons as it was for personal ones. Rosenberg used to do some
of his writing in the Odeon Coffeehouse. There he would sit at one
of the little round marble tables right next to the big front
window, where all the people could see him writing or "visibly"
thinking. Three or four tables or chairs around him would be covered with books and papers. Amann repeatedly pointed him out to

[6] In 1934 Hitler appointed Rosenberg as "The Commissioner of the Führer
for the Supervision of the Entire Intellectual and Ideological Indoctrination
and Education of the N.S.D.A.P.," a post he held for the rest of the Third
Reich.

me when we would pass by, with the words: "Look at 'im squat-
ting there, the fool-headed, stuck-up, undergraduate ninny! Writing 'works'—the Bohemian! Oughta be puttin' out a decent newspaper instead!" Without a doubt the Herr Publishing Director
hated his Managing Editor out of the fullness of his passionate
Bavarian heart. Obviously for him, Rosenberg, who came from an
area that was located even beyond Prussia, was the embodiment of
all those good-for-nothing Prussian yearling officers[7] who had once
made life miserable for him as a Bavarian sergeant.

Rosenberg's critics did him an injustice, however, when they
took all his abrasive qualities and attitudes as by-products of his
personality. Much must rather be attributed to his origins and his
career. In the party Rosenberg was thought of as a Baltic German
and he wanted to be thought of as such. In reality he was not that
and even his commitment to the German nation came after years
of wavering and then was probably primarily a result of logical
political calculation.

According to all my information, Rosenberg, born in 1893 in
Reval, came from a family of Estonian cottagers who, as frequently happened in the Baltic states in the middle of the nineteenth century, took the name of their German landlord and kept
it even after they moved from the country into the city. They
apparently also kept the feeling of belonging to the German
middle classes since otherwise it would be somewhat difficult to
understand Rosenberg's joining the Rubonia Corps[8] while he was
a student at the Riga Technical Academy. Its membership consisted of students of German origin from Russia or the Baltic
states and also those who felt German without having definite
German ancestry, such as could only be found in this area with its
shifting and transitory cultures and its rigid social distinctions.

After the outbreak of the war in 1914 Rosenberg must have
experienced a change of heart. Whether he became conscious of his
Estonian heritage or of belonging to the "Russian fatherland" can
no longer be determined. In any event by 1917 he was in Moscow

---

[7] *Einjähriger*. Gymnasium graduates in Prussia were privileged to serve only
one year in the army in imperial days, and that as officers. The only analogy in
America is the ROTC and the attitude toward them held by Regular Army
noncoms.

[8] A dueling fraternity

where he experienced the outbreak of the Russian Revolution and the first months of its course. How he came to be in Moscow, whether of his own volition or as a Russian soldier, is something I have tried to discover without success. He himself always evaded questions about this. But however that may be, what is indicative of his entire mental attitude in those days is that after he became known as a foe of the revolution he did not join the Baltic militia, as the entire Baltic-German youth did, but joined the stream of Russian émigrés to Paris.[9] There he became acquainted with the writings of Gobineau. These, he believed, could decipher the secret causes of the Russian Revolution, which he had just experienced himself. Thus they became the basis of his life philosophy.

From Paris Rosenberg wanted to go to London because, on the strength of his newly discovered insight, he thought that Great Britain, as the purest Germanic Great Power of the Old World, was alone in a position to combat Bolshevism with hopes of success. But London refused to grant him an entry visa, certainly not because he was the young unknown Mr. Rosenberg but because he was the Russian émigré Rosenberg from whom political trouble was to be feared whether he might be a tsarist or a Communist agent.

Rosenberg then went to Munich and probably still not in quest of Germany in this city but rather only to attach himself to the headquarters of German anti-Bolshevism, where activists and émigrés from eastern and southeastern Europe were gathering around Max Erwin von Scheubner-Richter.[10] Here in Munich there ensued the encounter with Nazism and, through that, with the particularly German problems, troubles, and tasks. But it was only slowly and incompletely that he made himself familiar with them. His essential and primary concern remained, as before, the "World Struggle" against "Jewish Bolshevism," against "Western-Jewish" Freemasonry, and against "Oriental-Jewish" Christianity. Seen thus,

[9] This information came from the political police and was supplied by Brüning to Habermann and the DHV (*Krebs' note*—W. S. A.).

[10] Max Erwin von Scheubner-Richter (1884–1923) was a Baltic German close to extreme conservative circles in Germany. He established the first contact between Hitler and Ludendorff and was later killed in the Putsch of 1923. See Karl Dietrich Bracher, *The German Dictatorship* (New York, 1970), p. 90 and *passim*.

Rosenberg was definitely no nationalist in the customary sense of the word. That is, he occasionally employed nationalistic terminology and appealed to nationalistic or racialist emotions, but these emotions were completely lacking in reality for him since he had no true roots in any nation. They were rather only pieces of scaffolding for his doctrinaire thought constructs. It seems no accident to me that Rosenberg was the only one who had nothing to say when he went to the gallows at Nuremberg. For him there was no legacy and no heritage.

CHAPTER 9

Gregor Strasser

The end of Gregor Strasser's life is well known. Toward noon on June 30, 1934, he died under the pistol shots of SS men who were surely convinced that they were executing one of the greatest traitors to the cause of Nazism and the *Führer*. The "plot" that was supposedly kept from fulfillment by Hitler's prompt intervention at that moment in Munich, Berlin, Hamburg,and Dresden was, as they saw it, hardly Strasser's first open betrayal. He had already betrayed the *Führer* in December 1932 when he resigned his national offices in the party in order to terminate a long-planned conspiracy with its enemies. Despite this he had been forgiven and had even been permitted an important and well-paid position in the chemical industry. But he had shown himself unworthy of the pardon. Patience was at an end: "Traitors must die, even when they are among the party's oldest fighters and have earned the greatest merit!"

Today we know that, from the standpoint of the convinced Nazi, Gregor Strasser could in fact be justifiably called a traitor. At the very latest, from the time of Hitler's failure in the presidential campaign, which Strasser had foreseen and also predicted to me, he was no longer willing to follow passively and without objection the course Hitler was steering for the party. Yet the beginnings of his political disaffection lay further back. Very likely it was already by 1930 that Strasser established connections with all sorts of groups and people without reporting this fully to Hitler or without informing him at all. But the first decisive blow against what was probably originally an unqualified confidence in Hitler came at the Bamberg Conference of February 1926, as will be described presently. Thus Strasser's willingness to separate from Hitler, to lend his hand toward splitting the party, and to abandon the party's claim to total power by cooperating with General Schleicher's cabinet was only the final stage of a long development determined by internal and external factors.

Therefore it is erroneous to explain Strasser's change of heart as having been caused solely by the party's poor financial position after the 1932 presidential elections, which allegedly led Strasser to doubt the ultimate victory of Nazism. It is equally erroneous to explain it by the supposed lure of becoming vice-chancellor. The party's finances, given the high costs of its organization and propaganda, were *always* strained. The strain had by no means reached catastrophic dimensions in the summer of 1932, or in any event was hardly greater than in some of the earlier years. One must not use the experiences of the middle-class parties as a standard of comparison for a party with regularly collected dues and systematically gathered contributions, not to mention several sound businesses (the publishing houses, insurance firms, quartermaster's stores). All this provided a financial understructure that would assure continued freedom of movement even if individual contributions from industrial and financial circles became more meager. As for the temptation of the vice-chancellorship, a victorious Hitler would have had offices to offer a loyal Strasser with far greater and more tangible power in them. No, it was not because of doubts over the likelihood of Hitler's victory that Strasser split with him, but rather because Strasser believed that such a victory —and it could only be a total one—would be disastrous. He no longer desired a victory for Hitler because he had come to understand what that would portend for the German people.

Gregor Strasser, the pharmacist from Landshut, was externally and internally a thorough Bavarian: coarse, full of battle lust, devoted to all the pleasures and joys of life whether gross or fine, a man of mercurial temperament and unquiet blood but simultaneously also cautious and full of peasant slyness, obstinacy, and devotion to the customary and traditional. He recounted with triumphant pleasure the story of how his battery had been received in the autumn of 1918 by the representative of the Soldiers' Soviet of Landshut:[1] "There he stood, the lousy bum, and chattered and

---

[1] In the last four days of World War I revolutionary "soviets" sprang up all over Germany, which seized control of the various towns. They were still in command when most of the German army returned home to be demobilized.

clattered on with his stupid swine grunts that he had learned by heart about the International, the victorious proletariat, the blood-thirsty generals and warmongers, the sweat-squeezing capitalists and stockbrokers. I sat up there on my nag, which I secretly nudged against the guy so that he was always having to step backward again and again, and I said nothing and slowly collected a whole mouthful of spit. Finally the guy got to the end and screamed out: 'Deliver up your weapons! Rip up your flags and insignia! Vote for the Soviet of Soldiers!' And by then I was ready: I let him have the whole mouthful of spit right in the middle of his face; I *flooded* the bum away. And then I gave the order 'Battery . . . trot!' and we marched back into Landshut the same way we had marched out in 1914."

That was the same Gregor Strasser who in meeting-hall battles, despite his diabetes, would whip off his coat, leap down from the speaker's podium, grab a chair and slug away with it. Or who would disrupt the Reichstag with a raucous tumult. But there was also another Strasser who kept the friendship of artists and writers, for example, with a man of such delicate sensitivity as the Baltic lyricist Otto von Taube, and who read widely, even during his sickness, Homer in the original Greek. Apart from that what distinguished Strasser from most of Hitler's other early collaborators was that he had not only acquired a middle-class profession but actually also practiced it, at least during the first years of his political activity. The pharmacist from Landshut had a bit of ground under his feet, which assured him his spiritual freedom and protected him from sliding off into the ranks of the political managers and literateurs.

Perhaps Gregor Strasser's brother, the Capuchin priest, also incorporated the forces of attachment and tradition for him, while his other brother, Otto, played the role of the nihilistic Mephistopheles who through negativism goaded one to a critical analysis of men and events. How much influence each of these brothers had upon Gregor would surely be something to which only an intimate friend of Strasser's could testify. Insofar as I was acquainted with Otto, I would not overestimate his influence. He himself, in speaking with me, repeatedly used the expression "My big brother has deigned to decide (big, please note, only in size). . . ." "In my estimation this formula was not just an expression of irony but also of a certain opposition and envy. On the other side Gregor occasionally spoke of his "super smart, ink-slinging kid brother" in a tone of voice that was equally evident of something less than pure brotherly love. Also he apparently had a poor opinion of Otto's collaborators: Herbert Blanck, von Schapke, and Hinckel. I admit that his first happened at a time when Gregor had already almost reached full human and political maturity.

In my opinion Gregor Strasser was the only real politician among the leading Nazis prior to 1933, if you include the property of political "Arete" (virtue) and not just political "Eros." That is, in addition to passion, ambition, combativeness, decisiveness, and willingness to take risks, also the ability to be moderate, to await the fullness of events, to differentiate, to recognize reality and build on the basis of it, to aspire to serve and be capable of respect.

Now that does not mean that Gregor Strasser possessed all of these attributes together or even that they were fully developed in him. But at least he tried and this attempt protected him from that sterile doctrinaire attitude prevailing not just among most Nazis but among very many German politicians: that definition of means and ends by the laws of an ideology drunk with illusions, that imaginary world of "as if." Thus Strasser was capable of change, of growth. He learned from experience, not just from association with men and events, but from evaluating them. It is true that the other Nazi leaders also grew with their assignments—Hitler, Goebbels, Goering, Himmler, Rosenberg, Schwartz, Amann—but they grew only in one dimension: horizontal extension. Strasser, on the other hand, grew in depth and height and thus uncovered in himself new well-springs of perception and saw broader perspectives. And therefore he was even ultimately prepared to change his political goals and to abandon favorite conceptions far beyond what could be expected of other members of the "front-lines generation" from the World War after 1918.

I first met Gregor Strasser in 1924 at the convention in Weimar of the National Socialist Liberation Movement, where the attempt was made, with only partial success, to unify the South German Nazis with the North German Racial Liberationists under the patronage of Ludendorff. As is generally known, Strasser supported this attempt while Esser and Streicher gave wild rabble-rousing speeches against the proposed unification and on behalf of their so-called Greater German Racial Community which had its main groups in Nuremberg and Munich.[2]

For Strasser's position, the following viewpoints were apparently decisive. According to the speech he gave to the assembled delegates, Strasser at that point in time was still like most of the young people of his class: far more counterrevolutionary than revolutionary. For him the Nazi party was less a party in the customary sense, trying to set itself off from other parties through its program, than it was the iron edge of a wedge that consisted of the broad "national movement" made up of many groups. This wedge was being driven into the Weimar Republic. The Munich Putsch of November 1923 had shattered it and robbed it of its most eloquent spokesman. On the other hand the May elections of 1924 had brought the movement its first thirty-two delegates to the Reichstag, including Strasser himself. In this situation what would be more likely for a man who himself admitted that he had never even properly read the Twenty-Five Points of the Nazi program and who had only a sympathetic smile for the sharply defined principles of Feder's theories than to try to regather the splintered segments of the wedge and at least assure himself of a loose electoral backing even if this meant blurring the fine philosphical distinctions? These thoughts differentiated him from the rigidly doctrinaire stance of Streicher and Esser, whom he found repulsive anyway.

To judge by the success of the moment it was actually not Strasser but Esser and Streicher who made the correct decision at Weimar. The National Socialist Liberation Movement under Ludendorff never got beyond a paper proclamation, and after the December elections of 1924 its followers were able to send only

---

[2] In an addendum to his memoirs Krebs later noted that yet another group was present at this convention, consisting chiefly of students from Göttingen University, including Rudolf Haase, Adalbert Volck, and Reinhardt Sunkel. This group derided the Racial Liberationists as rhetorical in their radicalism, antiquarian in their anti-Semitism, and comic in their Teutonic cultism. They opposed any parliamentary or electoral activity as a betrayal of revolutionary ideals and called for the formation of cadres for direct revolutionary action. Subsequently, they exercised little influence in the Nazi party though they were active in the Nazi Student League. After 1933 they were all relegated to secondary roles.

fourteen delegates into the Reichstag. When Hitler was released from Landsberg Fortress it collapsed completely. But if you look at it from a long-range viewpoint, Strasser's actions at Weimar were the correct ones. The winning of North Germany for Nazism, which organizationally at least was his accomplishment, was possible for him only on the basis of the contacts and relationships that he had developed since Weimar. For a long time, from about 1925 to 1929, Strasser's name meant almost more north of the German midlands than Hitler's, not just in the party but above all in the outer ring of watching, sympathizing racialist and nationalist groups among whom Nazism was seeking influence. Also the politics pursued in the Reichstag, insofar as a seven-man group can be said to pursue politics at all, was largely determined by Strasser even though Frick was officially the caucus leader.

As Hitler's commissioner for North Germany Strasser also conducted the membership meeting in Hamburg in November 1926, which, after some shilly-shallying, elected me Local Group leader. Strasser found it pretty hard to approve of the choice because he foresaw the difficulties which would arise for me out of my insufficient acquaintance with Hamburg. I had just moved to the city in June and knew little of its conditions in general and of the people and circumstances in the party there in particular. Furthermore he perceived from the scarcely three-minute-long speech I gave accepting the nomination how little I was qualified as a popular orator and how much I lacked personal ambitions. I have mentioned this actually insignificant incident because it seems to me characteristic of Strasser the politician. He did not ask: "How long has this Dr. Krebs been in the party?" He did not put my ideology or opinions to the test but did in fact examine in a sense my competence under those particularly unique conditions as he assumed them to be. That was the way he considered things. It was an approach that I was to encounter among none of the other Nazi leaders that I came to know. With all the others ideological prejudice dominated to an extent that permitted the sober recognition of the given reality only peripherally but never in its entirety.

Even Otto Strasser, who without a doubt was gifted with the ability to analyze men and affairs critically, immediately made faulty judgments whenever he thought he could detect agreement with his radically "socialist" ideology. Since beyond that he was considerably wanting in inner and external discipline, his "Black

Front"[3] later became a collection of noodleheads and political Bohemians.

Naturally even Gregor Strasser's sense of reality had its limits. They were to be found in his basic convictions, which had led him into politics in the first place and which defined friend and foe for him. Yet precisely in those years his convictions were changing. He was no longer a counterrevolutionary, as he had been initially, but rather found himself developing into a national revolutionary. Thus he was swept by the current that bore along the majority of the front-line's generation and the succeeding generation of youth. They came to realize that you could not go home again to the Bismarckian Reich; they hated the Weimar Republic, above all because it seemed to be justifying the defeat of 1918 by making, in front of the whole world, unfair and politically influenced accusations against their own people and their own heritage. They were in quest of a "Third Reich" with new life forms for the state, the economy, and society—forms that were neither Eastern nor Western.

I do not know the extent to which it was Strasser's own reflections or the influence of other people's ideas that led him to tread new paths. It was a feature of those years that many men in different places drew the same conclusions from the same assumptions quite independently of one another. On the other hand I also know that Strasser, again in contrast to many other leading Nazis, did not disdain relationships with the most diverse groups and individuals associated with the "national revolution." He also read books and writings that were not published by Eher & Co. in Munich. Thus he was familiar with the work of the Fichte Society in Hamburg and with "German Folkdom," the circle around Jünger and Schauwecker, with Nieckisch, Moeller van den Bruck,[4]

---

[3] After Otto Strasser split with Hitler in 1930, he organized a dissident national socialist group of this name and fought the Nazis inside Germany until 1933 and then from Czechoslovakia during the Third Reich. When Hitler annexed Czechoslovakia the "Black Front" fell apart. Otto Strasser emigrated to Canada, experienced a re-conversion to Catholicism, abandoned politics, and returned to West Germany after World War II, where he still lives.

[4] Moeller van den Bruck was the neo-conservative theoretician who coined the term "Third Reich." His writings are analyzed in Fritz Stern's *The Politics of Cultural Despair*, paperback (New York, 1961). Jünger, Nieckisch, and the Fichte Society are identified by footnotes in earlier chapters.

and the "Racial Studies" texts of Lehmann Publishing House, of which, by the way, he had a rather low opinion.

Despite all this it was not theory but concrete problems that absorbed Strasser's primary attention. His work in the party and his publications (the Combat Press in Berlin, editing the *National Socialist Correspondence*) were also devoted to pragmatic goals. That is, they served to give the movement a clearer, more unambiguous profile, especially in the areas of economic and social policy, and to define more sharply the revolutionary line, the thrust toward the future. Since the first Nazi newspaper for Hamburg, the weekly *Volksblatt*, was an insert of the Combat Press for a long time, I became rather closely acquainted with these interrelationships. They, in turn, relate closely to the Bamberg Conference of 1926, which I mentioned at the beginning of this chapter.[5]

After the Nazi party was reestablished in the spring of 1925, as Strasser recounted it to me during a visit in 1928, there were initially some rather strong groups founded outside of Bavaria, primarily in the Ruhr where the tradition of the 1923 struggle against the French continued to have effects. In Elberfeld there arose a group calling itself the Working Community of the Northwestern Districts of the NSDAP, which created its own publishing organ, the *National Socialist Correspondence*. This group included, in addition to Gregor Strasser and some others, Karl Kaufmann and Dr. Goebbels. It produced the so-called "Elberfeld Principles," which were designed to expand on the original Nazi program and in some respects to alter it. Their general drift was to emphasize an anti-bourgeois socialistic stance: the rights of the young nations were proclaimed against the capitalistic West; workers, peasants, and soldiers were summoned to take up the struggle. The program was visibly influenced by Moeller van den Bruck, Nieckisch, and the earlier stages of Bolshevism when the liberation of the peasants and the system of soviets predominated, even though the basic principle of private property was maintained and Bolshevism as a whole was sharply rejected. Apart from that there was much that

[5] For a divergent interpretation of the Bamberg conference, see Joseph L. Nyomarkay, "Factionalism in the National Socialist German Workers' Party, 1925–26: The Myth of the 'Northern Faction,' " *Political Science Quarterly* (1965), p. 22; reprinted in Henry A. Turner, ed., *Nazism and the Third Reich* (New York, 1972).

was vague, and by the time Strasser described it to me he was no longer wholeheartedly behind the program.

But the "Elberfeld Principles" had yet another intent which concerned internal Nazi politics. It was aimed toward halting the "Munich" fascist trend and forcing upon Hitler himself a "constitution" that would have made him into *primus inter pares* but not absolute despot. At the Bamberg Conference, which was conceived as the meeting of a small circle of leaders, the North German representatives wanted to present their principles and try to get them accepted by means of a vote. But Hitler, who at that point in time could not rely on his authority alone, invited every available subleader from Franconia[6] to the conference and with their assistance thwarted the intentions of the North German representatives by means which were, in the formal sense, unchallengeably democratic. This was relatively easy since simply on the basis of their experiences these Franconian sub-leaders (they came from villages and small towns) either had no comprehension of the North Germans' concerns or else disapproved of them. Beyond that, even then they were already under the spell of Hitler's aura. Many of them had also belonged to Streicher and Esser's Greater German Racial Community and thus had acquired from it a strong mistrust of Gregor Strasser.[7]

After this, to be sure, Strasser did not wholly abandon his own conceptions but instead promoted them through the pages of the Combat Press's journals (*The National Socialist*) and in the *National Socialist Correspondence*, which he had gained control of. These newspapers and periodicals fought, so to speak, a two-front war. Their public struggle was against the Weimar Republic;

---

[6] The city of Bamberg is located in northern Franconia.

[7] This account incorporates Krebs' corrections of his memoirs, which were originally based, in this instance, upon oral information from Gregor Strasser. Strasser had told Krebs that it was Goebbels who treacherously alerted Hitler before the conference, enabling him to pack it with his Franconian supporters. In fact, as Krebs later wished to point out, Goebbels defended the "Elberfeld Principles" strongly at the conference and only in the following fortnight fell under Hitler's spell. Strasser too, though he did not subordinate himself emotionally to Hitler as Goebbels did, abandoned the "Elberfeld Program" after conversation with Hitler. The entire series of events is analyzed through new evidence in Orlow, I, pp. 66–75, and also in Max H. Kele, *Nazis and Workers* (Chapel Hill, 1972).

their covert one, recognized only by the initiated, was directed against "Munich" and the new Gauleiter of Berlin, Dr. Goebbels, who had been placed in this decisive position by Strasser himself in 1926. Strasser later complained: "Whatta super-stupe of a pig's ass I was!"

Anyone who wants to understand the internal factional struggles of the Nazi party in the years 1926 to 1930 will have to study these papers. Above all the *National Socialist Correspondence*, which was directed to only a small circle of readers, offers significant material. Almost every basic demand that was sacred to the party leadership in Munich was here at some time either treated as questionable or cut to ribbons: the "Heil Hitler" salute, the collective anti-Semitism, the fascistic *Führer*-principle, the anti-Bolshevist foreign policy, even the domestic struggle against communism. To be sure, there seldom stood a positive proposal behind the criticism. But above all the instrument increasingly slipped out of the hands of its creator.

With his growing responsibilities as organization leader of the party Gregor Strasser lost control over the newspapers. He was unable to concern himself sufficiently with their contents. In contrast to the tactically superior Joseph Goebbels, he treated little things as unimportant, though at times they must not be treated that way. Thus it ultimately came about that Otto Strasser, who was not a loyal steward, made his brother's megaphone into his own mouthpiece and in the summer of 1930, along with all his press organs, quit the party.

This loss weakened Gregor Strasser's position decisively; he now no longer had any newspaper at his regular and free disposition, since he was also not on particularly friendly terms with Rosenberg. Thus, in his conflict with Goebbels, Strasser suffered a second severe defeat after Bamberg. Goebbels' *Angriff* now became the most widely read Nazi newspaper in northern Germany, which he could use to speak directly to the masses even when he was not actually standing before them on the podium. With these practically unnoticed methods, he decided the outcome of the Goebbels-Strasser conflict, which for years had overshadowed the work of all the party groups in northern Germany, in his favor. The masses, who must be constantly spoken to lest they forget, now increasingly lost sight of Strasser and heard him infrequently. That is, they knew that he was sitting in Munich, organizing; he was known to hold many strings in his hands. But his personal impression faded and thus his personal influence lessened, ultimately even with Hitler, who knew how to judge his collaborators also by their effect upon the masses.

The question may be asked: Why did Strasser not join his brother and give him direction and leadership, since he generally shared his criticism, since at that point he still almost completely controlled the party organization, and finally, since he had the best relationship with the North German SA leadership? I cannot give an unambiguous, so to say, documented, answer. Above all I do not know what the relationship between the two brothers was at the moment when Dr. Otto Strasser left the party. From a parenthetical remark of Gregor's I have to assume that he was angry with his brother and viewed his action as desertion from the common cause. To be sure, other people held different opinions even then, and especially now. They view the entire action, the split and the subsequent creation of the "Black Front," as a prearranged play between the two brothers, which was supposed to provide Gregor at an opportune moment with the necessary basis (press and organizational cadres) for his own "Strasser Party." But the gambit failed to come off because an accident put Gregor Strasser in bed for months on end with a broken vertebra and thus incapacitated him.

As I have already suggested, I consider this an erroneous view. Apart from the remark cited above, which of course could have been purposefully designed as a cover up, Gregor Strasser must have recognized his brother's scatterbrained organizational incompetence, which would stack the deck and condemn the game to failure from the very beginning. But above all the state of consciousness that had developed in him since about 1930 would not have permitted him to share in the goals and approaches of the "Black Front." During those days I came into rather frequent contact with Gregor Strasser because of the founding of the *Hamburger Tageblatt*, being involved in the development of the Nazi Shop-Cell Organization, and my creation of a network of Nazi contact men inside the DHV. In the course of this I could detect, or rather was frequently distressed to note, that he was increasingly opposed to radical tactics and practices. At the time I attributed this partly to his physical condition—he had been ill with diabetes for years and on top of that now bore the results of his broken vertebra—which robbed him of his former buoyancy. And partly also I believed that his high offices were beginning to make him cautious and flaccid. But today I am convinced that, perhaps promoted by introspection during his illness, the true conservatism of his nature had begun to assert itself with increasing force. He no longer desired, as was customary within the nationalist movement of the 1920s, to surround himself with a tiny group of believers activated by particularly radical slogans and subtle ideology. Instead, he wanted to systematically develop his position as organization leader in order to make his ideas prevail within the existing Nazi party whose basic goals he continued to approve of and which had now grown into a considerable power factor. And at least initially he succeeded to a certain extent in doing this. In his Organization Office he acquired fellow workers on whom he could depend, or at least so he believed. With the Shop-Cell Organization, whose leaders, Walter Schuhmann and Reinhold Muchow, were loyally devoted to him, he created a medium for his social opinions and a sort of counterweight to the autocracy of some of the Gauleiters, which was particularly of some significance in Berlin where his old opponent Goebbels still held unlimited domain. Also, the formation of Organization Section II[8] under Konstantin Hierl, whom he prized highly, may be surely considered as a success for Strasser.

On the other hand, however, he fell into all those conflicts and perplexities that have always been the lot of conservative men who serve a thoroughly unconservative system. Thus he preceded the sorrowful experience of many conservative men who ten years later in the Third Reich were to discover the same thing practically every day. The practical demands and necessities of his office forced him to make decisions that were not only contrary to his own con-

[8] This was a subsection of Strasser's department in the Nazi central headquarters, ostensibly charged with planning for the coming Nazi state but actually involved with controlling and coordinating the affiliated Nazi sub-organizations, while Strasser administered the party itself. See Orlow, I, p. 203 ff and Pridham, p. 95, note 19.

science but also contrary to his own interest. But at the same time he was forced to discover that his by no means conservative opponents hardly bothered with observing the rules to which he subordinated himself. His situation of functioning under internal and external compulsion was something I experienced in a drastic, almost tragically grotesque, example.

In autumn of 1931 Strasser proposed that I take over the office of specialist for social policy in the party's national headquarters and thus enter into his Organization Section. He had various reasons for this. On the one hand, he wanted to solidify the friendly relationship he had personally established with the leaders of the DHV, especially Habermann, by adding to his staff a man whom the union also trusted. Secondly, he needed as a specialist for social policy and trade union affairs someone who, despite being connected with the DHV, would not be like Stöhr, Marschler, Murr, or Engels—that is, someone not overly taxed with parliamentary, organizational, and speaking obligations and who had maintained a certain independence of action and judgment. This was a particularly pressing need because in those months after the election victory of September 1930 the influence of industrialist and big capitalist circles was increasing within the Nazi party. The acceptance of Dr. Otto Dietrich and Dr. Paul Wagener[9] into the party leadership was visible evidence of this. Dr. Wagener was even placed in Organization Section II, at Hitler's expressed wish, and thus became a splitting wedge or at least an alien element in Strasser's own team. And finally, my summons to Munich would at last put an end to the intolerable Krebs-Kaufmann conflict in Hamburg, which was particularly distasteful to Strasser because he also counted Kaufmann as one of his adherents.

Strasser's plan found the approval of the union's leadership, who granted me a leave of absence to make me available for this duty. I alone was hesitant about accepting the assignment because I had no wish to become financially dependent upon the party. Then suddenly Strasser himself, most likely at Hitler's instigation, withdrew the offer. He did it on the grounds that my reticence and above all my increasingly critical attitude toward the party's activi-

[9] Charged, respectively, with Press and Economic Affairs, both of these men were previously linked with big business in Germany.

ties would no longer permit him, as party organization leader, to take the responsibility for my appointment. At the same time, however, he explained to me that he himself generally agreed with the actual content of my criticisms. Over and above that he also told me that he had been compelled to institute a twenty-four-hour guard over his offices in the Brown House to prevent "officially sanctioned" breaking and entry by other party figures. His desk had already once been broken into. He then introduced me to his especially trusted people: his brother-in-law and ex-First Lieutenant Schulz (Feme-Schulz).[10]

That, then, was Strasser's situation in those years. On the one hand, he was working to strengthen the power and the position of the Nazi party. On the other hand, he was recognizing with increasing clarity what dangers for Germany's future were involved in this growing power and how little the development of his own power position would avail to avert this danger since his position was being systematically undermined. Already by the spring of 1932 Dr. Robert Ley was brought into the Brown House in order to replace Strasser "in case of an emergency."[11]

After the above mentioned conversation with Strasser I can recall only one further meeting with him. That came during the presidential election campaign of spring 1932. On that occasion he had denigrating remarks to make about Hitler's candidacy and about the pernicious nature of party politics in general, in which he explicitly included the Nazi party. He said it was not through the parties that the true will of the people was expressed—democracies founded upon parties were thus either self-deluding or a conscious swindle—but rather only through the developed corporative organizations of the trade unions, the Agrarian League, Commerce, and so on. These organizations must therefore form the cornerstones of a new state and social order.

Strasser's remarks indicated what groups he had established relationships with or had influenced his thinking. Above all, as is gen-

---

[10] Both shared his fate on June 30, 1934, though Lieutenant Schulz managed in a highly adventuresome fashion to escape to Switzerland with the assistance of Dr. Grimm-Essen, despite severe wounds (*Krebs' note*—W. S. A.).

[11] Robert Ley did become, in December 1932, chief of Party Organization in addition to later heading the German Labor Front.

erally known, he was in close contact with the *Tat*[12] circle at that time. One has to know, however, that the *Tat* circle was itself not a closed, intellectually self-sufficient group but also both absorbed and transmitted political information and opinions via a network of cross connections. For example, the *Tägliche Rundschau* was more or less the official organ of the Popular Conservatives, but it also served as a megaphone for the evangelical-social movement and the DHV, for expressions of opinion transcending the area of general politics. And far in the background there probably also stood Brüning, who had come into contact with Strasser via Habermann.

On May 10, 1932, Strasser gave a major speech in the Reichstag on the Nazi program for employment creation. In it for the first time his changing assumptions and deviations from the previous party line became visible. This produced, though that only gradually became apparent, quite divergent effects. Strasser's phrases about "vast anti-capitalist yearnings" or "the front of working people within the bounds of the nation's cooperative enterprises" surely found far less approval from Hitler, Goering, and Goebbels than from the great mass of Nazi members. While the party's leaders were at that very moment trying to work out political and financial arrangements with "the capitalists," the average party member heard his own hopes and goals expressed again in such formulations. On the other hand though, the latter were undoubtedly astonished when they heard or read the sentence: "As long as I have been involved in politics I have regularly read *Vorwärts*[13] and recognized the cleverness of certain articles in it." How's that? In *Vorwärts*, that scandalous, rabble-rousing sheet, Party-Comrade Strasser found clever articles? And even less comprehensible for many Nazis must have been Strasser's benevolent comments on

[12] This was a journal of right-wing utopian thought, which exercised considerable influence upon conservatives in the Weimar Republic. The "circle" around it was analyzed in Klemens von Klemperer's *Germany's New Conservatism: Its History and Dilemma in the Twentieth Century* (Princeton, 1957). See also Herman Lebovics, *Social Conservatism and the Middle Class in Germany, 1914–33* (Princeton, 1969), and Walter Struve, *Elites against Democracy* (Princeton, 1973).

[13] The official newspaper of Germany's Social Democratic party, the bitterest and most consistent opponents to Nazism.

the Free Unions and the employment-creation program, which they had just developed and which had just been proclaimed by Theodor Leipart,[14] "with whom we are always ready to cooperate under appropriate conditions." The Free Unions, who had been cursed throughout a decade for their unreliable national feeling and their social failures?

It is quite probable that these remarks of Strasser's, which were to be followed by even more generous remarks in a *Sportpalast* speech to Berlin's NSBO in October,[15] cut the ground out from under Strasser's policy in the coming months. Overnight he threw away favorite assumptions and not least the party's major thesis that any fellow traveling with other groups must weaken your own strength and endanger the final victory. In doing this he was putting too great a demand upon the faith and the intellectual adaptability of the ordinary Nazi. Thus he himself abetted the accusation of treachery and desertion that his old rival Goebbels was to levy against him a half year later.

This is, of course, insight after the fact. At the time, in May 1932, my editorial staff was pleased with Strasser's speech. We saw it as a victory of the "revolutionaries" over the "reactionaries" inside the party, especially when it was published in the national propaganda office's *Kampfschrift* pamphlet series under the title "Work and Bread." We hoped that with this there would begin a more flexible policy, one not solely seeking the favor of and based upon the bulk of the masses. How much we deceived ourselves, however, was shown twenty days later when Brüning was overthrown, which would hardly have happened without Hitler's readiness, signified to General Schleicher, to tolerate the politically and

14 Theodor Leipart was chairman of the ADGB, the Socialist Free Unions.

15 Excerpts from his speech of October 20, 1932, which was not printed by a party publisher but by his brother, Otto's, Hempel & Co.: "Anyone who still today does not understand the origins of the German Labor movement has lost the right to be allowed to speak even a single word about German politics. . . . Already in my Reichstag speech of May 10, I offered my hand to anyone who is prepared to join us in solving the problem of Germany's distress. Here again, before 15,000 workers, I repeat that the National Socialist Movement is willing to collaborate with anyone who loves Germany and wants to save Germany with us. . . . He [Leipart] has used words which, if they are honestly meant, open visions of the future which can fill everyone, no matter what his party, with joy" (*Krebs' addendum*—W.S.A.).

socially reactionary cabinet of von Papen. My own expulsion from the party was designed to document publicly that this readiness was also honestly meant. Still more, however, was it a warning to Strasser: Watch out—even longtime party membership and considerable service is no protection for those who turn against the opinions and directives of Hitler.[16]

As for the later events connected with Strasser I had experience of only occasional segments, because of my separation from the party and subsequent lengthy illness. Most of my information came from Max Habermann, who did not approve of Strasser's voluntary resignation from his party offices[17] and dispatched an agent to find him after Strasser disappeared in a car with his family into Austria at the moment when Schleicher urgently needed him in Berlin. I also heard a few hints about the Gauleiters who gathered in Stuttgart at Strasser's invitation in autumn 1932. Among the southern Gauleiters, Bückel of Rhineland-Palatinate was especially said to have declared his willingness to support Strasser's plans. Among the Northerners, Karl Kaufmann, Josef Wagner, Karl Röver, Rudolf Jordan, and probably also Bernhard Rust and Helmuth Brückner were among Strasser's adherents.

In the spring of 1934 Habermann told me that he was continuing contact with Strasser, using Dr. Elbrechter as intermediary, and that they still hoped, after excluding the radical elements in the party (the SA above all)[18] and the reactionary elements in the government (Hugenberg), to work out somehow a more or less sensible solution. Strasser is further said to have written his other brother, the priest, a letter that also expressed hope for a "reconciliation" with Hitler on the basis of a previous conversation. Some

[16] The above three paragraphs replace the second paragraph on page 192 of the German edition of Krebs' memoirs at his subsequent request, since he found errors in his original version.

[17] Strasser resigned all offices in the Nazi party on December 7, 1932, after Hitler discovered that he had been negotiating a possible Nazi entry into General von Schleicher's cabinet. The circumstances are detailed in Alan Bullock's *Hitler, A Study in Tyranny*, rev. ed., paperback (New York, 1964), pp. 237–240.

[18] This account contradicts the official assertion of collaboration between Roehm and Strasser, which I do not believe anyway. Strasser once spoke very drastically about Roehm (*Krebs' note*—W. S. A.).

years later, to be sure, I heard that it was precisely this letter, whose contents became known in the upper echelons of the Nazi party, in conjunction with a subsequent article in *Tat* that had some obscure references to a forthcoming return of Strasser into politics, that became the signal which led Goebbels and Goering to decide to murder him.

Whether these last bits of information are true or not I cannot say; I cannot even recall their source exactly any longer. However, all these individual reports are inconsequential for an evaluation of Strasser as a man and a politician. Even if the above mentioned "reconciliation" between Strasser and Hitler ever took place it is my firm conviction that it would never have involved Strasser's intellectual or emotional capitulation to Hitler. The fateful conclusion in all probability would only have been postponed for another decade and instead of coming from a bullet would have come from a noose.[19]

19 The allusion here is to the assassination plot against Hitler that culminated in the attempt of July 20, 1944. The prime conspirators were hanged.

CHAPTER 10

Other Leading Nazis
(Amann, Bouhler, Buch, Buttmann,
Brückner, Ellendt, Esser, Feder,
Frick, Haupt, Himmler, Lohse, Ludin,
Marschler, Pfeffer von Salomon,
Reventlow, Röver, Rust,
von Schirach, Schwarz
van Berk, Streicher,
Telschow, Wegener)

The years of my membership in the Nazi party brought me into contact with most of its leaders at the upper and intermediate levels. With many of them all I had was such a superficial acquaintance that I was unable to gain a clear impression. Thus I can only evaluate them in very general terms. What one noticed primarily was that they were very young, with all the advantages and disadvantages of youth. Sociologically considered, the majority of them stemmed from the middle classes: They were retailers, artisans, and commercial or technical white-collar employees. Academicians, men of the old regime, former career officers in the army were represented, at least up to 1933, only by isolated outsiders. And after the unity negotiations of 1924[1] broke down, part of even these left the party again or else retreated into the background.

Seen as a whole, the party was thus an organization of "new men" who were breaking into the domain of politics with youthful obstreperousness, full of faith in their own mission and determined to use their eagerness at risk-taking to make the impossible possible. From the spiritual heritage of the past they took whatever they thought useful for their goals and purposes. That produced, especially in the beginning, a remarkable mixture of liberal, conservative, Marxist, reactionary, and revolutionary elements, though

---

[1] Krebs means the attempt to fuse right-wing extremist groups described in the preceding chapter.

probably very few of them were aware of this. When they did think about their historical predecessors or forebears, they felt themselves to be linked to the great popular movements of the nineteenth century, the movements against Napoleon and for the unification of Germany (insofar as this derived from 1813 and not 1789). By no means did they want to be unreservedly anti-democratic. But most of them surely shared a view that had preceded even Napoleon—that a dictatorship based upon plebiscites was the ultimate and purest culmination of democracy. Only a very small portion of the Nazi sub-leaders could have understood, even before 1933, that they were working to bring about a totalitarian Caesarist system. Many felt themselves to be true fighters for the liberation of the people, though admittedly they were thinking more in terms of international independence than domestic freedoms. But at the same time they also had little use for the spurious liberties of parliamentary democracy—and with some justification, it seems to me. For the rest, internal party discussions of political questions were rare, partly even suspect: only gabblers and intellectuals discussed things! Thus the views of the Gauleiters, section specialists, and editors whom one met at conferences and mass meetings could usually only be inferred from chance remarks. What prevented false inferences was a certain uniformity of terminology, which required no special explanation or clarification. Beyond that, the common goals eventually also produced uniform types, who showed simply by their bearing, their gestures, their favorite phrases, what sorts they were and how they viewed the world.

The individual descriptions of the people with whom for one reason or another I had closer contact will seldom fall outside the frame of this general portrait. A few lines may become sharper, a couple of colors and shadings may be differentiated more clearly. These sketches, therefore, will not be of much benefit for an analysis of the party's ideology or structure. On the other hand, some aspects of the development of the Nazi party may become more understandable to historians if an attempt is made to portray those responsible for its development not just in terms of their functions and their political views but also in terms of their human qualities. Admittedly these portraits will be incomplete because my observations were narrowly limited through the rarity and briefness of my encounters with the men involved.

MAX AMANN

Editor's note: *Amann made an important contribution to the rise of Nazism by managing the party's publishing house, Eher Company of Munich, whose profits became a significant source of funds for the party. He had been Hitler's company sergeant during the war and joined the Nazi party in 1920 at age twenty-nine. The following year he became the party's business manager and, in 1922 director of Eher. In 1923 he was arrested for involvement in the "Beer Hall" Putsch but received only a token sentence. During the party's period of prohibition he kept the Völkischer Beobachter alive and after the party was refounded in 1925 he devoted exclusive attention to managing the Eher Company, being accountable only to Hitler. In the Third Reich he was rewarded by being made a member of the Reichstag, a general in the SS, Nazi Reichsleiter for press affairs, and president of the Press Chamber. He used his power to acquire the largest publishing empire in the world and to become a multimillionaire. In 1948 a denazification court declared him a "major offender," confiscated his property, and sentenced him to ten years' hard labor. He died in poverty and obscurity. His personality and his role in Nazism are described in Oron Hale's* Captive Press in the Third Reich *(Princeton, 1964), pp. 21–33.*

Early in the summer of 1931 I had my first close contact with Max Amann, the director of Eher Publishing Company. I sought him out in the business offices of the *Völkischer Beobachter* in order to persuade him to absorb the *Hamburger Tageblatt* into the Eher company. Amann sat behind his desk and received me (my visit had already been announced by the party treasurer, Franz X. Schwarz) with gracious benevolence. But he did not offer me a chair. To be sure, neither was there such a piece of furniture available in his office. There were only two high-backed antique armchairs standing in one corner and they were obviously for decoration rather than use. So I spoke my first words while standing and then seated myself with half my bottom on the corner of his desk nearest to me. Amann wrinkled up his forehead: "Oho," he said, "is that the latest fad in Hamburg, squattin' on desks?"

I smiled kindly and answered: "Oh yes, whenever we aren't offered a chair to sit down on."

At that Amann let out a terrible roar, not, however, directed at me but at his secretary, Bauer, because the long since ordered chairs had still not been delivered. The roar concluded with a threat to "clout him one" the next time the secretary made the slightest lapse. As the door closed behind the unfortunate Bauer, I asked Amann whether "clouting" belonged to the customary practices of Eher House. If so, then if I were to become a co-worker of his I would fear the worst for him. "For me?" asked Amann staring at me in astonishment. "Yes," I said. "In Hamburg we never let our ears be boxed, least of all by superior officials, without immediately hitting back—and you, Herr Amann, are really too tiny for that." The former statement was an exaggeration, but the latter was the exact truth: Amann was of small, squat stature.

At first Amann reacted to my impudent words with an angry red face, but then he began to laugh like mad. "What?" he cried delightedly. "So right off you'd gimme one? That's rich! That I gotta tell Adolf!"

He was not upset or insulted at all and never subsequently held this conversation against me; on the contrary, he always showed himself sympathetic and benevolent toward me. That was demonstrated immediately when he acceded to my business request. It was demonstrated later, when he actually had become my superior official as head of the publishing company, in that he always treated the *Hamburger Tageblatt* with special consideration. Beyond that, he personally supplied me with extensive inside information on matters concerning the Nazi press, which he would not have dared to do had he not felt that I was personally trustworthy. For this internal information was generally quite unpleasant: it included offenses and instances of corruption involving very prominent people such as Goebbels, Dr. Ley, and some other Gauleiters. He also complained frequently and angrily about the editor-in-chief of the *Völkischer Beobachter*, Alfred Rosenberg, for whom Amann had no understanding whatsoever. The contrast between the cramped and intellectual Balt and the impulsive, coarse, and down-to-earth Bavarian was unbridgeable. To be sure, Rosenberg was much too cautious and reserved to let a denigrating judgment about his publisher escape his lips; Amann, on the other hand, was probably outspoken to others besides me. Presumably Hitler's rather disdainful treatment of Rosenberg may be attributed partly to Amann's contempt for him. In general I would credit Amann with a considerable role in the party's internal clique struggles and I would think it was dangerous to have him as an enemy. Certainly his attitude in this respect was just like those of all self-made men from simple origins, no matter what philosophy they pay homage to in theory: "Whoever gets in my way will get kicked aside! Whoever is my objective opponent is also my personal enemy and furthermore a bad guy!"

Amann never discussed general politics with me. I believe that they interested him only to the extent that they affected the fate of his publishing house. Though he had no professional training as a publisher, he not only came to be completely at home in it, but in time actually learned to be fully sovereign. To be sure, this mastery was primarily exercised in business and organizational areas, and in these matters he preferred simple, sometimes even primitive methods. He had little understanding of the intellectual side of publishing, or at least little theoretical understanding of it. On the other hand, he possessed an instinct and a born sense of taste which, for example, led him to characterize the *Stürmer* as "a filthy rag that I won't touch." Also he was fairly quick in acquiring a good understanding of the technical aspects of printing and the entire external composition of newspapers and magazines. When the *Illustrierter Beobachter* was getting started I heard him swearing over the initial issues. As usual his form was coarse and crude, but in substance he was quite right.

In the core of his being Amann was a Royal Bavarian master sergeant with all the merits and flaws of this type. Among the merits I consider primarily a love of orderliness, which very quickly made Eher Publishing Company into a correct, solid, and well-run business, whereas almost all the other party publishing houses remained highly dubious enterprises from an organizational and business perspective. I also count it as a merit that he had a certain personal decency and honesty that tolerated no corruption, not just in others but also in himself.

Philip Bouhler

Editor's note: *Though he became a* Reichsleiter *of the Nazi party and wrote several books on Nazism, Bouhler was never a major figure in the movement. He joined the party at age twenty-two, in 1921, and from the beginning served primarily in its business end,*

working with Amann. During its prohibition he was business man-
ager of the Greater German Racial Community, a Nazi cover orga-
nization in South Germany. With the party's reestablishment in
1925 he became its business manager and chief of the Führer's
chancellory—in effect the executive secretary of the national head
quarters and the man responsible for the routine execution of Hit-
ler's decisions. In the Third Reich he was made a member of the
Reichstag, a general in the SS, and chief of the Party Censorship
Committee for the Protection of National Socialist Literature. In
1945 he committed suicide. Bouhler typified the bureaucratic side
of the party hierarchy and as such has been described in Dietrich
Orlow's History of the Nazi Party, I, p. 59.

The figure of Bouhler has always remained rather pale and shad-
owy for me, even though I met him fairly often. In the Schelling-
strasse Headquarters he sat in the same office as Hess. In the Brown
House he directed the Chancellory and so every appointment had
to be made through him, unless one had a previously arranged
appointment or had such good connections that one did not need
to go through the Chancellory.

Bouhler gave the impression of being the complete civil servant,
whose ambition was to rise to the heights of undersecretary. He
was always polite, always self-effacing, spoke of nothing other than
the immediate question at hand, and was able, like his immediate
superior Hess, to listen quietly without expressing his own opinions. He was doubtless immersed in his work. Though his position
gave him many opportunities to exert influence it was obviously far
from his nature to desire any independent role in the game of
intrigue that flourished among the party's cliques. He was not the
type to put a personal desire for advancement ahead of the loyal
fulfillment of duty. In this respect he embodied the good tradition
of a bygone era that had emphasized order and clear, clean, unwav-
ering rules. It was his destiny that through his conviction, personality, and ability he made possible the construction of a brilliantly
organized and hard-hitting party apparatus, which was then
employed by men of an entirely different sort for goals that surely
had nothing in common with Bouhler's. When or if he came to
recognize this is something I do not know. His personal fate after
Hitler came to power certainly suggests that he recognized it rather

quickly. He would doubtless not have been shoved aside into what were, within the general framework of party and state, rather insignificant posts, had he not let his deviation from the "party line" become noticeable.

Apart from that, Bouhler administered his office as director of party literary affairs with so much decency and common sense (according to all accounts) that it must be assumed that even though he probably remained a convinced Nazi to the end, still he was given only very circumscribed decision-making powers. It was not Bouhler and his co-worker, Hederich, who determined literary policies in the Third Reich, but rather Goebbels, Rosenberg, and the SS Chief Security Office. To be sure, Bouhler also showed frequently that he lacked the energy to make his opinions stick. He simply did not have the make-up of a fighter but instead had that of a civil servant, a man who adheres to the directives, to the established procedures, to respect for superior offices. Moreover, he apparently shared the view held by Hess and many other sincere idealists within the party that its "great goals" justified every suppression of your own ideas, even of your own conscience.

Such people perceived without any illusions, at the very latest after Stalingrad, the approaching fate. They also perceived all the errors, lapses, and misdeeds committed by the party's leadership including Hitler himself. But the consequence of these insights was not a rejection of or even deviation from the party. On the contrary, they believed that now above all was the time for them to live by and promote the old ideals of loyalty unto death, unconditional obedience, uncompromising militancy, and even idolization of the *Führer*.

There may have been hidden within these beliefs the hope of being able to save the basic concept despite the experience of defeat, persecution, and disgrace. Or it may simply have been an inability to sustain oneself by one's inner resources if the whole structure of ideology and proud delusions should collapse. That does not matter. Nor do I wish to discuss the reasonableness or irrationality of such attitudes and reject or justify them. What is important is that these attitudes be recognized, since otherwise many of the actions and developments inside the party cannot be understood and individual personalities would be judged or condemned on the basis of false premises.

WALTER BUCH

Editor's note: *Major Walter Buch was a career army officer (1904–18) who joined the Nazi party in 1922 at age thirty-nine, and was active as an SA commander in the "Beer Hall" Putsch. From 1927 on he was chairman of the party's internal Investiga tion-Reconciliation Committee (the Uschla) and after its name was changed to the Party Court in 1933 he thenceforth held the title "supreme party judge." From 1928 on he was a member of the Reichstag and in the Third Reich was made an honorary general of both the SA and the SS. He was also the father-in-law of Martin Bormann. In 1945 he committed suicide. He and the institution he directed have been described by Donald M. McKale, The Nazi Party Courts: Hitler's Management of Conflict in His Movement, 1921–1945 (Lawrence, Kansas, 1974).*

What has been said of Bouhler applies equally to Major Buch, the unfortunate "supreme judge" of the party. The word "unfortunate" is not used in reference to Buch's suicide in 1945 but rather in reference to his position within the party—a position that in no way agreed with his attitude or his character. I had frequent dealings with Buch and in the process always found him to be an honorable man of the best intentions. Without a doubt he had the goodwill to operate his office in such a way as to keep out or remove all corrupt elements. But it is equally without doubt that he did not succeed in doing so. His concept of what constituted behavior injurious to the party differed from Hitler's so frequently that it was impossible for Buch to effectuate it. As a dry, somewhat pedantic man in his ideas and actions, Buch possessed neither the wit nor the charm that was needed to resist or even convince Hitler. That is, Buch presented opinions and proposals but then simply obeyed when Hitler held contrary opinions and ordered decisions in accordance with them. On the occasion of the Pfeffer affair, described earlier,[2] Buch openly admitted to me his attitude and his method, saying it was caused by his military training in obedience: "You just click your heels together and say 'yes, sir!'"

Precisely because he was supreme party judge, Buch felt obligated to appear as an exemplar of loyalty and obedience. But in

[2] See Chapter 7, Rudolf Hess.

doing this he very early, probably much earlier than Bouhler, became aware of the tragedy of his position and his office. He often made remarks indicating that. He also quickly recognized that Hitler always employed and exploited people of his sort only in certain kinds of jobs: "He needs a couple of good sheep dogs like Schwarz and Hess and Bouhler so that we can keep the whole heap from falling apart."

And actually Hitler did have a remarkable ability for picking the appropriate people for a specific job. Where he needed men devoted to orderly ways, such as in the buildup of the party organization, he drew orderly types to himself, flattered them by praising the virtues and traits that such self-disciplined men incorporated. Later he corrupted the generals by speeches of praise for Prussiandom and the soldierly attitude. But internally he had little in common with the virtues he was praising; he probably even had contempt for the men of order. But he made sure that the objects of his deception never noticed this.

My impression is that Buch did perceive the deception, as I have said, but he did not find the strength to act accordingly. Now and again he tried to use the powers of his office to regulate matters in accordance with his own standards by mitigating decisions or formulating them in such a way as to make a future appeal and revision likely. Even my expulsion decree, which I received weeks after the fact, was couched in terms like that—probably in collaboration with Hess. But these were only little ameliorations and defensive measures against the spiritual compulsion exerted by Hitler. Only once was Major Buch prepared to make a complete break and that was in autumn 1932 after Gregor Strasser resigned his offices. That this readiness did not lead to the actual deed is traceable to Strasser's refusal to summon his followers to split from the party.

Certainly Major Buch's attitude was partly due to the fact that he was dominated more by patriotic political emotions than by clear political conceptions. In his basic essence he belonged to those "nationalistic circles" from the *ancien régime* who expected Hitler and the party to restore the Bismarckian Reich with only those few necessary corrections and alterations that were demanded by the times. But since they themselves were incapable of developing an intellectual conception to formulate these hopes, they needed something to support and adhere to. Buch did that even after he had come to recognize the questionableness of his attitude and he did it to the bitter end. His suicide was then only the logical culmination of a man who had ultimately lost even his religious roots in the Nazi party.

Dr. Rudolf Buttmann

Editor's note: Buttmann was born in Bavaria, near Würzburg, in 1885, received a doctorate in law, and became a librarian in Munich, ultimately with the legislative library of the Bavarian parliament. After World War I he quit the German Nationalist party, which he thought was insufficiently nationalistic, to join the Nazis. He became leader of the Nazi caucus in the Bavarian parliament and in general was viewed as the key spokesman for the party in Bavarian affairs. After Hitler came to power Buttmann served briefly as head of the cultural affairs department of the Reich Ministry of the Interior and then, in 1935, was sent back to Bavaria where he played no further political role. He died in Munich in 1947.

Such a logical culmination as befell Major Buch certainly did not exist for Dr. Rudolf Buttmann, who became director of the Bavarian State Library during the Third Reich. I actually met Dr. Buttmann only once, when I spent an entire day with him in the year 1924. He came to my home town of Amorbach during the May election campaign to speak on behalf of the Racial-Social Bloc[3] (whose local campaign director I was) and then stayed overnight in my parents' house. Nevertheless, even this brief encounter, which was full of personal and political discussions around our dinner table, in the Monastery Archives, in the nave of the Abbey Church, transmitted a rather clear impression of this clever and lively man's personality.

If I remember correctly, Dr. Buttmann told of how he had become friends with Max von Scheubner-Richter, Ernst Pöhner, and Theodor von der Pfordten (who died on November 9, 1923).[4]

[3] A temporary successor to the then outlawed Nazi party. See the note in Chapter 2.

[4] Date of the "Beer Hall" *Putsch*. On Scheubner-Richter, see the note in Chapter 8. The others mentioned were also pioneers in the early racialist movement after World War I in Munich.

As they had, he viewed Hitler and his party as one hope for "Germany's rebirth," but without thereby being prepared to commit himself blindly and without reservations. On the contrary, and in contrast to Bouhler and Buch, Buttmann gave the impression of a man who not only had his own political conceptions and goals but was also willing to try to fight for them inside the Nazi party. If one were looking for a characterization, perhaps one could label Buttmann's views and attitudes as "free conservative."

Already in those May days of 1924 Dr. Buttmann had bitter words for Julius Streicher and Hermann Esser. There was an immediate reason for this since the work of the Racial-Social Bloc was being made much more difficult by the Greater German Racial Community led by Streicher and Esser. But Buttmann had more pertinent reasons. He flatly described the two chief managers of the Greater German Racial Community as Bolsheviks and made no bones about his conviction that there were certain military-Bolshevik elements at work in the movement. From this conviction he drew the personal conclusion that especially people from the so-called bourgeois circles ought to go into the Nazi party in order to form a counterweight.

Buttmann also had some critical remarks about Hitler, personally; in other words, they concerned Hitler the man as well as the politician. It seems not improbable to me that Buttmann's disappearance from the front ranks of Nazism was traceable to the growth of his critical attitude. That is, Buttmann continued to hold his seat in the Bavarian legislature after the party was re-founded, but he no longer played a prominent role in party affairs. (He did serve as Hitler's representative in the Concordat[5] negotiations, though.) Neither during my frequent visits to Munich nor at any of the party rallies did I ever meet him again. Whenever I asked Rudolf Hess about him, I was given cold and evasive answers.

WILHELM BRÜCKNER
Editor's note: *Brückner was born in 1884, served as an officer throughout World War I, and then in 1919 fought with* Freikorps

---

[5] In 1933 the Vatican signed a treaty with the Third Reich to regularize church-state relations, called "The Concordat." On its history and effects see Guenter Lewy, *The Catholic Church and Nazi Germany* (New York, 1964).

Epp. In 1922 he joined the Nazi party and participated in the "Beer Hall Putsch," for which he was sentenced to eighteen weeks' imprisonment. From 1930 on he served as Hitler's adjutant. In the early years of the Third Reich he was made a member of the Reichstag and a general of the Stormtroopers, but in 1942 he fell from favor and was returned to the army as a major for the rest of the war.

If strict alphabetical order were being followed, Lieutenant Brückner, the *Führer's* Adjutant, could complain that he had been unfairly held back. But as far as I knew him, he never took himself or his office so seriously that he would not have accepted this in order to permit the connecting theme of Bouhler-Buch-Buttmann to emerge.

Brückner always came across to me as the harmlessly snappy lieutenant from a Balkan operetta, a man who combined a healthy natural boyishness with born cordial courtesy and well-trained good manners. Politics as an intellectual discipline and a responsible assignment doubtless gave him headaches extremely rarely. He was totally unproblematical and completely without personal plans or intentions, excepting a naturally patriotic viewpoint. But precisely for these reasons he was superbly suited for his office. Hitler needed a few hands to work for him and a few mouths to speak for him in his immediate staff, but not heads that might think. Beyond that, Brückner, with his sparkling external appearance, made a respectable receptionist as well as a messenger for the orders of his lord and master.

Whether in the course of such duties he ever acted independently and meshed his own decisions into the political machinery I do not know. I heard reports that he was often at pains to be of assistance to petitioners, giving them access to Hitler or Hess. That he was of kindly disposition I could easily believe. During my final interview with Hitler he stood in the back of the room and gave me silent gestures of human sympathy which, since he had heard only one side of the story, bordered on dereliction of duty.

In the years after the Nazi seizure of power Brückner was occasionally accused of not passing unpleasant news on to Hitler, in accordance with the saying that "no shadow must fall upon the king." According to a firsthand account from Brinkmann, this happened to a memorandum written by Ulrich von Hassell (then still ambassador to Italy), which contained very skeptical remarks on conditions in Italy and especially about the minimal value of the Italian army. To be sure this "suppression" had a consequent justification. Hitler complained to Hassell about his insufficient reportage. Hassell consequently referred him to the memorandum, which was then finally delivered. As Hitler read its contents, there occurred what Brückner had foreseen. Hitler began to rage against its author because he was "maliciously trying to undercut the Axis with lying or unproved assertions." The end of the story was that Hassell was recalled as ambassador from Rome.

Why Brückner was removed from his office at the beginning of World War II was something I never could find out exactly. What I heard would have been appropriate for a "Balkan operetta," but perhaps the tales were lies or exaggerations.

FRAU ELLENDT

One of the strangest phenomena out of the early years of the movement was one Frau Ellendt, who in the years 1922–23 won hundreds, perhaps thousands of supporters for the party in Lower and Middle Franconia. Whether this woman's name really was Ellendt, where she came from, where she belonged, and where she was headed, was something no one knew with exactitude. By one story she was the widow of a naval officer who had died in the war. Another account insisted that she was the American or even the Mexican wife of a German spy who had been executed in the United States. In any case there was an atmosphere of far-off foreign lands about her—even just from her appearance.

About thirty to thirty-five years old, slim, and ladylike in clothes and bearing, she had dark skin and black hair. She wore a sport costume with a military cut plus a small trim hat like a Girl Scout leader's. What was noticeable (especially in those inflationary years) was the excellent quality of her clothes, which lent a certain probability to the rumors of their bearer's foreign origins. Another thing suggesting foreign, or at least secret, sources of money was the life-style of Frau Ellendt, which, not exactly luxurious, was generous. It indicated complete financial independence. Frau Ellendt received not a penny from the party, as I was repeatedly assured; at the most she would permit one of her numerous admirers to drive her in an automobile to her meetings.

This woman possessed an enrapturing eloquence, which worked with equal effectiveness upon Franconian peasants, the notables of small towns in Hessia, or educated audiences. It was hard to analyze the substance of this rhetoric. In any event the negativistic or demagogic content was limited. Like a modern Joan of Arc, Frau Ellendt summoned her audiences to take up the ancient virtues of courage, love of country, and community spirit. She clothed her criticism in the form of a lament for the misery and shame of the Fatherland and the wasted deaths of those millions who had fallen in the war. She also displayed knowledge, wit, and even irony, though she used these intellectual weapons only rarely. In general she depended upon an appeal to emotions and a projection of her feminine aura—and with such success that the peasants, students, and workers whom she enthralled would have gladly gone to their graves at her command. She was clever and moderate enough not to request such a thing and she also employed anti-Semitic utterances sparingly. Given her ability at whipping up passions, this reticence was doubtless a blessing for the many Jews who lived in Franconia in those days.

Frau Ellendt's political effectiveness was short-lived. Even before the "Beer Hall" Putsch of November 1923, she disappeared from the political stage as suddenly as she had surfaced. Whether she had met Hitler, whether he was responsible for her disappearance —he could not abide "woman politicians" like Frau Ellendt—I do not know. Unless I am mistaken, someone told me, many years later, that Frau Ellendt had been a "secret agent." On whose behalf was not said.

HERMANN ESSER

Editor's note: *Esser was born in 1900, served in the final year of World War I, and joined the Nazi party immediately after its formation in 1919. He was briefly editor of the* Völkischer Beobachter *and was the Nazi propaganda chief in 1923 and 1925, when he composed a pamphlet entitled "The Jews as a World Plague." In the early years he was one of Hitler's closest associates and in 1933 was rewarded by being made Bavarian minister of economics and vice-president of the Reichstag. Thereafter his influence declined precipitously and from 1935 on he was relegated to the tourists' division of the Propaganda Ministry. He survived World War II and lives now in West Germany.*

During the German Convention in Marktbreit in the spring of 1923, when I was able to observe Frau Ellendt closely, I also encountered Hermann Esser for the first time. But the only thing I can remember is that he gave a long and strident speech whose intellectual content was rather thin. He cursed vigorously against conditions in the Weimar Republic, against priests and Jews; nor did he have a single kind word to say about the Kaiser's days. The rumor that only a few years before he had been a speaker for the Spartacists[6] seemed very credible after hearing his speech.

While I was a party member in Hamburg there was a conference at which a district leader suggested that Esser be invited to speak at a mass rally. This proposal was bitterly opposed. In 1923 or 1924 Esser had been the speaker at the traditional May festival of the Hamburg Nazis in Wedel. After giving a very pretty speech on the German spring and the German woman, he behaved in a much less pretty way toward the Nazi women who were present, if not to say in a truly swinish manner. The Hamburg party-comrades had neither forgotten nor forgiven this.

Thereafter I came into closer contact with Esser only once, in the summer of 1931. He sat for about an hour in my cubicle in the offices of the *Hamburger Tageblatt*. At that time he was editor of the *Illustrierter Beobachter* and Max Amann had brought him along as a "technical specialist," during his survey of the *Tageblatt* preparatory to its absorption by the Eher publishing house. To be sure, the "specialist," elegant as a fashion model, spoke not a word but spent the whole time staring with stupid arrogance at the tips of his glittering, expensive, light brown oxford shoes. In the very modest, virtually poverty-stricken furnishings of our editorial offices he came across like a visitor from a foreign world; perhaps that was the way he thought of himself: an amazing and admired guest. In actuality, wherever he was seen, in the publishing offices, the editorial rooms, the printshop, he only aroused vigorous displeasure. People of his sort were not desired by the masses in the party as representative Nazis. My impression is that this attitude was not substantially changed here in Hamburg even in the years after the

[6] The Spartacists were the predecessors of the German Communist party. This rumor probably derived from the fact that Esser worked as a journalist for a short while in 1918–19 for the Munich Social Democratic newspaper.

seizure of power. Nobody here could understand why people like Streicher, Esser, and Christian Weber were not removed from the party. Hitler called it "loyalty."

GOTTFRIED FEDER

Editor's note: *Feder was the prime economic theorist in the early years of Nazism. He developed a distinction between "productive" and "exploitative" capital, which formed a major segment of the original (and "immutable") program of the party. He also coined the slogan "Break the Interest-Serfdom!" Hitler used his ideas sporadically without ever committing himself to them and used Feder as a popular speaker, but never assigned him any significant post, though he was given the title* Reichsleiter. *In the Third Reich Feder was rapidly thrust into obscurity; he lost his title and his Reichstag membership in 1936. He died in 1941.*

Among the most frequent Nazi speakers to appear in Hamburg before 1930 (next to Goebbels, Count Reventlow, and Strasser) was Gottfried Feder. There were two reasons for this, one objective, the other personal.

Reflecting the general Hamburg mentality, the Nazis of Hamburg were always interested in hearing something specific about the party's economic goals. Vague and noncommittal declamations or slogans such as "Against Capitalism and Marxism!" were not enough for sober Hamburgers with their close links to economic affairs. They demanded a plan, theoretical theses, so that they could analyze these, test them against reality, apply them in dialectical debate against political opponents.

The one man who had such a plan in the early years of the Nazi party and who also knew how to present it in rather generally comprehensible terms through his thesis on "Breaking the Serfdom of Interest" was precisely Gottfried Feder. Therefore the party-comrades always liked to have him speak, even though his dry manner of lecturing often undercut the effectiveness of recruitment efforts at mass rallies.

Beyond that, Feder had a circle of personal acquaintances in Hamburg who seldom failed to produce propaganda for "Nazism's leading economic theorist." A trip from southern Bavaria to Hamburg could be objectively justified and more easily financed if it were made in connection with a speaker's assignment. The financial aspect was always close to Feder's heart; as a free-lance writer he was heavily dependent on lecture fees.

On the occasion of almost every visit of Feder to Hamburg I met with him. He was not an enjoyable or interesting companion, being just as dry in conversation as he was in lectures. His interests were limited. Apart from his special hobby horse (which incidentally was foaled in the stables of Silvio Gesell) you could only converse with this graduate of engineering school about various technical problems. Furthermore, he inclined to behave like a prima donna because of his conviction that he was absolutely the one and only creative mind in the Nazi party.

It makes personal relations somewhat difficult when you always have to be presenting laurels to your conversational partner and may never contradict him in the matter under discussion. Feder brusquely rejected any critique of his views, even any discussion of them. In this respect he was the complete reformist who thought of his teachings as sacred truths and saw any doubts about them as sacrilege. Apart from that Feder showed himself as very much the bourgeois who was not much impressed by the revolutionaries inside the party or by revolutionary methods. Probably he viewed the party in general as only a welcome instrument for the realization of his theories, except that at the bottom of his heart he was convinced that in time these theories would prevail by themselves solely because of their scientific weight and their scholarly validity.

Feder's position and influence in the Nazi party decreased in direct ratio to the willingness of businessmen to comply with Hitler's need for money. The appointments of Dr. Wagener and Dr. Dietrich[7] to party headquarters was the first sign (for those in the know) of Feder's coming isolation. Feder accelerated the process by getting himself involved in various (and to me rather opaque) intrigues inside the party. Evidently, as he began to feel the ground slip beneath his feet, he tried to secure himself a post as Gauleiter somewhere. But he was not the kind of man who could win the sort of slugfest that was required to depose an incumbent from such a cushy post. Beyond that he lacked virtually all the specifica-

[7] Both thought of as spokesmen for orthodox economics and the business community.

tions for the job: oratorical talent, organizational ability, ruthlessness, political knowledge and skills, but above all the ability to handle men. He lost a great deal of prestige with the party leaders and Hitler himself through his radio debate with the Social Democratic Professor Eric Nölting. Even the simple party member who followed this debate could discern Feder's complete inferiority to Nölting and the weakness of his assertions and argumentation.

After 1933 Feder was made state secretary in the Reich Ministry of Economics and professor at the Berlin Technical Academy, but the public heard little of his doings. In any event there was no more talk about the "breaking of interest-serfdom." After Hjalmar Schacht was appointed president of the Reichsbank, Feder faded entirely from view; he was hardly mentioned any more even in the medium-sized and smaller Nazi newspapers. The news of his death in 1941 was passed over by the party, too.

Dr. Wilhelm Frick
Editor's note: *Born of an upper-middle-class family in 1887, Frick received a doctorate in law and then went into the Bavarian civil service, where he became an official in the Munich police. As an early Nazi sympathizer, he was of considerable service to Hitler in this post and ultimately became involved in the 1923 Putsch, for which he was sentenced to a prison term he never served. From 1924 on, he was a Nazi member of the Reichstag; in 1930–31 he was minister of education in the first Nazi state government in Thuringia. In 1933 he became Reich minister of the interior, a post he held until 1943 when it was given to Heinrich Himmler, while Frick became "Reich protector" of Bohemia and Moravia. In 1945 Frick was convicted of war crimes at Nuremberg and hanged.*

Among the principled revolutionaries and *avant-garde*, Dr. Wilhelm Frick was known as the "Royal Bavarian Nazi." One joke said that he never carried out Hitler's orders without first getting them countersigned by ex-Crown Prince Ruprecht. Naturally that was a malicious exaggeration, not least because it suggests that the Bavarian Crown Prince played a role as a secret wire-puller in politics. But if jokes have the same virtue as caricatures, that is, to illustrate sharply the essence of men and matters, then the mocking title "Royal Bavarian Nazi" certainly accomplished this. In fact, Dr. Frick, viewed from the Nazi perspective, always did remain the former Royal Bavarian civil servant. The party people could count on his ideological purity only with reservations; they could depend completely, however on his obedience and his fulfillment of duty.

Ideologically, Dr. Frick belonged to that group of people whom, like Dr. Buttmann, I have labeled "free conservatives." But this concept had a different meaning in Bavaria than it did in North Germany.[8] The line of demarcation between them and the "old conservatives," especially such as were gathered into the right wing of the Bavarian Peoples' party,[9] was sharper, one might almost say more hostile, than was the case in East Elbian Prussia. This opposition strongly affected Bavarian developments after 1918. Those representatives of the intelligentsia and the leadership strata who came over to Hitler did so because of a sort of political homelessness. They were fed up with the rigid conservatives, especially those from the areas south of the Danube, with their exaggerated sectionalist emotions, but they could not break loose from their social and intellectual traditions enough to establish some sort of relationships with the various descendants of liberalism. They were not petty bourgeois; they did not think in mercantile or industrial terms as did the "grand liberals" in Franconia and the few big cities of Bavaria. And so they took a bold leap into the newly unfolding popular movement of Hitler in the hopes of keeping up their ideas inside it, and possibly even becoming leaders of it. These hopes were by no means illusionary, at least not in the beginning. South Germany had, in comparison with the North, much weaker class contradictions and the special intellectual and sociological structure of its population provided favorable conditions for the development of a popular movement in which even the old leadership groups could play an appropriate role. The *Führer* of this popular movement at first proclaimed so modestly that he was the "drummer," the "path-breaker," the "town crier,"

---

[8] In Bismarck's Reich the "free conesrvatives" were the extreme right except for the "old conservatives" who, as Prussian patriots, were even opposed to the formation of the Second Reich, since it apparently diminished Prussia's significance.

[9] An extreme states' rights party in the Weimar Republic, linked with the Catholic Center party.

that even convinced monarchists could array themselves among his followers without sacrificing their ideology, at least provisionally. That it did not remain provisional was more a result of fate than fault. The "drummer," the "path-breaker," transformed himself into the "summoned leader," the *Führer* who usurped the rights of kings and thereby caught the former king's men in the net of their own traditions and rules.

Hitler the revolutionary bound the men with roots in the *ancien régime* to him and to his destiny by misusing their peculiar value commitments to oaths, loyalty, obedience, honor, sense of duty, and incorruptibility. After they had sworn fealty to him, men like Frick, Walter Buch, Franz von Epp, Ernst Pöhner, August Schneidhuber, and Hans Ludin could not break out of this allegiance without breaking their personality patterns and their traditions.

Whether Dr. Frick himself recognized what kind of net he was caught in is something I cannot say with certainty. While I was active as party leader in Hamburg he visited the city two or three times at the most. He was not a passionate orator for mass meetings. The themes of his lectures made demands upon the abilities of his audiences, which could seldom be fulfilled by those who generally attended political rallies and not at all by the ones in the big cities. The educated grand bourgeoisie were not used to satisfying their political requirements at mass meetings. But in those early years of Nazism there were no intimate political circles in the party. Since, apart from that, I was never an elected representative of the party—for Nazi parliamentarians, Dr. Frick was, in those early days, the most prominent leader—I met him, with the exception of his visits to Hamburg, only at the national conventions of the party. On those occasions he always showed himself to be a charming, dignified, educated man who could also (in contrast to the dry manner of his lectures) converse in an interesting and humorous way. The only questions he hated to touch upon were political ones. In this he revealed the training of the good civil servant who has been taught not to chatter outside the office. Party work was also an "office" to him and the functionaries who were his equals or of higher rank counted as his colleagues or superiors. He found it distasteful to make value judgments about colleagues or superiors.

There were only two instances that I can remember when Frick

deviated from his customary avoidance of political discussions or
even political utterances. But especially these two cases seem to me
particularly instructive.

During the Reich party rally of 1929 I had breakfast with Dr.
Frick in our Nuremberg hotel. From outside came the marching
music of the units that were assembling themselves. We listened
for a while in silence and then Frick asked cautiously: "What do
you think about these parades? Do you believe that one can really
influence and win over people with them?" I responded that in my
estimation the masses surely could be won over with such specta-
cles even though I myself found them unattractive and would have
preferred silent marches with symbols of mourning. Frick nodded,
stared silently into the air for a few moments, and then finally said
with a sigh: "In any case it would be dreadful if nothing more
than marching came of all this! Sometimes one has such unpleasant feelings . . ."

Following my expulsion from the Nazi party, Frick sent greetings to me via Representative Franz Stöhr, plus a message of gratitude for my telling Hitler the truth. What was meant by "the
truth" was my characterization of Hitler as an Oriental despot, as
was stated in the press release I gave out after being expelled. So
Frick knew how it was with Hitler.

DR. JOACHIM HAUPT

Editor's note: *Haupt is noteworthy only as a sometime leader in
the Nazi Student League and as the founder, in 1933, of a set of
schools—called "NAPOLA's"—which trained a youth "elite" for
the Third Reich. The Nazi Student League was one of the party's
early successes. In the Weimar Republic, higher education was
almost exclusively for the middle classes and the faculties were
heavily nationalistic. Furthermore, the economic conditions of
those years made it increasingly impossible for graduates of
German universities to obtain suitable employment. The result
was a radicalized student body that was easily recruited for
Nazism. The organizational instrument for this was the Nazi Student League, founded in 1926 and led in a social revolutionary
style by Kurt Temple until 1928, when he was replaced by the
more conservative Baldur von Schirach. Schirach cooperated with
the traditional student groups, such as the fraternities, and by 1930*

the Nazi Student League had become the largest and most influential organization in the German universities. But Schirach also changed the character of the Nazi Student League, deemphasizing its social radicalism.

The inclusion of Dr. Joachim Haupt in my report, which is supposed to be primarily based upon my own experiences, is not completely legitimate. I heard Dr. Haupt speak only once, before Hamburg students, and conversed with him only briefly afterward. As I recall, his talk attempted to establish links between the original *Burschenschaft* (Lutzow's Free Corps and the Wartburg Festival),[10] the Revolution of 1848 (the St. Paul's Church parliament, the liberation struggle in Schleswig-Holstein), the Youth Movement (Hohe Meissner oath and Langemarck),[11] and the National Socialist movement. I can no longer recollect what was discussed in our personal conversation.

So this direct experience was not very comprehensive. Perhaps the contents of Haupt's address justifies mentioning him and his topic, because it indicates the historical roots of Nazism. It might be objected that these were only the opinions of an outsider. However, anyone familiar with Nazi writings from those years knows that similar ideas repeatedly emerged in articles and speeches. But above all Dr. Haupt was by no means an outsider; instead, he was the leading figure in the Nazi Student League at the beginning of the 1930s, especially in northern Germany. According to the wish

[10] When Prussia went to war against Napoleon in 1812, student volunteers formed a cavalry unit called Lutzow's Free Corps. Veterans from this group, plus other nationalistic students later organized the *Burschenschaft*, political fraternities that agitated for a united Germany and against reactionary oppression. Their agitation culminated in the Wartburg Festival in 1817, which touched off a wave of repression inside Germany. For their subsequent history see Rolland Lutz, "The German Revolutionary Student Movement, 1819–1833," *Central European History* (September 1971), p. 215.

[11] Germany's Youth Movement began in the 1890s as a naturalistic adolescent rebellion against the strictures of Victorian bourgeois society. In 1913 the various separate clubs assembled at Hohe Meissner and swore to uphold their ideals. A year later many of the members volunteered for the German army and died in great numbers at the Battle of Langemarck. Further information may be found in Walter Laquer, *Young Germany: A History of the German Youth Movement* (New York, 1962).

of the students in 1931, Haupt would have become *Reichsführer* of the Student League in place of Baldur von Schirach, had Hitler not intervened on Schirach's behalf and nullified Schirach's dismissal which had already been decided by the democratic process.

The reasons for Hitler's intervention were evident. First of all, in principle he dared not recognize decisions reached democratically since that would endanger his own leadership claims. Schirach had been appointed Student Leader by Hitler and thus only Hitler could remove him from this office. Secondly, Dr. Haupt was a much too independent thinker and personality for Hitler to tolerate in such a key position. Hitler viewed academicians as potentially dangerous anyway. He wanted at least the new academic generation to be raised in a "new spirit" whose precondition was to be not freedom but faith—not in the religious sense but as a commitment to the thesis that all knowledge must thenceforth fulfill a purely functional purpose in the service of the community. The supreme protector and agent of the community, however, was Adolf Hitler. Thus the education of the students in a "new spirit" meant educating them for Adolf Hitler to a belief, exclusive of every free judgment, in Hitler as the genius leader of the Germans in the twentieth century. For such a task Dr. Haupt was simply not suited; in this Hitler was completely correct. Baldur von Schirach, with his ecstatic adoration of the *Führer* was undoubtedly the better man for this assignment.

To be sure, the effect of Dr. Haupt's defeat upon the Nazi Student League was stagnation in its organizational development, a stagnation that was only overcome after the seizure of power and then by means of compulsion. The intellectual stagnation was never overcome. All that was later offered as intellectual inspiration was confined to the areas of organization and propaganda.

After 1933 Dr. Haupt himself was taken on by Bernhard Rust in the Ministry of Education. Very soon there began a disgusting hate campaign against him, with charges of homosexuality being leveled against him on the basis of his previous membership in the Youth Movement. Himmler and perhaps Schirach, too, had discovered the usefulness of the laws against homosexuality as a weapon against political opponents and used them especially against people in their own ranks who made them uncomfortable but against whom the customary ideological charges could not be brought. Unfortunately, Minister Rust was not brave, stubborn, and strong enough to defend his own colleagues. Dr. Haupt had to leave the ministry in order to become a lecturer or instructor at Greifswald University, if my sources are correct.

His fate was shared by virtually all the Student League leaders of the early days. They were fobbed off with offices and jobs devoid of significance. They were not to be trusted. It was feared that they could come up with the insane idea of transforming their youthful ideals into reality and thereby attempting a second revolution.[12] One need have no such fears about the bandwagon Nazis of later years and the unpolitical "pure bureaucrats." They followed every directive and order anyway, in order to prove their ideological loyalty.

HEINRICH HIMMLER

Editor's note: *Heinrich Himmler joined the Nazi party in 1925 though he was involved in the "Beer Hall" Putsch as a member of one of the* Freikorps. *He served as an assistant Gauleiter and then, in 1929, was named* Reichsführer *of the SS, which at that time had fewer than three hundred members. The methods by which he built this organization into the prime terrorist instrument of the Third Reich are described in Heinz Höhne,* The Order Under the Death's Head, *paperback (New York, 1971).*

In the spring of 1929 I spent part of a day alone in a train compartment with Heinrich Himmler, traveling from Elberfeld to Hamburg. I had met him at the Elberfeld Gauleiter's office, where I had dropped in after a lecture tour for the DHV. He was on a tour of Germany to inspect the first SS units and to assist in establishing others. Since he had to go to Hamburg and Schleswig-Holstein anyway and since he needed information about local conditions there, he joined me. Thus we had about six hours of unbroken conversation, which he exploited down to the very last minute to his heart's content, with the result that I had the whole incident traumatically etched into my memory.

Himmler was not a man of engaging or attractive properties; in this he was completely different from Goebbels and Hitler who, if

[12] The idea of a "second revolution" to complete Hitler's "national revolution" of 1933 by introducing vague but sweeping social changes was associated with Ernst Roehm, whom Hitler had murdered in 1934, ostensibly to prevent such a "second revolution."

it served their purpose, could be thoroughly gracious and charming. Himmler, on the contrary, conducted himself in a decidedly stiff, dour fashion. He was ostentatiously crude and lower class in the manner of an old trooper, though this was obviously his way of covering up a native gaucherie and social insecurity. But that alone would have been tolerable. What made him practically unbearable company on that trip was the stupid and fundamentally empty claptrap to which he ceaselessly subjected me.

Even today I think I may say without exaggeration that I have never been served so much political nonsense in such a concentrated form, and that from a man with a university education and a professional involvement with politics. Himmler's exegesis was a remarkable mixture of martial bombastics, petty-bourgeois barbershop prattle, and the zealous prophecy of a revivalist preacher. Thus he explained that he would shortly be setting up an SS unit in Hamburg with a strength of five hundred men. My objection that conditions in Hamburg were in no way comparable to those in Munich and southern Bavaria and that the total number of *party* members in Hamburg was barely five hundred was dismissed by him with a wave of his hand. Circumstances were not crucial—everything depended on having the right men. The trouble with Hamburg was that the right men just hadn't been found yet.

And in fact the circumstances concerned him so little that he was extremely ill-informed about aspects of the general internal situation of the party in Hamburg which everyone else knew about. The only things he had put into his notebook were the addresses of a few SA and SS leaders. What he was really concerned about were the "secret" circumstances. Did ex-Lieutenant Z. really have a Jewish or half-Jewish wife? How did SA Leader Conn come to have such a remarkable name? Was that a disguised form of "Cohen"? What about the bank in which Gauleiter Lohse had previously been employed? Could he have thus become dependent in some way upon the Jews?

And it went on in this way. To steer him away from this I told him of my work for the DHV. But Himmler knew from a "most trustworthy" source that the DHV's general chairman had invested money in Jewish stocks and that the district chairman in B belonged to the Freemasons. The Bavarian DHV only appeared to receive its directives from the Hamburg headquarters; in reality it followed the orders of Archbishop Faulhaber. Naturally the leaders of the German army were also all blood relatives of Jews, in-laws of Freemasons, and pupils of the Jesuits.

Now, the phantom images of the "Wise Men of Zion," world Freemasonry, and the Jesuit conspiracy did belong to the intellectual arsenal of the movement. But for most of the Nazi leaders these things formed more of a propaganda subterfuge than an actual conviction. At the very least they were conscious of the exaggerations involved. But after this conversation with Himmler I could only conclude that he actually lived with these specters, that they were the very stuff of his world in the face of which the real, actual world, with its problems and demands, faded completely into the background. Thus it was utterly impossible to have anything approaching a discussion, in the sense of an exchange or even a comparison of opinions, with him. One could only agree, contradict, or be silent. I myself chose, from Osnabrück on, to sit mutely shaking my head and shrugging my shoulders. This was after the failure of my attempt to break off Himmler's dreadfully boring platitudes by trying to lure him into the dining car. Himmler would have nothing to do with dining cars. To him they were (at least then) a symbol of bourgeois decadence. Only weaklings or voluptuaries would not prefer to go hungry for six hours, or to live from a sandwich previously stuffed into an overcoat pocket.

HINRICH LOHSE

Editor's note: *Hinrich Lohse was born in 1896, was wounded in World War I, joined the Nazi party in 1923, and in 1925 became the Gauleiter of Schleswig-Holstein, the province that fills the German part of the Danish peninsula. In the Third Reich he was made a member of the Reichstag, a Prussian state councillor, and the governor of Schleswig-Holstein. He also became a general of the Stormtroopers and, in 1941, Reich commissar for the Baltic countries, where he helped carry out the murder of the Jews in Estonia, Latvia, and Lithuania. In 1945, after an unsuccessful attempt to escape to South America in a submarine, Lohse was captured and sentenced to ten years' imprisonment. He was released in 1951 for reasons of health and died in his birthplace in Schleswig-Holstein in 1964.*

Although Schleswig-Holstein was our neighbor as a Gau and there was close cooperation between Hamburg and the adjacent towns of Altona and Wandsbek (which at that time were still part of Schleswig-Holstein), it was only rarely that I met with my neighboring Gauleiter, Lohse. After 1929 I hardly ever saw him again. One reason for this was purely objective. As a consequence of the agrarian crisis at the end of the 1920s, the Nazi movement in Schleswig-Holstein was mainly growing among the rural people in the Dithmarschen district. Thus Lohse spent most of his time there and had little opportunity or leisure (since in those early days he was still also working as a bank employee) to foster neighborly relations. But the inclination to do this was also not very strong. The minor and major frictions that constantly arose from the close meshing of the Hamburg, Wandsbek, and Altona organizations left a residue of unfriendly feelings on both sides. We tried to avoid expressing these by avoiding each other whenever possible.

Perhaps these tensions could have been lessened if there had been better personal contacts between Lohse and me. But that was prevented by the differences in our personalities, differences that actually led to misunderstandings even when there was little cause for them either in substance or in good or bad will. It may be that these personality differences have also soured my retrospective judgment and if so, one should take that into account and treat what follows with the necessary caution.

I cannot recall ever discussing the problems and goals of Nazism with Lohse in any profound way. Presumably, he would also have fended off any attempts at such a conversation as a fruitless waste of time. His sober and practical nature was devoted to organizational work and to the immediate problems of the day. In dealing with these he undoubtedly displayed skill, but at the same time he was lucky, since conditions in Schleswig-Holstein and the distress of the rural people along its west coast played directly into his hands.[13]

---

[13] From 1925 on, Germany's farmers were in an economic crisis marked by declining income plus increasing tax and mortgage foreclosures. This was especially true of Schleswig-Holstein, where farmers at first fought back through a variety of futile pressure groups and parties, then turned to the bombing of tax offices and other violent agitation, and finally flooded into the ranks of Nazism.

Even the revolutionary Peasants' Movement led by Klaus Heim, which at first threatened to be a dangerous competitor for the favor of the Dithmarschen people, proved in the end to be abortive and an assistance. Once the bombs brought in by the activists (Kaphengst, von Salomon, etc.), who rushed to the scene from the cities, were exploded and the peasant demonstrations had run their course with only limited momentary success, there could be no further escalation of methods by the Peasants' Movement leaders in attempting to win their goals. The personal and objective preconditions for a nationwide farmers' revolution were also lacking. Even the hill farmers of Schleswig-Holstein joined the agitation of their neighbors in Dithmarschen only in hesitant and tepid ways. The attempt to carry the peasants' "black flag" into Lower Saxony, Mecklenburg, Brandenburg, and Pommerania either failed or produced only limited results. Thus the leaders came to the end of their rope; since they were fundamentally opposed to parliamentary methods, they had nothing more to offer the excited peasant. Beyond that, one part of the leadership got themselves arrested and sent to the penitentiary while others went over to the Communists.

The smiling inheritor was the Nazi party, since the majority of the peasants could not possibly return to the parties of the Weimar system. (That was only natural since an attempt had been made to teach them love for the Republic with tax foreclosures, penal sentences, and policemen's truncheons.) The administrator of the inheritance was Hinrich Lohse, who came from Dithmarschen himself and understood the peasants. They were not concerned about the "Third Reich" as an idea to be realized in the future; what mattered to them was their farms and freedom from the tax officials, which does not mean that they were so narrow minded as not to know that the farm and the Reich were somehow tied up with each other. Lohse too, in my impression, was concerned about "the farm." That is, what mattered to him was taking care of the tasks that lay directly before him. He always seemed to me as one of the "bourgeois" Gauleiters, who could

By 1932 the Nazis had an absolute majority in this area; it was the most Nazified of any district in Germany. The reasons have been given a classic analysis in Rudolf Heberle's *From Democracy to Nazism: A Regional Case Study on Political Parties in Germany* (New York, 1970).

have fit in just as easily with the Economic party or one of the other middle-class parties, not just in his positive effects but also in his hardheaded purposeful efforts to enhance his own position.

I often asked myself in those days what, aside from the special political situation in Schleswig-Holstein, had led Lohse to Nazism. As I assume from some of his remarks, it was primarily the struggle against Jewish finance capitalism or for the "breaking of interest-serfdom." As a bank employee he had ample opportunity to become acquainted with the undeniably vast influence of Jewish financial capital upon the German economy in the Weimar era. Apart from that, however, he was probably like many people who approach their own immediate sphere of life with complete sobriety: they incline, once they get outside their own experience, knowledge, instinct, and intuition, toward boundless speculation and fanatically doctrinaire obstinancy. For people of that sort the idea of "breaking interest-serfdom" was just as much a holy conviction as in other places belief in an immediate Second Coming is. Political and religious sectarianism always prospers best when based upon a one-sided rationalist half-education that recognizes no deficiencies in itself and yet hungers for wholeness, that is, for something complete and unconditional, precisely because of an unconscious sense of self-deficiency.

Like most functionaries whose authority derives more from the organization and their position within it than from their own personality, Lohse was very concerned to protect and maintain this authority. He was zealous in his efforts to make sure that no one outgrew him or could actually push him out of his post. The natural result of this was that the level of leadership selection and replacement remained the level of Lohse. Anyone superior to that would have to retreat voluntarily into the background and hide his light under a basket or else would be pushed, in countless internal conflicts, into the background—sometimes completely into the outside. It was thus indicative that when Lohse went to Riga as Reich commissar in autumn 1941 he brought with him for his staff men who were virtually all from the ranks of old (in age as well as length of membership) party members. Had they possessed, in addition to this qualification, other substantive qualities, then no one could have objected. Regrettably that was the case only to a very limited extent, thanks to unsavory personnel policies. Outside of the civil service sector and that of other specialists, eight years of Nazi rule had produced hardly any new forces among the purely political leaders. The remarkable complex of leadership—a mix of mistrust, fear, inferiority feelings, and sentiments of loyalty—prevented the growth of replacements. In fairness one must concede that in this respect the Nazi party was simply following the wretched tradition of the German parties in general.

If nowadays there are large groups who incline to simplify and level out the phenomenon of Nazism by employing only a few value categories and classifications, they are following the example of Adolf Hitler himself. From the beginning he was concerned to bring about a comprehensive uniformity and simplification of opinions, views, and principles within the party. The slogan, so frequently employed after the seizure of power, of *Gleichschaltung*[14] also expressed the intention of the party leadership to create a uniform type for political leaders, SA and SS commanders, Labor Front functionaries, League of German Girls leaders. It must be conceded that the intention was partly realized. Especially with the younger generation, who lacked the contact with the spiritual traditions of the past, and the members of the SS units, who were subject to particularly strict discipline, the attempts at creating a human type so to say out of a laboratory flask (or, as I once heard at an indoctrination session, out of "Adolf's toy box") produced some success. In the poorly informed environment of Hitler's opponents inside Nazi Germany, however, I found that the extent of this success was regularly overestimated. On the one hand, what was accomplished was more the eradication of old values rather than the creation of new ones. And secondly, the success was frequently one of appearances based on a camouflage, which was by no means always consciously and purposefully applied. There were many who camouflaged themselves like endangered animals, out of a pure instinct for survival. They howled with the wolves to keep from being torn to pieces.

But in addition to these there were individuals and groups, after as well as before 1933, and even inside the core formations of the

---

[14] Usually translated as "coordination," this term meant the subjugation of all social and political entities by the Nazi party. But its literal meaning is closer to "equalization."

party, who maintained their own personalities and their individual independent way of thinking. Thus free discussions were possible, in fact common, in most of the leadership circles of the Hitler Youth, and they did not even shrink from a cautious criticism of Hitler. At the SS cadet school in Tölz there was open talk of the complete failure of Germany's eastern policy and a demand for a European conception, which still presumed a leadership position for Germany on the basis of Nordic racial theory, but which rejected purely dictatorial methods and proposed a rule by "European elites." And finally, from party members of all ranks who entered the army after 1939 and thereby won a certain perspective by their removal from the party[15] while also gaining insight through their soldierly experiences into the many mistakes that had been made, you very often heard a view that expressed itself in the words: "Just wait until the war is over and we'll clean out the pigsty and the rule of the local *Führers* quick enough!" And even if that was put in exaggerately crude soldier's talk and gave too much credit or blame to the "local *Führers*" as sources of the "pigsty," still I can well believe that if the war had been won there would have been a violent struggle to change the Third Reich's system. And it would have been led by just those members of the Nazi party who had maintained their own opinions and their own judgments.

HANS LUDIN

Editor's note: *In September 1930 three young army officers were tried for spreading Nazi propaganda in the barracks: Lieutenants Wendt, Scheringer, and Ludin. Hitler testified at the trial, proclaiming that his party would come to power legally. This was a significant step in his wooing of Germany's military-political elites. The Nazi officers, however, were sentenced to short prison terms. Scheringer was converted to communism by a fellow prisoner, Wendt joined Otto Strasser's "Black Front," and Ludin became a leader of the Nazi Stormtroops. At that time he was twenty-six. When Hitler came to power, Ludin was made a member of the Reichstag and a general of the Stormtroopers, in command of the*

---

[15] Until 1944 the German army followed its traditional rule of permitting no soldier to be a member of any party.

Southwest District. In 1940 he was appointed Germany's minister to the puppet state of Slovakia, a post he held for the remainder of the war. In 1945 Ludin was captured and returned to Czechoslovakia, where he was executed on December 11, 1948. For further information see F. L. Carsten, The Reichswehr and Politics, 1918–1933 *(Oxford, 1966), pp. 315–320.*

Lieutenant Hans Ludin, who became widely known through the so-called "Reichswehr Trial," was a man of independent opinion and judgment. After his dismissal from the army Ludin became a professional SA leader in Karlsruhe. I sought him out there, on the occasion of a business trip to southern Germany in autumn 1931, because of my interest in both his case and his personality. I had misgivings about the idea of forming cells in the army officer corps, as did Gregor Strasser and even Rudolf Hess. My misgivings were rather fundamental in nature while Hess and Strasser were afraid that the Communists would copy this example. In fact, this fear was not wholly groundless, as evidenced by Scheringer's subsequent conversion to communism and by certain "national Bolshevik" tendencies among the earlier Free Corps officers. But everything I had heard about Ludin was favorable as was the impression made by his conduct during the trial. Any honest and politically unbiased assessment of the defendant would have to concede his decency, personal courage, patriotism, and consistency. During my visit with Ludin I learned that to these qualities one should add an intelligence well above normal.

I met Ludin at the Karlsruhe Stormtrooper headquarters. Just the external impression of this headquarters contrasted favorably with most of the other offices of a similar sort with which I had become acquainted. A clean and obvious orderliness prevailed, such as is customary and necessary in places where soldiers gather. There was none of the atmosphere of a freebooter camp: no smell of stale beer, semiprofessional ruffians lounging around, loud singing, and general confusion. The responsible leader had stamped the rooms with a Prussian style, which was not just something that had been learned but was a matter of internal approval and commitment.

This was no easy accomplishment twelve years after the end of universal military training and within the framework of a revolu-

tionary political movement that measured "discipline" by obedience rather than orderliness. Furthermore, the headquarters was
being used as a soup kitchen for unemployed Stormtroopers.
Anyone who has ever had to deal with such matters even once
knows how easily all the bonds of discipline can break down
among a compacted gathering of men condemned to idleness, in
bitter humor, near despair, and therefore potentially mutinous.
Here, however, everything proceeded in a calm and frictionless
way. The men got their meals, ate, and disappeared. There was no
unnecessary waiting around; indeed, not even any superfluous conversation. Given the garrulous and gregarious temperament of the
average Badenese, this struck me as a particular indication of good
discipline. To be sure, most of the men (and this struck me as a
second noteworthy item, in comparison with conditions in northern Germany) were older, from the generation that had fought in
the war. These veterans were easier to keep under discipline than
the young people who formed the mass of the Stormtroopers in
Hamburg, Essen, Berlin, Brunswick, and who had already been
affected by the general dissolution of standards of the '20s.

Yet this factor diminished Ludin's accomplishment only margin-
ally. Granted that in the South the proportion of older men in the
Stormtroopers was always larger than in the North because of the
earlier and stronger growth of Nazism there. But by late autumn
1931 the increasing bitterness and brutalization of the struggle had
led here, too, to a rapidly increasing withdrawal of the older generation. That was not just because of the obvious reluctance of men
with wives and children to expose themselves to the dangers of
street fighting and meeting-hall battles; the cause lay more in the
difference between the reasonableness of mature men as opposed
to the untrammeled wildness of young lads. One could express it
more strongly: the veterans felt repelled by the rowdiness that was
sometimes promoted and pampered inside the Stormtrooper units.
So they withdrew, or else transferred into the so-called Reserve
Stormtroopers.

On this point it was possible to determine Ludin's attitude. I
asked him directly: Since he was still pretty young himself, how
did it happen that his SA unit had what seemed to me such a high
percentage of veterans? The answer was given me in a roundabout
way through one of the Stormtroopers, an artisan or worker from

his external appearance. This short, fortyish party-comrade said, with a sly grin: "Oh no, he won't let the young bums say anything!" Ludin smilingly confirmed that, even though he was practically a "young bum" himself, he was intentionally strengthening and supporting the veteran elements inside the SA for the sake of tradition and the maintenance of discipline.

We then got into a lengthy conversation about the party and the SA in which Ludin presented his own ideas openly and clearly. As was the case with many young people of his age and education, Ludin's decision to work within the Nazi party derived from lengthy reflection and was by no means the result of a sudden emotional impulse. Ludin had an exact awareness of the shortcomings and errors of the movement; it seemed to me also that he was at least skeptical about Hitler as a man. In his opinion, however, these shortcomings were heavily outweighed by the conviction that the Nazi movement was the legitimate continuation of the German people's development into a historical nation. This development had begun in August 1914 and had only been temporarily interrupted by the defeat and revolution of 1918. In fact, so he declared, it was precisely because of the party's shortcomings that every true patriot should join it. "If you deliver the party over to the 'young bums' and the thugs," he said, bringing the conversation back to our point of departure, "then you shouldn't be surprised to see that it has fallen into bad hands."

Naturally we also talked about the army. As far as its military achievements were concerned, Ludin was full of praise. But Hans von Seeckt's[16] concept of the unpolitical soldier seemed outmoded, unrealistic, and dangerous. The sentence "The army serves the state and only the state, for it is the state"[17] could only lead to one of two conclusions, if it was more than rhetoric. Either the army would constantly run the danger of being misused by a bad set of state leaders for bad purposes, or it would have to take over state power itself as had the Praetorian Guards of ancient Rome.

[16] General Hans von Seeckt commanded the German army from 1919–26. One of the ideas he bequeathed was that it must be strictly neutral in politics. See Gordon Craig, *The Politics of the Prussian Army* (New York, 1955), pp. 382 ff.

[17] Hans von Seeckt, *Gedanken eines Soldaten* (Berlin, 1929), p. 116.

Both these consequences were unacceptable. Beyond that, the years after 1918 had clearly proven that the army generals, Seeckt included, were not competent to take over the state precisely because of their lack of political training and understanding. The demand of the hour, therefore, was for "political soldiers" as had been the conception of the Prussian reformers.[18] Seeckt's notion was that since the destruction of the monarchy had removed the supreme commander, this vacuum could be filled by the abstract concept of "the state." In Ludin's view this was an error which would produce bitter consequences.

To be sure, Ludin had no clear idea of how the "political soldier" was to have his voice heard inside the state, without thereby threatening the authority of the state and thus sliding into the role of the Praetorians. But what was truly tragic was that his apprehensions about unpolitical soldiers being misused by a wicked leadership for evil purposes were to come true precisely in the party to which he had turned because of his determination to become politically active. Ludin had accurately prophesied the submission of the unpolitical officer corps to Hitler, whom it identified with Seeckt's abstract "state." But Ludin himself suffered the same fate. He became a victim of the same misuse which he wanted to escape through his withdrawal from the army. In contrast to, for example, Stauffenberg, who in 1933 as a young officer also accepted Hitler[19] but then won back his inner independence, Ludin evidently remained loyal to Hitler's cause to the end. In any case, I never heard his name mentioned in resistance circles, even though I often made cautious inquiry about him because of my memory of our conversation in Karlsruhe. Perhaps it was just this that explains his behavior after the collapse of the Third Reich, as was described in Ernst von Salomon's *Fragebogen*.[20] By refusing every opportunity to escape his impending delivery to the Czechs and

[18] In the Napoleonic era, such Prussian military reformers as Scharnhorst, Gneisenau, and Clausewitz worked to create a civilian army to replace Prussia's previously professional one.

[19] Colonel Claus Schenk von Stauffenberg attempted to kill Hitler on July 20, 1944. The assumption that he had been pro-Nazi in 1933 has since been refuted in Joachim Kramarz's *Stauffenberg* (New York, 1967).

[20] In English translation as *The Answers of Ernst von Salomon to the 131 Questions in the Allied Military Government "Fragebogen"* (London, 1954).

thus a sure death on the gallows, Ludin accepted responsibility for his share of the misdeeds of the regime he had served, although I remain convinced that he had personally behaved with purity and integrity.

WILHELM MARSCHLER

Editor's note: *Marschler was born in 1893, served in the army throughout World War I, then joined the DHV and the Nazi party. In 1931 he was elected to the Thuringian state legislature and in 1933 was made governor, that is, minister-president, of Thuringia. He was also appointed to the Reichstag and made an honorary general of the SA. He served out the Third Reich as an administrator in an unnoteworthy manner and survived its collapse.*

Like Gauleiter Forster of Danzig and Gauleiter Murr of Wurtemberg, Wilhelm Marschler, the minister-president of Thuringia, came from the ranks of the DHV. In the early '30s when he was state councilor and vice-president of the Thuringian legislature, I corresponded with him in connection with my development of the organization of Nazi contact men inside the DHV. About the same time he also participated in one of the week-long indoctrination workshops I conducted, and during those eight days spent together at an inn in the forest near Ilmenau, we had ample opportunity to get to know each other.

Though Marschler's was not a complicated nature (in fact his casualness sometimes bordered on boorishness), neither was he an easy man to understand. Between the instincts he inherited from his peasant forebears and the routines he had learned as a union tactician, he had developed a cautiousness, particularly with regard to politics, that could neither be outwitted nor circumvented. We talked politics for hours on end during the training sessions and sometimes got into vigorous arguments with each other. But he always knew how to avoid committing himself to anything that might be dangerous or might have unforeseeable consequences.

Marschler was often harshly critical of the DHV's policies and frequently sparred around with the union's employees in his district but, in contrast to Forster and many other Nazi members of the union, he never let it come to an open break. He was equally vociferous about his misgivings over some of the party's policies and personalities. But he expressed this only in small, closed circles and if he brought himself to act against malpractices in the party it was only when he could calculate precisely all the potential consequences of his decision. But then, to be sure, this squat, broad-shouldered man could unleash considerable energy.

Still, it would do Marschler an injustice to portray his caution as only the result of slyness plus perhaps a by-product of his rather extensive personal ambition. Along with this there went a large portion of wisdom gained through experience and through knowledge of his fellow man. He was only about ten years older than I, but he often advised me not to expect or demand from the world anything more than the absolute minimum: every human being had to walk with his feet on the ground; there was no place where trees grew into the heavens. Anyone who wanted too much would wind up accomplishing nothing and would only injure himself.

Apart from his individual attitude, Marschler was a representative of that segment of the white-collar and skilled workers who rejected the Socialist slogans of "proletariat" and "class war" and instead were pushing their way into the middle classes. For Marschler this attitude derived already from his longtime membership in the DHV. This helped him combine a commitment to the middle classes with a decidedly nationalistic stance in the sense of the racialist or national socialist movements from the beginning of the century. In this he resembled most members of new political classes. He took seriously ideas and ideals that the traditional bourgeoisie had already begun to question and he pursued them with the fresh energy usually found in newly emerging groups.

Significantly, he had no time at all for the concept of a national socialist "revolution." For him the Nazi party existed in order to fulfill older hopes and goals, such as had been proclaimed by Adolf Stöcker and Friedrich Naumann.[21] In contrast to many of the younger party members, Marschler was pleased with the democratic-parliamentary development peculiar to Nazism in Thuringia. He

[21] Adolf Stöcker was the leader of a radical anti-Semitic Christian Social party in the 1880s (see Peter G. Pulzer, *The Rise of Political Anti-Semitism in Germany and Austria*, New York, 1964). Friedrich Naumann tried unsuccessfully to bridge the gap between liberalism and socialism with a National Social movement in the decade prior to World War I.

was quite comfortable as vice president of the legislature and happily played the democratic game of committee sessions and parliamentary votes. In the years in which I had contact with him, he was certainly not pursuing the goal of one-party rule; such a thing hardly even occurred to him. When this nevertheless came about, he definitely made no attempt to fight the course of events but continued to serve, now as minister-president, to the end.

In 1945 the Americans put Marschler into an internment camp. But in spite of the high position he had held, he was not subject to any prosecution or indictment. That, too, evidences his personal integrity. Upon his release he settled in Karlsruhe as a businessman and died there in 1952.

FRANZ PFEFFER VON SALOMON

Editor's note: *Pfeffer, a scion of a Westphalian aristocratic family, was born in 1892 and began his adult life in the officer corps of the German army. During World War I he rose to the rank of captain. At the end of the war he retired from the army to form his own unit of the Free Corps, which became engaged in the struggle against the French occupation of the Ruhr. He joined the Nazi party and after its refoundation in 1925 was made co-Gauleiter for the Ruhr. In 1926 Hitler appointed Pfeffer supreme commander of the Stormtroopers, which at that time also included supervision over the Hitler Youth. From 1926 to 1930 Pfeffer put a strong militaristic stamp upon the development of the SA. This was contrary to Hitler's plan, which envisioned the Stormtroops as an internal terrorist organization rather than an army. Hence Hitler forced Pfeffer to resign at the end of August 1930, and himself took the rank of supreme commander of the SA with Ernst Roehm as chief of staff. Pfeffer became head of the SA quartermaster's store, an utterly insignificant post. He played no important role in the Third Reich, except as a member of the Reichstag and was even dismissed from that in 1941. In 1944 the Gestapo imprisoned him, apparently in the panic arrests following the assassination attempt on Hitler. He survived the end of the war and lives in West Germany today.*

The brown uniform, cut to measure for him by a tailor, suited him excellently. Certainly the field gray uniform he once had worn had

looked equally handsome on him. In a business suit Stormtrooper
Commander Pfeffer von Salomon seemed far less impressive. That
could be said of many men; for only a few does it seem to me as
characteristic of their entire personality. Without much exaggeration one could say of Pfeffer that it was the uniform alone that
made him a man and gave him self-confidence, stability, and a purpose. Without the uniform it became all too apparent that he
inclined toward the existence of an adventurer, a careless playboy.

These inclinations were doubtless congenital to a certain extent.
This slim man inherited restless blood and an incessantly critical
head. Both qualities inhibited him from orderly activity and from
a recognition of any authority. People like Pfeffer always feel something approaching primal hatred and contempt for the world of
the "citizen." In a well-regulated situation, therefore, they make
excellent professional soldiers. It was particularly fateful for Pfeffer
and many of his peers of a similar age and status that they were
introduced to a "well-regulated situation" only in the years of their
early youth. Beginning with the war, which they entered as fresh-
cheeked soldiers, there commenced the first relaxation and dissolution of the bonds of order. They could still learn the external
forms and requirements of their profession, including how to die
courageously, but they could not be taught the spiritual values,
and metaphysical content of the life of a soldier and an officer. So
they remained arrested in a state of spiritual and intellectual adolescence. They learned the techniques and routines of the soldier's
craft, but they never became military leaders, officers in the traditional sense. It was therefore sensible for the *Reichswehr* to refuse
admittance to the many Free Corps officers despite their extensive
battle experience. How could they have maintained and transmitted the ethos of the soldier through the long peacetime period
when they had never absorbed it themselves?

As I reported earlier,[22] Pfeffer took only the concept of obedience from the entire complex of values included in the term "soldierly discipline" when he came to train the Stormtroopers. For
him it was enough that the SA men follow the orders of their
immediate superiors. Apart from that they were free to be, in fact
they ought to be, thugs. In this approach Pfeffer reflected the

[22] See Chapter 2.

triumph of the civil-war mentality in that segment of the German officer corps which had never grasped the true morality of the soldier or else had forgotten it and abandoned it in the confusion of the war and the postwar era.

Now the civil-war mentality is one that is keenly concerned with direct results. As one of the most inhuman forms of war, civil war requires a fanatically blind obedience that disregards every law of God and man in the execution of orders received. To this extent, Pfeffer's training rules for the development of the SA as a civil-war army were thoroughly appropriate. Similarly, his decision to organize the Hitler Youth in the form of the previous youth defense corps followed this rule. But it was precisely my argument with him about the organizational form and life-style of the Hitler Youth that showed me most clearly how Pfeffer was influenced not so much by clear conceptions as by resentments and uncontrollable drives.

The civil-war mentality had come to control him; he did not choose it for himself consciously. Just like his cousins Bruno and Ernst von Salomon,[23] Pfeffer was a revolutionary not out of a desire to build something forward-looking but out of reactionary negativistic sentiments. He hated the Weimar Republic because he thought it had destroyed the better and more beautiful past. Among the qualities of this past was the glory of the soldier, which now seemed to him to be connected with the youth defense corps and the external soldierly forms that reflected his own memories and his own education. He lived out his memories, his hatreds, his compulsion to action first in the Free Corps, then in the Nazi party, without giving much thought to the ideological connections or justification of his actions. He enjoyed playing the role of the "eternal lieutenant," always available where there was a need for people of his sort, the man who goes into action without a qualm but who also lets himself be put into action. He went along with things and did his job. He lacked the seriousness to ask whether or not he ought to be going along with things. In case of need he dug a few appropriate sounding reasons out of his memory chest.

[23] Ernst von Salomon was associated with the Free Corps terrorist organization "Consul," which assassinated Walther Rathenau in 1922; Bruno von Salomon was responsible for bomb attacks on government offices in Schleswig-Holstein in the late 1920s and from there went on to join the Communist party.

Thus Pfeffer also held onto his job with the Nazi party as long and as profitably as possible without ever being, I am convinced, a true National Socialist. For the party's program he had only scorn. He was smart enough to recognize its deficiencies and errors. But helping to remove these deficiencies, contributing to an attempt to develop National Socialism as an intellectual movement, that he would not do. For this he lacked, as I said, the seriousness, perhaps also the ability—not the intellectual ability but the spiritual.

Insofar as Pfeffer criticized the party, he was undoubtedly supported or even encouraged to do so by his wife. Her repugnance for many leading Nazis, especially Hitler himself, derived from her unhindered instincts and her still solid appreciation of real values and rules. I met Frau von Pfeffer at a visit to the home of Rudolf Hess. As I recall, she belonged to the Westphalian aristocracy. She resembled Frau Hess in her clear, calm personality.

Pfeffer's boldly critical attitude against the actual political goals of the party was not without effect, incidentally. As I recounted earlier[24] he tried, at least behind the scenes, to promote the Stennes rebellion. Perhaps that was what he used the DHV's lost 30,000 marks election contribution for. One could conclude from this that he, like Stennes and many other high SA leaders who had been professional army officers, wanted to convert the party into an instrument for a new class of "political soldiers." To be sure, in Pfeffer's case the content of such a desire was probably even vaguer than that of his comrades.

The attempt cost him his position as supreme commander of the SA; he was exiled to the quartermaster's store. After 1933 he was taken into favor again and named chief of police in one of the West German cities.[25] But he was unable to hold on to it. For reasons unknown to me he was removed from office and imprisoned by the Gestapo.

COUNT ERNST ZU REVENTLOW
Editor's note: *Count Reventlow, born in 1869, was one of the few living links between Germany's nineteenth-century anti-Semitic movements and the Nazi party. He was an active promoter of the*

24 See Chapter 7.
25 Actually Kassel.

pre-World War I racialist parties, particularly noted for his ideological writings, and after World War I he helped found a new party that competed with Hitler's: the German Racial Liberation party or DVFP. This was strongest in North Germany where it had a well-developed system of local organizations and a membership vastly greater than the Nazi party's. However, the DVFP lacked Nazism's dynamism and was already in decline when, in February 1927, Reventlow and several of its other leaders went over to Nazism. This destroyed the Racial Liberationists and gave Hitler a firm base in North Germany; consequently, Hitler tried to keep on good terms with the ex-DVFP leaders. Reventlow continued to hold his Reichstag seat, now as a Nazi, and to publish the Reichswart, once the official DVFP newspaper. But he never exercised much influence within the Nazi party nor did he hold any significant posts in the Third Reich. He died in 1943.

A few weeks after I resigned as Gauleiter of Hamburg, Count Reventlow came to the city to give a lecture. Even before he visited the party headquarters, however, this eminent and very elderly man took the trouble to visit me at the DHV building. He considered it an act of loyalty, he explained, to let me tell him the reasons for my decision, which he much regretted. At the party headquarters, he said, he would probably hear only negative judgments, in accordance with the deplorable German custom (particularly widespread in the party) of damning the predecessor in order to pile up credits for any accomplishments that might occur in the future.

This little episode, which cannot be fully assessed without the added fact that I had met the Count only once or twice beforehand, has always struck me as characteristic of Reventlow's behavior as a man and a politician. I have deliberately said "man" first. I do not share the view, widely held by the Count's friends and enemies, that politics was a sort of sport for him, that is, an activity for someone who would otherwise have been idle. On the contrary, one could call Reventlow a professional politician in the literal sense of the word since he was economically dependent upon the proceeds of his political publications. On one occasion he told me of the concern caused him by the growing authoritarian centralism in the party, which affected him personally in that it threatened

the continuing publication of his weekly newspaper, *Der Reichswart*. There were repeated open or hidden attacks on the organizational or editorial independence of the paper. Threats of a boycott
or prohibition alternated with generous promises to make him the
salaried editor of an official party newspaper. But the *Reichswart*,
he said, had value to him only as his personal loudspeaker and thus
all the offers were unacceptable from the outset. But what would
happen if the threats were meant seriously? "Since I lost practically
all my property in the inflation, I live by the earnings of my newspaper and its connected press; a few party circulars and notices in
the *Völkischer Beobachter* and I'd be wiped out . . . and I am
already an old man." That was the approximate conclusion which
the Count drew from his tale. That despite this he continued to
defend his independence is evidence, just like the incident described
above, as to what impelled Reventlow to political action.

A man in politics for the money would have accepted the deal
and exchanged his independence for a well-paid job as editor. A
careerist concerned about his own personal advancement would
have treated the Hamburg incident by jettisoning his own personal
links and obligations, adopting the judgment of the prevailing
party officials, and thus openly demonstrating his acceptance of
party discipline. By doing neither of these things and thus violating the customary cannons of "political cleverness," Reventlow
actually undermined his own ability to put across his political goals
and conceptions. In fact he ultimately made this impossible: His
influence in the Nazi party shrunk year by year until it was virtually insignificant. But this also makes apparent Reventlow's
subordination of political considerations to his own individually
designed rules and values, which stemmed from his character as a
man.

Already in the Kaiser's time Reventlow had become a professional politician out of passion. But his vocation derived more
from internal than external impulses, more from his personal
views than from the objective situation. That is why his political
behavior was determined more by personal than objective needs.
Reventlow would do nothing contrary to his own idea of honor,
liberty, moderation, openness to every man, and the courage to
accept truth, even when he knew that to act thus would injure his
own cause. That is not to deny that at times he could be silent and

accommodating. Significantly, it never came to an open conflict between him and Hitler. But even his gestures of silence and submission were so eloquent that sometimes they were more expressive than loud protests. For the rest the Count was never afraid to state views that deviated from the party line either in the columns of the *Reichswart* or in personal correspondence. It was just that he did so with such sophisticated irony as to obviate any sweeping effect, which also probably spared him from possible enmities and persecutions. In the conceptual world of the secret police there is no category for irony.

All these characteristics caused Reventlow to be a unique figure among the Nazi leaders. He cannot be lumped together with people like Frick, Buttmann, Pöhner, the former professional officers, in short, the representatives of the tradition-bound "conservative" wing of Nazism. Reventlow's political views were much more "revolutionary" than theirs; his political methods, based on his particular human attitude, were much more "reactionary" than theirs. Somehow he reminded one of certain noblemen in the French Revolution. He joined the popular revolutionary movement, became its spokesman on platforms and in writing, sacrificed to it outmoded political views and the interests and privileges of the aristocracy. What he did not offer up was his purely human set of values and standards, and that was because of the conviction that they would be indispensable for the period of reconstruction once the period of destruction and change had passed. In this he was truly conservative even to the extent of denying himself external success. And so he maintained stoutly and without discourage-ment his independence, his freedom of thought and expression.

The thoughts and reasons that led Reventlow to join the Nazi party can only be derived from the course of his political development and his occasional hints. He had joined the first racialist-social movement founded by Adolf Stöcker, Friedrich Naumann, Theodor Fritsch, and the founders of the DHV. After 1918 he was one of the leaders of the Racial Liberation party of North Germany and served as its representative in the Reichstag. Along with Wilhelm Kube and Franz Stöhr he went over to the Nazi party in 1927. An evident reason for this step must have been the realization that there was no further justification for the existence of the Racial Liberation party in the space between the Nazis and the

Nationalist party. One would have to choose between them, and that leads us to the deeper cause: Reventlow chose what he hoped would be the clearly social revolutionary course.[26]

For there can be no doubt from Reventlow's speeches and writings that he, who had lived so many years in Berlin, had recognized the sociopolitical problems of the big-city workers and employees and that he desired the true solution to their problems—that is, the complete incorporation of these groups into the economic, social, and political structure. He had no use for the patriarchal would-be solutions proposed from time to time by the circles around Alfred Hugenberg.[27] But he was equally opposed to the total welfare state, which would have required people to pay for the dubious gift of economic security by giving up their freedom.

Incidentally, it always astonished those who were caught up in prejudice and slogans how friendly the workers and little people showed themselves toward Reventlow's speeches. I cannot recall that there was ever a demonstration against him, the Count and the *Junker*, in Hamburg. Nor did either the Socialist or Communist press ever try to whip up such a demonstration.

Reventlow's prime concern, however, was not social policy but rather foreign policy and an attempt at a religious revival or extension of the Reformation. Since he set forth his views on these questions in many articles and several books, they do not require any basic explication. But a few special points should be underlined which were to be significant for his position inside the party.

Reventlow viewed England as the real enemy of Germany; therefore he felt that the worst mistake in Germany's foreign policy since the dismissal of Bismarck was the renunciation of the Reinsurance Treaty.[28] The Bolshevization of Russia hardly changed his attitude. Obviously such views angered Rosenberg, the anti-Comintern people, and ultimately Hitler himself. For this reason, the hopes of his friends (and perhaps also his own) that Reventlow would someday become the foreign minister of a Nazi Germany

[26] For documented corroboration of Krebs' analysis, see Noakes, p. 61.

[27] Leader of the Nationalist (i.e., conservative) party.

[28] From 1873 to 1890 Germany maintained some sort of treaty relationship with Russia, the last of these being the Reinsurance Treaty of 1887. With the non-renewal of this treaty in 1890 there began an estrangement between the two powers, which culminated in war in 1914.

were shown to be unfulfillable already by the beginning of the '30s. The columns of the *Reichswart* showed that he himself had reached that conclusion, in that he treated foreign policy matters with increasing rarity and caution.

Reventlow's Anglophobia was closely connected with his anti-Semitism. For him the Jewish Question was least of all a racial question; he viewed it as a multifaceted spiritual problem whose historical, social, and above all religious aspects had vastly more significance than the matter of biological heritage. He believed that a prime danger for Germany was to be found in (to put it crudely) the symbiosis between Anglo-Saxon Puritanism and Jewish Talmudism. This danger was not just political but resided much more on the general spiritual-philosophical level. He thought that this would threaten to produce a situation in which the still "unformed" German race would be unable to resist the thoroughly developed otherness of the Anglo-Saxons and Jews. Were there a true German race, or more accurately, a German nation, then there would be no anti-Semitism. Such, approximately, was Reventlow's thesis.

Naturally such views put Reventlow on the extreme periphery of the party, whose simplistic black-white propaganda required the German, the Aryan, to be noble and the Jew to be subhuman, According to Reventlow's views, however, one could assume almost the exact opposite. Anyone who held views like that was something like a potential traitor to the doctrinaire Nazi, but at the very least a shifty fellow. Therefore, it was small wonder that fanatical anti-Semites attributed what they saw as Reventlow's wavering, fuzzy, weakly humanistic attitude on the Jewish Question to the Count's marriage to a French woman. Anyone who could marry a French woman, and beyond that a typical specimen of Mediterranian racial characteristics, would probably also marry a Jewess (and, in fact, as I have since learned, the Countess actually was half-Jewish). Admittedly such were the opinions of the extremists who were speaking only for themselves. Nonetheless, they throw an indicative spotlight on Reventlow's position inside the party. Hitler undoubtedly had similar thoughts about the Count, only he would have given different reasons for his assessment. Above all, Hitler, apart from his differences over foreign policy, could have employed against Reventlow the basic formula that emerged from the struggle with Arthur Dinter at the 1927 party rally: "The Nazi party is a political movement that has no business with religious questions." Admittedly this basic rule was fictitious. The party and Hitler himself were very much concerned with religious questions if only in their negative intention to destroy every connection with transcendental values. They did that with the clear understanding that one can only bring men to total obedience to wordly powers if one has already destroyed their image of the other-worldly Power. Had Reventlow provided assistance in this negative effort by adding pseudoreligious concepts to the false phrases "believer in a deity" or "providence", then he would have rendered great service to the party. But in actuality the Count was deeply concerned with religion despite his rejection of the official church beliefs. I almost want to say that he was even concerned with the Christian religion. My brief correspondence with him on the occasion of my essay attacking Gustav Frenssen's "Faith of the North Mark" showed me that very clearly. Reventlow was a serious religious seeker and was firmly convinced that without a profound religious revival Germany and Europe would sink into a decline. People without a God or gods, he said, lost the basis of life; even a Caesar of vast success and genius could not revoke this historical law, not even if he took upon himself the name of a god. The example of the Roman Caesars was evidence enough.

With such views, Reventlow increasingly separated himself internally and externally from the party. His death, which I recall occurring in the second to last year of the war, was therefore given little notice in the party, even though Frick gave the graveside oration and laid down a wreath from Hitler.

KARL RÖVER

Editor's note: *Röver was born in 1889, educated in a business school, employed in Africa, 1911–14. In the last three years of World War I he served in the army's propaganda department. After 1918 he worked in his father's store in Oldenburg, joining a predecessor of the Nazi party before the "Beer Hall" Putsch and the party itself in 1925. In 1928 he was made Gauleiter of the newly created district of Wesser-Ems. From 1928–30 he was city councilman in Oldenburg, then Reichstag delegate. In 1932 he*

*became minister-president of Oldenburg and gained national noto-
riety for a campaign to prevent an African Lutheran minister from
preaching in one of Oldenburg's churches on the grounds that "a
circus would be a more suitable place to exhibit a Negro." When
Hitler came to power, Röver was appointed Reich commissar for
Oldenburg and Bremen and made a general of the SA. He held no
significant posts in the Third Reich and died in 1942 of natural
causes. For further information see Noakes, pp. 90, 228 ff.*

Toward the end of November 1931, when I was spending a few
days giving speeches in Gau Oldenburg, Gauleiter Röver sent word
that he wanted to see me at party headquarters. When I arrived he
was in a state of considerable agitation. He was a big heavy man
with the broad peasant's face so common to that area. Though we
hardly knew each other and he could only have known my views
through the *Hamburger Tageblatt* and from occasional remarks by
Gregor Strasser, Röver began our conversation without beating
around the bush by unleashing an extraordinarily candid criticism
of actions taken by the party leadership including Hitler himself.
Above all, there were two matters that excited Röver's dismay and
also his apprehension: the formation of an "out and out reactionary and capitalistic" economic advisory council in the national
headquarters and Hitler's orders that Röver should be a candidate
for the office of minister-president of Oldenburg.

Röver was a simple man and doubtless not overendowed with
intellect. But he was honest and responsible enough to recognize
his limitations and to draw the necessary conclusions from that
recognition. " 'This won't do,' Röver told Hitler, 'Old Karly Röver
as minister-president—the whole of Oldenburg would split their
sides laughing!' I practically begged him on bended knee not to
ask of me more than I can do and not to make me a liar and a
clown in front of my own people. For six years I've cursed the
political bosses. Now they'll point their fingers at me: 'Look at old
Karly Röver, become a big boss himself; wants to do things he
can't understand and never learned!' " Thus Röver's account,
which has remained in my memory practically word for word over
all the years because it was the expression of an admittedly uncom-
plicated but honest, "simple" believer in Nazism at the moment of
his first doubts.

In fact Röver was in a state of near desperation in that conversation, which went on for more than an hour. Repeatedly he asked me (and himself) questions like: "Have we just been lied to again? Are all the accusations and demands of Nazi propaganda just like those of the other parties: lures to get the mass votes so that the string-pullers and party officials can climb into the saddle? Is even the Führer thinking more about his own power than about Germany and the German people?"

Like a large number of the North German Gauleiters, Karl Röver was also a follower of Gregor Strasser. He was, therefore, particularly upset at the social reactionary trends that from about 1930 on were increasingly evident in the party's leadership. He may have been lacking in formal education, but he was thoroughly capable of assessing the events that were taking place in and around the newly formed economic advisory council. Furthermore, he had maintained sufficient intellectual independence to express his judgment openly. To be sure, he also had no real idea as to what should or could be done to put a stop to the undesirable evolution of the party. And I, to whom he had turned for advice, had to disappoint him with a shrug of my shoulders. Since the attempts by Otto Strasser and Major Stennes had run their course, it had become clear to me that the only prospect for success would be in a united rebellion against Hitler by the top party leaders. But who should organize such a united front? Goebbels was out of the question. As for Strasser, it was known how critical he was of many of the measures of the "sheepsheads" in Munich, but up to then he had given no signs of a desire to undertake open resistance. "Maybe he'll do it anyway," said Röver, after I had set forth my doubts to him. In any event, he intended to speak to Strasser and I should try to win over all the northern Gauleiters I had access to for an action similar to the Bamberg meeting of 1925. "Let Adolf say what he wants! Adolf can't treat us like stupid kids. We need a leader, not a tyrant. No, no tyrant!"

I made it clear to Röver that it was out of the question for me to play the role he wanted to assign me, for the simple reason that most of the North German Gauleiters did not even know me. But Röver stuck to his plan and spoke with great warmth to me, though frankly I had the impression that the longer he spoke of his plans the less seriously he believed in their realization. For the moment it was consolation enough for him to make a plan, in order to get over his anger and concern. As I took my leave of him he seemed calmer and more confident, despite my refusal and expression of doubts.

That evening, after the meeting, I spent a few more minutes talking with him. He was even stronger about the morning's decision and urged me once again to join his efforts. That was the last I heard from Röver. Nor did I ever learn whether, or to what extent, he had been informed of Strasser's intentions after his resignation or whether he approved of them. But it seems to me that the above episode suffices for an assessment of Röver's personality. Furthermore, I am willing to believe that people like Röver were by no means rare inside the Nazi party. Only most of the men like him were spared his glance behind the scenes. Therefore, they were also unable to react in the way he did.

After 1933 one didn't hear much about Röver. I do not know the extent of his responsibility or participation in the outbreak of the conflict over crucifixes in the schools of the southern (Catholic) parts of Oldenburg. That he had, like many North German Protestants, an anti-Catholic complex is something that I can well assume in view of some of his comments. As I recall, Röver died shortly after the outbreak of World War II. His successor was Paul Wegener, about whom I will have more to say below.

DR. BERNHARD RUST
Editor's note: *Rust was born in Hanover in 1883 and became a high-school teacher in 1909. He served as an officer throughout World War I and was severely wounded. After the war he became a company commander in the Home Guards and a member of the Nationalist party. In 1922 he quit the Nationalists and founded the Hanover branch of the German Racial Liberation party or DVFP. In 1925 he led his branch into the Nazi party and was made Gauleiter of Hanover. Rust belonged to the Strasser wing of Nazism and was a frequent critic of the party's "insufficient social radicalism." In 1930 he was dismissed as a teacher on grounds of improper behavior toward a girl student; he pleaded, in defense, temporary insanity caused by his war wounds. That same year he was elected to the Reichstag. When Hitler came to power Rust was made first Prussian minister of education, then Reich minister*

of education. Until 1940 he also held the post of Gauleiter of South Hanover-Brunswick. On May 8, 1945, Rust committed suicide.

Anyone who might conclude from *Reichminister* Rust's 1945 suicide that he was a particularly fanatical Nazi, who could not hope to survive the collapse of his temporal and spiritual world, would be deceiving himself. There was undoubtedly no need for Rust to fear prosecution. What dismissals occurred within the domain of his ministry on racial or political grounds came about because of general laws for which he bore neither more nor less responsibility than all the other ministers. I never heard that he himself took any particular initiative in this respect; on the contrary, what I repeatedly heard was that in Rust's domain the dismissals and forced retirements took place as correctly as possible and, when applicable, even followed the laws of the Weimar Republic. No, it was not fear of prosecution that drove Rust to take his own life, or in any case not justifiably. On the other hand, I know that Rust was tortured from virtually the day of his entry into the Nazi party by doubts as to whether he had taken the right step.

On the return trip from the Nuremberg party rally of 1929, I spent several hours conversing with Rust and Friedrich Wilhelm Heinz, whom Rust had just recruited as the editor of his Gau newspaper. The theme of our discussion was whether Hitler was truly the man to entrust with the fate of the German people. We did not agree upon a clear answer even though Rust's entire nature was such that he would have liked to have been able to answer with a joyful "yes." He repeatedly tried to mitigate his own and our doubts by referring to the words that Hitler had just uttered at the party rally, which Rust had written down with pedantic accuracy in his notebook. The outcome of our long, fundamental, and sometimes heated discussion was that Heinz and I concluded that one should "wait and see," while Rust produced a rather forced melodramatic "one must be able to compel himself to have faith."

With this formulation, Rust himself clearly and accurately characterized his own position in the party and his relationship to it. It was the tenuous position of a man who wanted to have faith and trust but was not really able to. It was caused by his rather soft nature, which was extensively deficient in the power to make clear decisions. He suffered from heart disease as a consequence of his service in the war, as I understand, and that may have increased his weakness and softness. But these qualities also derived from Rust's political background.

Like Buttmann, Frick, Bouhler, Epp, and numerous other Nazis who had formed their political goals before or during the World War, Rust belonged to that wing of the party which consciously sought to link the present and the future to the past. Therefore, his question "dare we entrust Hitler with Germany's fate?" was not simply rhetorical. On the contrary, it grew out of very definite assumptions and visions that had been formed in the racialist groups of Northwest Germany long before the emergence of Nazism. These were modeled on the ideas of Paul de Lagarde, Julius Langbehn, Willibald Hentschel, Ludwig Schemann, and Houston Stewart Chamberlain.[29] They stressed the folk rather than the state, inner moral renewal rather than the development of external power, a return to origins rather than progress toward the perfection of a mechanism. To be sure, there had been only limited advancement toward these goals: The wishful vision of working through tiny circles and minuscule groups, which would become the "secret of the country" and would ferment the whole nation like a leaven, had not been realized. Thus they turned to Hitler's mass movement, as it stretched its grasp farther and farther from South Germany in the second half of the '20s, because they thought they saw in it certain related characteristics and so permitted themselves to hope that through it they might achieve their own goals. And so, for lack of self-critical faculties and because they failed to recognize that in a mass movement there were forces that would inevitably produce radicalization and intellectual leveling, they imagined that they could become something like an intellectual general staff for this movement. They assumed that the existing leaders of the Nazi party, including Hitler, would play the role of tribunes of the people, demagogues, or, as one representative of these racialist circles once told me, political "market criers."

[29] For a description of this ideological heritage see Fritz Stern, *The Politics of Cultural Despair: A Study in the Rise of the Germanic Ideology* (New York, 1961).

Whether Rust had these same notions when he seceded from the Racial Liberation party to join the Nazis is something I do not know. By 1929 at least, he had come to realize that the presumptive division of duties (general staff vs. political trench fighters) was a foolish, unrealistic scheme. Precisely as the 1929 party rally had demonstrated to any sharply observant onlooker, Hitler had gathered practically unlimited control over the party in his hand, and, therefore, the fate of the Nazi movement and (if one believed that it would be victorious) also Germany's fate would depend completely upon the abilities, the beneficent or evil qualities, of this one man. Rust recognized this fact, as his question proved. His resigned conclusion ("one must be able to have faith") admittedly proved also that he was unable to surmount the reservations and doubts that derived from his personality and his political background. Thus there ultimately remained for him, along with his willingness to cooperate and be loyal, only the sober and modest decision: "Wait and see."

After 1929, even though I saw and spoke with Rust once or twice, I had no occasion to exchange thoughts with him in a fundamental way. So I cannot give a conclusive judgment as to when or whether he ever rescued himself from his schizophrenia. But if one may draw conclusions from his activity as minister of education, then I would conclude that he never escaped his split condition but also that he increasingly withdrew back to his original point of departure.

In the Third Reich little was heard of Rust's ministry and therefore it was also not considered to be very significant. In fact, however, it accomplished more than meets the eye. Admittedly, it generally shrank from confrontations with party offices, such as Rosenberg's[30] or the Propaganda Ministry. Rust's whole nature was not that of a fighter and his doubts and concerns about the evolution of the party probably made him even more unsure of himself and more willing to compromise in struggles with party representatives over conflicting competencies. Thus he allowed

[30] Rosenberg's office was charged with the supervision of ideological education for the Nazi party and therefore was likely to conflict with Rust's Ministry of Education, as was, for that matter, the Hitler Youth, the SS, the Labor Front, etc., all of which set up their own schools. Unresolved overlapping competencies were a prime characteristic of the Third Reich.

Goebbels to push him almost completely out of the cultural sector. Thus he refused to resist the pretensions of the Rosenberg office and the Hitler Youth, even though resistance was not only objectively justified but also could have been successful without much risk or effort. For example, when we in Hamburg sent a request for advise to Rust's ministry regarding modes of founding a planned school of music and theater, the response we received was that the founding of music academies was now under the control of the Reich Youth Leader's office. Rust's ministry regrettably could not advise us, though it reserved the opinion that music schools were purely educational matters and therefore should be under the direction of the Ministry of Education or else the educational and cultural administrative bodies of the individual states.

That was, for Rust's ministry, a typical response. They did not dare fight out a justified legal claim but at least maintained it in theory in hopes that it might be recognized again in better times. In Hamburg this advice from the ministry was taken as a broad hint, the school was founded as a municipal institution, and eventually also won (as was almost always the case in the Third Reich when people dared to represent their standpoint openly and objectively) the approval of the Reich Youth Leader's office.

The constant retreats that Rust's ministry undertook whenever faced with a struggle over competence areas is therefore neither deniable nor, with a few exceptions, excusable. Nevertheless, it would be wrong, as I already said above, to adjudge all of its actions negatively. Nor were its accomplishments solely limited to the fact that certain disreputable or even harmful practices, which were common to other offices during the Hitler era, were either unknown or rare in Rust's ministry. Alongside the lack of arbitrary and illegal measures, for example in hiring and firing officials, there was also a discernible will and ability to work for constructive laws and administration. The German library system, for example, experienced an extraordinary growth under the guiding initiative of Rust's ministry. Ideas for improvement flowed into the museums, though admittedly the coming of the war kept them from being realized. But it seems to me that what is even more important for a judgment of Rust's personality is that the methods employed and the prevailing atmosphere in his ministry suggest that he had very specific intentions during these last years of his life. He may not have resisted; he—who was never a real revolutionary—never became a counterrevolutionary or escaped into the "inner emigration" (this, incidentally, would hardly have been possible for him to do, given the structure of the Hitlerian state). But he did attempt to create in his domain a germ-cell of tradition, a place for the realization of his ideals. One of Rust's co-workers told me once: "We know that people out there in the country are upset with or scornful of our bureaucratic slowness and ponderousness. But they deceive themselves; we are not being bureaucratic but fundamental. We admit to intentionally cultivating occasionally ponderous ceremonies in the application of our work in order to point up and maintain the contrast between our methods and the frivolous thoughtlessness of other people. We wish to present and preserve a bit of Prussiandom."

Whether Rust as a Lower Saxon was concerned for the preservation of explicitly Prussian values is neither here nor there. But that in setting these goals for his ministry he was, as I said above, consciously seeking to return to his political point of departure, seems definite to me. He was granted only moderate success; as is always the case in revolutionary times, the conservative politician loses out against the activist, especially when, contrary to all his basic views, he comes to be a follower of the activist. But anyone who inquires not simply about success but also about intentions will have to judge Rust as a politician and a man more justly than before.

BALDUR VON SCHIRACH

Editor's note: *Schirach was born in 1907; his father, a former Prussian officer, was the director of the Court Theater in Weimar; his mother was American. He studied at the University of Munich where in 1925 he joined the Nazi party. Two years later he was appointed national leader of the Nazi Student League and in 1931 Reich Youth Leader, which made him head of the Hitler Youth too. When Hitler came to power this title was expanded to cover all German youth organizations. By the outbreak of World War II Schirach had fallen from Hitler's favor and was demoted to Gauleiter of Vienna, while his former second-in-command became Reich Youth Leader. In 1946 Schirach was condemned by the Nuremberg Court to twenty years' imprisonment. He completed*

this term and now lives in West Germany. For further informa-
tion and analysis of him see Joachim C. Fest, The Face of the
Third Reich: Portraits of the Nazi Leadership *(New York, 1970),*
pp. 333–344.

Near the end of the '20s, if I remember correctly, the *Weltbühne*
compared the SA with the *jeunesse dorée*[31] of the French Revolution, whose uprising was put down by the rule of the Jacobins and
who therefore paved the way for the coming dictatorship. At first
glance the comparison is somewhat seductive. In actuality, however, the propagandistically simplified scheme of Communist-
Jacobin revolution vs. bourgeois-nationalistic reaction does not
accord with reality. In 1930 there was no unified bourgeois youth
with a common political will. Nor can one equate the anti-commu-
nism of the SA with "pro-bourgeois." The *jeunesse dorée* of
1929–30 were not to be found in the ranks of the SA and the Nazi
party, with a few exceptions, but instead belonged to the *Stahlhelm,* the "Werewolves," the Young Germanic Order, and all the
other paramilitary organizations whose primary goals in domestic
politics could be expressed by the slogan "Restoration of the
Order-State."

One of the exceptions was Baldur von Schirach, who was to
become Reich Youth Leader. That he derived from an educated
and propertied family was not of decisive importance in this. In
the early days of the party you could find several hundred members with similar origins. But that Schirach was never able to shake
off the marks of his origins, that his whole bearing constantly characterized him as a child of the upper bourgeoisie, justifies his inclusion among the *jeunesse dorée* of 1929. And he was also viewed as
an outsider by the overwhelming majority of the party's membership, even though that membership usually held no firm opinions
about its leaders.

Before Schirach was made leader of the Hitler Youth he acted
as leader of the Nazi Student League, having been appointed to
this position by Hitler personally, as I recall. It was in this capacity

---

[31] The comparison is linguistically imperfect since the expression actually
means "easy living youth," while it was used here to mean the propertied bourgeoisie (*Krebs' note—W. S. A.*).

that I first made his acquaintance at a meeting of Nazi students in Hamburg. I heard him speak and then afterward spent a while with him in a small group.

In his speech Schirach's theme was political students whose task was to maintain and carry forward in the present the heritage of the Wartburg Festival. In contrast to Dr. Joachim Haupt, however, he pretended that these were his own original ideas and that the Nazi Student League was the only legitimate heir of the original *Burschenschaften*. As a result, he aroused the displeasure of those who knew better without satisfying the remainder, since his eloquence did not suffice for this. Schirach spoke with conscious rhetoric and was full of stylized pretensions. But his ideas were all half-baked and did not fit into the gilded baroque frame. He was simply too young to be able to exhaust his subject formally and in substance. As a general impression, I recall a mixture of academic lecture and lyrical poem.

Schirach's deficiencies as a speaker probably contributed strongly to his unpopularity. The mass of party members used to judge the value of the "leaders" according to the quality of their gift of gab and their mastery of the polemical arts, the crude and scornful insults that were especially highly prized. That Schirach lacked these arts, or refused to employ them, was taken by many as indicating weakness or even dishonesty.

Now it may be that part of his weakness was that of the overbred intellectual and aesthete—there were all kinds of wicked stories about his girlishly decorated apartment—but Schirach was not dishonest in his attitude toward the party. They were confusing dishonesty with artificiality, which was apparent the moment Schirach adopted the pose of a man of the people or the youth leader, neither of which fit him. He came across then like a Berliner in Bavarian *Lederhosen* or a pale snob on a sport field. On the other hand, Schirach was only being consistent when he did not want to hear anything about the Youth Movement, or when he stayed at the Vier Jahreszeiten Hotel rather than the Hein Godewind[32] on the occasion of a Hitler Youth meeting in Hamburg. He was simply sticking to his life-style, which was a mixture of the bourgeois and the Bohemian.

[32] Approximately the differentiation between the Waldorf-Astoria and the YMCA.

In personal conversation Schirach showed himself to be rather open-minded. You could talk to him about the most diverse questions. Thus, for example, when I told him about the unpleasant differences that had developed between the DHV and the party, he showed unexpected understanding and promised to support my position at the national headquarters. I do not know whether he kept his promise though.

He was also willing to listen to political heresies and even to offer them space in the columns of the *Bewegung*, the newspaper of the Nazi Student League. At his instigation I wrote an article for it entitled "Between East and West" that was slanted toward a clear rejection of Alfred Rosenberg's anti-Russian policy. Schirach also occasionally voiced opposition against Rosenberg's cultural attitude. Unfortunately, his opposition was generally restricted to declamations that led to no practical results. In any case, he made Rainer Maria Rilke acceptable again in the Third Reich, made it possible for the Association of Bibliophiles to continue its work by becoming a member, and in 1942 even tried to resist the cultural dictatorship emanating from Munich and the "House of German Culture" by sponsoring an exhibition of modern art in Vienna. To be sure, this attempt was very quickly nipped off when Hitler stepped in personally and forbade any disruption of his cultural policy. Schirach's commissioner, who had also negotiated with the cultural offices in Hamburg, was subjected to disciplinary measures without Schirach being able to protect him.

Part of Schirach's style included a very conscious projection of himself as being intellectually superior, which came across in the earlier years as simple arrogance. Thus at the above mentioned gathering he also spoke about the behavior of soldiers at the front. He, who had never been a soldier and knew the war only from reading about it, knew much better than those who had been soldiers and had experienced the war in person. When I pointed out his errors he clapped me benevolently on the shoulder and said, "Just believe me, my dear Dr. Krebs; it was exactly the way I told you!" When that produced a shaking of heads by some of those present, while the rest just laughed out loud, Schirach glanced around the room in surprise. He was completely unable to comprehend how silly he had made himself with that remark.

Though Schirach was unambiguously a part of the bourgeois wing of the party by origin and behavior, one cannot assume a sim-

ilarly clear ideological identification at the time of our acquaintance. As a student, Schirach was still too young to be able to
decide among the ideologies being pressed upon him. His broad
flat face suggested, to be sure, that he never would achieve an
intellectual profile and would always live a secondhand life intellectually and spiritually. This probably also explains his boundless
devotion to Hitler, which certainly derived from an honest conviction that lasted to the end of the war. On the other hand, it was
probably also Schirach's uncompensated lack of substance that
contributed heavily to his unpopularity among youth. This unpopularity led already by the early '30s to a revolt within the Nazi
Student League, which would have cost Schirach his position as
leader had not Hitler intervened on his behalf. Later on in the
Hitler Youth one also encountered expressions of this unpopularity
everywhere. I am not in a position to decide whether this was
objectively justified, since I lack a thorough knowledge of conditions in the Hitler Youth leadership. One thing that is probably
sure is that Schirach himself desired the struggle against the Youth
Movement.[33] By nature he was undoubtedly an unpolitical and
totally unsoldierly man. Beautiful decorations, pictures, and books
meant more to him than helmets and weapons. He only played at
the other things: youth leader, Reich commissar, proclaimer of the
national revolution and the greater Germanic Reich. He tried to
make a life from literature. It was, as I already said, a secondhand
life.

HANS SCHWARZ VAN BERK
Editor's note: *Krebs chose this otherwise generally insignificant
figure to illustrate the development of Nazi journalism. For further
information see Oron J. Hale,* The Captive Press in the Third
Reich *(Princeton, 1964), and Ernest K. Bramsted,* Goebbels and
National Socialist Propaganda *(East Lansing, Mich., 1963).*

Just as the organizational development of the Nazi press proceeded
very slowly, so also there was a slow development of characteristic

---

[33] In the Third Reich the previous Youth Movement (or *Bündische
Jugend*) was prohibited, even though the Hitler Youth had taken much of its
style from them. By 1936 the Hitler Youth had no competition for the allegiance of young Germans.

types among Nazi journalists and writers. In the beginning those who wrote for Nazi newspapers were preeminently men from the old racialist movement plus professional soldiers, unemployed because the war was over. Thus in the *Völkischer Kurier*, edited by ex-Captain Wilhelm Weiss, one could find among the staff a whole series of names previously familiar through the publications of the Lehmann Press and the Pan German Society. Only a part of them went on to write for the *Völkischer Beobachter*, which became the official organ of the Nazi party after the dissolution of the *Kurier*. Of these I recall only a few names, such as Dr. Gregor Stolzing-Czerny, Dr. Buchner, Dr. A. Wirth, von Koerber, Weberstedt, and above all Dietrich Eckart, who, however, had died in December 1923. It was Eckart especially who embodied in his articles, poems, and plays the intellectual world of the prewar racialist-nationalist groups. (Significantly, Goebbels and Strasser were probably the only Nazi leaders to recognize this.) Nevertheless Alfred Rosenberg, and Hitler too tried very hard to make Eckart the party's leading poet and to get his poem "Sturm, Sturm, Sturm" accepted as the official party anthem. To be sure, they were not successful. Rosenberg's book on Dietrich Eckart was hardly noted in party circles, while the poem, despite various musical renditions and repeated directives from Munich that it should be sung at party ceremonies, was ill received. The young Nazis hardly knew what to think of it since it tried to satisfy their enthusiasm and lust for combat by giving them, in excessively melodramatic language, only "Judah" as an enemy. Even the simple Stormtrooper, who used to shout his "Croak Judah!" at demonstrations and rallies more out of a rowdy love of shouting than from true internal conviction, felt that there had to be more to it than this.

Even after the party was refounded it still took a long time before there evolved something like an independent style of Nazi journalism. Trained journalists played virtually no role in this. The few representatives of this element who sought positions in the slowly emerging Nazi press were rarely masters of their craft. They did not come in order to wield their pens for newly acquired views and opinions but rather because of the lamentable fact that no one else needed their blunted pens any more. People of that sort, however, insofar as they found employment at all, were naturally not in a position to create a new image, jargon, terminology for the

Nazi combat sheets. On the contrary, this task was accomplished, admittedly only after countless fiascos and false starts, by pure amateurs. Even in retrospect it seems astounding what powers and abilities were awakened in men of the most diverse origins and educational levels by the revolutionary élan of the movement. The old saw that he who has nothing to say also has nothing to write was, however, not disproved. On the other hand, the widespread overevaluation of formal education (especially so in Germany) was basically disregarded. Naturally every self-made Nazi editor ultimately had to acquire the knowledge and dexterity that belonged to his craft. But what deserves to be noted and remembered is that they had to acquire it on the job, without any special training, evening courses, or graduation certificates.

The first newspaper to introduce the new style, and simultaneously the emerging new generation of journalists, was the *National Socialist Correspondence*. Though its publisher, Gregor Strasser, was a Bavarian, most of its writers were party members from northern and western Germany. The initial place of publication was Elberfeld, the then center of the party's organization in the Ruhr. At that time Dr. Goebbels was still cooperating; I do not know whether or to what extent he was responsible for the consciously bold and aggressive tone of the paper. After Goebbels and Strasser increasingly parted company, the *Correspondence* was moved to the Combat Press in Berlin. Strasser remained the publisher; Herbert Blanck was editor.

In the *National Socialist Correspondence* there emerged for the first time the names of Friedrich Wilhelm Heinz, Dr. Herdieckerhof, Dr. Ispert, Richard Schapke, Reinhold Muchow, Dietrich Klagges, Dr. Otto Strasser, Bodo Uhse, Edo Wandel, Otto Bangert. They loved to write their commentaries under such revolutionary pseudonyms as Jäcklin Rohrbach, Wendel Hipper, Thomas Münzer, Ulrich von Hutten, and so on. They were equally concerned to be revolutionary in their demands and their writing style. In their commentaries they undoubtedly took the *Weltbühne* as their stylistic model.

While the Munich party circles tried to avoid taking a stand on individual problems as much as possible, limiting themselves to a few major questions, there was no area of life on which the *National Socialist Correspondence* did not take a position. That was not done with deeply scrutinizing scholarly thoroughness, but was almost always hard-hitting, spritely, and full of gusto. Anyone who compared, say, Rosenberg's *Weltkampf* or the *National-sozialistische Monatshefte* with the *Correspondence* must have had the impression of two entirely different intellectual worlds. In Munich they quickly drew conclusions from this disparity and as early as February 1927 issued an official party declaration in the *Völkischer Beobachter*: "The *National Socialist Correspondence* is not a party organ but rather an independent newspaper. Its articles do not have the character of official party positions but instead only that of discussion materials or academic treatises. . . ." The implied rejection in this declaration became even stronger in ensuing years as the "socialistic" tendency of the *Correspondence* increasingly came to light. Rosenberg and Hess repeatedly mentioned it to me in very critical terms. When the group around Otto Strasser broke away and converted the paper to the organ of the Militant Association of Revolutionary National Socialists (beginning with the issue of August 1, 1930), the Munich people considered that their own critical apprehensions had been proved justified. But they thereby also forgot that they had made no attempt to link themselves to the dynamic forces that were struggling to express and evolve themselves in the *National Socialist Correspondence*, that they had not tried to form and use it for their own goals.

I can no longer recall how long after 1930 the *National Socialist Correspondence* continued to be published. Given Dr. Otto Strasser's deficiencies as an organizer and the faction fights that rapidly broke out within the "Black Front" (which soon evolved out of the Militant Association of Revolutionary National Socialists), its publication probably ceased very quickly. Its circulation was never very large anyway, since it always made severe demands upon its readers. What is incontestable is that the *National Socialist Correspondence* made a serious attempt to develop clearly the ideas implicit in national socialism and to create an intellectual elite. That this attempt was not fully realized was partly due to circumstances, partly to the men who undertook it. Dr. Otto Strasser's slogan, from the above mentioned August 1930 issue, "We see ourselves as the Jacobins of the German revolution," shows too much of a nihilistic and destructive basis. Jacobins can never accomplish anything permanent; at most they can clear away the ruins of the past. It may be significant that the staff of the *Corre-spondence* never grew beyond negativism into a working collective firmly anchored by common goals. That is, almost all of the erst-while staff played a role in one place or another after the paper col-lapsed, just as beforehand they had contributed measurably to the development of the Nazi press in northern Germany. But the places where they went to work showed them pointed in the most diverse directions. The talented Bodo Uhse, who edited the party's *Schleswig-Holsteinische Tagezeitung* for a while, went from the Black Front to the Communists' Peasant International. Reinhold Muchow became editor of *Workerdom*, the organ of the Nazi Shop-Cell Organization. Friedrich Wilhelm Heinz joined the army in 1933 and there became involved in the plans of the military re-sistance groups. A few stuck with Otto Strasser and had to go into exile with him or else wound up in prisons, like Blanck and I think also Schapke. Others cooperated with the Third Reich in more or less significant positions. Probably they all mutually considered each other as traitors, as happens in revolutionary eras. Only the passage of time permits one to recognize how closely they were linked to each other through the same revolutionary impulse, through the same serious conviction that they were pioneers of a new historical epoch.

Among the staff of the *National Socialist Correspondence* there was one Hans Schwarz, though he was not particularly prominent there, as I recall, under that name. He first became well known after splitting away from Otto Strasser's group, which decision he emphasized by changing his name to Hans Schwarz van Berk.

A few months after we began publishing the *Hamburger Tage-blatt*, Hans Schwarz van Berk came to see me in our editorial offices in order to apply for a job as political editor. He said he was no longer happy with his job at the *Pommersche Tagespost*, a newspaper of the Country People's Movement, though it was never clear whether the cause of his unhappiness was personal or objectively political. Since he had only belonged to the Nazi party as of 1930 (before that he had been a member of Erhardt's Free Corps), his profession as a journalist was probably more important to him than his membership in the party.

This is not to make a value judgment on Schwarz van Berk's personality but rather to register that a third level had been reached in the development of Nazi journalism. The first was characterized by the old racialist-nationalist and anti-Semitic writers from the prewar era. In the second stage the amateurs were forced to pick up the pens, glue pots, and scissors themselves. Now there appeared the "born" and "trained" journalists. Schwarz van Berk seems to me to be the prototype of this breed. Perhaps one could also have selected the subsequent Reich Press Leader Otto Dietrich or "Putzi" Hanfstängl, who both began to play a role in the party about this time, too, but neither of them were, in my opinion, as "authentic" journalists as Schwarz van Berk, either in their ability or their attitude.

Where the "authentic" journalists show up something is going on—either you find sweet honey or sweet poison. Therefore the appearance of a man like Schwarz van Berk was symptomatic, not just for the development of the Nazi press but for the entire Nazi party. He was not simply looking for a job (in addition to his work with the *Pommersche Tagespost* he was also a regular contributor to the magazine *Nahe Osten*); he was much more interested in going beyond his previous membership to participate immediately in events that his journalistic antennae told him were in the offing. Similar antennae led Mr. Knickerbocker of America[34] to make his initial visit to the Brown House about that same time. The limits and dangers of this sort of journalism have been recognized; Schwarz van Berk was unable to avoid the dangers because he did not respect the limits.

Since we could not meet his actually rather modest salary request, Schwarz van Berk went to work as editor of the Nazi weekly for Pomerania, the *Diktator*. In this position he composed a little pamphlet, "Prussiandom and National Socialism," subtitled "Seven Letters to a Prussian Junker," whose contents clearly demonstrated his violation of the limits. With vast stylistic skill and surprising empathy Schwarz van Berk (who came from western Germany) employed the terminology of Prussian conservatism in order to win over the Pomeranian nobility to the cause of Nazism. In fact, he not only used the terminology, he also pre-

[34] Presumably Hubert R. Knickerbocker (1898–1949), the Pulitzer Prize-winning correspondent for the New York *Evening Post* and International News Service in Berlin in the 1920s and 1930s.

sented himself and his party as a modern expression of Prussiandom adjusted to the needs of the time, even though he knew
better than that. He did this so skillfully that individual parts
could have been used ten years later as the basic position of the
Prussian conservative wing of the resistance movement.

In my judgment this was the point where his methods began to
be impermissible. Schwarz van Berk was smart enough to know that
to talk about the Nazi party as heirs to the historic tasks of Prussia
was to engage in a conscious deception. It is true that the party
contained Prussian conservative elements, though at the moment he
published his pamphlet they were already in retreat before a totally
un-Prussian demagogic radicalism. In masking this, in fact in con-
verting it, in order to promote the "sacred cause," into the exact
opposite, Schwarz van Berk was doing something that in subsequent years would bring misery to the cause he represented and to
himself. It is completely incontestable that the subsequent bitter
opposition of a large portion of the Pomeranian and East Elbian
Junkers against the Hitlerian state can be traced back to their disgust over the deception practiced against them and against the
"Spirit of Potsdam." These aristocratic gentlemen who, after a
long mistrustful hesitation, finally joined the Nazi party or at least
stopped opposing it, felt themselves insulted and betrayed by this
sort of propagandistic horse-trader trick. They then responded with
direct deeds, as Schwarz van Berk had urged them to do in his
pamphlet (though, to be sure, for quite different goals).

That was the objective consequence. The personal consequence
was that Schwarz van Berk debased himself and his work, even
inside the party. He made himself into a tool of propaganda
and lost his soul as a journalist of independent thought and attitude. After 1933, to be sure, Schwarz van Berk was editor of
Angriff for a while. Then like many Nazi newsmen he made a
world voyage on behalf of and paid for by the Nazi Press Office
and the Propaganda Ministry, sending back reports for six major
newspapers. Finally, from autumn 1939 on he served as political
editor of the weekly *Das Reich* and also ran a press bureau for the
foreign press section of the government.

But, despite all these undoubtedly somewhat significant positions, he was no longer able to give meaning and style to his own
work. He remained thenceforth the propagandist whose esteem

and effect was not comparable to his ability and intelligence. A tool of propaganda is not supposed to think; he is supposed to execute orders. If he refuses or even shows signs of independence, he will be shoved aside. According to everything I heard that is what regularly happened to Schwarz van Berk whenever he dared to open his mouth against his lord and master, Goebbels. Thus his significance for the internal and external development of the Third Reich was constantly reduced, even though his talents were such that he should have been one of its leading figures.

JULIUS STREICHER

Editor's note: Streicher was born in 1885 of middle-class parents. He became a grade-school teacher in Nuremberg and an early and vehement anti-Semite. After serving as an officer in the army in World War I, he became a prominent leader of one of the first proto-Nazi parties, the German Social party. In 1921 he engineered the dissolution of this party and the entry of most of its members into the Nazi party. Hitler rewarded him by making him Gauleiter of Franconia, the capital of which was Nuremberg. He achieved early notoriety as the editor of the semi-pornographic and scurrilously anti-Semitic weekly Der Stürmer; his personal style was so tyrannical and corrupt that he faced constant opposition within his own Gau both before and after Hitler came to power. He was given no significant posts in the Third Reich, apart from the chairmanship of various anti-Semitic committees and by 1940 the evidence of his financial corruption was so great that Hitler reluctantly dismissed him from his post as Gauleiter. In 1945 he was tried by the Nuremberg Court—the prison psychologist found that he had the lowest IQ score of any of the defendants—was found guilty of crimes against humanity and was hanged in Nuremberg in 1946. Further information on him is available in Eugene Davidson, The Trial of the Germans (New York, 1966), pp. 39–57.

An exact analysis of the curious personality of Julius Streicher, if done without the usual black-white depiction, would probably produce some valuable insights into the nature and the intellectual-spiritual substrata of anti-Semitism. It is equally probable, however that such insights would displease everyone, especially the spokesmen on all sides. My rare, and with one exception, quite superficial contacts with Streicher protect me from the danger of arousing universal dislike. I can only report about the single exception, though perhaps even that may uncover some of the delusion-filled substrata.

During the city elections of 1928 Streicher came to Hamburg to give a speech. Even as we were greeting him at the railroad station he declared that he was not feeling well. Someone had tried to poison his coffee in the dining car of the train. However, since he had been warned before he left Nuremberg that the Jews might attempt to assassinate him, he left the bitter brew alone after his first taste of it. This revelation caused us to shake our heads and essay a few expressions of doubt, whereupon Streicher became bitterly angry. He had long known, he fumed, that the North Germans had no notion of the insidiousness of Jewish fighting methods. In general, the clear anti-Semitic course of the party was being followed less and less so that he, Streicher, was forced to assume that agents and spies paid by the Jews had managed to infiltrate everywhere. For quite a while now he had been keeping an eye on a couple of people and when the time came he would rip the masks from their faces.

And so it continued in the same style. But ultimately we engineered a sensible conversation with him. Streicher was neither stupid nor uneducated; he was well informed about the history of his hometown; he had a peasant's sly appreciation of men and events and he would even let himself be contradicted as long as one kept away from the Jewish question. His account of the poisoned coffee we wrote off as a propaganda atrocity tale. We did not wish to attribute to a man who spoke with so much expertise about sociological problems in the Nuremberg area the absurdity of actually believing in such fairy tales. On the other hand, it was easy to assume that, in his demonic fanaticism, he made them up and spread them around.

However he *had* meant his story seriously. Streicher actually *was* convinced that an attempt would be made to murder him in Hamburg. We discovered this when we came to discuss the technical arrangements for the meeting. He was supposed to be taken by automobile from his hotel to the Sagebiel Hall and returned the same way. As usual the SA would form a line on either side of his path between the auto and the entrance to the hall. Streicher, however, demanded a quadruple security cordon with two lines on each side, one meter apart, both outer lines to face outward. By this means Streicher hoped to make it impossible for the lurking murderer to accomplish his pistol or hand-grenade attack.

Rather bewildered, we tried to talk Streicher out of his fears, above all by referring to the fact that acts of individual terrorism were scarcely common in Hamburg. In the ensuing argument it became clear the Streicher's fears had nothing to do with ordinary cowardice. It was simply that he would find it intolerable if the hated Jews were to have the satisfaction of seeing him, the world's number one fighter for anti-Semitism, successfully assassinated. Therefore, he also showed himself completely unaffected by every argument based on reason so that finally I had to refuse to fulfill his wishes point-blank. I did so with reference to the bad effect on the morale of the Stormtroopers who, after all, actually were exposed to frequent assaults when they went home at night, without our being able to supply them with a security escort.

After some heated shilly-shallying Schleicher finally gave in and of course there was not a sign of any assassination attempt. The whole episode demonstrates, however, how some of the roots of anti-Semitism reach so deeply as to be inaccessible to soundings by reason.

OTTO TELSCHOW

Editor's note: *Telschow was born in 1876, the son of a farmer, and was educated at a Prussian military school, following which he served in the army, 1893–1901, and then in the Hamburg police until dismissed in 1924 for subversive political activity. From 1905 he belonged to the German Social party, a tiny racialist organization. After World War I he joined the Racial Liberation party and was made one of its district leaders in 1922. In 1925 he went over to the Nazis and was made Gauleiter of East Hanover, which consisted of the pastoral and heath country between Hamburg and Hanover. He acquired no other significant posts in the Third Reich but held the distinction of being the oldest Nazi Gauleiter.*

Among Hamburg's neighboring Gauleiters I have the faintest memories of Otto Telschow. He was hardly ever a speaker for us.

On his frequent visits to our headquarters we usually tried to compliment him out the door as quickly as possible because he kept us from working and also had nothing particularly clever to contribute to a conversation. Thus I only know now that ex-police officer Telschow was a man of undoubtedly honest intentions but not equipped with any noteworthy abilities. In the area between Lüneburg and Cuxhaven he gradually used his rumbling folksy oratory to establish himself and win a following, which then quickly led him to a not inconsiderable vanity.

Telschow conducted his agitation campaigns primarily against the Freemasons and the Jews. That corresponded to his deficient political knowledge and understanding. Since he knew nothing about the interconnections, background, and effective forces of politics or history, he sought enlightenment on both themes ("the key to world history") by turning to the little popularly written pamphlets provided by the party. He memorized their contents and then presented them with the necessary force of conviction to his absorptive audiences. He had significant success, since these audiences had approximately the same level of understanding of the Jewish Question as Telschow himself did.

Very few Jews actually lived in Telschow's district. Thus the stories he and his *Niedersachsenstürmer* told about them stirred up the imagination and curiosity of his readers and audiences mightily. That is, they had no way to test the validity of his yarns, but they accepted their accuracy in the same way that the tales of a world traveler get accepted, as long as there is no reason to doubt his honesty. "He's been there; he must know about it." And so Telschow feasted on the crumbs of the big successful party demagogues who pulled the masses out of their customary mental ruts and took them in tow by creating new concepts and images, by lambasting previously unknown and unimagined wire-pullers and enemies.

The Freemasons presented a different problem. Most of the towns of eastern Hanover had members of lodges or even lodges themselves. Generally they were composed of representatives of the propertied and educated middle classes. The fact that it was just these bourgeoisie who showed the least receptiveness to Nazi agitation was all too eagerly presented as the results of secret Masonic activity. "Now you see," one could argue, "here is evidence for what the writings on the secret doings of international Freemasonry have disclosed. Who won't come to our meetings? Who combats us openly or secretly? All those who are caught in the golden strands of the international Jewish-Masonic web! Your own eyesight proves the correctness of our assertions. . . ."

Thus the situation meshed with Telschow's own aptitudes and inclinations. But perhaps he would have chosen another whipping boy for his agitation if the emergence of the Tannenberg League had not forced him to select that same object. Just as in Schleswig-Holstein, the Ludendorff movement got an early start and spread itself rapidly along the lower Elbe and in the Lüneburg Heath. To combat it you either had to expose the exaggerations of their campaign against the Jews, Freemasons, and Jesuits or you had to outbid it. The method used in Hamburg, of simply ignoring the Ludendorff people, was probably possible only with a city population, which had other problems more directly pertinent to their lives. Telschow opted for outbidding the Tannenberg League.

How successful he was in detail is something I no longer know. It could surely be determined from the election statistics.[35] Significantly, in Harburg, the biggest and practically the only industrial town in his district, Telschow and his methods found little receptivity and even less success. The Nazi party in Harburg increasingly linked itself more and more closely to Hamburg: intellectually, organizationally, and finally also in its newspaper work. Initially this caused some friction and arguments but ultimately Telschow voluntarily moved the center of his efforts out into the countryside and the small towns. It can surely be assumed that Telschow was expressing a recognizable self-criticism by this decision. He was simultaneously displaying, however, an approach that was not usually to be expected from a Nazi Gauleiter.

Telschow was basically, as he once voluntarily explained to me, a Guelph.[36] Given his peasant origins that was by no means surprising. Furthermore, the racialist circles of North Germany had

[35] Available in James K. Pollock, "An Areal Study of the German Electorate, 1930–1933," *American Political Science Review* (1944), pp. 89–95.

[36] Prussia's annexation of the Kingdom of Hanover in 1866 caused localistic resentments, which lasted well into the twentieth century. Since the Hanoverian royal house was known as the "Guelph" line, those who felt this way called themselves Guelphs.

always taken an authentically Guelph position with their partisan attitude toward Widukind and Henry the Lion.[37] But that was mostly a historical memory whose contemporary consequences were usually satisfied by the struggle against excessive papal influence. Telschow, on the other hand, with his simple, straightforward emotions, drew from racialist theory the not illogical conclusion that one must remove the "super-state" of Prussia and restore the old Duchy of Lower Saxony. Even in later years, when the Nazi party had long since incorporated the "position of Charlemagne," Telschow stuck firmly to his views. Probably he was completely unconscious of the way in which this was a protest against Nazism. For him it was enough to be the "Duke of Lüneburg" or at least to be called that by his followers, half in scorn, half in flattery.

I never learned how he ran his ducal business nor did I ever personally encounter him after 1936. I know he committed suicide in 1945.

PAUL WEGENER

Editor's note: Wegener was born in 1908, educated in a business school, then went to work as a white-collar employee in Bremen, where he also joined the Nazi party and rapidly rose to the rank of county leader. But his real career began when he was taken under the wing of Martin Bormann, who saw to it that Wegener advanced quickly within the Nazi hierarchy. From 1934 to 1936 he served as Bormann's adjutant; he was Deputy Gauleiter of Kurmark, the area around Berlin, 1936–40; from 1940 to 1942 he was head of the Nazi organization in Norway, adviser to Vidkun Quisling, and Deputy Reichskommissar. Upon the death of Karl Röver in May 1942, Wegener was named Gauleiter of Weser-Ems and Reichsstatthalter, or governor, of Oldenburg and Bremen. In 1944 he capped his career as a Nazi by becoming Goebbels' deputy commissioner for Total War and a general in the SS.

At the end of April 1932 I traveled to Dornum Castle in East Frisia to give two lectures (on socialism and on foreign policy) at

---

[37] Medieval defenders of Lower Saxony against the centralizing tendencies of, respectively, Charlemagne and the Holy Roman Empire.

a weekend conference for Gau and district orators sponsored by Gau Weser-Ems. I remember this conference well, since its organization contrasted favorably with the usual party conferences, which had increasingly degenerated into sessions for the distribution and explication of orders and directives. There was rarely an opportunity for open discussion with cross criticism and depth analysis of the complexities of a subject. At Dornum Castle, however, thanks to the way its organizer had structured the conference, there developed real discussions lasting for hours, in which gradually the usual slogans were forgotten and the arguments came to center on the actual question itself. What also helped make this possible was, to be sure, the nature of the participating group, which had obviously been chosen with deliberate selectivity. Among the overwhelmingly young participants there were hardly any superficial chatterers or demagogues. Most of the assembled fifteen to twenty Gau and district orators were seriously interested in using the sessions to gain a firm understanding for their work, which was, of course, only possible through questions, counterquestions, and a careful consideration of opinions.

Sociologically speaking, the participants came from all strata— even the sons of peasants were represented—though, as I recall, white-collar workers predominated. That reflected the general structure of the Nazi party, of course, but in this particular instance it was probably also because the propaganda leader for Gau Weser-Ems, Schulze, was a member of the DHV and had recruited substantial numbers of his colleagues into the Nazi party.

Organizationally and intellectually the conference was directed by Paul Wegener, the later Gauleiter and *Statthalter* of Weser-Ems. In conducting the discussions he was assisted by party-comrade Meyer, a teacher from Bennekkenstein in the Harz, who was later to become, during the war, the Deputy Gauleiter of South Hanover. Meyer also gave some lectures himself, but I missed them since I did not arrive until Saturday evening.

Both before and after 1945 I heard various unpleasant tales about Gauleiter Wegener. Whether or to what extent these stories were true I could not determine with surety, but they surprised me because the Wegener I had met at Dornum Castle had made the best of impressions on me. This impression was based on more than just his generally decent behavior. He treated Meyer and me with polite modesty, which was by no means something to be taken for granted from the young Nazis of those years. He was also comradely toward the participants and avoided ordering them around unnecessarily. In private conversation, too (we spent practically the entire evening of my arrival alone together, since Meyer was finishing up the discussion that followed his lecture), he showed characteristics that were rare in the party even then. That he was smart was no special distinction. That despite his cleverness he had preserved a sincere though risky independence of thought and critical judgment indicated, however, a commendable inner attitude.

Our conversation was primarily concerned with the evolution of the Nazi party since autumn 1931. I did not spare Wegener any of my doubts and concerns and must have destroyed several of his illusions, since in consequence of his youth he was probably still a believer. He listened quietly to me and agreed or disagreed according to how he viewed the matter himself. He never resorted to the authority of the *Führer* or the party program as a justification or a threat, the way a fanatic might have. Nor did he act differently the following day when I lectured to the conference participants and in the process made several heretical remarks. It was precisely these remarks that he picked up in initiating the discussion and thus directed it toward that fruitful debate that I mentioned above. That was by no means without risk for him personally, since by then there had already developed a spy system within the party which, either from limited conviction or calculating competitiveness, sought to bring down every outsider, every man of independent opinions. One had to assume, precisely at semiprivate conferences such as this one, that one or another of the participants would fill his notebook with dangerous-sounding statements in order to show them to the nearest party headquarters. Wegener was surely aware of this possibility but nevertheless refused to change his approach and thereby showed that political courage which, as is well known, has been all too rare in Germany.

Having had this experience with Wegener, I could never fully understand how his personality could change in such a way as to cause the previously mentioned unfavorable judgment of some of his actions and behavior during his years in office. I cannot assume that he pretended, with me, to have qualities that he did not, in fact, possess: He was too young for such a trick. Nor am I quite willing to believe that he was corrupted by being given power at an early age. He would have shown a susceptibility to this at Dornum Castle, where his position as conference leader gave him ample opportunity to manifest a lust for power. The most likely explanation is the uncanny power shown by the Nazi party apparatus in stamping a personality completely into the mold of the perfectly behaving functionary. With this party apparatus one could no longer apply the old folk wisdom that sometimes you have to howl with the wolves. Here, in order to save his own skin a man had to pull on wolves' clothing and hunt and tear with the pack. The higher the position one held the more powerfully one was subject to the rules of the machinery that one had bound oneself to.

FOR FURTHER READING

The following list of books and articles is limited to works in English, which should be readily available in most college libraries. More complete bibliographies may be found in the books by Bracher and Gay, listed below.

Weimar Germany and the Rise of Nazism

Abel, Theodore. *The Nazi Movement: Why Hitler Came Into Power. An Answer Based on the Life Histories of 600 of His Followers.* Englewood Cliffs, 1938, and New York, 1966 (paperback).

Allen, William Sheridan. *The Nazi Seizure of Power: The Experience of a Single German Town, 1930 to 1935.* Chicago, 1965, and paperback.

Bracher, Karl Dietrich. *The German Dictatorship: The Origins, Structure, and Effects of National Socialism.* New York, 1970, and paperback.

Carsten, Francis L. *The Reichswehr and Politics: 1918 to 1933.* Oxford, 1966, and Berkeley, 1973 (paperback).

Comfort, Richard A. *Revolutionary Hamburg: Labor Politics in the Early Weimar Republic.* Stanford, 1966.

Eschenburg, Theodore, et. al. *The Path to Dictatorship, 1918–1933,* trans. John S. Conway. New York, 1963, paperback.

Eyck, Erich. *A History of the Weimar Republic.* 2 vols. New York, 1970, and paperback.

Friedrich, Otto. *Before the Deluge: A Portrait of Berlin in the 1920's.* New York, 1972, and paperback.

Gay, Peter. *Weimar Culture: The Outsider as Insider.* New York, 1968, and paperback, 1970.

Gordon, Harold J., Jr. *Hitler and the Beerhall Putsch.* Princeton, 1972.

Grunberger, Richard. *Germany 1918–1945.* London, 1964, and New York, paperback, 1967.

Grunfeld, Frederic V. *The Hitler File: A Social History of Germany and the Nazis, 1918–45.* New York, 1974.

Hale, Oron J. *The Captive Press in the Third Reich.* Princeton, 1964.

Heberle, Rudolf. *From Democracy to Nazism: A Regional Case Study on Political Parties in Germany.* Baton Rouge, La., 1945, and rev. ed., New York, 1970, paperback.

Herzstein, Robert Edwin. *Adolf Hitler and the German Trauma, 1913–1945: An Interpretation of the Nazi Phenomenon.* New York, 1974.

Kele, Max H. *Nazis and Workers: National Socialist Appeals to German Labor, 1919–1933.* Chapel Hill, N.C., 1972.

Klemperer, Klemens von. *Germany's New Conservatism: Its History and Dilemma in the Twentieth Century.* Princeton, 1957, and paperback.

Lane, Barbara Miller. *Architecture and Politics in Germany, 1918–1945.* Cambridge, Mass., 1968.

Laqueur, Walter Z. *Young Germany: A History of the German Youth Movement.* New York, 1962.

Lebovics, Herman. *Social Conservatism and the Middle Classes in Germany, 1914–1933.* Princeton, 1969.

McKale, Donald M. *The Nazi Party Courts: Hitler's Management of Conflict in His Movement, 1921–1945.* Lawrence, Kans., 1974.

Mayer, Milton. *They Thought They Were Free: The Germans, 1933–1945.* Chicago, 1955, and paperback.

Merkl, Peter H. *Political Violence Under the Swastika: 581 Early Nazis.* Princeton, 1975.

Meyer, Henry Cord (ed.). *The Long Generation: Germany from Empire to Ruin, 1913–1945.* New York, 1973, paperback.

Mosse, George L. *The Crisis of German Ideology: Intellectual Origins of the Third Reich.* New York, 1964, and paperback.

Nicholls, Anthony J. *Weimar and the Rise of Hitler.* New York, 1968, and paperback.

Noakes, Jeremy. *The Nazi Party in Lower Saxony, 1921–1933.* Oxford, 1971.

———, and Geoffrey Pridham. *Documents on Nazism, 1919–1945.* New York, 1975.

Nyomarkay, Joseph. *Charisma and Factionalism in the Nazi Party.* Minneapolis, 1967.

Orlow, Dietrich. *The History of the Nazi Party, 1919 to 1933.* Pittsburgh, 1969.

Pridham, Geoffrey. *Hitler's Rise to Power: The Nazi Movement in Bavaria, 1923–1933.* London, 1973.

Remak, Joachim. *The Nazi Years: A Documentary History.* Englewood Cliffs, N.J., 1969, paperback.

Snyder, Louis L. *The Weimar Republic: A History of Germany from Ebert to Hitler.* Princeton, 1966, paperback.

Stern, Fritz. *The Politics of Cultural Despair: A Study in the Rise of the Germanic Ideology.* Berkeley, 1961, and paperback.

Stern, J. P. *Hitler: The Führer and the People.* Berkeley, 1975.

Struve, Walter. *Elites Against Democracy: Leadership Ideals in Bourgeois Political Thought in Germany, 1890–1933.* Princeton, 1973.

Turner, Henry A. (ed.). *Nazism and the Third Reich.* New York, 1972, paperback.

———, *Stresemann and the Politics of the Weimar Republic.* Princeton, 1965.

Waite, Robert G. L. *Vanguard of Nazism: The Free Corps Movement in*

Postwar Germany, 1918–1923. Cambridge, Mass., 1952, and New York, 1969, paperback.

ARTICLES

Broszat, Martin. "National Socialism, its Social Basis and Psychological Impact," in E. J. Feuchtwanger, *Upheaval and Continuity: A Century of German History.* Pittsburgh, 1974, pp. 134–151.

Campbell, F. Gregory. "The Struggle for Upper Silesia, 1919–1922," *Journal of Modern History* (December 1970), pp. 361–385.

Chanady Attila, "The Disintegration of the German National People's Party, 1924–1930." *Journal of Modern History* (March 1967), pp. 65–90.

———. "The Dissolution of the German Democratic Party in 1930." *American Historical Review* (June 1968), pp. 1433–1453.

Chickering, Roger P. "The Reichsbanner and the Weimar Republic, 1924–26." *Journal of Modern History* (December 1968), pp. 524–534.

Edmondson, Nelson. "The Fichte Society: A Chapter in Germany's Conservative Revolution." *Journal of Modern History* (June 1966), pp. 161–180.

Farquharson, John. "The NSDAP in Hanover and Lower Saxony, 1921–1926." *Journal of Contemporary History* (October 1973), pp. 103–120.

Gates, Robert A. "German Socialism and the Crisis of 1929–33." *Central European History* (December 1974), pp. 332–359.

Gerth, Hans. "The Nazi Party: Its Leadership and Composition." *American Journal of Sociology* (1940).

Jones, Larry Eugene. "'The Dying Middle': Weimar Germany and the Fragmentation of Bourgeois Politics." *Central European History* (March 1972), pp. 23–54.

Lane, Barbara Miller. "Nazi Ideology: Some Unfinished Business." *Central European History* (March 1974), pp. 3–30.

Layton, Roland V., Jr. "The *Völkischer Beobachter,* 1920–1933: The Nazi Party Newspaper in the Weimar Era." *Central European History* (December 1970), pp. 353–382.

———. "The Early Years of the Nazi Press in Hamburg." *University of Virginia Essays in History,* Vol. 7 (1961–1962), pp. 20–36.

Lerner, Daniel, *et al.* "The Nazi Elite," in Harold Lasswell and Daniel Lerner (eds.), *World Revolutionary Elites: Studies in Coercive Ideological Movements.* Cambridge, Mass., 1966, pp. 194–318.

Loewenburg, Peter. "The Psychohistorical Origins of the Nazi Youth Cohort." *American Historical Review* (December 1971), pp. 1457–1502.

Mitchell, Otis C. "Criminals of the Dream: Nazi Stormtroopers During the Drive to Power and the Early Days of the Third Reich," in Otis C. Mitchell (ed.), *Nazism and the Common Man.* Minneapolis, 1972, paperback.

Phelps, Reginald H. "'Before Hitler Came': Thule Society and Germanen Orden." *Journal of Modern History* (September 1963), pp. 245–261.

Stern, Howard. "The Organization 'Consul.'" *Journal of Modern History* (March 1963), pp. 20–32.

Turner, Henry A., Jr. "Big Business and the Rise of Hitler." *American Historical Review* (October 1969), pp. 56–70.

Weinberg, Gerhard L. "National Socialist Organization and Foreign Policy Aims in 1927." *Journal of Modern History* (December 1964), pp. 428–433.

Prominent Individuals Discussed by Krebs

Bramsted, Ernest K. *Goebbels and National Socialist Propaganda, 1925–1945.* East Lansing, 1965.

Brecht, Arnold. *The Political Education of Arnold Brecht: An Autobiography, 1884–1970.* Princeton, 1970.

Bullock, Alan. *Hitler, A Study in Tyranny.* New York, 1964 (rev. ed. paperback).

Davidson, Eugene. *The Trial of the Germans: An Account of the Twenty-two Defendants before the International Military Tribunal at Nuremberg.* New York, 1966, paperback.

Fest, Joachim C. *The Face of the Third Reich: Portraits of the Nazi Leadership.* New York, 1970, paperback.

———. *Hitler.* New York, 1974.

Goebbels, Joseph. *My Part in Germany's Struggle.* London, 1934.

———. *The Early Goebbels Diaries,* edited by Helmut Heiber. New York 1963.

Hanfstaengel, Ernst. *Unheard Witness.* Philadelphia, 1957.

Heiber, Helmut. *Goebbels.* New York, 1972.

Hitler, Adolf. *Mein Kampf,* translated by Ralph Mannheim. Boston, 1962, paperback.

———. *Hitler's Secret Book,* translated by Salvator Attanasio. New York, 1961, paperback.

Jäckel, Eberhard. *Hitler's Weltanschauung.* Middletown, Conn., 1972.

Jenks, William A. *Vienna and the Young Hitler.* New York, 1960.

Ludecke, Kurt. *I Knew Hitler.* London, 1938.

Manvell, Roger, and Heinrich Fraenkel. *Dr. Goebbels: His Life and Death.* New York, 1960, paperback.

———. *Hess: A Biography.* London, 1971.

Maser, Werner. *Hitler: Legend, Myth, and Reality.* New York, 1973, and paperback.

——— (ed.). *Hitler's Letters and Notes.* New York, 1974.

Rauschnigg, Hermann. *The Revolution of Nihilism.* New York, 1937.

———. *The Voice of Destruction.* New York, 1940.

———. *The Conservative Revolution.* New York, 1940.

Rosenberg, Alfred. *Memoirs,* edited by S. Lang and E. von Schenck. New York, 1949.

Schramm, Percy E. *Hitler: The Man and the Military Leader,* edited and translated by Donald S. Detweiler. Chicago, 1971.

Smith, Bradley F. *Adolf Hitler: His Family, Childhood, and Youth.* Stanford, 1967.

Strasser, Otto. *Hitler and I.* Boston, 1940.

ARTICLES

Binion, Rudolf. "Hitler's Concept of Lebensraum: The Psychological Basis." *History of Childhood Quarterly* (1973), pp. 187–215.

Heyl, John D. "Hitler's Economic Thought: A Reappraisal." *Central European History* (March 1973), pp. 83–96.

Loewenberg, Peter. "The Unsuccessful Adolescence of Heinrich Himmler." *American Historical Review* (June 1971), pp. 612–641.

Lenman, Robin. "Julius Streicher and the Origins of the NSDAP in Nuremberg, 1918–1923," in Anthony Nicholls and Erich Matthias, eds. *German Democracy and the Triumph of Hitler.* New York, 1971.

Nicholls, Anthony. "Hitler and the Bavarian Background to National Socialism," in Anthony Nicolls and Erich Matthias, eds., *German Democracy and the Triumph of Hitler.* New York, 1971, pp. 99–128.

Struve, Walter. "Hans Zehrer as a Neo-conservative Elite Theorist." *American Historical Review* (July 1965), pp. 1035–1057.

Stürmer, Michael. "Parliamentary Government in Weimar Germany, 1924–1928," in Anthony Nicholls and Erich Matthias, eds., *German Democracy and the Triumph of Hitler.* New York, 1971, pp. 59–68.

INDEX

Amann, Max, 99, 104, 117, 118, 189, 195, 220, 244–246, 256

André, Edgar, 58, 95

Angriff, 96, 201, 233, 306

Anti-Semitism, 8, 46–47, 308–311. *See also* Jewish question

Bamberg Conference, 1926, 202*n*, 224, 231–232

Bangert, Otto, 302

Bank crisis, 1931. *See under* Germany

Barlach, Ernst, 218

Bavarian People's Party, 148, 260

Bechly, Hans, 9, 18, 32, 181, 207

"Beer Hall" Putsch, 1923, vii, 5, 151, 175*n*, 228, 244, 249, 251*n*, 253

Berns, Peter, 16

Bewegung, 299

"Black Front," 185, 230*n*, 234, 304

Blanck, Herbert, 227, 302, 304

Blunk, Hans Friedrich, 126

Böckenhauer, Arthur, 41, 48–50, 68, 70, 73

Bormann, Martin, 210, 249, 312

Bouhler, Philip, 170, 172, 246–248

Braun, Otto, 26

Brinkmann, Edgar, 33, 44–47, 64, 68, 71, 88, 91, 93, 98, 104, 114, 123

Bröcker, Paul, 8

Brückner, Lieut. Helmuth, 240

Bruckner, Wilhelm, 252–254

Brüning, Heinrich, 13, 20, 25, 26*n*, 116, 120, 121, 168–70, 183, 204

Buch, Maj. Walter, 174, 208, 249–251

Buchner, Dr. (Nazi newspaper contributor), 301

Bückel (Gauleiter), 240

Bülk, Richard, 95

Bündische Jugend. *See* Youth Movement

Burat (Nazi party member, Hamburg), 134

Burmester (privy councillor), 128–129

Busch, Dr. Harald, 127

Buttmann, Dr. Rudolf, 251–252

Christian Social Movement, 39,
  278n
Coburg, 143
Combat Press, 67, 88, 231, 232
Communists, 142, 143, 256n
Concordat, 252
"Consul," 149n, 281n
Curtius, Julius, 29

DHV. See German Nationalist
  Merchant Apprentices'
  Association
DVP. See People's Party
Dawes Plan, 9, 97
Deutsche Ring, 28, 33, 115
Deutscher, Der, 116
Dickszas (Hamburg shop-cell
  organizer), 84, 86
Diederichs, Eugen, 219
Dietrich, Hans, 150
Dietrich, Otto, 104, 118–119,
  215, 236, 258, 305
Dinter, Arthur, 167, 288
Disarmament, 168
Droege, Dr., 113

Eckart, Dietrich, 301
Eckhart, Meister, 218, 219
Eher Verlag, 117n, 117–118, 244
"Elberfeld Principles," 231–232
Elbrechter, Dr., 240
Ellendt, Frau, 254–255
Ellerhusen (stormtrooper), 57
Engel, Johannes, 79, 80
Erhardt, Capt. Hermann, 149,
  175
Erzberger, 149n
Escherich, Maj. Georg, 150n
Esser, Hermann, 144, 227, 228,
  252, 255–257

Estonia, 267

Feder, Gottfried, 58, 257–259
Fichte Society, 92, 230
Forster, Albert, 23, 24, 25, 32,
  37, 174
France, 146
Free Corps, 69, 141, 142, 145,
  149n, 281n
Freemasons, 44, 310–311
Freikorps. See Free Corps
Frenssen, Gustav, 288
Frick, Dr. Wilhelm, 31, 195,
  259–262
Funk, Dr. Walther, 104

GDA (union), 83
Gerig (Reichstag delegate), 15
German Labor Front. See
  Labor Front
German Nationalist Merchant
  Apprentices' Association
  (DHV), 4–34, 82, 83, 116,
  121, 174, 178–179, 204
German Nationalist People's
  Party (DNVP). See Nation-
  alist People's Party
German Office Workerhood,
  36–37
German Racial Liberation Party
  (DVFP). See Racial Liber-
  ation Party
German Social Party, 307
German Youth Movement. See
  Youth Movement
Germany
  bank crisis of 1931 in, 27, 183,
    217
  elections: 1924, 228; 1928, 38,
    67–68; 1930, 13, 38, 98,

Germany, elections: continued
100, 168, 183, 236; 1932,
31–32, 131–133, 186, 237
farmers in, 268n–269n
laws, 157n
middle-class and white-collar
workers in, 3, 7
mobilization, 1939, 184
monarchy, 141–142
political parties, 30
press, 112
See also Weimar Republic
Gestapo, 105n
"Geusen," 91
Gilbert, 69
Glatzel, Frank, 15, 16
Gloy, Walter, 41, 88
Goebbels, Joseph, 58, 77, 79n,
134–135, 174n, 186, 188,
191–205, 209, 231–233, 239,
248, 295, 301, 302
Goering, Hermann, 168n
Goltz, 107–108
Great Depression, 87
Greater German Racial Com-
munity, 228, 247, 252
Grimm, Hans, 179
Groener, Gen. Wilhelm, 188
Gruber, Kurt, 52
Grünwedel, Albert, 219

HAPAG (shipping firm), 82, 86
Haase, Rudolf, 228n
Habedank (Nazi shop-cell
leader), 86
Habermann, Max, 4, 5, 7, 10,
13, 18, 21, 22, 23, 29, 30, 35–
36, 120, 180, 181, 207, 209,
240

Hamburg
city council elections, 1928,
15, 88, 308
election law, 1927, 61, 65
Hitler visits, 15, 63, 151–156
Nazi party in, 38–74
Nazi press in, 87–137
shop-cell organization in,
75–86
Hamburger Nachrichten, 99
Hamburger Tageblatt, 29, 33,
98–137 passim, 188–189,
203–204, 217, 218, 256
Hamburger Volksblatt, 67, 88–
92, 95, 195, 231, 244
Handelswacht, 10, 11
Hanfstängl, Ernst, 305
Hank, Hugo, 53
Hansische Warte, 33, 90, 93,
95, 202
Harke, C. G., 90, 95
Harzburg Front, 104, 173
Hassell, Ulrich von, 254
Haupt, Dr. Joachim, 262–265
Haushofer, Karl, 211
Hederich (Office of Party
Literary Affairs), 248
Heim, Klaus, 269
Heinemann, Lt. Gen. Bruno, 42
Heinz, Friedrich Wilhelm, 162,
184, 292, 302
Henning (city councilor,
Hamburg), 112
Herdieckerhof, Dr. (political
writer), 302
Hess, Frau, 209–210
Hess, Rudolf, 21, 30, 35, 52, 67,
88, 91, 99, 104, 117, 157, 174,
179, 181, 183–184, 195, 206–
214, 273, 303

Hierl, Konstantin, 235
Himmler, Heinrich, 259, 265–267
Hinckel (collaborator of O. Strasser), 227
Hindenburg, Paul von, 31, 133n, 186, 188
Hitler, Adolf, 141–190
  assassination plot against, July 20, 1944, 22, 241n, 276n
  "Beer Hall" Putsch, 151
  Brüning, arrangements for meeting with, 25, 168–174
  early leadership, vii, 146–151
  election of 1932, 31, 186–187
  England, 154
  Frick on, 262
  hypochondria, 164–165
  Krebs, relations with, 103, 105, 156–157, 162–163, 188–190
  Mein Kampf, 17n, 117n, 211
  Nazi Party Conference of 1928, 158–160
  Nazi party purge, June 30, 1934, 49n, 177, 224, 237n, 265n
  Nuremberg rallies, 161
  rages, 162–163
  salute, 162
  trade unions, 29, 178–179, 181
  visits to Hamburg, 15, 63, 151–156
  views of: on army leadership, 175–176; cultural policy, 299; factory workers, 77; Nazi party, 166, 180–183, 208; Pfeffer affair, 174;

Hitler, views of: continued
  press, 187–188; Reventlow, 160; Rosenberg's Der Mythus, 220; two-front war, 211
  Young Plan, 10
Hitler Youth, 281
Hoeger, Fritz, 127
Hoover, Herbert, 27n
Hugenberg, Alfred, 10, 173, 286
Humbert (editor), 116, 117
Hüttmann, Wilhelm, 66–67, 74, 88–90

Illustrierter Beobachter, 246, 256
Ispert, Dr., 302
Italy, 254

Jacobi, Hans, 136
Jewish financial influence, 270
Jewish question, 193, 287
Jordan, Rudolf, 240
Jung deutsche Orden, See Young Germanic Order
Jünger, Ernst, 96, 230
Junkers, 306

Kahr, Gustav von, 149, 150, 151n
Kampf Publishing House, 206
Kaufmann, Karl, 35, 74, 81, 93, 117, 119, 133, 190, 197, 231, 240
Killinger, Heinz, 69
Klagges, Dietrich, 302
Klant, Josef, 38–42, 61
Knickerbocker, Hubert R., 305n
Koenig, Frieda, 59
Koerber, von, 301

Kohlmeyer, Wilhelm, 53
Krebs, Albert, ix–xi
  DHV, 4–5
  editor of: *Hamburger Tage-*
    blatt, 34, 98–137; *Ham-*
    burger Volksblatt, 91–95;
    Hansische Warte, 93–98
  Gauleiter of Hamburg, 38–74;
    resignation, 14, 70–74, 88,
    156–157
  Nazi party: membership, 13;
    expulsion from, 35, 137,
    162–163, 188–190, 203, 240
  Nazi shop-cell organization,
    leader of, in Hamburg,
    75–86
  nervous breakdown, 137
  relations with G. Strasser, 236
  resigns from German Office
    Workerhood, 37
  views on Brüning, 121–122
Kube, Wilhelm, 9, 77

Labor Front (DAF), 25n, 33,
  75, 78, 84, 179
Lambach, Walter, 9n, 10, 11, 15
Latvia, 267
Lauerbach, Friedrich, 134
Leipart, Theodor, 239
Ley, Robert, 13, 25, 33, 36, 237
Lithuania 267
Lohse, Hinrich, 24, 74, 157,
  267–272
Lossow, Otto van, 151n
Ludendorff, General, 57, 194,
  227, 228
Ludendorff, Mathilde, 154–155
Ludin, Hans, 272–277

Marschler, Wilhelm, 277–279
Marxist parties. *See* Commu-
  nists
Massman, K., 92
Meyer (Gauleiter), 313
Meyer, Hellmuth, 4
Meyer-Christian, Wolf, 29, 92,
  188
Militant Association of Revolu-
  tionary National Socialists,
  303
Moeller van den Bruck, 230, 231
Muchow, Reinhold, 13, 80, 235,
  302, 304

Nachtpost, 89n
National Socialist Correspon-
  dence, 16, 231, 232, 302, 303
National Socialist German
    Workers party (NSDAP)
  art, 127
  conference of 1928, 16, 78,
    158–160, 212
  development of, 142–147
  discipline in, 72
  Habermann on, 5, 22
  Hamburg, 38–74
  idealists in, xi–xii, 109–111
  leadership of, 271–272
  membership of, 27, 40–41,
    43–48, 87, 242–243
  policies of, 157
  press, 103–104, 187–188,
    215–216, 233, 300–307
  Reichstag, 26
  trade unions, 3–37, 75–86
National Socialist Liberation
    Movement, 194, 227–229, 242

National Socialist Pupils League, 91
National Socialist Shop-Cell Organization (NSBO), 18, 75–86, 235, 304
National Socialist Student League, 91, 262–263, 299, 300
Nationalist People's Party (DNVP), 5, 9
Nationalsozialistische Betriebs-zellen Organization (NSBO). See National Socialist Shop-Cell Organization
Nationalsozialistischen Briefe. See National Socialist Correspondence
Naumann, Friedrich, 278
Nazis. See National Socialist German Workers party
Nieckisch, Ernst, 216, 230, 231
Nieland, Hans, 81, 117
Nölting, Eric, 259
Nuremberg Party Rally, 1927, 60–61, 161

Okrass, Hermann, 95

Pan German Society, 301
Papen, Franz von, 183
Penzhorn, 41
People's party (DVP), 124
Peters, Arnold, 51–52
Petersen, Albert, 110–112
Pfeffer von Salomon, Franz, 28n, 52, 71, 171, 174–175, 195, 208, 210, 249, 279–282
Pfeffer von Salomon, Frau, 282
Pfordten, Theodor von der, 251
Pöhner, Ernst, 251

Poland, 145, 184–185
Popular Conservative League, 9n, 10

RBA, 81
Racial Liberation party (DVFP), 61–62, 283, 285
Racial-Social Bloc, 61, 251, 252
Rathenau, Walther, 112n, 149n, 281n
Raubal, Angela, 171n
Raubal, Geli, 171n, 172
Reemtsma, Philipp, 123–124
Reich Party Convention of 1929, 159
Reichsbanner, 55n
Reichswart, Der, 283–284
Reinke, Helmuth, 43, 44, 64, 66, 81, 84, 88
Reinsurance Treaty of 1887, 286n
Reparations, 9n, 22, 27, 169, 217
Reventlow, Count Ernst zu, 61, 64, 160, 282–288
Reventlow, Countess, 287
Rhineland, 97
Rilke, Rainer Maria, 299
Ritter von Leisser, Hans, 151n
Roehm, Ernst, 6, 69, 171n, 175–177, 240n, 265n
Römer, Beppo, 145
Rosenberg, Alfred, 11, 20, 104, 183–184, 192, 195, 215–223, 245, 248, 294n, 299, 303; Der Mythus des 20. Jahrhunderts, 218n–219n
Röver, Karl, 240, 288–291
Ruhr, 145, 146

Rust, Bernhard, 240, 264,
    291–296

SA (Sturmabteilung). *See*
    Storm Troopers
SD (SS Security Service), 105
SS (Schutzstaffel), 106
Salomon, Bruno von, 48, 281*n*
Salomon, Ernst von, 69, 281*n*
Schacht, Hjalmar, 104*n*, 259
Schapke, Richard von, 227, 302,
    304
Schauwecker, Franz, 69, 191, 230
Scheringer, Lieut., 272
Scheubner-Richter, Max von,
    222, 251
Schirach, Baldur von, 20,
    262–263, 296–300
Schlageter, Albert Leo, 145
Schleicher, Gen. Kurt von, 32,
    183, 188, 203, 204*n*
*Schleswig-Holsteinische Tage-
    zeitung*, 304
Schlotterer, Dr., 123
Schmidt, Ludwig, 92
Schneider, 35
Schranz, Helmuth, 43, 50–51
Schuhmann, Walter, 13, 80, 235
Schulz, Lieut., 237
Schulze (propaganda leader),
    313
Schwarz, Franz Xaver, 21, 28,
    117, 174
Schwarz van Berk, Hans,
    300–307
Seeckt, Gen. Hans von, 69,
    175–176, 275, 276
Seldte, Franz, 10
Silesia, 145

Social Democratic Party (SPD),
    238
Socialist Free Unions, 75
South Tyrol, 104
Spartacists, 142, 256*n*
Stahlhelm. *See* Steel Helmets
Stanick, Friedrich, 32
Stapel, Dr., 7
State party (Staatspartei), 124
Stauffenberg, Col. Claus Schenk
    von, 276
Steel Helmets, 10*n*, 41
Stegerwald, 116
Stennes, Walter, 174*n*, 199
Stennes Putsch, 174*n*, 194,
    202, 210, 282
Stöcker, Adolf, 39*n*, 278
Stöhr, Franz, 9, 24
Stolzing-Czerny, Gregor, 301
Storm Troopers (SA), 49, 57,
    65, 68–73, 106, 143, 160, 171,
    198–199, 202, 240, 274, 280
Strasser (Capuchin priest), 226
Strasser, Gregor, 20, 29, 30, 32,
    43, 61, 67, 79–81, 99, 120,
    188, 195, 202*n*, 204, 205, 207,
    224–241, 250, 273, 301, 302
Strasser, Otto, 172, 206, 216,
    226–227, 229, 230*n*, 233, 234,
    302, 303
Streicher, Julius, 6, 144, 227,
    228, 252, 307–309
Stresemann, Gustav, 8*n*, 9, 124*n*
Stürmer, Der, 6*n*, 88*n*, 246, 307
Sunkel, Reinhardt, 228*n*

Tägliche Rundschau, 116, 238
Tannenberg League, 154–155
Tat, 238

Taube, Otto von, 226
Telschow, Otto, 58, 309–312
Temple, Kurt, 262
Thiel, Otto, 11, 15
"Third Reich," 230n
Thoma (shop-cell organizer), 82
Treaty of Versailles, 8, 22, 47, 97, 192
Treviranus, Gottfried, 9n, 168

Uhse, Bodo, 302
Universities, 91–92, 126n
Uschla, 208

VWWA (union), 83
Vatican, 252n
Volck, Adalbert, 228n
Völkischer Beobachter, 11, 20n, 77–78, 117n, 244, 255, 301
Völkischer Kurier, 219, 301
Völkisch-Sozialer Block. See Racial-Social Bloc
Vorwärts, 238

Wagener, Otto, 12, 13, 28
Wagener, Paul, 181, 236, 258
Wagner, Josef, 240
Walter, Robert, 110–111

Wandel, Edo, 302
Weber, Christian, 144
Weber, Friedrich, 219
Weberstedt, 301
Wegener, Paul, 312–315
Weimar Republic, 3–4, 24n, 32n, 79, 102, 128n, 183
Weiss, Capt. Wilhelm, 301
Wendt, Lieut., 272
Werewolves, 41
Westarp, Count, 9n
Westphal (Communist), 58
Winnig, August, 189
Winter (director of DHV), 21, 33, 117
Wirth, A., 301
Woermann, Kurt, 123
Workerdom, 80, 304
Wüstenhagen, Karl, 129–131

Young Germanic Order, 41
Young Plan, 9, 10, 97, 124, 173
Youth Movement, 59, 202, 263n, 300n

Zentralverband der Angestellen, 12
Zidek, Frau, 59
Ziegler, Benno, 4, 11